AF793031

Mental Health Law

Mental Health Law

Abolish or Reform?

KAY WILSON

Melbourne Social Equity Institute

University of Melbourne

OXFORD
UNIVERSITY PRESS

OXFORD
UNIVERSITY PRESS

Great Clarendon Street, Oxford, OX2 6DP,
United Kingdom

Oxford University Press is a department of the University of Oxford.
It furthers the University's objective of excellence in research, scholarship,
and education by publishing worldwide. Oxford is a registered trade mark of
Oxford University Press in the UK and in certain other countries

© Kay Wilson 2021

The moral rights of the author have been asserted

First Edition published in 2021

Impression: 1

All rights reserved. No part of this publication may be reproduced, stored in
a retrieval system, or transmitted, in any form or by any means, without the
prior permission in writing of Oxford University Press, or as expressly permitted
by law, by licence or under terms agreed with the appropriate reprographics
rights organization. Enquiries concerning reproduction outside the scope of the
above should be sent to the Rights Department, Oxford University Press, at the
address above

You must not circulate this work in any other form
and you must impose this same condition on any acquirer

Crown copyright material is reproduced under Class Licence
Number C01P0000148 with the permission of OPSI
and the Queen's Printer for Scotland

Published in the United States of America by Oxford University Press
198 Madison Avenue, New York, NY 10016, United States of America

British Library Cataloguing in Publication Data
Data available

Library of Congress Control Number: 2020952992

ISBN 978–0–19–284325–8

DOI: 10.1093/oso/9780192843258.001.0001

Printed and bound by
CPI Group (UK) Ltd, Croydon, CR0 4YY

Links to third party websites are provided by Oxford in good faith and
for information only. Oxford disclaims any responsibility for the materials
contained in any third party website referenced in this work.

Preface

This book contains my PhD dissertation with minor modifications which I completed part-time at Melbourne Law School, University of Melbourne, Victoria, Australia between 2013 and 2019. I have been working and studying in the fields of mental health, disability, and human rights law for over ten years part-time. I began as research assistant for Professor Bernadette McSherry at the Centre for the Advancement of Law and Mental Health (CALMH) at Monash University for four years and later for two years when Professor McSherry became the foundation director of the Melbourne Social Equity Institute (MSEI) where I worked on a seclusion and restraint reduction project for the National Mental Health Commission with a team of interdisciplinary researchers. I am also currently an honorary fellow of MSEI.

I obtained a combined Bachelor of Arts/Bachelor of Laws degree with first class honours from Monash University graduating in 2000 and I am a qualified lawyer who in a previous life practiced commercial law at a major Australian law firm and in corporate law for a statutory authority in the energy sector. However, my interest in mental health and disability law arises from my undergraduate and honours degree in psychology which sparked my interest in understanding human behaviour and two publications in psychology based on my honours thesis (noted below). My interest is also personal as I have the lived experience of supporting many persons with mental health and disability issues among my own circle of family and friends, including my father who is a Vietnam War veteran diagnosed with anxiety, depression, and post-traumatic stress disorder, and children who are on the autism spectrum. While I have no intention of turning my book into an autobiography as I would rather rely on the published research, I would like to say that I know people with mental impairments who are very dissatisfied with their experiences of involuntary detention and treatment, but I also know others who are only still alive because of mental health law, or who have suffered enormously (and caused people around them to suffer) because they have been unable to obtain the mental health care they needed when they needed it. I have also seen the positive difference that psychiatric care can make in improving *some* people's lives and allowing them to chase their dreams. So while I am *very* sympathetic to abolitionists and I agree that their contribution to the debate is *very* important, I cannot accept that their views on mental health law are the one and only truth or that they are the *only* stakeholders and rights-holders in this field.

Carer-led research is rare in the mental health and disability field probably because caring is often thankless, exhausting, gendered work which leaves little time for research. Nonetheless, such perspectives add an important dimension to the literature, especially since all proposals for providing support for legal capacity regardless of whether mental health law is abolished or reformed assume a large, selfless, and unpaid role for carers (even if the use of professional supporters is also envisaged). My lived experience also informs my research in that I am well aware of some of the practical difficulties of trying to implement supported decision-making, even if I view it as an exciting development which is worthy of further research. For instance, there are times where after much time and effort I have been given a clear 'no' only to be told a few minutes later 'I wanted that why aren't you giving it to me?' This is usually in relation to everyday issues such as what to have for lunch, rather than serious and complex questions about potentially life-saving medical treatment. It also underscores my concern that the strong British Social Model of Disability and the abolitionist approach may not appropriately reflect the realities of those living with mental and cognitive impairment.

In addition to writing this book, I have published a number of journal articles on my own and with Bernadette McSherry and Penelope Weller and I have given a few conference papers, some of which I draw on in various parts of this book. I set out details of those papers below.

Publications

Kay Wilson, 'The Convention on the Rights of Persons with Disabilities and Mental Health: the Conflict about Abolition, Dilemmas of Implementation and Untapped Potential' *Disability Law and Human Rights: Theory and Policy* (Pan MacMillian) (forthcoming).

Kay Wilson, 'The COVID-19 Pandemic and the Human Rights of Persons with Mental and Cognitive Impairments Subject to Coercive Powers in Australia' (2020) 73 *International Journal of Law and Psychiatry* 101605.

Kay Wilson, 'The Abolition or Reform of Mental Health Law: How Should the Law Recognise and Respond to the Vulnerability of Persons with Mental Impairment?' (2020) 28(1) *Medical Law Review* 30–64.

Kay Wilson, 'The Call for the Abolition of Mental Health Law and the Right to Life: The Challenges of Suicide and Accidental Death,' (2018) 18(4) *Human Rights Law Review* 651–88.

Bernadette McSherry and Kay Wilson, 'The Concept of Capacity in Australian Mental Health Law Reform: Going in the Wrong Direction?' (2015) 40 *International Journal of Law and Psychiatry* 60–69.

Melbourne Social Equity Institute, *Seclusion and Restraint Project Report* (University of Melbourne, 2014) 'The Regulatory Framework for Seclusion and Restraint' (Chapter 2).

Kay Wilson, 'Law Reform or Systemic Reform? Stakeholder's Perceptions of Resource Constraints in Mental Health in Australia, New Zealand and Canada' (2013) 20(4) *Psychiatry, Psychology and Law* 553–77.

Bernadette McSherry and Kay Wilson, 'Detention and Treatment Down Under: Human Rights and Mental Health Laws in Australia and New Zealand' (2011) 19(4) *Medical Law Review* 548–80.

Kay Wilson and Penelope Weller, 'Benevolent Paternalism or a Clash of Values: Motherhood and Refusal of Medical Treatment in Ireland' (2011) *Journal of Mental Health Law* 108–19.

Kay Wilson and Eleonora Gullone, 'The Relationship between Personality and Affect over the Lifespan' (1999) 27 *Personality and Individual Differences* 1141–56.

Kay Wilson, Eleonora Gullone, and Simon Moss 'The Youth Version of the Positive and Negative Affect Schedule: A Psychometric Validation' (1998) 15(3) *Behaviour Change* 187–93.

Travelling Fellowships

Transnational Law Summer Institute 2016, 'Transnational Lawyering and Judging', King's College London, 21–30 July 2016, including paid accommodation, meals and tuition (fellowship awarded on a competitive basis).

John Harber Phillips Travelling Fellowship to the Greek/Australia International Law and Medical Conference, Thessaloniki, Greece, 31 May–6 June 2015 (academic prize included paid flights, accommodation and tours and the opportunity to give my award-winning conference paper, noted below).

Teaching Fellowship

Teaching Fellowship 2017, Melbourne Law School, University of Melbourne, Human Rights and Global Justice.

Conferences

Kay Wilson, 'The Future of Mental Health Law and the Disputed, Competing and Unknown Facts about Mental Impairment.' *Melbourne Doctoral Forum on Legal Theory*, Melbourne Law School, December 2018.

Kay Wilson, 'Reckoning and Reconciliation: The Equality of Persons with Mental Impairments under the United Nations Convention on the Rights of Persons with Disabilities.' *Melbourne Doctoral Forum on Legal Theory*, Melbourne Law School, December 2016.

Kay Wilson, 'A Celebration of Law and Medicine': Law and Medicine Working Together to Reduce Seclusion and Restraint in Health-Settings' *Greek/Australia International Law and Medical Conference*, Thessaloniki, Greece, June 2015.

Kay Wilson, 'The Evolution of the Concept of Legal Capacity: A New Vision of Persons with Disabilities' *Endeavour Foundation Symposium*, Brisbane, Australia, June 2014.

Acknowledgements

As feminists and disability theorists have pointed out, while we often think of achievement as something that belongs to the individual, it usually does not happen without the right support. While I have always been a fairly self-directed student, since starting my PhD I have learnt that it actually takes three people to write a thesis (which now forms this book with minor amendments). I am deeply indebted to the guidance and intelligent and useful advice I've always had from Professors Bernadette McSherry and Dianne Otto. I have found that even the smallest of their suggestions can make a significant difference to my work. There are also times where a few words of encouragement have gone a long way to keep me focussed and to press on in my PhD journey.

The other woman in my life who deserves acknowledgement is my mother Adriana Wilson, who has always been very supportive, especially in helping me to care for my children Caitlin and James. Her belief in me and her practical assistance have made this PhD possible.

I would also like to thank Professors Genevra Richardson and John Dawson who examined my PhD dissertation for their generous praise, the valuable contribution of the anonymous reviewers of this book, and the editors, production staff, and academic board at Oxford University Press. This research has been made possible by an Australian Government Research Training Program Scholarship and the James and Valarie McNiff Top-Up Scholarship 2015 and 2017.

Table of Contents

List of Abbreviations

AIHW	Australian Institute of Health and Welfare
ALRC	Australian Law Reform Commission
Art	Article
CEDAW	Convention on the Elimination of Discrimination Against Women
CERD	Convention on the Elimination of Racial Discrimination
Ch	Chapter
CRPD	Convention on the Right of Persons with Disabilities
DPOs	Disabled Persons Organizations
ECHR	European Convention on Human Rights
ECT	Electroconvulsive therapy
ed	editor
ICCPR	International Covenant on Civil and Political Rights
MCA	Mental Capacity Act
MHA	Mental Health Act
MHRSA NT	Mental Health and Related Services Act
n	note
NDIS	National Disability Insurance Scheme
s	section
tr	translated by
UN	United Nations
VCLT	Vienna Convention on the Law of Treaties
VLRC	Victorian Law Reform Commission

1
Introduction

1.1 Introduction

This book explores a single overarching question: should mental health law be abolished or reformed? While I explain in detail what I mean by mental health law in section 1.2 below, in short, I mean the legal power to detain in hospital and treat persons with mental impairment without their consent. I have chosen this topic because since the entry into force of the United Nations *Convention on the Rights of Persons with Disabilities* (CRPD) in 2008[1] and over a decade of international debate about the future of mental health law, it remains an important, multifaceted, and perplexing question which needs further research and rigorous scholarly attention. The abolition or reform of mental health law is an issue which has attracted interest from a wide range of interdisciplinary scholars, policy-makers, law reformers, and disability and human rights activists past and present, so I am not on my own. However, few have examined the question of whether mental health law should be abolished or reformed as directly, deeply, or as broadly as I do. As Peter Bartlett points out, now that the CRPD 'party'[2] is over and we are working out what the CRPD means and how to implement it, 'proper and detailed theoretical analysis matters'.[3]

While my research question assumes that mental health law should be abolished or reformed, rather than be left untouched, it would only be the most superficial reading of the CRPD which could conclude that existing mental health law is already CRPD compliant and does not require *any* further reform.[4] Indeed, as set out in section 1.3 below and in Chapter 3, the CRPD Committee, some scholars, and disability and human rights advocates (whom I collectively refer to as 'abolitionists') have put forth a compelling critique of mental health law that I believe deserves serious consideration, even if I do not agree with all of their solutions. Further, the contention that the CRPD requires at least *some* reform is supported by the actual behaviour of States Parties many of which have already engaged in a number of reviews and reforms to mental health law post-CRPD (see section 1.3.3 below), even if they have not contemplated actual abolition. The CRPD has also influenced case law in many domestic judicial decisions and in regional human rights courts.

However, in order to understand my 'big' overarching question about whether mental health law should be abolished or reformed and then to begin to answer it

[1] *Convention on the Rights of Persons with Disabilities*, open for signature 30 March 2007, UNTS 2515 (entered into force 3 May 2008) (hereafter CRPD).

[2] Peter Bartlett, 'The United Nations Convention on the Rights of Persons with Disabilities and Mental Health Law' (2012) 75(5) MLR 752, 777 (hereafter Bartlett UN Convention).

[3] ibid 778.

[4] ibid 754.

Mental Health Law. Kay Wilson, Oxford University Press. © Kay Wilson 2021. DOI: 10.1093/oso/9780192843258.003.0001

I need to break it up into a series of smaller, more manageable, questions. First, what do I mean by mental health law? Second, what is the abolition of mental health law, where has the call for abolition come from, why has it emerged now, and why should anyone take it seriously? Third, how will I determine whether mental health law *should* be abolished? In other words, given I am asking what is essentially a normative question, what are my conceptual framework, methodology, and scope? Fourth, if I conclude that mental health law should *not* be abolished (which I do), then how do I propose it *should* it be reformed?

It is the answers to these four complex and inter-linked questions which form the basic structure of my introduction and my overall contention that:

> mental health law should NOT be abolished, but be reformed by decreasing coercion and increasing social support to persons with mental impairments to maximize their dignity (including autonomy), equality, and participation in accordance with the overall object and purpose of the CRPD.

I argue that the CRPD demands a 'package' of systemic, social, and legal reforms and that the effectiveness of changes in mental health law is often dictated more by resource constraints than abstract legal principles.[5] In my view it is indisputable that the principle of reciprocity—that those whom society compels to accept mental health care also have a right to actually receive high quality dignified care in a safe environment—ought to underpin mental health law.[6] However, resources for those undergoing involuntary treatment should not come at the expense of bolstering the voluntary mental health system, access to services, and the provision of supports to persons with mental impairments to actually enable real 'choice'.[7] I, along with many other scholars, have also become increasingly interested in the way in which the availability of a range of high quality services, as well as alternatives to traditional psychiatry, and wider social changes could be used to reduce the use of involuntary detention and psychiatric treatment and possibly even to try to avoid the need for mental health law altogether.[8] However, as a lawyer my primary focus in this book is on whether, when, and how legal compulsion should *ever* be permitted in relation to persons with

[5] Kay Wilson 'Law Reform or Systemic Reform? Stakeholder Perceptions of Resource Constraints in Mental Health in Australia, New Zealand and Canada' (2013) 20(4) Psychiatry Psychol & L 553 (hereafter Wilson, 'Law Reform or Systemic Reform?'); Bernadette McSherry and Kay Wilson, 'The Concept of Capacity in Australian Mental Health Law Reform: Going the Wrong Direction?' (2015) 40 Int J Law Psychiatry 60–69, 66 (hereafter McSherry and Wilson, 'Capacity').

[6] Report of the Expert Committee, *Review of the Mental Health Act 1983* (November 1999), [3.2] (hereafter 'Richardson Report').

[7] McSherry and Wilson, 'Capacity' (n 5) 66.

[8] McSherry and Wilson, 'Capacity' (n 5). Kay Wilson, 'The Call for the Abolition of Mental Health Law: The Challenges of Suicide, Accidental Death and the Equal Enjoyment of the Right to Life' (2018) 18(4) Hum Rights Law Rev 651, 686 (hereafter Wilson, 'Right to Life'); Kay Wilson, 'The Abolition or Reform of Mental Health Law: How Should the Law Recognise and Respond to the Vulnerability or Persons with Mental Impairment?' (2020) 28(1) Med Law Rev 30 (hereafter Wilson, 'Vulnerability'); Jillian Craigie and others, 'Legal Capacity, Mental Capacity and Supported Decision-Making: Report from a Panel Event' (2019) 62 Int J Law Psychiatry 160, 166 (hereafter Craigie, 'Panel Event'); Piers Gooding and others, *Alternatives to Coercion in Mental Health Settings: A Literature Review* (Melbourne Social Equity Institute, University of Melbourne 2018) (hereafter Gooding, 'Alternatives to Coercion').

mental impairment under the CRPD, an issue which can still stand on its own even if it is closely related to, and is often dependent on, the wider systemic and social context.[9] Nonetheless, I emphasize the importance of mental health resources and socio-economic rights in my holistic approach to interpreting the CRPD set out below.

To support my arguments, I have developed what I call the 'interpretive compass' of the CRPD by which I have explored the meaning and scope of dignity (including autonomy), equality, and participation as key values that underpin the objects and purpose of the CRPD and as an aid to interpretation of what I argue is an 'incompletely theorized agreement'. I compare what I have identified as the three *main* legal models (although I accept that there may be others) which have emerged in the mental health literature in the wake of the CRPD.[10] The first is the complete abolition of mental health law and its replacement with a support model ('Abolition with Support'). The second is to bring mental health law into line with general medical law by changing the civil commitment criteria from a harm-based to a mental capacity-based model and to combine that with a support model ('Mental Capacity with Support'). The third model is to provide persons with mental impairment with support in the first instance and to only use coercion as a last resort if a person's decision-making is unclear and they are at risk of harming themselves or others ('Support Except Where There is Harm'). Within each of the three models there are different variations put forward in legislation and by different scholars and law reformers, which I explore throughout the book, but especially in Chapter 3 and Chapters 4 to 8. There is also some overlap between the three models. All models use the provision of support in various ways to assist persons with mental impairments to make decisions and thereby each aims to reduce legal compulsion to various extents. However, only the Abolition with Support model requires the absolute banning of involuntary detention and psychiatric treatment. Of these three main approaches, I argue in Chapter 8, that at present the Mental Capacity with Support model is the most consistent with what I see as the overall vision of the CRPD which is to improve the lives (especially the dignity, autonomy, equality, and participation) of persons with mental impairments and disabilities generally.

I understand that the arguments which make up the book are multi-layered and multi-textured, rather than being the straightforward exposition of a single idea, but I argue that the debate about the future of mental health law demands the embracing of complexity and nuance. While one of the key strengths of the Abolition with Support model is its apparent simplicity, there is a difference between advocacy which is best framed by a clear political demand and scholarship which involves the exploration of knowledge without necessarily being driven by a particular ideology or outcome. In fact, I criticize the Abolition with Support model for being too simplistic in responding to the actual and varied needs of persons with mental impairments.

To further explain my approach to answering my overarching research question, and to set out the background that sits behind it, I address each of my four sub-questions in turn.

[9] Particularly resource constraints. See Wilson, 'Law Reform or Systemic Reform?' (n 5).
[10] Wilson, 'Right to Life' (n 8) 655–61; Wilson, 'Vulnerability' (n 8).

1.2 What is Mental Health Law?

Mental health law authorizes what would otherwise be illegal: the involuntarily detention and psychiatric treatment of persons with severe mental impairment (usually thought to be at risk of harming themselves or others), thereby, legitimating psychiatric power.[11] At the same time, mental health law limits the scope of this authority[12] and provides persons who are involuntarily detained and treated with legal protections and safeguards well beyond what is available to 'voluntary' or 'informal' patients under general medical law.[13] As Clive Unsworth observes 'law actually constitutes the mental health system, in the sense that it authoritatively constructs, empowers, and regulates relationships between the agents who perform mental health functions'.[14]

Given the 'negative and positive function'[15] of mental health law in both authorizing and controlling involuntary detention and psychiatric treatment, it is not surprising that it has been conceptualized in a number of different ways. These range from being seen as a form of *parens patriae* (or as offering protection to the vulnerable),[16] risk management,[17] a therapeutic tool,[18] a system of social control,[19] a preventive detention regime,[20] an exercise of tutelary authority,[21] and more recently a substitute decision-making regime[22] and a form of torture.[23]

While Genevra Richardson observes that 'mental health law' broadly defined refers to the entire body of laws that pertain to persons with mental impairment,[24] in this book I refer to mental health law in the literal sense. That is, as the power of the

[11] Tina Minkowitz, 'Abolishing Mental Health Laws to Comply with the Convention on the Rights of Persons with Disabilities' in Bernadette McSherry and Penelope Weller (eds), *Rethinking Rights-Based Mental Health Laws* (Hart Publishing 2010) 151, 151 (hereafter Minkowitz, 'Abolishing Mental Health Laws').

[12] ibid.

[13] For instance, the *Mental Health Act* 2014 (Vic) is almost exclusively drafted for the involuntary patient. That said, the position of a 'voluntary' patient is beginning to be regarded as closer to that of an 'involuntary' psychiatric patient, than a general patient: *Rabone v Pennine Care NHS Foundation Trust* [2012] UKSC 2 [27]–[34] (hereafter *Rabone v Pennine Care NHS Foundation Trust*).

[14] Clive Unsworth, *The Politics of Mental Health Legislation* (Claredon Press 1987) 5 (hereafter Unsworth, *Politics of Mental Health*).

[15] ibid.

[16] See Chapter 2.

[17] See Chapters 2 and 3.

[18] David B Wexler, *Mental Health Law: Major Issues, Perspectives in Law and Psychology* (Plenum Press 1981) (hereafter Wexler, *Mental Health*).

[19] Michael Cavadino, *Mental Health Law in Context: Doctor's Orders?* (Dartmouth Publishing Company 1989) 11 (hereafter Cavadino, *Doctor's Orders*).

[20] Bernadette McSherry, *Managing Fear: The Law and Ethics of Preventive Detention and Risk Assessment* (Routledge 2014) (hereafter McSherry, *Managing Fear*).

[21] Philip Fennell, 'Institutionalising the Community: The Codification of Clinical Authority and the Limits of Rights-Based Approaches' in Bernadette McSherry and Penelope Weller (eds), *Rethinking Rights-Based Mental Health Laws* (Hart Publishing 2010) 13, 23 (hereafter Fennell, 'Institutionalising the Community').

[22] Committee on the Rights of Persons with Disabilities 'General Comment No 1 (2014) Article 12: Equal Recognition before the Law' (11 April 2014) UN Doc CRPD/C/GC/1 (hereafter 'General Comment 1').

[23] UNHCR, 'Report of the Special Rapporteur on Torture and other Cruel, Inhuman or Degrading Treatment or Punishment, Juan E. Méndez' (1 February 2013) UN Doc A/HRC/22/53, [89(b)] (hereafter Mendez, 'Torture Report').

[24] Genevra Richardson, 'Reforming Mental Health Law: Principle or Pragmatism' (2001) 54 Curr Leg Probl 415, 415 (hereafter Richardson, 'Principle or Pragmatism').

state to detain and treat persons with severe mental health problems without their consent whether or not that power is found in a specific Mental Health Act, or is scattered across general legislation.[25] I describe this power as '*involuntary* detention and psychiatric treatment' rather than 'compulsory' or 'forced' as I believe that 'involuntary' more accurately describes both the situation where people are unable to make decisions for themselves, as well as where people are detained or treated against their express will and preferences. I explore the different ways in which mental health law is conceptualized, how it has developed and its core functions, purposes, and justifications in Chapter 2. In my understanding of mental health law, as discussed in section 1.5 below which sets out the scope of this book, I do not include criminal doctrines such as fitness to be tried and the insanity defence, which are very complicated topics in themselves deserving of their own volume.

At this juncture, I want to point out that while the numbers of persons against whom mental health law is invoked are significant, the majority of persons with mental impairments receive treatment either on a voluntary basis or no treatment at all.[26] For example, the Australian Institute of Health and Welfare has reported that about 8.5 million people (around 45 per cent) from 16 to 85 suffer from mental health problems during their lifetime with around 20 per cent of the Australian population suffering from a mental health problem per year, with similar proportions occurring in other comparable western nations.[27] Of these, about 4 million Australians received mental health prescriptions in 2016–2017[28] whereas only about 41,197 people experienced involuntary hospital admission for psychiatric treatment in 2011–2012.[29] In addition, a further group received involuntary treatment in the community. For example, in Victoria alone about 5,000 people per year (or 98.8 per 100,000) are on Community Treatment Orders, the highest in Australia.[30] In England the rate of persons detained in hospital under mental health law was 115.7 per 100,000 in 2015–2016 (or 49,551 in 2017–2018) and has more than doubled since 1984.[31] In England the rate of CTOs was 4,784 in 2017–2018, that is, 10.8 per 100,000 for males and 6.4 per 100,000 for females.[32] It is also well documented that some people who voluntarily agree to hospital

[25] OECD, *Making Mental Health Count: The Social and Economic Costs of Neglecting Mental Health Care* (OECD Health Policy Studies, OECD Publishing 2014) 216–17 (hereafter OECD, 'Making Mental Health Count').

[26] McSherry and Wilson, 'Capacity' (n 5) 66.

[27] Australian Institute of Health and Welfare, *Mental Health Services in Australia 2018*, <https://www.aihw.gov.au/reports/mental-health-services/mental-health-services-in-australia/report-contents/summary-of-mental-health-services-in-australia> (last accessed 25 October 2019) (hereafter AIHW, 'Mental Health 2018'); 'Law Reform or Systemic Reform?' (n 5) 555.

[28] AIHW 'Mental Health 2018' (n 27).

[29] Australian Institute of Health and Welfare, Admitted Patient Mental Health Related Care, <https://www.aihw.gov.au/getmedia/71900b8a-fe09-4a6b-9b3c-350698cc82c9/Mental-health-related-admitted-patient-care-2011-12.pdf.aspx> (last accessed 25 October 2019) (hereafter AIHW, 'Admitted Patient').

[30] Edwina M Light and others, 'Community Treatment Orders in Australia: Rates and Patterns of Use' (2012) 20(6) Australas Psychiatry 478, 480 (hereafter Light, 'CTOs').

[31] Patrick Keown and others, 'Changes in the use of the Mental Health Act 1983 in England 1984/85 to 2015/16' (2018) 213 Br J Psychiatry 595, 596 (hereafter Keown, 'Changes in Use of MHA'); NHS Digital Mental Health Statistics Annual Figures 2017–2018 (9 October 2018) https://files.digital.nhs.uk/34/B224B3/ment-heal-act-stat-eng-2017-18-summ-rep.pdf (last accessed 6 May 2019) (hereafter NHS, 'Digital').

[32] NHS Digital (n 31).

admission and treatment do so to avoid coercion under mental health law, whereas due to resource constraints some voluntary patents end up being detained under mental health law in order to be able to access treatment, so there is some overlap between the voluntary and involuntary categories. The application of mental health law is also influenced by a number of non-legal factors. For example, comparisons of involuntary detention and treatment indicate differences between different countries, cultures, and even mental health facilities as well as demographic factors such as the type of mental impairment a person has as well as race, gender, and ethnicity.[33]

Nevertheless, even though *any* use of legally sanctioned coercion is always a matter of human rights concern and carries with it the prospect of abuse, it should also be remembered that mental health law only applies to a relatively small proportion of persons who suffer from mental health problems and an even smaller proportion of the general community. That is, persons involuntarily detained and treated under mental health law are not the 'norm' and there are millions of persons with mental impairment globally who are voluntarily choosing mental health treatment, presumably because they believe it provides them with some benefits. It is true, as Sascha Callaghan and colleagues point out, that not all persons with mental impairment who are involuntarily detained and treated are thankful for the intervention in retrospect.[34] But, it is estimated that a substantial proportion (between 40 and 80 per cent) are grateful, especially if they perceived the admission procedures to be fair[35] and the treatment was successful in causing mental capacity to be regained.[36] There are also a significant number of persons with unmet need who have difficulty accessing any treatment at all, or who would like to access treatments which are not currently offered.[37]

1.3 What is the Call for the Abolition of Mental Health Law, Where Has it Come From, Why Has it Emerged Now, and Why Does it Matter?

1.3.1 What is the Call for the Abolition of Mental Health Law?

By 'the call for the abolition of mental health law' I mean the repeal of mental health law and with it the removal of any form of legal compulsion for hospital admission or psychiatric treatment in any and all circumstances.[38] Instead, abolitionists propose that persons with mental impairment would be offered various formal and informal supports to assist them in considering their situation and in ascertaining their

[33] Gooding and others, 'Alternatives to Coercion' (n 8).

[34] Sascha Callaghan and others, 'Risk of Suicide Is Insufficient Warrant for Coercive Treatment of Mental Illness' (2013) 36 Int J Law Psychiatry 374, 383 (hereafter Callaghan, 'Risk of Suicide').

[35] Stefan Priebe and others, 'Patients' Views and Readmissions 1 Year After Involuntary Hospitalisation' (2009) 194 Br J Psychiatry 49, 53 (hereafter Priebe, 'Patients' Views').

[36] Gareth S Owen and others, 'Retrospective Views of Psychiatric In-Patients Regaining Mental Capacity' (2009) 195 Br J Psychiatry 403, 405 (hereafter Owen, 'Retrospective Views').

[37] Emmanuel Umama-Agada and others, 'Variations in Involuntary Admission Rates at Three Psychiatry Centres in Dublin Involuntary Admission Study (DIAS). Can the Differences Be Explained?' (2018) 57 Int J Law Psychiatry 17 (hereafter Umama-Agada, 'Variations in Involuntary Admission').

[38] General Comment 1 (n 22) [28], [42].

individual will and preferences.[39] In rare cases where a person's will and preferences cannot be determined, a supporter or facilitator may need to make a decision for the individual in accordance with 'the best interpretation of his or her will and preferences'.[40] More recently, abolitionists have become divided between whether the abolition of mental health law means the absolute banning of legal coercion of any kind,[41] or whether some forms of legal coercion may be permitted by the CRPD provided it does not discriminate against persons with disabilities, that is, so called 'disability neutrality' although most still oppose involuntary detention and treatment.[42] I explain the Abolition with Support model in detail in Chapters 3 and 4 to 7.

While the 'fusion model' in Northern Ireland could be claimed to be the 'abolition' of mental health law as it abolishes separate stand-alone mental health legislation, it still permits substituted decision-making in the best interests of persons who lack mental capacity and to this extent is only a change in form, rather than substance.[43] It has been widely criticized by abolitionists as being non-compliant with the CRPD,[44] and in my view is better characterized as a 'reform' of rather than the 'abolition' of mental health law (see my discussion of the Mental Capacity with Support model in Chapter 8). While the repeal of mental health law would mean that persons with mental impairments would be governed by general medical law, that is, the Mental Capacity with Support model, most abolitionists would require the abolition of compulsion with respect to persons lacking mental capacity as well. However, some legislation regulating supported-decision making and spelling out suitable safeguards would probably be required by abolitionists.

1.3.2 Where Does the Call for the Abolition of Mental Health Law Come From? Why Has it Emerged Now?

Given that mental health law is a form of state-sanctioned coercion and has always been controversial, it is hardly surprising that calls for the abolition of mental health

[39] Piers Gooding, *A New Era for Mental Health Law and Policy: Supportive-Decision Making and the UN Convention On the Rights of Persons with Disability* (Cambridge University Press 2017) 118 (hereafter Gooding, *A New Era*).

[40] General Comment 1 (n 22) [26]; Anna Arstein-Kerslake and Eilionoir Flynn 'The General Comment on Article 12 of the Convention on the Rights of Persons with Disabilities: A Roadmap for Equality Before the Law' (2016) 20(4) Int J Hum Rights 471, 477 (hereafter Arstein-Kerslake and Flynn, 'Article 12').

[41] See for example, Tina Minkowitz, 'CRPD and Transformative Equality' (2017) 13 Int J Law Context 77 (hereafter Minkowitz, 'Transformative'); Amita Dhanda, 'From Duality to Indivisibility: Mental Health Care and Human Rights' (2016) 32 S Afr J Hum Rights 438 (hereafter Dhanda, 'From Duality to Indivisibility').

[42] Jill Stavert, 'Paradigm Shift of Paradigm Paralysis? National Mental Health and Capacity Law and Implementing the CRPD in Scotland' (2018) 7 Laws 26, 28 (hereafter Stavert, 'Paradigm Shift'); Piers Gooding and Eilionoir Flynn, 'Querying the Call to Introduce Mental Capacity Testing to Mental Health Law: Does the Doctrine of Necessity Provide an Alternative?' (2015) 4 Laws 246, 261 (Gooding and Flynn, 'Mental Capacity Testing'); Eilionoir Flynn and Anna Arstein-Kerslake, 'State Intervention in the Lives of People with Disabilities: The Case for a Disability-Neutral Framework' (2017) (13) Int J Law Context 39, 57 (hereafter Flynn and Arstein-Kerslake, 'State Intervention').

[43] *Mental Capacity Act* 2016 (Northern Ireland).

[44] Ad Hoc Joint Committee on the Mental Capacity Bill 'Report on the Mental Capacity Bill' 25 January 2016 (NIA 353/11-16), [23], [29]–[34] (hereafter 'Northern Ireland Bill Report').

law are not new. I set out a detailed history of where the call for the abolition of mental health has come from in Chapter 3. However, the most recent iteration of the call for the abolition of mental health law emerged after the negotiation and entry into force of the CRPD in 2008. Since then, mental health law has been increasingly criticized on the grounds that it is discriminatory and is an unnecessary interference with individual liberty and bodily integrity. While it may not yet be a mainstream view, the abolition of mental health law and other substitute decision-making regimes (which allow a third party to make decisions contrary to the will and preferences of the person with disabilities) has for the first time been articulated by abolitionists as a clear political goal.[45]

The CRPD is unique among international human rights treaties in that it was negotiated between States Parties with strong involvement from civil society, especially Disabled Persons Organizations (DPOs). While there are different accounts of the negotiation of the CRPD from various people who participated in it,[46] what is clear is that the negotiations with respect to the abolition of mental health law, particularly the right to legal capacity in Article 12, were especially fraught, at one point even threatening to derail the whole convention.[47] Unfortunately, the status of involuntary detention and psychiatric treatment was left deliberately unresolved, as states refused to agree to abolish mental health law and disability advocates decided that the CRPD should not mention the issue at all for fear of giving the retention of mental health law legitimacy.[48] While Amita Dhanda has claimed victory for abolitionists in that the CRPD does not contain a positive right permitting States Parties to use involuntary detention and psychiatric treatment,[49] this seems rather hollow given that most states already have a mental health law of some kind, making the issue of abolition rather than permission key to implementation. In the circumstances, the concept of a strategically motivated 'negotiated silence' on the future of mental health

[45] For example, Minkowitz, 'Abolishing Mental Health Laws' (n 11); Amita Dhanda, 'Universal Legal Capacity as a Universal Human Right' in Michael Dudley, Derrick Silove, and Fran Gale (eds), *Mental Health and Human Rights: Vision, Praxis and Courage* (Oxford University Press 2012), 177 (hereafter Dhanda, 'Universal Legal Capacity'); Kristen Booth Glen, 'Changing Paradigms: Mental Capacity, Legal Capacity, Guardianship, and Beyond' (2012) 44 Colum Hum Rts L Rev 93 (hereafter Booth Glen, 'Changing Paradigms'); Eilionoir Flynn and Anna Arstein-Kerslake, 'Legislating Personhood: Realising the Right to Support in Exercising Legal Capacity' (2014) 10(1) Int J Law Context 81 (hereafter Flynn and Arstein-Kerslake, 'Legislating Personhood'); Mary Keys, 'Article 12 [Equal Recognition before the Law]' in Valentina Fina, Rachele Cera, and Giuseppe Palmisano (eds), *The United Nations Convention on the Rights of Persons with Disabilities: A Commentary* (Cham: Springer 2017) 263 (hereafter Keys 'Article 12'); Theresa Degener, 'Disability in a Human Rights Context' (2016) 5 Laws 35 (hereafter Degener 'Disability'); General Comment 1 (n 22).

[46] For example, Anna MacQuarrie and Connie Laurin-Bowie, *Our Lives, Our Voices: People with Intellectual Disabilities and Their Families* (University of Pennsylvania Press 2013) (hereafter MacQuarrie and Laurin-Bowie, Our Lives, Our Voices); Richard M Duffy and Brendan D Kelly, 'Rights, Laws and Tensions: A Comparative Analysis of the Convention on the Rights of Persons with Disabilities and the Who Resource Book on Mental Health, Human Rights and Legislation' (2017) 54 Int J Law Psychiatry 26, 28 (hereafter Duffy and Kelly, 'Rights, Laws and Tensions').

[47] Craigie, 'Panel Event' (n 8) 165.

[48] Rosemary Kayess and Phillip French, 'Out of Darkness into Light? Introducing the Convention on the Rights of Persons with Disabilities' (2008) 8(1) Hum Rights Law Rev 1, 30 (hereafter Kayess and French, 'Out of Darkness').

[49] Dhandra, 'From Duality to Indivisibility' (n 41) 444.

law, as advocated by Annegret Kämpf seems to be a more accurate description of what occurred.[50]

Nonetheless, post-CRPD abolitionists argue that collectively the general principle of non-discrimination (Article 4) and the rights to equality (Article 5), legal capacity (Article 12), liberty (Article 14), bodily integrity (Article 17), independent living (Article 19), health (Article 25), and the ban on torture and cruel and unusual punishment (Article 15), all require the abolition of mental health law. As Melvyn Freeman and colleagues have remarked 'countries that originally ratified the CRPD are facing intense pressure to implement far reaching changes that challenge fundamental principles of mental health care and treatment hitherto widely accepted as reflecting a human rights perspective . . . '[51]

The abolition of mental health law has been repeatedly and consistently advocated by the CRPD Committee, the international human rights body responsible for interpreting and monitoring the implementation of the CRPD, in its concluding observations to states' reports,[52] General Comment No 1 (Article 12, Equal Recognition before the Law),[53] the Guidelines on the Right to Liberty and Security of Persons with Disabilities,[54] and recently in General Comment 6 (Article 5, Equality and Non-Discrimination).[55] In particular, in General Comment No. 1, which is probably the clearest and most pointed instruction to states to abolish mental health law, the CRPD Committee has unequivocally and controversially stated:

> State parties' obligation to replace substitute decision-making regimes by supported decision-making requires both the abolition of substitute decision-making regimes and the development of supported decision-making alternatives. The development of supported decision-making systems in parallel with the maintenance of substitute decision-making regimes is not sufficient to comply with article 12 of the Convention [equality before the law/ legal capacity];[56]

[50] Annagret Kampf, 'Involuntary Treatment Decisions: Using Negotiated Silence to Facilitate Change?' in Bernadette McSherry and Penelope Weller (eds), *Rethinking Rights-Based Mental Health Laws* (Hart Publishing 2010) 129, 144–46 (hereafter Kampf, 'Negotiated Silence').

[51] Melvyn Colin Freeman and others, 'Reversing Hard Won Victories in the Name of Human Rights: a Critique of the General Comment on Article 12 of the UN Convention on the Rights of Persons with Disabilities' (2015) 2 Lancet Psych 844, 844 (hereafter Freeman, 'Reversing Hard Won Victories').

[52] For example, Committee on Rights of Persons with Disabilities, 'Concluding Observations on the Initial report of Australia, adopted by the Committee at its tenth session' (2–13 September 2013) CRPD/C/AUS/CO/1 (hereafter 'Concluding Observations Australia') [34], and more recently, Committee on Rights of Persons with Disabilities, 'Concluding Observations on the United Kingdom' (3 October 2017) CRPD/C/GBR/CO/1) [31] and [55] (hereafter 'Concluding Observations UK'); George Szmukler reports that the CRPD Committee has called for the abolition of all substitute decision-making regimes in over twenty state reports: George Szmukler, 'Compulsion and "Coercion" in Mental Health Care' (2015) 14 World Psych 259, 260 (hereafter Szmukler, 'Compulsion and "Coercion" ').

[53] General Comment 1 (n 22).

[54] CRPD Committee, Guidelines on Article 14 of the Convention on the Rights of Persons with Disabilities: The Right to Liberty and Security of Persons (14th Session, September 2015), [6] and [10] (hereafter 'CRPD Guidelines').

[55] CRPD Committee, General Comment 6: Equality and Non-discrimination (Article 5), 9 March 2018, [30].

[56] ibid [24] (hereafter 'General Comment 6').

and

> State parties must abolish policies and legislative provisions that allow or perpetuate forced treatment, as it is an ongoing violation found in mental health laws across the globe, despite empirical evidence indicating its lack of effectiveness and the views of people using mental health systems who have experienced deep pain and trauma as a result of forced treatment.[57]

Similarly, the United Nations Special Rapporteur on Torture, Juan E. Méndez, has called for 'an absolute ban on all forced and non-consensual medical interventions against persons with disabilities'[58] including those with mental impairments, although he has subsequently indicated that this call may not apply where there is a risk of harm to self or others.[59] The call for the abolition of mental health law has also been recently endorsed by Dainius Puras, the Special Rapporteur on the Right of Everyone to the Enjoyment of the Highest Attainable Standard of Physical and Mental Health,[60] an independent expert who reports to the United Nations Human Rights Committee. He has stated that:

> Considering that the right to health is now understood within the framework of the Convention on the Rights of Persons with Disabilities, immediate action is required to radically reduce medical coercion and facilitate the move towards an end to all forced psychiatric treatment and confinement. In that connection, States must not permit substitute decision-makers to provide consent on behalf of persons with disabilities on decisions that concern their physical or mental integrity; instead, support should be provided at all times for them to make decisions, including in emergency and crisis situations.[61]

Notably, rather than call for the immediate abolition of mental health law, the Special Rapporteur has instead proposed that States Parties take steps towards the abolition of mental health law, such as developing mainstream alternatives to coercion in policy and practice, developing a plan to reduce with a view to eliminating coercive medical practices in consultation with persons with mental impairment, increasing investment in research, and sharing good practices between countries.[62] Nevertheless, the abolition rather than the reform of mental health law is the ultimate aim.

The call for the abolition of mental health law, emerging as a result of the so-called 'paradigm shift' of the CRPD, has also spawned a growing literature.[63] Abolitionists use their individual involvement in and the voices of disabled persons' organizations

[57] ibid [38].
[58] Mendez, 'Torture Report' (n 23) [89(b)].
[59] Gooding, *A New Era* (n 39) 78.
[60] UNHRC, 'Report of the Special Rapporteur on the Right of Everyone to the Enjoyment of the Highest Attainable Standard of Physical and Mental Health' (28 March 2017) A/HRC/35/21, [63]–[66].
[61] ibid [65].
[62] ibid [66].
[63] For example (n 45).

in the negotiation and implementation of the CRPD to give their arguments moral force.[64]

However, Australia, Canada, and a number of other jurisdictions, have made interpretive declarations that they do not interpret the CRPD as requiring the abolition of substituted decision-making, although substitute decision-making is only permitted on a limited basis, such as where it is a 'last resort' and subject to safeguards, which is still a high standard.[65] Notably, the United Kingdom did not make any such declaration. Mary Donnelly speculates that the reason was 'not because of a plan to abolish compulsory treatment',[66] but because it was never seriously contemplated that the CRPD could require the abolition of mental health law.[67] This is confirmed by the UK Office of Disability Issues which has taken the view that the *Mental Health Act* 1983 (UK) and *Mental Capacity Act* 2005 (UK) are compliant with the CRPD, despite providing for substitute decision-making.[68] Further, the most recent independent review of mental health law in the United Kingdom by Simon Wellesley has rejected the abolition of mental health law advocated by the CRPD Committee as both undesirable and as unnecessary to recognize the United Kingdom's human rights obligations under the European Convention on Human Rights (ECHR) and the CRPD, although he proposes a series of reforms (see Chapter 8 section 8.4).[69] Since the CRPD has come into force, no state has abolished mental health law, although substitute decision-making has been recently abolished with respect to guardianship law in Columbia and Peru. Language barriers make it difficult for me to evaluate the Columbian and Peruvian legislation, although I note that Antonio Martinez-Pujalte argues that the Peruvian legislation has gone too far in granting autonomy to persons with disabilities in respect of making them responsible for arranging their own supports.[70] While it will be interesting to see whether the abolition of substitute decision-making with respect to guardianship in Columbia and Peru really does result in significant benefits and freedom for persons with disabilities in those jurisdictions, mental health contains some unique challenges such as the effects of episodic illness, delusions, self-harm, suicide, and how to deal with persons in acute crises which may explain why States Parties are reluctant to abolish mental health law. As Oliver Lewis observes, it is 'unprecedented in international human rights law for a treaty body to articulate as a norm something that is not reflected in a law anywhere'.[71]

[64] For example, Flynn and Arstein-Kerslake, 'State Intervention' (n 42) 39, 42; Dhanda, 'From Duality to Indivisibility' (n 41) 448.

[65] CRPD, declarations and reservations, <http://treaties.un.org/Pages/ViewDetails.aspx?src=TREATY&mtdsg_no=IV-15&chapter=4&lang=en> (13 October 2013) (hereafter 'CRPD Interpretive Declarations').

[66] Mary Donnelly, *Healthcare Decision-Making and the Law* (Oxford University Press 2010) 2 (hereafter Donnelly, *Healthcare Decision-Making*).

[67] ibid.

[68] Office of Disability Issues, UK Initial Report on the UN Convention on the Rights of Persons with Disabilities (2011) 1, 40–41 (hereafter 'Office of Disability Issues Report').

[69] Independent Review of the MHA 1983, 'Modernising the Mental Health Act: Increasing Choice, Reducing Compulsion' (UK Government, Final Report, December 2018) (hereafter 'Wellesley Report').

[70] Antonio Martinez-Pujalte, 'Legal Capacity and Supported Decision-Making: Lessons from Some Recent Legal Reforms' (2019) 8 Laws 4, 17 (hereafter Martinez-Pujalte, 'Legal Capacity').

[71] Craigie (n 8) 165.

Further, not all international and regional human rights bodies have demanded the abolition of mental health law. For example, the Human Rights Committee, which monitors the International Covenant on Civil and Political Rights (ICCPR), noted in General Comment 35, contradicting the CRPD Committee, that the deprivation of liberty of persons with disability may be justified in some circumstances:

> the existence of a disability shall not in itself justify a deprivation of liberty but rather any deprivation of liberty must be necessary and proportionate, for the purpose of protecting the individual in question from serious harm or preventing injury to others. It must be applied only as a measure of last resort and for the shortest appropriate period of time, and must be accompanied by adequate procedural and substantive safeguards established by law.[72]

The Subcommittee on the Prevention of Torture and Other Cruel, Inhuman and Degrading Treatment and Punishment has also interpreted the CRPD as not only allowing involuntary detention and psychiatric treatment where persons lack mental capacity and are at risk of harming themselves or others, but points out that a failure to do so may also be a form of discrimination and cruel, inhuman, and degrading treatment and punishment.[73]

Similarly, the European Convention on Human Rights (ECHR) permits states to deprive persons of 'unsound mind' of their liberty where it is warranted due to medical necessity.[74] Under the ECHR involuntary detention and psychiatric treatment must also be subject to fair and speedy review procedures, a person must be held in a suitable facility (a hospital not a prison) and it must be proportionate.[75] While the European Court of Human Rights has considered the CRPD as being relevant, it has not joined the call for the abolition of mental health law.[76] In fact, the abolition of mental health law conflicts with jurisprudence on the right to life from the European Court of Human Rights and the English courts that the state has a heightened positive operational obligation to take reasonable steps to prevent the suicide of persons who are under the control of the state: prisoners,[77] administrative detainees,[78] military conscripts,[79] voluntary and involuntary psychiatric patients in hospital,[80] and

[72] UN Human Rights Committee, General Comment 35 Article 9 (Liberty and Security of the Person) 16 December 2014, CCPR/C/GC/35 (hereafter 'General Comment 35').

[73] Subcommittee on the Prevention of Torture and Other Cruel, Inhuman, or Degrading Treatment or Punishment, *Approach of the Subcommittee on Prevention of Torture and* Other Cruel, *Inhuman or Degrading Treatment or Punishment regarding the rights of persons institutionalized and treated medically without informed consent* CAT/OP/27/2 26 January 2016, [14]–[15] (hereafter 'Torture Subcommittee 2016 Report').

[74] Article 5(e), European Convention on Human Rights, opened for signature 1950 (entered into force 1 June 2010) (hereafter 'ECHR').

[75] John Dawson and Annagret Kampf, 'Incapacity Principles in Mental Health Laws in Europe' (2006) 12(3) Psychol, Psych and Law 310, 316 (hereafter Dawson and Kampf, 'Incapacity Principles')

[76] *N v Romania* App No 59132/08, 28 November 2017, [141]–[147] (hereafter *N v Romania*).

[77] *Keenan v United Kingdom* App No 27229195, 3 April 2001 (hereafter *Keenan v UK*).

[78] *Slimani v France* App No 57671/00, 27 October 2004 (hereafter *Slimani v France*).

[79] *Perevedentsevy v Russia* App No 39583/05, 13 October 2014 (hereafter *Perevedentsevy v Russia*).

[80] *Savage v South Essex Partnership NHS Foundation Trust* [2008] UKHL 74 (hereafter *Savage v South Essex Partnership NHS Foundation Trust*).

vulnerable persons in the community.[81] Such reasonable steps include a duty to involuntarily detain and treat persons with mental impairment who are at risk of suicide in certain circumstances.[82] Not surprisingly, those states which have conflicting obligations under the ECHR and the CRPD have tended to give precedence to their ECHR obligations, which are usually more embedded in domestic law.[83] Further, the ECHR and its jurisprudence is based on a reliance on the power of medical expertise and ethics that is well entrenched in western societies.[84]

In addition, the call for the abolition of mental health law has divided scholarly opinion. Some scholars, especially those involved in drafting the CRPD and the CRPD Committee, argue that the Abolition with Support model is the only way to implement the 'paradigm shift' in accordance with the letter and the spirit of the CRPD.[85] Others like me are more cautious and critical.[86] While they see some merits in the Abolition with Support model, as I explain below, they believe that the CRPD does not go that far and prefer significant legal and systemic mental health reform to complete abolition. Still others, such as Paul Appelbaum, do not believe that the abolitionists have wrongly interpreted the CRPD at all (despite States Parties never agreeing to the Abolition with Support model), but are critical of the CRPD itself and believe that the CRPD rather than the Abolition with Support model is what needs to be undone.[87]

1.3.3 Why Does the Call for the Abolition of Mental Health Law Matter?

Given that States Parties are unlikely to abolish mental health law as a political reality, (and it is my argument that mental health law should *not* be abolished), why then does

[81] *Mammadov v Azerbaijan* App No 4762/05, 17 March 2010 (hereafter *Mammadov v Azerbaijan*).

[82] *Rabone v Penine Care NHS Foundation Trust* [2012] UKSC 2 (hereafter *Rabone v Penine Care NHS Foundation Trust*); *Reynolds v United Kingdom* App No 2694/08, 13 March 2012 (hereafter *Reynolds v United Kingdom*).

[83] For example, Northern Ireland Bill Report (n 44) para 23.

[84] Philip Fennell and Urfan Khaliq, 'Conflicting or Complementary Obligations? The UN Disability Rights Convention, the European Convention on Human Rights and English Law' [2011](6) EHRLR 662, 671–72 (hereafter Fennell and Khaliq, 'CRPD and ECHR').

[85] For example, n 41, n 42, and n 45.

[86] For example, Wilson, 'Right to Life' and 'Vulnerability' (n 8); Gavin Davidson and others, 'An International Comparison of Legal Frameworks for Supported and Substitute Decision-Making in Mental Health Services' (2016) 44 Int J Law Psychiatry 30, 31 (hereafter Davidson 'International Comparison'); Matthew Burch, 'Autonomy, Respect, and the Rights of Persons with Disabilities in Crisis' (2017) 34(3) J App Philos 389; Matthe Scholten and Jakov Gather, 'Adverse Consequences of Article 12 of the UN Convention on the Rights of Persons with Disabilities for Persons with Mental Disabilities and an Alternative Way Forward' (2017) 44 J Med Ethics 1 (hereafter Scholten and Gather, 'Adverse Consequences'); Katrine Del Villar, 'Should Supported Decision-Making Replace Substituted Decision-Making? The Convention on the Rights of Persons with Disabilities and Coercive Treatment under Queensland's Mental Health Act 2000' (2015) 4 Laws 173 (hereafter Del Villar 'Supported Decision-Making'); David Bilchitz, 'Dignity, Fundamental Rights and Legal Capacity: Moving Beyond the Paradigm Set by the General Comment on Article 12 of the Convention on the Rights of Persons with Disabilities' (2016) 32(3) S Afr J Hum Rights 410 (hereafter Bilchitz 'Dignity, Fundamental Rights and Legal Capacity').

[87] Paul S Appelbaum, 'Protecting the Rights of Persons with Disabilities: An International Convention and Its Problems' (2016) 67(4) Psychiatr Serv 366, 368 (hereafter Appelbaum, 'Protecting the Rights of Persons with Disabilities').

the call for the abolition of mental health law matter? In this book, I argue that the call for the abolition of mental health law is important for five reasons. First, as discussed below, the CRPD is one of the most widely adopted conventions in the world and is regarded as the leading international human rights instrument governing the rights of persons with disabilities. Therefore, the views of the treaty body responsible for interpreting and monitoring the CRPD, while not binding on States' Parties, have weight and cannot be simply dismissed out of hand.

Second, the call for the abolition of mental health law brings into the debate about the future of mental health law the voices of a sub-group of persons with mental impairment who often call themselves 'psychiatric survivors' (although I contend they are not representative of *all* persons with mental impairment).[88] I also believe that the call for the abolition of mental health law amplifies the voices of all persons with mental impairment (regardless of whether they agree with abolition or not) which is necessary to include persons with mental impairments in policy-making and to honour the dignity, equality and participation of all persons with mental impairments. The call for the abolition of mental health law also provides a valuable critique of mental health law: it draws attention to the weaknesses of mental health law in theory and practice and how it might be improved. It is, however, important to acknowledge that for some 'patient advocate groups upholding rights to refuse treatment . . . is not a negotiating position'[89] and that for them anything less than the abolition of mental health law will not suffice.

Third, while radical ideas like the abolition of mental health law may never come to fruition, they often have the effect of shifting the ground of the entire debate, making ideas which were once rejected as extreme seem more plausible (such as, the Mental Capacity with Support model), and have a role in opening up discussion of new alternatives and reforms. For instance, the call for the abolition of mental health law has inspired a number of alternative interpretations of the CRPD which stop short of calling for the abolition of mental health law, but which aim to reduce coercion and to support more persons with mental impairment to make their own healthcare decisions. What all of these approaches have in common is a new emphasis on recognizing and respecting the subjective will and preferences of the individual, albeit to different extents. That is, since the adoption of the CRPD the development of the law has shifted away from the traditional model of care, welfare, and protection as reflected in mental health law towards liberty, autonomy, self-determination, and non-discrimination. In addition, the CRPD may be influencing the development of the 'best interests' test in general medical law which, in recent English cases, has begun to give greater weight to individual wishes and preferences, at times over a person's objective medical best interests.[90]

[88] Anne Plumb, 'UN Convention on the Rights of Persons with Disabilities: Out of the Frying Pan into the Fire?' in Jill Anderson and Bob Sapey Helen Splander (eds), *Madness, Distress and the Politics of Disablement* (Policy Press 2015) 184, 187 (hereafter Plumb, 'Out of the Frying Pan').

[89] Alan Rosen and others, 'The Human Rights of People with Severe and Persistent Mental Illness: Can Conflicts between Dominant and Non-Dominant Paradigms be Reconciled?' in Michael Dudley, Derrick Silove, and Fran Gale (eds), *Mental Health and Human Rights: Vision, Praxis and Courage* (Oxford University Press 2012) 297, 306 (hereafter Rosen 'Severe and Persistent Mental Illness').

[90] For example, *X NHS Trust v B* [2015] EWCOP 60 (hereafter *X NHS Trust v B*).

Fourth, the call for the abolition of mental health law and the CRPD has sparked widespread mental health and guardianship law reform activity. For instance, in Australia, Tasmania,[91] Victoria,[92] Western Australia,[93] the Australian Capital Territory,[94] and Queensland[95] have all enacted new mental health laws post-CRPD and New South Wales[96] and South Australia[97] have conducted reviews and reforms to their mental health laws. The Australian Law Reform Commission has also completed a report on Equality, Capacity and Disability in Commonwealth Laws in November 2014.[98] As Sascha Callaghan and Christopher Ryan observe, each of these reviews and reforms were prompted by the CRPD to make domestic legislation more compliant with human rights.[99] Internationally, there have also been a number of post-CRPD reviews and reforms. As noted above there has been an Independent Review[100] of mental health law in England and Northern Ireland has adopted a 'fusion model' which will abolish stand-alone mental health law, but still permit substitute decision-making in the best interests of persons who are assessed to lack mental capacity.[101] The CRPD has led to supported decision-making legislation being enacted in Ireland.[102] In Canada, the CRPD has prompted provinces that did not already have supported decision-making, such as Newfoundland and Labrador and Prince Edward Island to create such systems, influenced the development of disability jurisprudence, and been part of various reviews, reports, and programmes.[103] In New Zealand, the compatibility of the *Mental Health (Compulsory Assessment and Treatment Act) 1992* with the CRPD was reviewed as part of the Disability Action Plan 2014–18[104] and a recent inquiry into mental health and addiction proposes reform to bring mental health law into line with the CRPD (although it appears not go so far as abolition).[105]

[91] *Mental Health Act* 2013 (Tas) (hereafter MHA Tas).

[92] *Mental Health Act* 2014 (Vic) (hereafter MHA Vic).

[93] *Mental Health Act* 2014 (WA) (hereafter MHA WA).

[94] *Mental Health Act* 2015 (ACT) (hereafter MHA ACT).

[95] *Mental Health Act* 2016 (Qld) (hereafter MHA Qld).

[96] *Mental Health Amendment (Statutory Review Act)* 2014 (NSW) amending *Mental Health Act* 2007 (NSW) (hereafter MHA NSW).

[97] *Mental Health (Review) Amendment Act* 2016 (SA) amending *Mental Health Act* 2009 (SA) (hereafter MHA SA).

[98] Australian Law Reform Commission, *Equality, Capacity and Disability in Commonwealth Laws* (Australian Government 2014) (hereafter 'ALRC Report').

[99] Sascha Callaghan and Christopher Ryan 'An Evolving Revolution: Evaluating Australia's Compliance with the Convention on the Rights of Persons with Disabilities in Mental Health Law' (2016) 31(2) UNSWLJ 596, 597 (hereafter Callaghan and Ryan, 'An Evolving Revolution').

[100] Wellesley Report (n 69).

[101] *Mental Capacity Act* 2016 (Northern Ireland) (hereafter MCA NI).

[102] *Assisted Decision-Making (Capacity) Act* 2015 (Ireland) (hereafter 'Assisted Decision-Making Ireland').

[103] Steven Hoffman and others, 'Is the UN Convention on the Rights of Persons with Disabilities Impacting Mental Health Laws and Policies in High-Income Countries? A Case Study of Implementation in Canada' (2016) 16(28) BMC Int Health Hum Rights <https://www.ncbi.nlm.nih.gov/pmc/articles/PMC5105274/> accessed 24 November 2020 (hereafter Hoffman, 'Implementation of CRPD on MHL in Canada').

[104] <https://www.health.govt.nz/our-work/mental-health-and-addictions/mental-health/mental-health-and-human-rights-assessment> accessed 24 November 2020 (hereafter 'NZ Mental Health Review').

[105] Government Inquiry into Mental Health and Addiction 'He Ara Oranga: Report of the Government Inquiry into Mental Health and Addiction' (Crown, 2018) <https://mentalhealth.inquiry.govt.nz/inquiry-report/he-ara-oranga/> accessed 24 November 2020 (hereafter 'NZ Mental Health and Addiction Inquiry').

Fifth, while many scholars and law reformers have since claimed that certain models of mental health law reform are 'CRPD-compliant', the issue of what a 'human rights model' of mental health law looks like remains highly contested. Therefore, even if mental health law is not abolished two questions remain: how should the CRPD be interpreted and what does the CRPD require states to do with mental health law? These two questions inform my conceptual framework, methodology, and scope, discussed in the next section.

1.4 How Will I Determine Whether Mental Health Law Should be Abolished or Reformed?

There are, of course, many different ways of answering my overarching research question of whether mental health law should be abolished or reformed. A common approach has been to list and analyse all of the arguments for and against the abolition and reform of mental health law and to argue a position one way or the other.[106] However, this has resulted in the division of the literature into 'camps' for and against the abolition of mental health law, which loosely resemble the three models I have identified above, and has done little to resolve the current impasse between abolitionists and States Parties. To be able to break the deadlock, it is necessary to gain a deeper understanding of the problem and what is driving the arguments for and against the abolition of mental health law, as I do in Chapters 2 and 3, rather than to skip ahead to defend a particular solution. However, in attempting to chart a middle course through such contested territory, I find myself being at once too conservative and too radical, and in danger of being attacked from all sides. I realize that by arguing against the abolition of mental health law, I am, as John Dawson puts it, arguing 'somewhat against my legal training'.[107] But, like John Dawson I argue for a vision of disability rights which goes beyond non-interference and negative liberty, to intervention that may empower individuals to maximize their positive liberty using both medical and social support to live full lives.[108]

Despite such a risk I rely on the strength of the breadth and depth of my research and the rigour of my reasoning to support my arguments. It is also necessary to analyse the problem using an appropriate conceptual framework. I have chosen the CRPD and international human rights law as my conceptual framework which I have used to develop 'the interpretive compass', based on dignity (including autonomy), equality, and participation. However, my approach to considering whether mental health law should be abolished or reformed is not purely doctrinal. Instead I have used what might be called a 'jurisprudential' or 'ethical' approach by exploring the deep principles or values which underpin the CRPD and international human rights law, namely those I have selected for my 'interpretive compass' dignity (including autonomy), equality, and participation. I explain each of my approaches below.

[106] See, for example, n 45 and n 86.

[107] John Dawson, 'Concepts of Liberty in Mental Health Law' (2009) 12(1) Otago LR 23, 23 (hereafter Dawson, 'Concepts of Liberty').

[108] ibid 29.

1.4.1 The CRPD and International Human Rights Law as My Conceptual Framework

Whether the CRPD is the 'paradigm shift' it is widely claimed to be, or simply the latest 'fad' in the 'fashions and cycles'[109] of mental health law, the use of the CRPD as my conceptual framework can be justified on legal, political, and moral grounds. From a legal perspective, the CRPD is a core international human rights treaty that is legally binding on Australia in international law with 161 signatories and 177 ratifications.[110] The CRPD is also widely regarded as the leading international human rights instrument governing the rights of persons with mental impairment. From a political perspective, the CRPD is the primary political tool that is being used to advance the rights of persons with mental impairment and is being taken seriously by Australian governments who have referred to it in the National Disability Insurance Scheme,[111] National Disability Strategy,[112] the ALRC enquiry, and the law reforms outlined in section 1.3.3 above. Finally, from a moral perspective, the CRPD in furthering the core human rights values of human dignity, equality, non-discrimination, freedom, universality, and human diversity has a strong moral weight in shaping a new vision of persons with disabilities as active participants in their own lives and society.

However, given the discord surrounding the negotiation of the CRPD explained above, it was not possible to achieve more than a fragile consensus, making the interpretation of the CRPD unusually difficult and contested. Djeffal Christian has remarked, 'at high level diplomatic discussions the law is sometimes left in a fuzzy state for the sake of achieving agreement'.[113] The result is that many international human rights treaties, including the CRPD, can be conceptualized as 'incompletely theorized agreements', especially where there is a key issue which is not directly addressed in the text of the convention and on which the parties vehemently disagree. As noted by Rosemary Kayess and Philip French, 'the CRPD, like all international instruments, is ultimately a negotiated text. It is therefore unrealistic to expect it to reflect a fully coherent or comprehensive exposition of disability rights'.[114] John Dawson also observes that 'many indicators that would usually be present in well-drafted legislation to show how different aspects of a code fit together seem deliberately omitted from the Convention to avoid controversy between those holding incompatible views in the drafting process'.[115]

In addition, interpretation during treaty implementation is often conceived of as an ongoing process, as parties work together to develop the meaning of the treaty and to

[109] Michael D Kirby 'Law Reform, Politics and Mental Health' (1983) 17(1) Aust NZ J Psychiatry 39 (hereafter Kirby, 'Law Reform').

[110] United Nations, Enable, <http://www.un.org/disabilities/> accessed 4 June 2019 (hereafter 'CRPD signatories and ratifications'.

[111] *National Disability Insurance Scheme Act* 2013 (Cth) s 3(a) (hereafter NDIS Act).

[112] Council of Australian Governments, *National Disability Strategy 2010–2020* (2011) 16 (hereafter 'Disability Strategy').

[113] Djeffal Christian, *Static and Evolutive Treaty Interpretation* (Cambridge University Press 2015) 7(hereafter Christian, *Treaty Interpretation*).

[114] Kayess and French, 'Out of Darkness' (n 48) 33.

[115] John Dawson, 'A Realistic Approach to Assessing Mental Health Laws Compliance with the UNCRPD' (2015) 40 Int J Law Psychiatry 70, 71 (hereafter Dawson, 'A Realistic Approach').

translate it into reality.[116] As Sandra Fredman puts it, human rights are no more than 'a value pre-commitment to which society as a whole is bound'[117] which 'anchors rather than concludes discussion'.[118] Therefore, the meaning of a treaty is not an objective artefact but must be forged and reforged as part of the deliberations of the relevant 'interpretive community'. As Oliver Lewis has observed, 'the CRPD is inspiring not because it codifies a pre-existing reality, but because it articulates a shared reality which has yet to be explained'.[119] Indeed, the CRPD expressly contemplates that persons with disability will participate in that process of treaty implementation and monitoring,[120] and as I set out in Chapter 7 section 7.6, participation is an important principle in its own right and is part of recognizing the dignity and equality of persons with disability.

It also means that my interpretation of the CRPD, being formulated without direct consultation with persons with disability (although after reviewing materials that have been produced by disability organizations and the CRPD Committee), can only be regarded as at best provisional, as 'an' interpretation, rather than 'the' interpretation. To do more than that would be to go beyond what the treaty drafters themselves were able to achieve. However, despite this inevitable limitation it is my intention (and hope) that my interpretation will provide some useful insights to all of those who have an interest in this debate, even if they do not agree with all of my conclusions.

While I have adopted the CRPD as my conceptual framework, I nonetheless reject the abolitionist interpretation set out above that the CRPD requires the abolition of mental health law. I argue that it relies on a narrow and selective reading of the human rights and fundamental freedoms the CRPD guarantees for persons with disabilities based on what is often called the 'strong interpretation' of the social model of disability. That is, the abolitionist interpretation may be viewed as being based on a 'shopping list' of rights which have been selected to support a particular outcome, rather than an integrated interpretation of the CRPD and what it seeks to achieve for persons with disabilities in its entirety. While treaty interpretation has long been described as an 'art' rather than a 'science'[121] and there is no doubt that it is a burgeoning and technical field, it is not my intention to engage in an exhaustive explanation of it or to provide a new theory of treaty interpretation. Instead, I argue that the CRPD needs to be interpreted using a more holistic approach in accordance with the tools and conventions of international human rights law, particularly the text of the CRPD and Articles 31 and 33 of the *Vienna Convention on the Law of Treaties* and the *interactive* model of social disability. I note that this methodology has also been recently used by Andrea

[116] Oliver Lewis, 'The Expressive, Educational and Proactive Roles of Human Rights: An Analysis of the United Nations Convention on the Rights of Persons with Disabilities' in Bernadette McSherry and Penelope Weller (eds), *Rethinking Rights-Based Mental Health Laws* (Hart Publishing 2010) 97, 105–106 (hereafter Lewis, 'Expressive, Educational and Proactive Roles').

[117] Sandra Fredman, *Human Rights Transformed: Positive Rights and Positive Duties* (Oxford University Press 2008) 110 (hereafter Fredman, *Human Rights Transformed*).

[118] ibid 106.

[119] Lewis, 'Expressive, Educational and Proactive Roles' (n 117) 100.

[120] CRPD, Art 33(3).

[121] Ulf Linderfalk, 'Is Treaty Interpretation an Art or a Science? International Law and Rational Decision-Making' (2015) 2(1) EUR J Int Law 169, 170 (hereafter Linderfalk 'Is Treaty Interpretation an Art or Science?')

Broderick[122] and Francesco Seatzu[123] to interpret the CRPD, especially the meaning of equality, and my book also relies and expands upon the methodology.

1.4.1.1 The Vienna Convention on the Law of Treaties (VCLT)

As a starting point, it is impossible to ignore Articles 31 to 33 of the Vienna Convention on the Law of Treaties (VCLT)[124] which are widely assumed to reflect customary international law and which have been praised for their flexibility in providing a process, rather than a prescription for interpretation. As Daniel Rietiker remarks 'while they avoid taking a firm stand on any of the great doctrinal debates on interpretation, it is hard to think of any approach to interpretation that would be totally excluded from Articles 31–33.'[125] Articles 31 to 33 of the VCLT have also been recognized as providing a delicate balance between the objective (textual), subjective (intention of the drafters), and teleological (object and purpose) approaches to interpretation.[126] The primary provision is Article 31(1) which provides:

> A treaty shall be interpreted in good faith in accordance with the ordinary meaning to be given to the terms of the treaty in their context and in light of its object and purpose.

There are four key concepts here: 'good faith', 'ordinary meaning', 'context', and 'object and purpose'. The first concept of good faith is self-explanatory. It requires honesty, fairness, and reasonableness in the process of interpretation and a result that is 'not manifestly absurd or unreasonable'.[127] The 'ordinary meaning to be given to the terms of the treaty' puts the focus of the interpretation firmly on the text which is presumed to be a faithful representation of the intentions of the parties. It gives an objective meaning to the treaty and means that words must be given their plain and natural meaning in general usage, unless the parties can prove that they intended a special meaning. While there may be more than one 'ordinary meaning', the principles of interpretation favour the 'ordinary meaning' that best fits the 'context' and 'object and purpose' of the treaty. The 'context' of the treaty includes the entire text of the treaty including any preamble and annexures. In circumstances where the ordinary meaning is 'unclear or ambiguous' or where the result is 'manifestly absurd or unreasonable' reference to preparatory materials is permitted.[128] The context also includes

[122] Andrea Broderick, *The Long and Winding Road to Equality and Inclusion for Persons with Disabilities: The United Nations Convention on the Rights of Persons with Disabilities* (Intersentia 2015), Chapter 1 (hereafter Broderick, *The Long and Winding Road to Equality*).

[123] Francesco Seatzu, 'The Convention on the Rights of Persons with Disabilities and International Human Rights Law' (2018) 7 Int Hum Rights Law Rev 82, 83 (hereafter Seatzu 'CRPD and IHRL').

[124] Vienna Convention on the Law of Treaties, opened for signature 23 May 1969, 1155 UNTS 331 (entered into force 27 January 1980) (hereafter VCLT).

[125] Daniel Rietiker, 'The Principle of "Effectiveness" in the Recent Jurisprudence of the European Court of Human Rights: Its Different Dimensions and Its Consistency with Public International Law—No Need for the Concept of Treaty Sui Generis' (2010) 79 Nord J Int Law 245, 253 (hereafter Rietiker, 'The Principle of "Effectiveness"').

[126] ibid.

[127] Oliver Dorr, 'Article 31' in Oliver Dorr and Kirsten Schmalenbach (eds), *Vienna Convention on the Law of Treaties: A Commentary* (Springer 2012) 559, 588 (hereafter Dorr, 'Article 31').

[128] VCLT (n 125) Art 32.

the circumstances at completion, any related agreements at and post-completion,[129] and consistency with the general principles of public international law.[130] The 'object and purpose' of the treaty redirects the parties back to their shared goals and reasons for entering into the treaty which can be evident from the title, preamble, and entire text. As Birgit Schlűtter argues:

> the interpretation of a treaty in light of its object and purpose is probably the most important rule of article 31(1) of the VCLT, both in general international law and in human rights law. In contrast to the literal and contextual method, an interpretation following the object and purpose touches on the very content of the rule, and, in the human rights context, on the values enshrined in it.[131]

The object and purpose can refer to the treaty as a whole and to the object and purpose of specific provisions.[132] Each of the four concepts in Articles 31–33 of the VCLT are of equal weight and operate in combination with each other, rather than hierarchically and I will use them that way in interpreting the CRPD.

1.4.1.2 Beyond the VCLT: Social and Political Aspects Including the Social and Human Rights Models of Disability

While the VCLT codifies the international customary law on treaties, it is not the exclusive source of law on treaty interpretation in international law and it is not without its limitations. For example, the 'rule of effectiveness' posits that treaties should be interpreted to give the fullest effect to all of their articles which is an independent rule of international law, even if the rule of effectiveness could also be interpreted as being part of 'good faith' and the 'objects and purpose' of the treaty under Article 31(1) of VCLT.[133] Other relevant principles include the rule of law,[134] and the presumptions of rational interpretation. For example, there are presumptions that the special should be given precedence over the general (*lex specialis derogate legi speciali*) and that later agreements should be given precedence over earlier ones (*lex posterior derogate legi priori*).

Further, the meaning of a human rights convention is not static, but can change over time both as a matter of treaty interpretation and of treaty implementation. First, 'evolutive' or dynamic theories of treaty interpretation in which treaties are conceptualized as a 'living instrument' have been influential in human rights jurisprudence and scholarship.[135] However, 'evolutive' interpretation is unlikely to be of great relevance to the CRPD at present, as it has only relatively recently been negotiated (coming into force on 3 May 2008) and there has been little time for legal and social changes to

[129] ibid Art 31(2).
[130] ibid Art 31(3)(c).
[131] Birgit Schlutter, 'Aspects of Human Rights Interpretation by the UN Treaty Bodies' in Helen Keller and Geir Ulfstein (eds), *UN Human Rights Treaty Bodies: Law and Legitimacy* (Cambridge University Press 2012) 278 (hereafter Schlutter, 'UN Treaty Bodies').
[132] ibid 281.
[133] Rietiker, 'The Principle of "Effectiveness"' (n 125) 253.
[134] Schlutter, 'UN Treaty Bodies' (n 131).
[135] Christian, *Treaty Interpretation* (n 114); Rietiker,'The Principle of "Effectiveness"' (n 125) 263.

occur since completion that would alter its meaning. Further, as Andrea Broderick argues 'it is also important to bear in mind that the interpretation of the CRPD should not be overly dynamic, in the sense that it should not be based on wishful thinking'.[136] It should also be noted that the meaning of key human rights concepts such as dignity, equality, and discrimination (Chapters 4 to 7) have evolved over time. Secondly, reference can be given to 'subsequent agreements' and 'subsequent practice' (including inaction in implementing the treaty terms) to determine the current understanding of the parties of the meaning of the agreement.[137] David McGrogan argues that 'the monitoring practice of human rights treaty bodies can itself be conduct constitutive of subsequent practice, provided the necessary criteria are met: that the conduct is intended to be interpretive, that it is concordant, common and consistent, and that there is no disagreement'.[138] The implications of 'subsequent practice' may partly explain the unwavering insistence of abolitionists on the abolition of mental health law post-CRPD and the continuing deadlock with States Parties.

Human rights treaties are also often argued to have a 'special character' as they are not entered into as a reciprocal agreement between states, but involve the state undertaking to the international community that they will abide by the principles of international human rights law for the benefit of the individuals in their own and other jurisdictions.[139] This has given rise to the *pro persona* principle that human rights treaties should be interpreted for the benefit of the individuals intended to be protected, rather than to preserve state sovereignty. That said, the issue with respect to the abolition of mental health law is not so much about eroding state sovereignty as how all the rights of the CRPD should be interpreted to provide the most benefit to persons with mental impairments where exactly what is beneficial is unclear.

In the disability context, the VCLT has been criticized for reducing interpretation to an entirely 'juridical exercise' in an effort to retain exclusive legal control over meaning. As Teodor Mlandenov argues:

> The extent to which such juridical meta-rules can effectively arrest the dynamics of meaning and cope with "ambiguity and obscurity" is a matter that needs to be resolved on a case-by-case basis. Notwithstanding concrete cases though, interpretation always involves a social and political aspect that cannot be effaced through purely juridical means.[140]

By focussing on the 'social and political' aspects of attributing meaning, Teodor Mlandenov characterizes the VCLT as 'juridical meta rules' and conceptualizes the

[136] Broderick, *The Long and Winding Road to Equality* (n 123) 9.

[137] VCLT (n 125), Art 31(3)(a) and (b).

[138] David McGrogan, 'On the Interpretation of Human Rights Treaties and Subsequent Practice' (2014) 32(4) Netherlands Q Hum Rights 347, 363 (hereafter McGrogan, 'Interpretation of Human Rights').

[139] Frederic Megret, 'Nature of Obligations' in Daniel Moeckli and others (eds), *International Human Rights Law* (Oxford University Press 2014) 97 (hereafter Megret, 'Nature of Obligations').

[140] Teodor Mlandenov, 'The UN Convention on the Rights of Persons with Disabilities and its Interpretation' (2013) 7(1) ALTER Eur J of Disability Research 69, 74 (hereafter Mlandenov, 'CRPD and Interpretation').

principles of legal interpretation as being embedded within language and the wider socio-political context. He notes that:

> in a number of areas crucial for disability equality—for example, with regard to 'reasonable accommodation', 'independent living' or 'legal capacity'—the CRPD can only invite certain responses and open up possibilities for the deployment of certain meanings and practices, but it cannot determine these responses, meanings and practices. Neither is it possible to fix them through legal instruments such as the VCLT.[141]

One of the 'social and political' aspects of interpretation Teodor Mlandenov identifies is the significant time and resource constraints that are experienced by the CRPD Committee and which have a negative impact on its ability to provide in-depth interpretation.[142] The other important socio-political factor is the need to understand the CRPD within the conceptual framework of the social model of disability. The social model of disability refers to a range of approaches which focus on the structural and social barriers and environment including, laws, policies, and social attitudes, which effectively 'disable' persons with various kinds of impairment.[143] It involves the wholesale rejection of the medical model in which the source of disability is conceptualized as an individual biological impairment where people are offered medical treatment and therapy and are expected to live with and struggle to overcome their inevitable limitations. Rannveig Traustadottir has identified three different social models of disability. First, the 'political' British social model of disability, or 'strong interpretation' of the social model of disability, in which disability is seen as the failure of an oppressive society to support and enable persons with disability.[144] Second, the less radical Nordic Relational Approach which understands disability as a 'poor fit' between persons with impairment and their environment and third, the North American Minority Group Approach which conceptualizes disability as a civil rights issue and persons with disability as part of a socially disadvantaged minority group.[145] The social model of disability has been extremely influential as a theoretical foundation for the emergence of critical disability studies, as a simple and effective strategy in disability advocacy and politics, and in motivating disabled persons themselves who 'do not need to be ashamed of "being abnormal" or feeling sorry for themselves, instead they ... [can] ... be angry at society for discriminating against them'.[146] By conceptualizing disability as a form of social injustice, the social model of disability demands social change.[147] However, the theory that personal characteristics are 'socially

[141] ibid 75.
[142] ibid 76.
[143] Tom Shakespeare and Nicholas Watson, 'Defending the Social Model' (1997) 12(2) Disabil Soc 293, 293 (hereafter Shakespeare and Watson, 'Defending the Social Model').
[144] Rannveig Traustadottir, 'Disability Studies, the Social Model and Legal Developments' in Oddny Mjoll Arnadottir and Gerard Quinn (eds), *The UN Convention on the Rights of Persons with Disabilities: European and Scandinavian Perspectives* (Martinus Nijhoff Publishers 2009) 3, 9, 12, and 14 (hereafter Traustadottir, 'Disability Studies').
[145] ibid.
[146] ibid 10.
[147] Linda Barclay, 'Justice and Disability: What Kind of Theorizing Is Needed?' (2011) 42(3) J Soc Philos 273 (hereafter Barclay, 'Justice and Disability').

constructed' and create social disadvantage is not unique to persons with disability, but has also been used by other groups to claim human rights and social inclusion by demonstrating that gender, race and sexuality are also 'socially constructed'.[148] To this extent, the 'paradigm shift' that arises from the social model of disability may not be as radical as is often claimed.

While the political success of the social model of disability is undisputed, within the discipline of disability studies many disability scholars are concerned that it is not a realistic representation of disability.[149] Specifically, it has been argued that the social model puts too much emphasis on social barriers and ignores the actual effect of and lived experience of impairments.[150] That is, it overlooks the impact of pain, deterioration, and limited functioning that is caused by impairments; it falsely assumes that social change is always preferable to medical intervention; and that designing a society that does not disadvantage *somebody* may not be possible.[151] In the mental health context, the social model of disability has also been criticized by Anne Plumb as being derived from the needs of persons with physical impairments without being sufficiently developed to be able to properly apply to the unique experiences and needs of persons with mental impairments.[152] The CRPD needs to apply to persons with all types, combinations of, and levels of severity of impairments some of whom may have significant support needs. While this may be a criticism of the disability rights movement and the CRPD itself—that it is not sufficiently sensitive to individual differences—I argue that it is also an issue for interpretation. Even though *express* reference to the social model of disability never appears in the treaty text, it can be seen in the separation between the concepts of 'impairment' and 'disability' and the focus of the CRPD on eliminating social and environmental barriers.[153] Therefore, the social model of disability is used as an 'interpretive device in commentaries and guidelines that seek to clarify the meaning of the CRPD's principles and provisions'.[154]

Nevertheless, it is the British social model of disability and the radical social constructionist view of disability that have been most influential in the conceptualization of disability in the CRPD by abolitionists. The effect of this is that the CRPD is a wholesale rejection of the formerly dominant 'medical model' and according to Rosemary Kayess and Philip French the drafting by civil society was 'most influenced by an uncritical, populist, understanding of the social model of disability'.[155] More recently, scholars such as Theresia Degener and Francesco Seatzu have argued that the CRPD has moved away from both the medical and social models of disability and has instead produced the 'human rights model' of disability.[156] The 'human rights model'

[148] I discuss the cross-fertilization between different movements in Chapter 3. See also, Ryu P Cheng, 'Sociological Theories of Disability, Gender, and Sexuality: A Review of the Literature' (2009) 19 J Hum Behav Soc Environ 112 (hereafter Cheng, 'Sociological Theories').

[149] Christopher A Riddle, 'Defining Disability: Metaphysical Not Political' (2013) 16 Med Health Care Philos 377, 379 (hereafter Riddle, 'Defining Disability').

[150] Traustadottir, 'Disability Studies' (n 145) 3, 10–12.

[151] Barclay, 'Justice and Disability' (n 148) 276.

[152] Plumb, 'Out of the Frying Pan' (n 89) 184.

[153] CRPD, Art 1.

[154] ibid 74.

[155] Kayess and French, 'Out of Darkness' (n 48) 33.

[156] Degener, 'Disability' (n 45); Seatzu, 'CRPD and IHRL' (n 124) 87.

of disability is claimed to further develop the social model of disability by recognizing that rights cannot be removed on the basis of personal features.[157] It is also claimed to ground the social model of disability in human rights norms, such as human dignity and respect for human diversity, and to be able to incorporate the impact of the pain and restriction of the impairment itself on the person with disability.[158] That said, Degener does not actually explain *how* the human rights model overcomes the limitations of the social model of disability, particularly, how it recognizes the lived experience of impairment any better than the social model of disability.[159] In fact, it seems no different from the British social model of disability except couched within the language and moral weight of international human rights law. Therefore, I argue in the next section that the CRPD is actually based on the *interactive* rather than the social model of disability and the so-called human rights model put forward by abolitionists.

1.4.1.3 Applying the Principles of Human Rights Treaty Interpretation to the CRPD

By taking a holistic approach to interpretation, I argue that the abolition of mental health law is only one possible interpretation of the CRPD and that abolition is not the most consistent with the text, context, and object and purpose of the CRPD, as well as the socio-political aspects including the interactive model of disability. In interpreting the CRPD to reject the abolition of mental health law, I argue that contrary to claims by the abolitionists, the CRPD is not in fact grounded in the strong British social model of disability or the so-called human rights model of disability. That is, I argue that a 'critical realist' account which views disability as both real in an objective sense (as opposed to being constituted by 'labels') and as an *interaction* between individual and social/environmental factors, put forward by Tom Shakespeare presents a far more complex and nuanced approach to understanding persons with mental impairment.[160] The *interactive* account of the social model of disability is much like the Nordic Relational Account, discussed above in section 1.4.1.2. While Tom Shakespeare's critique of the social model of disability is controversial within Disability Studies, it has still been an influential alternative to and arguably a more fulsome account of the experience of disability. Other theorists which take a similar approach are Michael Bury,[161] Jenny Morris,[162] Julie Mulvany,[163] and Johnathan Burns.[164] Such an approach is also consistent with the text of the inclusive description

[157] Seatzu, 'CRPD and IHRL' (n 124) 87.
[158] Degener, 'Disability' (n 45).
[159] ibid.
[160] Tom Shakespeare, *Disability Rights and Wrongs* (Routledge 2013), 75 (hereafter Shakespeare, 'Disability Rights').
[161] Michael Bury, 'Social Constructionism and the Development of Medical Sociology' (2008) 8(2) Sociol Health Illn 137.
[162] Jenny Morris, *Pride Against Prejudice: Transforming Attitudes to Disability* (The Women's Press 1991) (hereafter Morris, 'Pride Against Prejudice').
[163] Julie Mulvany, 'Disability, Impairment or Illness? The Relevance of the Social Model of Disability to the Study of Mental Disorder' (2000) 22(5) Sociol Health Illn 582, 589 (hereafter Mulvany, 'Disability, Impairment or Illness').
[164] Johnathan Kenneth Burns, 'Mental Health Inequity: A Human Rights Approach to Inequality, Discrimination, and Mental Disability' (2009) 11(2) Health Hum Rights 19, 22 (hereafter Burns, 'Mental Health Inequity').

of disability in the CRPD as being an *interaction* between the different types of impairment and various barriers which may hinder a person's full and effective participation in society and the context of the competing rights described above within the CRPD.[165] Further, Andrea Broderick argues that the inclusive description of disability and the preamble of the CRPD were actually drafted to reflect an *interactive* rather than a socially constructivist model of disability after the Australian delegate pointed out that a purely social and environmental conceptualization of disability would be unworkable.[166] She also argues that an understanding which leaves out impairment is undesirable and incomplete.[167] Therefore, I do not interpret impairment as being completely socially constructed and I consider the impact of mental impairment on a person's functioning as being as relevant to understanding their human rights in addition to the removal of social and environmental barriers.

According to Article 1, the 'object and purpose' of the CRPD is to 'to promote, protect and ensure the full and equal enjoyment of *all* human rights and fundamental freedoms by *all* persons with disabilities, and to promote respect for their inherent dignity'.[168] It is clear from the text and context of the CRPD that it actually has a number of 'objects and purposes'. One of those is to promote the liberty, autonomy, and self-determination of persons with mental impairment, but it is also to protect their right to life (Article 10), security of the person (Article 14), freedom from exploitation, violence, and abuse (Article 16), independent living (Article 19), the right to health (Article 25), and rehabilitation (Article 26), opportunity to participate in education (Article 24), and the rights to work and employment (Article 27), and an adequate standard of living (Article 28). That is, on an holistic interpretation persons with disability are viewed as persons who should be supported to make their own decisions wherever possible, but who also have interests in achieving the same quality of life persons without disabilities take for granted and who should not be deprived of those opportunities, experiences, and benefits, because their mental impairment may impede their recognition of their desire for and enjoyment of those rights. It could be argued that whether and to what extent persons enjoy their rights to life, security of the person, education, employment, and so on should be a matter of personal choice. However, I note that these other 'rights' appear repeatedly throughout the international human rights framework and that it is reasonable to infer that these rights have universal value to most humans and that they ought not be easily waived, especially where there is good reason to doubt that the person does not understand the full implications of doing so and are likely to suffer significant disadvantage or death.

An interpretation of the CRPD which assumes that people are always autonomous and that support is always sufficient, regardless of the severity and nature of their mental impairment, is unrealistic in that it reinforces an able-bodied norm of the independent, self-sufficient, invulnerable person, and does not sufficiently recognize human vulnerability.[169] As Anne Plumb argues, persons with mental impairment

[165] CRPD, Art 1.
[166] Broderick, *The Long and Winding Road to Equality* (n 123) 77–79.
[167] ibid.
[168] CRPD, Art 1 (my emphasis).
[169] Wilson, 'Vulnerability' (n 8).

have some unique experiences which set mental impairment apart from other types of problems and while valid and often meaningful to persons with mental impairments these experiences can still leave them in a very bad place.[170] The unintended consequences of the abolition of mental health law could include irreparable harm to self and others, including death, loss of relationships, and reputation and the stigma of criminal conviction and imprisonment in a less than therapeutic environment. From this perspective, the abolitionist's interpretation could be considered to produce a result that is 'manifestly absurd and unreasonable'[171] and that another interpretation must be sought. In the words of George Szmukler, 'it is hard to imagine a society in which it would be seen as right that persons who are seriously incapable of exercising autonomy or expressing their will and preferences would be allowed to act so as to incur grave harms including death'.[172]

The abolitionist interpretation also gives the most extreme or 'purist' rather than the more moderate interpretation of each right. For example, John Dawson and Genevra Richardson have argued that Article 12(4) of the CRPD is ambiguous and can be read as permitting substitute decision-making in limited circumstances provided it is for the shortest possible time and subject to safeguards such as external judicial review, rather than requiring the abolition of mental health law.[173] The right to bodily integrity could be read to prohibit all interference with a person's body: or, as Bernadette McSherry points out, only as prohibiting unbeneficial and overly intrusive treatment.[174] Similarly, even though there are undoubtedly situations in which use of mental health law could amount to torture or cruel, inhuman or degrading treatment or punishment, to say that involuntary detention and psychiatric treatment *always* qualifies overlooks the purpose of the perpetrator (which is usually to relieve suffering and to heal)[175] and that failure to treat might also amount to torture or cruel, inhuman, or degrading treatment or punishment.[176] Further, to say that the right to health prohibits involuntary detention and psychiatric treatment, ignores the requirement to provide medical 'services designed to minimise and prevent further disabilities',[177] and that the requirement that services be provided 'on the basis of free and informed consent'[178] might only be possible where a person is capable of giving free and informed consent (leaving a person not so capable unable to access any medical treatment without mental health law).

170 Plumb, 'Out of the Frying Pan' (n 89) 189.
171 Dorr, 'Article 31' (n 127).
172 Szmukler, 'Compulsion and "Coercion"' (n 52).
173 Dawson, 'A Realistic Approach' (n 116) 74; Genevra Richardson, 'Mental Disabilities and the Law: From Substitute to Supported Decision-Making' (2012) 65 Curr Leg Probl 333, 346 (hereafter Richardson, 'Mental Disabilities').
174 Bernadette McSherry, 'Protecting the Integrity of the Person: Developing Limitations on Involuntary Treatment' (2008) 26(2) Journal of Law in Cont 111, 122 (hereafter McSherry, 'Protecting the Integrity of the Person').
175 Michelle Farrell, 'Just How Ill-Treated Were You? An Investigation of Cross-Fertilisation in the Interpretive Approaches to Torture in the European Court of Human Rights and International Criminal Law' (2015) 84(3) Nord J Int Law 483, 501, and 512 (hereafter Farrell, 'Just How Ill-Treated Were You?').
176 *D v United Kingdom* (1997) 24 EHRR 423 (hereafter D v United Kingdom).
177 CRPD, Art 25(b).
178 CRPD, Art 15(d).

Further, the CRPD was deliberately drafted to cover only the rights of persons with disabilities.[179] The rights of families are only mentioned once in the preamble and only then with respect to the obligation of the state to support families in supporting persons with disabilities.[180] The CRPD does not consider the rights of others in the community who might be at risk of harm from persons with mental impairments which would be found in other treaties, such as the International Covenant on Civil and Political Rights ('ICCPR'), but which are no less important in wider international human rights law.

Even some abolitionists are aware that an absolute ban on involuntary detention and psychiatric treatment may not be a realistic interpretation of the CRPD in emergency situations. However, the prospect of hiving out exceptions creates a dilemma about what exceptions might be justified to recognize rights other than a person's legal capacity. As Piers Gooding notes:

> These matters tend to give rise to a fundamental question in debates about supported decision-making and the broader support framework of the CRPD; that is, when can coercive responses be justified? There seems to be a broad consensus that at least some crises warrant some form of coercive intervention. Yet the literature on the CRPD includes little to identify what those crises are, how they might be determined or what CRPD-compliant 'coercion' might look like. In part, this gap has opened up where proponents of universal legal capacity do not wish to 'lock in' exceptions, which historically have placed people with disabilities on a slippery slope towards having their rights denied—but what are the consequences of this?[181]

Of course, no human right is absolute and the difficulty of reconciling conflicting human rights within a particular treaty, between different treaties, and between an individual and the community, has long been a criticism of human rights law. As Nikolas Rose laments, while philosophers have created various ways to attempt to resolve conflicts between competing rights, in the mental health context rights still remain 'interminable' and the 'appeal to rights can provide no effective means of substantiating demands that claims are valid and should have priority over others'.[182] One method has been for courts to try to balance competing rights between individuals and the state, using some form of 'proportionality' analysis to determine whether a proposed limitation on a right relates to a legitimate aim, is necessary, and is the minimum needed to intrude on the individual right.[183] However, the role of 'proportionality analysis' in balancing rights is controversial and has been criticized for trying to compare rights which are incommensurable as being irrational and as undermining the purpose of rights in defending the minority against the majority.[184] Further, given that the way

[179] MacQuarrie and Laurin-Bowie, *Our Lives, Our Voices* (n 46) 32.

[180] CRPD Preamble [24].

[181] Gooding, *A New Era* (n 39) 13.

[182] Nikolas Rose, 'Law, Rights and Psychiatry' in Peter Miller and Nikolas Rose (eds), *The Power of Psychiatry* (Polity Press 1986) 177, 207 (hereafter Rose, 'Law, Rights and Psychiatry').

[183] Aharon Barak, 'Proportionality and Principled Balancing' (2010) 4(1) LEHR 2, 6–7 (hereafter Barak, 'Proportionality').

[184] Steven Greer, '"Balancing" and the European Court of Human Rights: A Contribution to the Habermas-Alexy Debate' (2004) 63(2) Camb Law J 412, 414 (hereafter Greer, 'Balancing'); Basak Cali

the CRPD has been negotiated has left many 'gaps' within the treaty, any attempt to 'balance' competing rights using proportionality analysis seems premature. As Jeremy Waldron points out, rights usually contain externally justified limitations on their exercise as well as internal limitations on their scope, which can be determined by doing a qualitative analysis of their meaning.[185] Therefore, I argue that a better starting point is to first seek a deeper understanding of the scope and meaning of certain apparently conflicting CRPD rights, their boundaries, and how they might overlap.

I took such a qualitative approach to interpretation in a journal article which explores the meaning and scope of the right to life in Article 10 of the CRPD and how it might interact with the abolitionist and reform models.[186] However, in this book, rather than focus on other competing rights, I focus on the general principles in Article 3 of the CRPD, particularly, the principles of inherent dignity (including autonomy), equality, and participation. While I discuss my justification of these three values in detail in Chapter 4, there is no doubt that these three general principles feature prominently in the text of the CRPD, were intended by the drafters to be an aid to interpretation of the entire text of the CRPD, and to create a more detailed explanation of the object and purpose of the CRPD set out in Article 1.[187] According to Oliver Lewis 'the principles represent the moral basis of the CRPD, explaining the reasons for its existence, and providing guidance for national authorities, courts and the treaty monitoring body on how to interpret the CRPD'.[188] More broadly, the principles of dignity, equality, and participation underpin all international human rights treaties and firmly anchor the CRPD within wider international human rights law, giving it the normative weight of other human rights treaties and separating it from prior disability instruments.[189] As Gerard Quinn argues, dignity, autonomy, and equality are part of the core legacy values for which CRPD serves as 'a mirror before society':

> It makes us face up to our own values—to our so-called 'legacy values' of dignity, autonomy equality and social solidarity. It forces us to acknowledge the large gap that still exists between the 'myth system' of our values and the 'operations system' of how these values are in fact dishonoured in daily practice.[190]

Further, in General Comment No. 1, the CRPD Committee has called for the abolition of mental health law by explicitly basing its interpretation of equality before the law

'Balancing Human Rights? Methodological Problems with Weights, Scales and Proportions' (2007) 29 Hum Rights Q 251, 270 (hereafter Cali, 'Balancing Human Rights?').

[185] Jeremy Waldron, 'Dignity, Rights, and Responsibilities' (2011) 43(1) Ariz St L J 1112 (hereafter Waldron, 'Dignity').

[186] Wilson, 'Right to Life' (n 8).

[187] Valentina Della Fina, 'Article 3 [General Principles]' in V Della Fina and others (eds), *The United Nations Convention on the Rights of Persons with Disabilities* (Springer International Publishing 2017) 120, 121 (hereafter Della Fina 'Article 3').

[188] Lewis, 'Expressive, Educational and Proactive Roles' (n 117) 102.

[189] Seatzu, 'CRPD and IHRL' (n 124) 88, 90.

[190] Comments of Professor Gerard Quinn, The UN Convention on the Human Rights of Persons with Disabilities, Presentation to the Irish Human Rights Commission (Dublin, 19 April 2007) in Andrea Broderick, *The Long and Winding Road to Equality* (n 123) 120, 2.

(Article 12) on the general principles in Article 3 of the CRPD.[191] However, as Jillian Craigie has recently observed:

> . . . it is unclear how the step from these principles to the conclusions in General Comment No.1 was made. Indeed, it seems plausible that the application of these principles might sometimes yield conflicting guidance that would need resolution. The requirements to respect the inherent dignity and value the independence of persons, for example, do not always point in the same direction. Much depends on the situation that is being considered, and how these principles are understood.[192]

For this reason, a rigorous analysis of the principles of dignity (including autonomy), equality, and participation is likely to be very useful to persons who are trying to interpret the CRPD and in finding a way through the existing stalemate about the future of metal health law. As Alex-Ruck Keene has recently observed 'there are dilemmas, including at the heart of the CRPD, that are simply not resolvable by assertion'.[193]

Inherent dignity, autonomy, equality, and participation are complex, developing, and highly disputed concepts which do not have a single 'plain and ordinary' meaning. For this reason, I examine the text of the CRPD, the *travaux preparatoires* or records of drafting the CRPD, and the context of these concepts in the CRPD, the CRPD literature, and wider international human rights law and philosophy. First, I argue that inherent dignity includes, but has a wider meaning than respecting autonomy, that autonomy is a state of fact rather than a 'right', and that at times a person with mental impairment may not be autonomous even with support. Second, I argue that equality and non-discrimination are rights to substantive and transformative rather than formal equality, so that equality and non-discrimination in the mental health context does not mean treating differently placed persons with and without mental impairment as 'the same'. I also point out many of the difficulties in applying equality and non-discrimination with respect to persons with mental impairments in the debate about the abolition or reform of mental health law. Finally, I argue that participation and inclusion means consultation and negotiation in a way that is respectful of a person's inherent dignity and equality (see Chapter 7 section 7.6). I then consider how the 'interpretive compass' applies to the Abolition with Support, Mental Capacity with Support, and support except where there is harm models in Chapters 4 to 8. However, just because I do not agree with the abolitionist's conclusion that mental health law should be abolished, does not mean I believe that the abolitionists concerns should be discarded. On the contrary, I argue that taking the views of the abolitionists seriously, understanding their reasons for holding them, and accommodating their concerns as far as reasonable and practicable, is vital for the future of mental health law reform

[191] General Comment 1 (n 22) [4].

[192] Craigie, 'Panel Event' (n 8) 160–61.

[193] Alex Ruck-Keene 'Deprivation of Liberty, Restraint, and the CRPD: The View from the German Federal Constitutional Court' Mental Capacity Law and Policy blog-post 4 December 2018 <http://www.mentalcapacitylawandpolicy.org.uk/deprivation-of-liberty-restraint-and-the-crpd-the-view-from-the-german-federal-constitutional-court/> accessed 21 June 2019(hereafter Ruck-Keene, 'Deprivation of Liberty, Restraint, and the CRPD').

and the dignity, equality, and participation of persons with disability, even if it may not produce the exact results the abolitionists are advocating.

1.4.2 A 'Jurisprudential' or 'Ethical' Approach

While I apply the rules of treaty interpretation, as noted above, I have not taken a purely doctrinal or narrow 'black letter law' approach to my research question that focuses exclusively on an internally self-sustaining set of legal principles based on the text of relevant treaties, legislation, and court decisions. Rather, I do a deeper 'jurisprudential' or 'ethical' analysis of the core human rights values of dignity (including autonomy), equality, and participation and how they should inform the interpretation of the CRPD. My 'jurisprudential' or 'ethical' approach is consistent with the methods of legal philosophers, such as Ronald Dworkin, who argue that the conventional methods of legal interpretation are inadequate without deliberation and reflection about the moral and social traditions on which they are based.[194] I show where these three values are supported in the text of the CRPD and in international human rights law more generally and debate their meanings by drawing on multi-disciplinary ethical and jurisprudential literature as well as material from sociology, disability studies, psychology, medicine, and history. I then apply these meanings in evaluating the abolitionist position and the options for the reform of mental health law and practice.

I have also couched my 'jurisprudential' or 'ethical' analysis within the wider socio-historical context of the development of and opposition to mental health law in the common law world (particularly, England) which I set out in Chapters 2 and 3. By doing so I trace the social forces which have shaped mental health law and practice and the current debates surrounding its abolition and reform which may continue to influence the existence and direction of mental health law in the future. I also write with an awareness of the likely social effects of the abolition and reform of mental health law on persons with mental impairments, those around them, and society as a whole. My 'jurisprudential' or 'ethical' analysis is further supplemented by drawing on published personal accounts by persons with mental impairments, my studies in psychology, and my own lived experience of mental impairment as a family member and carer which enriches my perspective (see 'Preface' above).

1.5 Scope

While I accept that the values of liberty and autonomy are more culturally embedded in western societies than others and that there are other cultural responses to mental impairment, I have confined this book to western societies because it is difficult to generalize between countries with well-developed mental health systems and those which offer little formal medical treatment and incorporate vastly different religious and cultural beliefs about the origins of mental impairment. While there can be some

[194] For example, Ronald Dworkin, *Taking Rights Seriously* (Bloomsbury Publishing 2013) 20 (hereafter Dworkin, *Taking Rights Seriously*).

benefits to non-western approaches to mental impairment in terms of social support, in many countries without a mental health system or mental health law, families are unable to cope with the behaviour and unproductivity of their loved ones and people with mental impairment are often poorly treated, in some cases being chained or caged indefinitely in 'prayer camps' with no medical treatment and little prospect of recovery.[195]

Similarly, even though 'it is no longer tenable to regard the prison estate as a system separate from the mental health system',[196] my book will focus on civil rather than criminal law (excluding issues like fitness to plead, the abolition of insanity defences, or sentencing diversion programmes). The application of the CRPD to the abolition of criminal law provisions which cater specifically to persons with mental impairments raise a number of complex issues about how well conventional general criminal law concepts such as *mens rea*, voluntariness, mistake of fact, and duress can be enlarged to deal with persons with mental impairments as well as the potentially destructive consequences to the lives of persons with mental impairments if the existing defences were abolished.[197] For reasons of time and space these issues which have their own vast literature and history are beyond the scope of this book. However, the role of prison as a de facto mental health service,[198] the inherently punitive rather than therapeutic nature of prison,[199] and the historically low quality of prison mental health services[200] are matters of serious concern when considering the consequences of the abolition of mental health law.

As already discussed above and as indicated by the title this book is about mental impairment and mental health law with its many unique issues (such as the effects of episodic illness, delusions, self-harm, suicide, and how to deal with persons in acute crises) not cognitive impairment and guardianship law. However, mental health and guardianship law have been historically linked, at times being regulated by the same legislation, and there is likely to be some overlap between some of the arguments in the book about the interpretation and implementation of the CRPD with guardianship. There is also no doubt that the problems with guardianship law and the need for

[195] Benedict Carey, 'The Chains of Mental Illness in West Africa' *The New York Times* 11 October 2015 (hereafter Carey, 'Chains of Mental Illness'); Burns, 'Mental Health Inequity' (n 165) 25; Peter Bartlett 'Thinking About the Rest of the World: Mental Health and Rights Outside the 'First World' in Bernadette McSherry and Penelope Weller (eds), *Rethinking Rights-Based Mental Health Laws* (Hart 2010) 397, 407 (hereafter Bartlett, 'Thinking About the Rest of the World').

[196] Peter Bartlett and Ralph Sandland, *Mental Health Law: Policy and Practice* (3rd edn, Oxford University Press 2007) 63(hereafter Bartlett and Sandland, *Mental Health Law*).

[197] Michael Perlin, '"God Said to Abraham/Kill Me a Son": Why the Insanity Defense and the Incompetency Status are Compatible With and Required by the Convention on the Rights of Persons with Disabilities and Basic Principles of Therapeutic Jurisprudence' (2017) 54 Am Crim L Rev 477, 480 (hereafter Perlin, 'Insanity Defence').

[198] 'Locked in' The Economist (3 August 2013) (hereafter 'Locked in').

[199] Danny H Sullivan and Paul E Mullen 'Mental Health and Human Rights in Secure Settings' in Michael Dudley and others (eds), *Mental Health and Human Rights: Vision, Praxis and Courage* (Oxford University Press 2012) 292–93 (hereafter Sullivan and Mullen, 'Mental Health and Human Rights in Secure Settings').

[200] Michael Perlin, '"There are no Trials Inside the Gates of Eden" Mental Health Courts, the Convention on the Rights of Persons with Disabilities, Dignity and the Promise of Therapeutic Jurisprudence' in Bernadette McSherry and Ian Freckelton (eds), *Coercive Care: Rights, Law and Policy* (Routledge 2013) 193 (hereafter Perlin, 'Mental Health Courts').

substantive change to the treatment of persons with disabilities is as great as it is for mental health law.[201]

My book is limited to adults with mental impairments. The law in relation to children has added complexity which I have not touched on in this book.

1.6 Terminology

The definition of mental disorders or impairment beyond 'something not working properly in the mind' is complex and dependent on the context and purpose for which the term is used.[202] As noted by the Australian Law Reform Commission, there is a problem of language in the entire disability field as terms that were once considered socially acceptable to describe people with disabilities become derogatory and then a new lexicon is adopted and the process begins again.[203] The language used at various times and with various groups captures the way in which those individuals and their differences have been conceptualized by society and the way in which they conceptualize themselves. For this reason, my book (particularly in chapters 2 and 3) will use terms like 'mental illness', 'madness', 'insanity', 'lunatics', and 'idiots', but it will specify how those terms are being used, whether that be to reflect social attitudes at particular times, or self-identification and empowerment. My use of language in this way recognizes the way in which the power to 'name' and 'label' is an important element of power relationships and why people with mental impairment feel misunderstood by society.

Obviously terminology is problematic in this field and often reflects the author's political leanings. I have chosen 'mental impairment' as my default term because it is the term that is used in Article 1 of the CRPD which, when interacting with social and environmental barriers, is claimed to produce disability. The term 'mental impairment' is consistent with the interactive model of disability which recognizes both the effects of the impairment on the person and the social and environmental causes of disability. By the term 'mental impairment' I mean persons with severe psychiatric conditions including schizophrenia, bipolar disorder, depression, anxiety disorders, eating disorders, obsessive-compulsive disorder, and post-traumatic stress disorder which may be treatable by psychiatric intervention, rather than persons with cognitive impairments such as intellectual disability, autism, and dementia (although there is some overlap in the legal issues raised by the two groups). While I have no difficulty with the idea that society has a role in constructing and dismantling disability, the term 'persons with disabilities' is too general to capture some of the specific issues faced by persons with mental impairments that are not encountered by persons with physical, intellectual, and sensory impairments.

[201] Michael Perlin, '"Striking for the Guardians and Protectors of the Mind": The Convention on the Rights of Persons with Mental Disabilities and the Future of Guardianship Law' (2013) 117 Penn St L Rev 1159 (hereafter Perlin, 'The Future of Guardianship Law').

[202] Jamie Walvisch, 'Defining "Mental Disorder" in Legal Contexts' (2017) 52 Int J Law Psychiatry 7, 17–18 (hereafter Walvisch, 'Defining "Mental Disorder"').

[203] ALRC Report (n 99) [2.20–2.23].

As noted by George Szmukler and colleagues, the notion of whether all mental impairments, even those that are short term and episodic, are sufficiently 'long term' to fall within the inclusive description in Article 1 of the CRPD raises questions of how well mental impairment fits within the disability paradigm.[204] However, I assume for the purposes of this book that 'mental impairment' falls within the inclusive description regardless of whether it is sufficiently long term.

1.7 Conclusion

In this book I explore the issue of whether mental health law should be abolished or reformed in light of the entry into force of the CRPD in 2008. By mental health law I mean laws which enable the involuntary detention and treatment of persons with mental impairments. By abolition I mean the repeal of mental health law and its replacement with a Support model in which a person with mental impairment cannot be admitted to hospital or treated without their consent (although there may be some exceptions for non-discriminatory coercion). It is my contention that, contrary to the assertion of abolitionists, mental health law should not be abolished but should instead be reformed by decreasing coercion and increasing social support for persons with mental impairments. In reaching this conclusion my book uses a conceptual framework based on the CRPD and international human rights law. Given that the CRPD is an 'incompletely theorized agreement', I argue that by adopting a holistic approach to interpretation in accordance with the VCLT and socio-politic aspects of interpretation and using the 'interpretive compass' of inherent dignity (including autonomy), equality, and participation, the CRPD does not require States Parties to abolish mental health law, although some reform is required. I use the 'interpretive compass' to compare three options: (1) the Abolition with Support, (2) Mental Capacity with Support, and (3) Support Except where there is Harm models. As they are presently articulated, I conclude that the Mental Capacity with Support model is compatible with the CRPD and is to be preferred. However, systemic and social reform is still required. In reaching my conclusions, I use a jurisprudential or ethical analysis methodology, by examining the development of mental health law and the emergence of the call for the abolition of mental health law within its socio-historical context. I also take a jurisprudential or ethical approach in developing the 'interpretive compass' and comparing the three models drawing on theoretical and empirical research.

[204] George Szmukler and others, 'Mental Health Law and the UN Convention on the Rights of Persons with Disabilities' (2014) 37 Int J Law Psychiatry 245, 246 (hereafter Szmukler, 'Mental Health Law and CRPD').

2
The History, Justification, and Purpose of Mental Health Law

2.1 Introduction

The purpose of this chapter is to explore the development, justifications, and purpose of mental health law in England.

An historical perspective illustrates that the evolution of mental health law is based on what Genevra Richardson calls a mixture of 'principle and pragmatism'.[1] While there is no comprehensive 'grand theory' (or theories) of mental health law, the conceptual basis of mental health law has its origins in the twin pillars of the so-called 'police powers' of the state and the doctrine of *parens patriae*, as justifying exceptions to a far more dominant 'grand theory'—liberalism.

The 'police powers' of the state are derived from the sovereign power and obligation of the state to use coercion, but only if necessary, to protect the public and promote safety. The 'police powers' of the state should not be confused with the power of the police force to take people who appear to have a mental impairment to hospital for a psychiatric assessment under various mental health laws. Rather, the term 'police' comes from the words 'politia' (the state), 'polis' (the city), and 'politeia' (citizenship).[2] The police powers go to the core function of the state as the only actor with the power to regulate, tax, and spend public funds[3] and to co-ordinate action for the 'common good' to protect and promote the health, safety, morals, and general welfare of the community.[4] Lawrence Gostin notes that the police powers also have another secondary meaning of 'cleanliness' based on the association between hygiene, sanitation, and public health.[5]

By contrast, the doctrine of *parens patriae* is grounded in the individual need of the recipient and the social need of the law to allocate responsibility for meeting it. That is, *parens patriae* only applies where other social processes for care, support, and protection are unavailable or are inadequate. In the much-quoted words of Lord Eldon in the nineteenth century child custody case of *Wellesley v Beaufort (the Duke of)*, the jurisdiction derives from:

[1] Genevra Richardson, 'Reforming Mental Health Law: Principle or Pragmatism' (2001) 54 Curr Leg Probl 415 (hereafter Richardson, 'Principle or Pragmatism').

[2] Lawrence O Gostin, *Public Health Law: Power, Duty, Restraint* (2nd edn, University of California Press 2008) 92 (hereafter Gostin, *Public Health Law*).

[3] James F Childress and others, 'Public Health Ethics: Mapping the Terrain' (2002) 30 J Law Med Ethics 170.

[4] Gostin, *Public Health Law* (n 2) 92.

[5] ibid.

Mental Health Law. Kay Wilson, Oxford University Press. © Kay Wilson 2021. DOI: 10.1093/oso/9780192843258.003.0002

> ... the king, as parens patriae, having care of those who are not able to care for themselves, and is founded on the necessity that the law should place somewhere the care of those who cannot take care of themselves, particularly in cases where it is clear some care should be thrown around them.[6]

As Lord Goff described it in *Re F*, the doctrine of *parens patriae* reflects the principle of necessity to ensure that people are able to obtain access to much needed healthcare, even if they are unable to consent to it in an emergency or on a permanent basis.[7] In the mental health context Robert Schopp notes that *parens patriae* involves 'promoting well-being through effective treatment'.[8]

The rationales contained within the police powers of the state and the doctrine of *parens patriae* find expression in what Genevra Richardson calls the 'three broad goals' of mental health law being 'the provision of access to health care, the protection of the patient and the protection of others'.[9] Further, the police powers and *parens patriae* justifications are reflected to varying degrees in the text of most current mental health laws which contain civil commitment criteria such as those that refer to the 'prevention of harm to self and others', mental deterioration, inability to care for oneself, and mental capacity.

In this regard, mental health law can be seen as a way of providing some structure and substance to the otherwise nebulous boundaries of the police power of the state and the doctrine of *parens patriae.* For example, contemporary mental health laws typically require that a person has a mental illness (as legally defined), the production of evidence to support the seriousness and imminence of harm to self or others,[10] that a mental illness must be of a kind for which treatment is available,[11] that detention must be for the purposes of safety not punishment, and that a person be offered 'the least restrictive alternative'[12] to involuntary detention and treatment.

This chapter does not intend to provide an exhaustive account of the history of mental health law (as that would be an impossible task) and there are already several excellent works.[13] I will, however, give a selective history for the specific purpose of tracing the origins of mental health law, including the role of the police powers of

[6] *Wellesley v Beaufort* (*The Duke of*) 2 Russ 20, 243 (hereafter *Wellesley v Beaufort*).

[7] *F v West Berkshire HA* [1991] UKHL 1 (17 July 1990) 23 (Lord Goff) (hereafter *F v West Berkshire HA*).

[8] Robert Schopp, *Competence, Condemnation and Commitment: An Integrated Theory of Mental Health Law* (American Psychological Association 2001) 61 (hereafter Schopp, *Competence, Condemnation and Commitment*).

[9] Genevra Richardson, 'Balancing Autonomy and Risk: A Failure of Nerve in England and Wales?' (2007) 30 Int J Law Psychiatry 71, 71 (hereafter Richardson, 'Balancing Autonomy and Risk').

[10] For example, the *Mental Health Act* 2014 (Vic) (hereafter MHA Vic) has lifted the threshold from harm to 'serious' harm, s 4.

[11] *Mental Health Act* 2007 (UK) s 4 (hereafter MHA UK).

[12] Gostin, *Public Health Law* (n 2) 50.

[13] For example, Clive Unsworth, *The Politics of Mental Health Legislation* (Claredon Press, Oxford 1987) (hereafter Unsworth, *The Politics of Mental Health*); Jacqueline Atkinson, *Advance Directives in Mental Health: Theory, Practice and Ethics* (Jessica Kingsley 2007) Ch 3 (hereafter Atkinson, *Advance Directives*); Peter Shea, *Defining Madness* (Hawkins Press 1999) (hereafter Shea, *Defining Madness*); Roy Porter, *Madness: A Brief History* (Oxford University Press 2002) (hereafter Porter, *Madness*); Andrew Scull, *Madness: A Very Short Introduction* (Oxford University Press 2011) (hereafter, Scull, *Madness*).

the state and *parens patriae,* and what has shaped its current form. I also treat those histories with an element of caution, given that Tomi Gomory and colleagues have pointed out that the leading historians of psychiatry all unquestioningly accept the medicalization of mental illness, creating an inherent and unacknowledged bias in their approach to the subject.[14]

Piers Gooding points to the continuation of involuntary detention and treatment, the doctrine of *parens patriae* and the police powers of the state as the primary justifications for state intervention, and the perception that people with mental impairment require special legal treatment, as important constants in mental health law.[15] However, my account emphasizes change in the 'fashions and cycles'[16] of mental health law which has always been in a continual state of reform, the call for abolition perhaps being the latest iteration. I trace the historical shifts in responsibility for the supervision and care of persons with mental impairment between society and the state and more recently, since the emergence of the abolitionist movement, calls for that responsibility to be given back to persons with mental impairment themselves. Further, contrary to the perception of the abolitionists, the supporters of mental health law have not always stood impervious to the criticisms of opponents, but, as argued by Nikolas Rose, have sought to respond and adapt to those criticisms, creating a strong history of legal and systemic reform.[17]

2.2 Before the First Specific Stand-Alone Mental Health Law

While mental impairment may be as old as humankind, there was no dedicated stand-alone mental health law until the end of the nineteenth century. To the extent the law did regulate mental impairment it did so through a range of different legislative schemes for different social classes. The development of the law is also tied to how mental impairment has been conceptualized and understood and what treatments (if any) were available.

Greek and Roman law provided for the appointment of guardians, sought to prevent the mad (as they were then called) from causing harm to person and property, and prohibited the mad from entering the cities.[18] Like today, the Ancient Greeks conceived of madness as a medical problem with a somatic (rather than spiritual or demonic) cause and there are records that Ancient Greek physicians used informal

[14] Toni Gomory and others, 'Madness or Mental Illness? Revisiting Historians of Psychiatry' (2013) 23 Curr Psychol 119 (hereafter Gomory, 'Madness or Mental Illness?').

[15] Piers Gooding, 'Change and Continuity in Mental Health Law: The Long Road to the United Nations Convention on the Rights of Persons with Disabilities and Its Implications for Mental Health and the Law Today' (2014) 20(3) Web JCLI 367 (hereafter, Gooding, 'Change and Continuity').

[16] Michael D Kirby, 'Law Reform, Politics and Mental Health' (1983) 17(1) Aust NZ J Psychiatry 39, 39 (Hereafter Kirby, 'Law Reform').

[17] Nikolas Rose, 'Psychiatry: The Discipline of Mental Health' in Peter Miller and Nikolas Rose (eds), *The Power of Psychiatry* (Polity Press 1986) 43(hereafter Rose, 'Psychiatry').

[18] Porter, *Madness* (n 13) 95.

coercive strategies to convince patients to accept medical treatment.[19] For example, Soranus of Ephesus wrote in respect of the treatment of mania:

> Now if there is a person whom the patient has customarily feared or respected, he should not be brought into the sickroom repeatedly. For this frequent repetition gives rise to a lack of regard. But when circumstances require it, as when the patient does not submit to the application of a remedy, this person should then be brought in to overcome the patient's stubbornness, by inspiring fear or respect.[20]

In England the doctrine of *parens patriae* can be traced to the king's jurisdiction over the person and property of infants, idiots, and lunatics (as they were then called) under the Royal Prerogative from 1324. *Parens patriae* was not so much a power as a moral responsibility which resided in the person of the sovereign who undertook the role of a 'benevolent benefactor'[21] and 'father and protector of his people'.[22] While *parens patriae* was a duty that extended to all people who lacked mental capacity, in practice the sovereign was only interested in caring for and protecting those with property, taking the rents and profits of the land, and converting the incapacitated individuals to his wards.[23] This is an early example of the use of the *parens patriae* doctrine where state intervention was motivated more by the sovereign's own benefit than for the benefit of his ward. While lunatics were treated more favourably than idiots, in recognition that lunatics once had their reason and of the fluctuating nature of their impairment, Henry Theobald notes that such discrimination did not always occur in practice, as juries resented the harsh treatment of idiots and tended to find lunacy rather than idiocy.[24] Those without wealth were left to care for themselves or to live in the workhouse or prison.

In medieval England various religious orders occasionally took responsibility for mad individuals as part of the Christian duty of charity.[25] The Christian notion that a caring society has a moral responsibility to make provision for those who are less fortunate still survives in the current medical charitable model of disability. Patricia Allderidge argues that there is evidence that the mad were 'treated' by the church alongside people with other kinds of sickness and that their mental illness was not necessarily regarded as demonic possession or being of a spiritual nature.[26] The religious order St Mary of Bethlam established the earliest and most infamous asylum, confining lunatics at Bethlam hospital ('Bedlam') in the fourteenth century.[27] However,

[19] Soranus of Ephesus, 'Madness or Insanity (Greek Mania)' in Greg Eghigian (ed), *From Madness to Mental Health: Psychiatric Disorder and Its Treatment in Western Civilisation* (Rutgers University Press 2010) 39, 44 (hereafter Soranus, 'Madness or Insanity').

[20] ibid.

[21] 'The "Crime" of Mental Illness: Extension of "Criminal" Procedural Safeguards to Involuntary Civil Commitments' (1975) 66(3) J Crim Law Criminol 255, 255(hereafter, 'The "Crime" of Mental Illness').

[22] George B Curtis, 'The Checkered Career of Parens Patriae: The State as Parent or Tyrant?' (1976) 25(4) De P LR 895, 895(hereafter Curtis, 'Parens Patriae').

[23] Unsworth, *Politics of Mental Health* (n 13) 47.

[24] Henry Studdy Theobald, *The Law Relating to Lunacy* (Stevens and Sons 1924) 2–3 (hereafter Theobald, *Lunancy*).

[25] Porter, *Madness* (n 13) 96.

[26] Patricia Allderidge, 'Hospitals, Madhouses and Asylums: Cycles in the Care of the Insane' (1979) 134 Br J Psychiatry 321, 322 (hereafter Allderidge, 'Hospitals, Madhouses and Asylums').

[27] Porter, *Madness* (n 13) 96.

prior to the eighteenth and nineteenth century, responsibility for the care and supervision of people with mental impairment lay with the family, rather than the state.

The absence of mental health law, however, did not mean that the mad had an equal social status or were socially tolerated and included, as envisaged by those calling for the abolition of mental health law today. While the mad may have possessed a certain kind of social power as 'the holy fool, witch or man-possessed'[28] and had the liberty to speak their mind and mock their 'betters', their lives were at the mercy of the goodwill, skills, and resources of their families. It was common for the mad to be chained or caged, ill-treated and neglected, or left to beg on the streets.

Michel Foucault has described the locking away of socially undesirable, irrational, and unproductive individuals, including lunatics and idiots in seventeenth century Europe as the 'Great Confinement' and as an early example of the exercise of the 'police powers' of the state to protect public safety.[29] However, Roy Porter calls this interpretation 'simplistic' and 'overgeneralised' and doubts its application beyond France.[30] Andrew Scull goes further, arguing that the 'Great Confinement' 'remains a late 20th-century ideological construct, one with little or no contemporary relevance or resonance in the societies it purports to describe'.[31] Rather, Roy Porter and Andrew Scull attribute the emergence of the private madhouse in England as a response to the desire of wealthy families to outsource the shame and 'burden' of caring for their mad relatives, rather than from any direct action of the state.[32] Not all families embraced this development and many looked for other ways to cope such as employing servants to care for their relatives in the home or sending them away to live in remote places.

The new spontaneously arising 'trade-in-lunacy' in the eighteenth century was completely market-driven and unregulated. Not surprisingly, it quickly became a source of scandal and abuse, both as a way of taking the assets of and disposing of wealthy relatives (some of whom may have in fact been insane) and due to the terrible living conditions in the madhouses themselves. Accordingly, the *Madhouses Act* 1774 was passed to protect against wrongful confinement by requiring medical certification and appointing commissioners to licence and inspect private madhouses. Such certification is an early example of intervention based on an assessment of medical need, although it also served the purpose of a legal safeguard to address the fears of the public and to sort the sane from the insane.

Most people who were not supported by their families, however, did not have the means to afford private madhouses and were subsumed within the poor law and criminal justice system. Clive Unsworth describes the *Vagrancy Act* 1744 as 'a typical expression of the Whig oligarchy's anxiety to protect landed property against the property-less'.[33] It applied to a range of wandering persons from rogues, vagabonds, and beggars to the insane. The Act authorized the containment of dangerous persons locked in a safe and secure place (usually a prison) for the duration of their lunacy.

[28] ibid 98–99.

[29] Michel Foucault, *Madness and Civilisation: A History of Insanity in the Age of Reason* (Richard Howard tr, Pantheon Books 1965) 46 (hereafter Foucault, *Madness and Civilisation*).

[30] Porter, *Madness* (n 13) 99.

[31] Scull, *Madness* (n 13) 39.

[32] Porter, *Madness* (n 13) 100; Scull, *Madness* (n 13) 40.

[33] Unsworth, *Politics of Mental Health* (n 13) 53.

While it was not specifically aimed at the insane, it is considered to be an example of the exercise of police powers of the state and the origins of compulsory powers to detain in mental health law.[34] However, as Jacqueline Atkinson and Jacquie Reilly point out, it acknowledged the 'differentness' of the insane and their lack of moral responsibility for their own behaviour, as it prohibited them from being whipped (which was permitted for other classes).[35] However, the same law allowed 'dangerous lunatics' to be chained.[36] While the purpose of their confinement was not therapeutic, the Act envisaged that the insane may be cured and that their maintenance and cure would be at their own expense if they had assets to pay for it.[37]

The lunatics living in workhouses and prisons did not fit in. Often exploited by other inmates and considered troublesome to the authorities, by the early nineteenth century it became evident to social reformers that special provision should be made for them. That is, the separation of the insane from the rest of the incarcerated population and wider society developed as a response to an unmet individual and social need based on care rather than property. As noted by Tom Burns 'in our risk-obsessed days it is sobering to realize that asylums were proposed more to protect the deranged individual from society than vice versa'.[38]

Hence, the Act of 1808 subtitled 'for the better Care and Maintenance of Lunatics, being Paupers or Criminals in England' made provision for the counties to build asylums at public expense to house paupers and criminal lunatics and the *Lunatic Asylums Act* 1845 required it. Nevertheless, large numbers of pauper lunatics were never transferred to the asylum from the workhouses due to over-crowding and the higher cost of asylum accommodation.[39]

The building of asylums coincided with a sense of optimism in the power of the asylum to treat insanity and to restore reason. While the function of the asylum later became primarily custodial, its original purpose was not necessarily to segregate and lock away the insane. As Robert Ellis observes:

> While the new asylums had their own contemporary critics, it was the twentieth century that saw the apparently benign nature of the asylum subject to reinterpretation and revision.[40]

Rather, the removal of people from the stress and demands of society to a country setting with fresh air in the natural environment was intended to be a therapeutic and humane alternative to chaining and other more restrictive practices.[41] The provision

[34] ibid 52.

[35] Jacqueline Atkinson and Jacquie Reilly, 'The Recent History of Concepts of "Dangerousness" in Mental Health Law' (2011) 13(1) Hist and Phil of Psych 45, 45 (hereafter Atkinson and Reilly, '"Dangerousness" in Mental Health Law').

[36] ibid.

[37] ibid.

[38] Tom Burns, *Psychiatry: A Very Short Introduction* (Oxford University Press 2006) 36 (hereafter Burns, *Psychiatry*).

[39] Peter Bartlett, 'The Asylum, the Workhouse, and the Voice of the Insane Poor in 19th Century England' (1998) 21(4) Int J Law Psych 421, 422 (hereafter Bartlett, 'The Asylum').

[40] Robert Ellis, 'The Asylum, the Poor Law and the Growth of County Asylums in Nineteenth Century Yorkshire' (2008) XLV(2) Northern Hist 279, 279 (hereafter Ellis, 'The Asylum and Poor Law').

[41] Allderidge, 'Hospitals, Madhouses and Asylums' (n 26) 333.

of a structured environment and inpatient care and supervision is still regarded as 'treatment'.[42] Further, the concentration of individuals in institutions allowed closer medical observation of insanity aiding the development of psychiatry.[43]

Initially, the asylums were considered to be successful in assisting recovery and different institutions and jurisdictions (especially in England and the United States) even competed against each other for higher cure rates.[44] Peter Bartlett observes that for some people asylum life was attractive compared to living in the workhouse or the community.[45] Records indicate that some people tried to manipulate the poor law system to get admitted to an asylum and many were reluctant to leave.[46] The York Retreat and the Tuke family became famous for using the asylum as the setting for 'moral treatment' based on using kindness and reason to 'cure' lunatics.[47]

The statistics of patient improvement were important to convince donors and governments to invest in asylums rather than to leave the insane in the cheaper workhouses and prisons.[48] Some institutions in early phases of the asylum movement were able to boast cure rates of 90 per cent, but by 1885 the average rate was around 40 per cent[49] and this decreased to below 20 per cent by the end of the nineteenth century.[50] Theodore Porter notes that these numbers could be explained by manipulation of the statistics by asylum managers using techniques such as counting deaths as discharges, returning the incurable patients to the workhouses, and failing to correct for relapsed cases.[51] It was also quickly noted by asylum doctors that 'early and recent cases' had the best recovery rates as it allowed treatment to commence before 'the effects of a disorder penetrated deeply into the brain tissues'.[52] Since then the importance of prevention and early intervention in the recovery from mental impairment has become a key driver of mental health law and policy. It has also spurred the development of a wide range of mental health services outside the asylum walls, a focus on the mental health of children and young people (before mental impairment has the chance to become entrenched), and the general 'psychiatricisation'[53] of society. It is, perhaps, ironic that the medical profession's difficulty in effectively treating mental impairment has been used as the justification for giving the medical profession greater power to intervene in mental impairment at an earlier stage.

42 Nell Munro, 'Define Acceptable: How Can We Ensure That Treatment for Mental Disorder in Detention Is Consistent with the UN Convention on the Rights of Persons with Disabilities?' (2012) 16(6) Int J Hum Rights 903, 908 (hereafter Munro, 'Define Acceptable').

43 Ellis, 'The Asylum and Poor Law' (n 40) 288.

44 Theodore M Porter, 'Funny Numbers' (2012) 4 Cult Unbound 585, 589 (hereafter, Porter, 'Funny Numbers').

45 Bartlett, 'The Asylum' (n 39) 425–9.

46 ibid.

47 Louis C Charland, 'Benevolent Theory: Moral Treatment at the York Retreat' (2007) 18(1) History of Psych 61, 61 (hereafter Charland, 'Moral Treatment').

48 Porter, 'Funny Numbers' (n 44) 588.

49 Unsworth, *The Politics of Mental Health* (n 13) 83.

50 Porter, 'Funny Numbers' (n 44) 588.

51 ibid 590, 591.

52 ibid 589.

53 This term is widely used in the literature together with 'medicalisation' to describe the conceptualization of everyday life problems as medical and psychiatric phenomenon. It is difficult to pinpoint its exact source, but it can be found in Thomas S Szasz, 'Ideology and Insanity' (1973) 25(4) Int Soc Sci J 504, 507 (hereafter Szasz 'Ideology and Insanity').

Unfortunately, the later asylums became clogged with chronic and incurable cases and became unable to provide personalized care.[54] Stephen Garton argues that the decline of the asylum was not because asylums were inherently custodial, but was rather the result of the fact that doctors lost faith in and commitment to moral treatment and made a series of decisions which shifted their attention to the more lucrative and glamorous private clinic and out-patient practice, leaving the most serious cases to languish in the asylum.[55] Ironically, many of the 'alternatives' to psychiatry advocated by abolitionists today such as peer-run residential retreats and safe spaces,[56] have their historical roots in the moral treatment and respite from everyday life once provided by the asylum.[57]

2.3 The First Specific Stand-Alone Mental Health Act

The image of a pendulum swinging between legal and medical control[58] has almost become a cliché in describing the history of mental health law since the late nineteenth century.

The first stand-alone mental health law in English law was the *Lunacy Act* 1890. This Act has been dubbed by Kathleen Jones a 'triumph of legalism',[59] because it created a formal legal structure designed to allow legal oversight and restriction of medical discretion.[60] Some key provisions included that admission was based on an order of a judicial authority (of limited duration) and two medical certificates,[61] protections from collusion between doctors and the family,[62] rights to send letters unopened to various third parties including the lord chancellor, judges, and commissioners in lunacy,[63] and obligations on asylum managers to inform private patients of their right to send unopened letters and request a private interview with the chancery visitors.[64]

At this time, the supposed cause of insanity that could support a petition was divided into moral and physical causes including:

[54] Ellis, 'The Asylum and Poor Law' (n 40) 288; Scull, Madness (n 13); William R Breakey, *The Rise and Fall of the State Mental Hospital* (Oxford University Press 1996) 20–21(hereafter Breakey, *State Mental Hospital*).

[55] Stephen Garton, 'Seeking Refuge: Why Asylum Facilities Might Still Be Relevant for Mental Health Care Services Today' (2009) 11(1) Health and Hist 25, 41 (hereafter Garton 'Seeking Refuge'); Norman Dain, 'Critics and Dissenters: Reflections on "Anti-Psychiatry" in the United States' (1989) 25 J Hist Behav 3, 36–7 (hereafter Dain, 'Critics and Dissenters').

[56] Piers Gooding and others, *Alternatives to Coercion in Mental Health Settings: A Literature Review* (Melbourne Social Equity Institute, University of Melbourne 2018) (hereafter Gooding, *Alternatives to Coercion*).

[57] Loren Mosher, 'Sorteria and Other Alternatives to Acute Psychiatric Hospitalization' (1999) 187 J Nerv Ment Dis 142, 144 (hereafter, Mosher, 'Sortoria').

[58] Larry Gostin, 'Contemporary Social Historical Perspectives on Mental Health Reform' (1983) 10(1) J Law Soc 47, 47 (hereafter Gostin, 'Mental Health Reform').

[59] Kathleen Jones, *Mental Health and Social Policy 1845–1959* (Routledge and Kegan Paul Ltd 1960), Part 1 (hereafter Jones, *Mental Health and Social Policy*).

[60] ibid.

[61] Lunacy Act 1890, ss 4–8 (hereafter 'Lunacy Act').

[62] ibid ss 30–32.

[63] ibid s 41.

[64] ibid s 42.

> Moral causes—Domestic trouble (including loss of relatives and friends), adverse circumstances (including business anxieties and pecuniary difficulties), mental anxiety and worry (not included under the above two heads) and overwork, religious excitement, love affairs (including seduction), fright and nervous shock.
>
> Physical causes—intemperance in drink, sexual intemperance, venereal disease, sexual self-abuse, over exertion, sunstroke, accident or injury, pregnancy, parturition and the puerperal state, lactation, uterine and ovarian disorders, puberty, change of life, fevers, privation and starvation, old age, other bodily diseases or disorders, heredity influence, congenital defect, other causes. Several causes may, of course, be in combination.[65]

The commissioners and visitors were given the power to discharge because as the 1878 Select Committee observed:

> If it is important that every security should be taken against the risk of a sane person being consigned to an asylum, it is scarcely less so that the treatment of insane patients while under detention should cease as soon as they are no longer dangerous to themselves or others and are not likely to be benefited by further detention.[66]

The reference to 'danger to themselves and others' is an example of the harm criterion. It should be noted that the harm criterion was originally designed to narrow the scope of asylum admission to the most serious cases for whom residing in the community was impossible without resulting in harm to self or others. While the legalism of the *Lunacy Act* 1890 was criticized from the medical point of view as a 'disappointing and retrograde measure'[67] because it inhibited access to early intervention and the development of medical and social services, many of its provisions foreshadow those in current mental health law.

There is no doubt that the 'legalism' of the *Lunacy Act* was a response to continued public fears of the potential abuse of lunacy law to confine those who may be merely 'eccentric' rather than insane, fears that wrongful commitment in an asylum could make a sane person insane, concern at the spiralling numbers of people detained in asylums, and public distrust of the ability of medicine to deliver the miraculous cures it had promised.[68]

However, legalism was also based on a concern for the 'liberty of the subject' (at that time for the wrongfully committed, rather than for the insane), liberalism being a culturally embedded value of western societies since the Enlightenment. In this respect, the work of nineteenth century philosopher, John Stuart Mill, on utilitarian liberalism, has been influential both in defending liberty as a matter of individual freedom and

[65] ibid s 5(4), notes: these causes were taken from the Annual Reports of the Commissioners in Lunacy.

[66] Sydney George Lushington, *Archibald's Lunacy: Comprising the Lunacy Acts 1890 and 1891, the Lancashire County (Lunatic Asylums and Other Powers) Act 1891, and All the Statutory Rules, Orders, and Forms of Force Thereunder: Also the Statutes Related to Criminal Lunatics, the Lunacy (Vacating of Seats) Act 1886, and the Idiots Act 1886* (4th edn, Gale 1895) 113–14 (hereafter Lushington, *Archibald's Lunacy*).

[67] P Murray Deas, 'An Address Delivered at the Opening of the Section of Psychology. Lunacy Legislation and the Lunacy Act 1890' (1891) 2(1596) Br Med J 242, 243(hereafter Deas, 'Lunacy Legislation Address').

[68] ibid; Jones, *Mental Health and Social Policy* (n 60); Unsworth, The Politics of Mental Health (n 13), 64.

human diversity and in defining the limits of liberalism.[69] His book *On Liberty* has been described as 'the most passionate treatise on human freedom ever written, and a perennially sacred scripture to the world's civil libertarians'.[70] Utilitarian liberalism is also the basis most frequently used to justify the respect for individual autonomy in contemporary healthcare decision-making and medical ethics, overtaking Kantian deontology.[71] The limits on liberty Mill identified are on conduct which harms and interferes with the liberty of others[72] and the need for those whose liberty is respected by law to have sufficient maturity and 'an ordinary amount of understanding'.[73] These two limits can also be seen in the 'police powers of the state' and *parens patriae* justifications for mental health law. The effect of these limits is the exclusion of those not of full age and people with mental and intellectual impairment from the benefits and personal responsibility of liberalism. While the significance of Mill's work will be explored later in Chapter 5 section 5.2.2, at this point, I note that utilitarian liberalism has been used by both the abolitionists and the supporters of mental health law to support their arguments (within a human rights framework). Therefore, while the *Lunacy Act* 1890 was designed to protect liberty, that protection was limited to the sane, and its existence in permitting involuntary detention at all would be criticized by contemporary abolitionists.

2.4 The Medicalization of Mental Health Law

The 'legalism' of the *Lunacy Act* 1890 was somewhat relaxed in the *Mental Treatment Act* 1930 which equated the treatment of mental illness (the new conceptualization of madness) with that of physical illness. The Act aimed to circumvent the legalistic certification process in the *Lunacy Act* 1890 (which remained in effect) by providing other more informal avenues to improve access to early intervention in a way that was less stigmatizing than formal certification. In the words of the Board of Control 'from the point of view of both humanity and economy, treatment cannot begin too early'.[74] The main reform of the Act was the ability of voluntary patients to be admitted to hospital without certification. There was also the ability to admit a 'temporary non-volitional' patient being someone who is 'suffering from a mental illness and is likely to benefit by temporary treatment but is for the time being incapable of expressing himself as willing or unwilling to receive such treatment'[75] based on two medical certificates without approval from a judicial authority. There was some confusion about how widely this new category was intended to be applied with the government expressing the view that it was for rare cases where it was unclear whether a person was

[69] John Stewart Mill, in David Bronwich and George Kateb (eds), *On Liberty* (Yale University Press 2003) (hereafter Mill, *On Liberty*).

[70] Christopher Clausen, 'John Stuart Mill's "Very Simple Principle"' (2009) [Spring] The Wilson Quarterly 40, 40 (hereafter Clausen, 'John Stuart Mill').

[71] Mary Donnelly, *Healthcare Decision-Making and the Law: Autonomy, Capacity and the Limits of Liberalism* (Cambridge Law, Medicine, and Ethics 2010) 14 (Donnelly, *Healthcare Decision-Making*).

[72] Mill, *On Liberty* (n 70) 81.

[73] ibid 140.

[74] 'The Mental Treatment Act 1930' (1930) 2(3637) Br Med J 489, 489 (hereafter 'Mental Treatment Act').

[75] *Mental Treatment Act* 1930, s 5 (repealed) (hereafter, MTA).

consenting.[76] In some places, however, it was reported to be used for up to 34 per cent of admissions.[77] The Act also included the expansion of mental health services that could be provided on an out-patient basis. The continuation of involuntary detention and treatment in the *Mental Treatment Act* was justified by analogy to the detention of people with infectious diseases under the police powers. This amendment narrowed the number of patients that would require involuntary detention and treatment under mental health law, although the 'voluntariness' of a patient's consent may be influenced by the threat of involuntary detention and treatment.[78]

It should be noted that in the United States the medicalization of mental health law was even more pronounced during this period. The Great Depression led to a relaxation of harm based civil commitment criteria and a preference for a need-for-treatment standard.[79] It was not until the civil rights movement and the Supreme Court decision of *O'Connor v Donaldson*[80] in 1975 that mental health law in the United States was tightened so that:

> a state cannot constitutionally confine without more a non-dangerous individual who is capable of living in freedom by himself or with the help of willing and responsible family members or friends.[81]

The medicalization of mental health law reflected a change in the conceptualization of madness as having spiritual, social, physical, and moral causes, to being understood as having a biological and genetic origin. Modern psychiatry shifted away from the 'internal conflicts' and the understanding of one's self in respect of various social relationships in psychoanalysis, to a focus on 'neutral empirical data—in this case, the observable behaviour of the individual' without regard to the social and cultural context. Thus, from a biomedical perspective the 'psychic illnesses become "chemical imbalances" that result in observable behaviours'[82] and the goal of psychiatry becomes one of correct diagnosis, the prescription of medication, and short term cognitive-behaviour therapies to treat symptoms.[83] This approach was also socially influenced by the desire of psychiatry to 'regain … its footing in scientific medicine'[84] and insurance companies to restrict payments to psychiatrically diagnosed conditions.

The 'medicalising shift' of the twentieth century[85] was brought to its climax by the *Mental Health Act* 1959 which repealed the *Lunacy Act* 1890, the *Mental Treatment*

[76] Sidney Clark, 'Mental Treatment Act 1930: Temporary Patients' (1933) 2(3793) Br Med J 543, 543 (hereafter Clark, 'Temporary Patients').

[77] ibid.

[78] There is a body of empirical research which indicates that 'voluntary' psychiatric patients have similar levels of perceived coercion as involuntary psychiatric patients. For example, Brian O'Donoghue and others, 'Perceived Coercion in Voluntary Hospital Admission' (2014) 21(1) Psychiatry Res 120 (hereafter O'Donoghue, 'Perceived Coercion').

[79] Dan Moon, 'The Dangerousness of the Status Quo: A Case for Modernizing Civil Commitment Law' (2014) 20 Widener Law Rev 209, 212 (hereafter Moon, 'Modernizing Civil Commitment Law').

[80] 422 US 563.

[81] ibid 576.

[82] Kevin Aho, 'Medicalising Mental Health: A Phenomenological Alternative' (2008) 29 J Med Humanit 243, 246 (hereafter Aho, 'Medicalising Mental Health').

[83] ibid.

[84] ibid.

[85] Gooding, 'Change and Continuity' (n 15).

Act 1930, and the *Mental Deficiency Acts* 1913 to 1939 and brought mental illness and mental handicap into a single regulatory framework for mental disorder.[86] The extent to which mental health, guardianship, mental capacity, and other disability legislation are integrated or dealt with in separate laws is a matter which has varied over time in different jurisdictions[87] and is still a matter of debate.[88] The parallel historical evolution of guardianship, mental capacity, and other disability legislation has influenced the development of the call for abolition as part of the wider disability rights movement. However, the distinctions between guardianship, mental capacity and other disability legislation and mental health law are of little relevance to abolitionists who oppose substitute decision-making in all its forms and for all persons with disabilities.[89]

The *Mental Health Act* 1959 was intended to end the 'legalism' that had dominated mental health law for more than seventy years and to bring mental health within the National Health Service and framework of the emerging welfare state.[90] It can be seen as reflecting the state's interest in promoting the health of its citizens for the purpose of economic and social prosperity.[91] It also captures social expectations that individuals will take responsibility for their health so that those who are ill will seek medical assistance to become well so that they can return to their social roles.[92] Like the *Mental Treatment Act* 1930, its ethos was that mental health patients would be treated with as much informality as possible and that voluntary admission would predominate. The location of mental health services would shift from the institution to the community. Involuntary admission would be the exception that was reserved for that small 'residual' group that refused voluntary treatment. As Piers Gooding notes, the act of involuntary admission automatically authorized involuntary treatment and this needs to be understood in the context where medical paternalism was prominent and the doctrine of informed consent and patient autonomy were only starting to emerge.[93]

The civil commitment criteria were still based on risk of harm, that is, detention was 'in the interests of the patient's health or safety for the protection of other persons'[94] and the person needed to suffer from a mental disorder 'of a nature or degree which warrants the detention of the patient in hospital for medical treatment'.[95] However,

[86] *Mental Health Act* 1959 (Eng and Wales), s 1 (repealed) (hereafter MHA 1959).

[87] For example, in Victoria Mental Health and Guardianship were dealt with together in the *Mental Health Act* 1959 (Vic) until 1986 and the Victorian Law Reform Commission has recommended that they stay separate with the ability to appoint a person guardian: Victorian Law Reform Commission, *Guardianship: Final Report 24* (2012) [24.5]–[24.7] (hereafter VLRC, Guardianship); Mental Capacity Act 2016 (Northern Ireland) (hereafter MCA NI).

[88] For example, Rowena Daw, 'The Case for a Fusion Law: Challenges and Issues' in Bernadette McSherry and Ian Freckelton (eds), *Coercive Care: Rights, Law and Policy* (Routledge 2013) 93 (hereafter Daw, 'Fusion'); George Szmukler and Michael Bach, 'Mental Health Disabilities and Human Right Protections' (2015) 2 Glob Ment Health 1 (hereafter Szmukler and Bach, 'Mental Health Disabilities'); MCA NI.

[89] Committee on the Rights of Persons with Disabilities 'General Comment No 1 (2014) Article 12: Equal Recognition before the Law' (11 April 2014) UN Doc CRPD/C/GC/1, [7] (hereafter CRPD).

[90] United Kingdom, *Royal Commission on the Law Relating to Mental Illness and Mental Deficiency 1954–1957 Report* (1957) 109 (hereafter 'Percy Commission').

[91] Rose, 'Psychiatry' (n 17) 46.

[92] Micheal Cavadino, *Mental Health Law in Context: Doctor's Orders?* (Dartmouth Publishing Company 1989) 12 (hereafter Cavadino, *Doctor's Orders*).

[93] Gooding, 'Change and Continuity' (n 15).

[94] MCA 1959, s 26.

[95] MCA 1959, s 26.

while the harm criteria of the *Lunacy Act* 1890 remained, the Royal Commission that preceded the Act (the Percy Commission) justified the reforms contained in the *Mental Health Act* 1959 in terms that correspond more closely to the doctrine of *parens patriae*, rather than the police powers of the state. That is, the Percy Commission conceptualized mental illness as being a type of illness that requires involuntary medical intervention because:

> ... various forms of mental disorders do affect the patient's own reason and powers of judgment and his power to appreciate the effect on others of his own behaviour, there are likely always to be some who will refuse the offer of treatment or training in any form.[96]

That is, some people with mental illness lack sufficient mental capacity and 'insight'[97] into their condition to understand or accept that what they are experiencing is a mental illness and they require medical treatment to manage their symptoms, recover, and restore reason. However, it should be noted that the concept of 'insight', while widely used by psychiatrists and mental health tribunals in hospital discharge decision-making as a marker of severity of illness and future treatment compliance, is controversial and evolving.[98] Critics argue that 'insight' is often used as a 'blanket term' to dismiss the views and lived experiences of people with mental illness, even if they have genuine concerns about the treatment that is proposed for them.[99] Nevertheless, there is a significant body of literature around 'insight' as a neurological deficit and coping mechanism and psychiatrists often regard it as the most characteristic feature of severe mental illness, especially schizophrenia.[100]

In addition, the assessment of risk was on the basis of two medical certificates without judicial involvement and the Act abolished the board of control and previous mechanisms of external oversight of medical discretion. The new Mental Health Tribunal, composed of a medical, legal, and lay member, was to determine whether a person was fit for discharge rather than as a check on wrongful admission. The effect of these reforms was to concentrate power in medical hands on the assumption that doctor and patient had a shared interest in treatment and recovery. In 1975, Philip Bean noted however, that in practice 'it seems doctors will automatically assume a danger exists to self or others if the medical disorder is severe. In other words psychiatrists could still rely on a medical definition in order to cover any additional social requirements.'[101] That is, the harm criterion was interpreted and applied broadly making

[96] Percy Commission (n 91) 111.

[97] Ian Freckelton, 'Extra-Legislative Factors in Involuntary Status Decision-Making' in Bernadette McSherry and Penelope Weller (eds), *Rethinking Rights-Based Mental Health Laws* (Hart Publishing 2010) 203, 206–207 (hereafter Freckelton, 'Extra-Legislative Factors').

[98] Ibid; Kate Diesfeld, '"Insight" Unpacking the Concept in Mental Health Law' (2003) 10(1) Psychiatry Psychol & L 63(hereafter Diesfield, 'Insight').

[99] ibid 68.

[100] Xavier Amador and Henry Kronengold, 'Understanding and Assessing Insight' in Xavier Amador and Anthony David (eds), *Insight and Psychosis: Awareness of Illness in Schizophrenia and Related Disorders* (2nd edn, Oxford University Press 2004) 24–25 (hereafter Amador and Kronengold, 'Insight').

[101] Philip Bean, 'The Mental Health Act 1959: Some Issues Concerning Rule Enforcement' (1975) 2(2) J Law Soc 225, 227(hereafter Bean, 'MHA 1959').

it more akin to treatment on the basis of medical necessity or lack of mental capacity, than the risk of harm to the individual or society.

Not surprisingly, the unprecedented power conferred on the medical profession by the *Mental Health Act* 1959, did not take long to attract its critics along with the backlash of the anti-psychiatry movement and general public mistrust in institutions at that time. In the United States, Peter Miller identifies four different types of critiques of psychiatry. The 'theoretical critique' of the anti-psychiatry movement challenged the conceptualization of mental illness as an 'illness' and pointed out that psychiatric knowledge about the aetiology, diagnosis, and treatment of mental illness was still too uncertain to justify the unfettered medical authority in the new *Mental Health Act* 1959.[102] The 'institutional critique' was aimed at the abolition of the asylum based on the role of institutionalized care in producing mental illness.[103] The 'juridical critique' was based on the rights of patients and the status of people with mental illness as a citizen and the 'technological critique' described the regulation of institutions and different kinds of treatments.[104] Each of these critiques is evident in setting the scene for the reforms of the *Mental Health Act* 1983 and elements of them still underpin the arguments for abolition.

It is still controversial whether the motives for deinstitutionalization were humanitarian, libertarian, a result of the new pharmacological treatments, or economic given the high cost of psychiatric inpatient treatment and maintaining facilities. However, the *Mental Health Act* 1959 continued the policy shift towards the deinstitutionalization of people with mental illness, a process that is still continuing in western developed countries and has probably never been implemented fully.[105]

The abolition of the asylum and emphasis on community treatment did not solve 'the problem' of mental illness. Rather, it resulted in the transfer of people with mental illness back to their families (as in the eighteenth century)[106] and their 'transinstitutionalisation' to prisons, group homes, boarding houses, and the streets.[107] While the problems with deinstitutionalization have been attributed to under-resourcing and the lack of proper community services, it also requires a tolerant society that is able to accept and accommodate the difference of people with mental illness. As Henry Rollin remarked in 1963, 'as for "community care"—the current popular psychiatric catchphrase—the question arises: does the community care?'[108] The release of people with mental illness into the community fuelled fears that mental health law reform had gone too far and that too many people who were dangerous were at large within the community.[109]

[102] Peter Miller, 'Critiques of Psychiatry' in Peter Miller and Nikolas Rose (eds), *The Power of Psychiatry* (Polity Press 1986) 11, 13, 21–24 (hereafter Miller, 'Critiques of Psychiatry').

[103] ibid.

[104] ibid.

[105] Liz Jamieson and Pamela J Taylor, 'Mental Disorder and Perceived Threat to the Public: People Who Do Not Return to Community Living' (2002) 181 Br J Psychiatry 399(hereafter Jamieson and Taylor, 'Mental Disorder').

[106] Scull, *Madness* (n 13) 114.

[107] Ralph Slovenko, 'The Transinstitutionalisation of the Mentally Ill' (2003) 29 Ohio NU L Rev 641, 641 (hereafter Slovenko, 'Transinstitutionalisation').

[108] Hernry R Rollin, 'Social and Legal Repercussions of the Mental Health Act, 1959' (1963) 1(5333) Br Med J 786, 788 (hereafter Rollin, 'Social and Legal Repercussions').

[109] Unsworth, *The Politics of Mental Health* (n 13) 316.

The experience of deinstitutionalization, as the 'first' abolition, however, also offers three lessons for the abolition of mental health law. First, despite long-held fears that institutionalization could produce or exacerbate mental illness, the abolition of the asylum did not cause mental illness to disappear, just as the abolition of mental health law would not (at least on its own) cause mental impairment or disability to disappear. Secondly, to focus only on the evils of the asylum was to ignore the benefits of the asylum, in terms of providing accommodation, supervision, stability and care for people who may not have fared well in family, community care, or other institutions, such as, prison. Similarly, it is necessary to recognize the benefits of mental health law in ensuring that the most severely impaired people have access to care and treatment and to ensure that those benefits are not lost by its abolition. Finally, the past indicates that it is difficult to secure the level of investment in the resources necessary to provide the kind of community services required to potentially replace legal coercion without adverse consequences for people with mental impairment and the community (although that does not mean it should not be tried).

2.5 The 'New Legalism' and the Mental Health Act 1983

The wide discretionary power of medical professionals enshrined in the *Mental Health Act* 1959, did not adequately recognize or protect the legal rights of people with mental illness. This paved the way for a 'new legalism', the brain child of Lawrence Gostin, legal director of MIND (National Association for Mental Health), as a platform for reform. The involvement of MIND in the development of the *Mental Health Act* 1983 (UK) is an example of the growing participation of mental health consumer advocacy groups in mental health law reform. Lawrence Gostin argued that the 'new legalism' could be distinguished from the legal formalism of the *Lunacy Act* 1890 in that its focus was on increasing the liberty of patients (as opposed to protecting the sane), on applying the 'ideology of entitlement' to a range of mental health services as an enforceable legal right, and on restoring some of the legal status of people with mental illness as citizens (for example, the right to access the courts without leave and to vote).[110] Bernadette McSherry and Penelope Weller have referred to this new concern with rights as 'rights-based legalism'.[111] These concerns for liberty, provision of healthcare, and citizenship are taken up and extended by the abolitionists, as grounds for the abolition of mental health law.

While not all the reforms proposed by the 'new legalism' were enacted in the *Mental Health Act* 1983, those reforms provided a reintroduction of formal legal safeguards as a check on medical power. For example, mental health law was tightened up by measures such as narrowing the definition of mental illness so that it explicitly excluded those with 'sexual deviancy or dependence on alcohol or drugs', the 'treatability test' to prevent mental health law from being used for purely custodial detention where

[110] Gostin, 'Mental Health Reform' (n 59).

[111] Bernadette McSherry and Penelope Weller, 'Rethinking Rights Based Mental Health Laws' in Bernadette McSherry and Penelope Weller (eds), *Rethinking Rights-Based Mental Health Laws* (Hart Publishing 2010) 3, 5 (hereafter McSherry and Weller, 'Rethinking Rights Based Mental Health Laws').

no treatment exists, an expanded role for the social worker, increased opportunities for mental health tribunal review, restrictions on psychosurgery, electroconvulsive therapy, and medication for more than three months without consent, a second opinion, and establishment of the Mental Health Act Commission.[112]

Civil commitment criteria based on risk of harm to self and others remained unchanged, but the duration of compulsory orders was halved.[113] While the *Mental Health Act* 1983 increased procedural safeguards, wide medical discretion remained and its conceptual origins are still often viewed as being rooted in the paternalism of the Percy Commission and *Mental Health Act* 1959.[114]

In the 1990s and 2000s there was on-going debate about when involuntary detention and treatment should be used, including continuing concerns about public safety and violence in general,[115] early intervention and increasing the rights of people with mental impairment. Concerns about public safety arose from a number of high profile cases involving the release of people with personality disorder into the community because they were untreatable under the *Mental Health Act* 1983.[116] Martyn Pickersgill argues that there was a process of 'collaboration' between the state and psychiatry in making personality disorder treatable and changing the treatability test in the *Mental Health Amendment Act* 2007.[117] Nikolas Rose also identifies a general shift in thinking about protection from 'dangerous' individuals, to a paradoxical acceptance that risk of harm is ever-present, but still needs to be calculated, controlled, and eliminated.[118]

The other major reform of the *Mental Health Amendment Act* 2007 was the introduction of compulsory community treatment orders, which can be seen both as a way of reducing coercion by providing an alternative to detention in hospital, and as a way of 'institutionalising the community'.[119] The introduction of community treatment orders was particularly controversial in England and was seen as a way of increasing surveillance of and social control over people with mental illness in the community.[120] That said, community treatment orders have been widely used in other jurisdictions, like Victoria, since the *Mental Health Act* 1986 (Vic).

112 Gostin, 'Mental Health Reform' (n 59).

113 ibid.

114 Richardson, 'Principle or Pragmatism' (n 1) 415; Aisling Boyle, 'The Law and Incapacity Determinations: A Conflict of Governance' (2008) 71(3) MLR 413, 436 (hereafter Boyle, 'Incapacity Determinations').

115 Richard J Bonnie, 'Three Strands of Mental Health Law: Developmental Mileposts' in Richard J Bonnie and Lynda E Frost (eds), *The Evolution of Mental Health Law* (American Psychological Association 2001) 31, 32, 39–40 (hereafter Bonnie, 'Three Strands of Mental Health Law').

116 Atkinson and Reilly, '"Dangerousness" in Mental Health Law' (n 35) 47–49.

117 Martyn Pickersgill, 'How Personality Became Treatable: The Mutual Constitution of Clinical Knowledge and Mental Health Law' (2012) 43(1) Soc Stud Sci 30, 31–32 (hereafter Pikersgill, 'How Personality Became Treatable').

118 Nikolas Rose, 'Governing Risky Individuals: The Role of Psychiatry in New Regimes of Control' (1998) 5(2) Psychiatry Psychol & L 177 (hereafter, Rose, 'Governing Risky Individuals').

119 Philip Fennell, 'Institutionalising the Community: The Codification of Clinical Authority and the Limits of Rights-Based Approaches' in Bernadette McSherry and Penelope Weller (eds), *Rethinking Rights-Based Mental Health Laws* (Hart Publishing 2010) 13 (hereafter Fennell, 'Insitutionalising the Community').

120 Boyle, 'Incapacity Determinations' (n 115) 437–38.

Civil commitment criteria based on risk of harm to self or others came under fire for being too narrow, delaying early intervention and jeopardizing treatment success,[121] and unjustifiably treating people with mental impairment differently from general health patients.[122] The concern that harm criteria were too narrow prompted the expansion of the harm criteria through the amendment of mental health laws in the last twenty years to allow involuntary detention and treatment on the grounds of 'mental deterioration'.[123]

Self-proclaimed 'mad' activists,[124] and other critics have also criticized involuntary detention and treatment based on harm for being discriminatory and mental health law generally for depriving them of their rights.[125] This led to proposals, such as the Richardson Report, that the harm criteria be modified by criteria based on mental capacity which would make the law the same for people with mental and physical illness and give those who can prove their mental capacity the right to refuse treatment.[126]

The proposal to replace civil commitment criteria based on the risk of harm to self and others with mental capacity was rejected in England by the passing of the *Mental Health Act* 2007 (UK). The rejection of the Richardson Report proposal has been criticized as elevating the police powers justification of mental health law in the interest of risk management and public safety, over the *parens patriae* justification and concern with the health of the patient reflected in the proposed reform to involuntary detention and treatment on the basis of 'mental capacity'.[127] However, it should be noted that in Canada and the United States mental capacity criteria have been used to give people with mental impairment who are assessed to retain mental capacity the ability to refuse psychiatric treatment, even if involuntary detention based on harm is still permitted.[128] The inclusion of mental capacity criteria is also a current trend

[121] Matthew Large and others, 'Mental Health Laws That Require Dangerousness for Involuntary Admission May Delay the Initial Treatment of Schizophrenia' (2008) 43 (251–56) Soc Psychiatry Epidemiol 251 (hereafter Large, 'Mental Health Laws').

[122] Christopher James Ryan, 'One Flu over the Cuckoo's Nest: Comparing Legislated Coercive Treatment for Mental Illness with That for Other Illness' (2010) 8 Bioeth Inq 87, 89 (hereafter Ryan, 'One Flu over the Cuckoo's Nest').

[123] For example, *Mental Health Act* 2009 (SA), s 21(1)(b) (hereafter, MHA SA); John Ellery Gray and others, 'Australian and Canadian Mental Health Acts Compared' (2010) 44(12) Aust NZ J Psychiatry 1126, 1128 (hereafter, Gray, 'Australian and Canadian Mental Health Acts').

[124] Nick Crossley, 'Not Being Mentally Ill: Social Movements, System Survivors and the Oppositional Habitus' (2004) 11(2) Anthropol Med 161, 170 (hereafter Crossley, 'Not Being Mentally Ill').

[125] Tina Minkowitz, 'Abolishing Mental Health Laws to Comply with the Convention on the Rights of Persons with Disabilities' in Bernadette McSherry and Penelope Weller (eds), *Rethinking Rights-Based Mental Health Laws* (Hart Publishing 2010) 151 (hereafter Minkowitz 'Abolishing Mental Health Laws'); David W Oaks, 'Whose Voices Should Be Heard? The Role of Mental Health Consumers, Psychiatric Survivors, and Families' in Michael Dudley and others (eds), *Mental Health and Human Rights: Vision, Praxis and Courage* (Oxford University Press 2012) 566 (hereafter Oaks, 'Whose Voices Should Be Heard?').

[126] Report of the Expert Committee, *Review of the Mental Health Act 1983 November 1999* [2.15] and [5.18] (hereafter, 'Richardson Report').

[127] Boyle (n 114) 434; Richardson (n 9) 75; George Szmukler and Frank Holloway, 'Reform of the Mental Health Act: Health or Safety?' (2000) 177 Br J Psychiatry 196, 196 (hereafter Szmulker and Holloway, 'Reform of the Mental Health Act').

[128] For example, in Ontario Canada see Mental Health Act, RSO 1990, M 7, s 20 (hereafter, 'MHA Ontario').

in Australian mental health law reform, although risk criteria have been retained as well.[129]

However, mental capacity criteria are used in England and Wales to permit those with functional deficits other than mental impairment to make their own decisions, and people with mental impairment to make decisions about non-psychiatric treatment,[130] where mental capacity criteria are met under the *Mental Capacity Act* 2005. Those who are assessed to lack mental capacity, however, still have decisions made for them by a substitute decision-maker who must take their wishes and preferences, together with other objective medical considerations, into account when determining what is in their best interest.[131]

Meanwhile, the emergence of calls for the abolition of mental health law and the entry into force of the CRPD, has challenged the need for mental health law itself, regardless of whether the basis for intervention is medical necessity, risk of harm to self or others, or mental capacity (See Chapter 3). From this perspective mental impairment is conceptualized as a disability that is created by social conditions that do not adequately support people with impairments and has been described as an oppositional device to social oppression.[132]

2.6 Conclusion

Five important principles may be derived from the history of mental health systems. First, that the state does not—contrary to what is often implied by anti-psychiatrists and abolitionists—particularly *want* to intervene in the lives of persons with mental impairments. It only does so when other informal social care systems and self-help have failed. That is, the reluctance of states to abolish mental health law is not simply a matter of stubbornness, or lack of imagination, but is rooted in legitimate public policy concerns and social need. Second, that the absence of mental health law prior to the eighteenth century did not necessarily improve the liberty, autonomy, dignity, or quality of life of people with mental impairment (as envisaged by current abolitionists). Thus, the abolitionist project needs to extend well beyond the abolition of mental health law and supported decision-making as it is currently articulated. Third, less law does not necessarily mean more liberty, but that if the law creates too many formal barriers, people will look for 'work arounds' (for example, *Lunacy Act* 1890 and *Mental Treatment Act* 1930). Fourth, those proposing social change proclaim that

[129] Bernadette McSherry and Kay Wilson, 'The Concept of Capacity in Australian Mental Health Law Reform: Going in the Wrong Direction?' (2015) 40 Int J Law Psychiatry 60, 62 (McSherry and Wilson, 'The Concept of Capacity').

[130] For example, in *Nottinghamshire Healthcare NHS Trust (Applicant) v RC (Respondent)* [2014] EWHC 1317 (COP) (hereafter *Nottinghamshire Healthcare NHS Trust (Applicant) v RC (Respondent)*) where a person with mental illness who was also a Jehovah's Witness was considered to have sufficient mental capacity to make an advance statement refusing blood products.

[131] *Mental Capacity Act* 2005 (UK), s 4 (hereafter MCA).

[132] Mike Oliver, 'The Social Model of Disability: Thirty Years On' (2013) 28(7) Disabil Soc 1024, 1024 (hereafter Oliver, 'The Social Model of Disability'); Angherd E Beckett and Tom Campbell, 'The Social Model of Disability as an Oppositional Device' (2015) 30(2) ibid 270, 271 (hereafter Beckett and Campbell, 'The Social Model of Disability').

their proposals are more enlightened and humane than the current regime and those in the past.[133] The claims of contemporary abolitionists that only a complete 'paradigm shift' and break with the past will suffice contain echoes of the rhetoric of the abolitionists of the asylum that 'only a radical and complete break with the past, the abandonment of the attempt to patch up the mental hospital, offered the prospect of finally breaking free of this dismal, self-perpetuating cycle'[134] of imperfect reform. Finally, mental health law is heavily situated within is socio-historical and systemic context so that any reforms in the field (including abolition) will have far reaching and possibly unintended consequences.

Fortunately, the historical evolution of mental health law has indicated that while balancing competing individual and social needs is enormously challenging, mental health law is flexible and capable of achieving multiple purposes and functions. Similarly, the evolution of the police powers of the state and the doctrine of *parens patriae*, suggest a range of possible avenues of reform that could combine 'top-down' (power of the state through mental health law) and 'bottom-up' (empowering the person to make decisions for themselves) approaches. As Clive Unsworth observes, mental health law can authorize and legitimate involuntary detention and treatment, while at the same time limiting and protecting people with mental illness from unchecked medical power, provide external oversight, inspection and monitoring, harness and direct healthcare resources, and allocate responsibility between medical professionals, the family, and the state.[135] It may even be able to give more responsibility, social support, inclusion, and empowerment to people with mental impairment. In the words of Joseph Dute mental health law 'must be perfected, not abolished'.[136]

[133] Andrew Scull, 'Deinstitutionalization and the Rights of the Deviant' (1981) 37(3) JSI 6, 7–8 (hereafter Scull, 'Deinstitutionalization').

[134] ibid.

[135] Unsworth, *The Politics of Mental Health* (n 13) 9–18.

[136] Joseph Dute, 'Should Substituted Decision-Making Be Abolished?' (2015) 22 Eur J Health Law 315, 320.

3
The Case for the Abolition of Mental Health Law

3.1 Introduction

Even though it is my contention that mental health law should not be abolished but be reformed, I argue it is crucial to understand fully the call for the abolition of mental health law, what is driving it, and why it has emerged now. It is also important to provide an in-depth analysis of the Abolition with Support model so as to counter potential criticisms from abolitionists that I have built a 'straw man' because I have not understood the call for abolition. Understanding what sits behind the call for the abolition of mental health law is also necessary to be able to assess to what extent the Abolition with Support model actually addresses the concerns of persons with mental impairments and whether alternative proposals may provide equally good if not better solutions.

Moreover, there has been little scholarly analysis of the history of calls for abolition or attention given to the 'resistance' to psychiatric power by opposition groups:[1] the other side of the history set out in Chapter 2. As Michael Perlin has recently observed, 'this voice is typically ignored' and 'there is little evidence that these groups are taken seriously by lawyers or academics'.[2] Such neglect may be explained by a perception that the arguments for abolition are so extreme and unlikely to be implemented that they have remained at the fringes of a debate about the width of clinical discretion that has not examined whether that discretion should exist at all.[3] However, the marginalization of the arguments for the abolition of mental health law, and of those who voice and identify with them, can be interpreted as a reflection of the very prejudices and power-relationships that are challenged by the abolitionists. As argued in Chapter 1 (section 1.3(c)), taking the criticisms of abolitionists seriously is necessary to properly value the inherent dignity, equality, and participation of all persons with mental impairments.

The purpose of this chapter is to attempt to fill that void by focussing on the call for the abolition of mental health law. I trace the emergence of the arguments for the abolition of mental health law and how they are related to the different ways in which mental health law is often conceptualized. I 'drill down' into what lies beneath those

[1] Nick Crossley, 'Not Being Mentally Ill: Social Movements, System Survivors and the Oppositional Habitus' (2004) 11(2) Anthropol Med 161 (hereafter, Crossley, 'Not Being Mentally Ill').

[2] Michael Perlin, *International Human Rights and Mental Disability Law: When the Silenced Are Heard* (Oxford University Press 2012) 16 (hereafter Perlin, *International Human Rights and Mental Disability Law*).

[3] Genevra Richardson, 'Reforming Mental Health Law: Principle or Pragmatism' (2001) 54 Curr Leg Probl 415, 418 (hereafter, Richardson, 'Principle or Pragmatism').

Mental Health Law. Kay Wilson, Oxford University Press. © Kay Wilson 2021. DOI: 10.1093/oso/9780192843258.003.0003

calls and analyse their conceptual substratum and socio-historical context. Section 3.2 of this chapter will explore the emergence and development of the arguments for abolition, including the experiences that have informed those views and the gradual incorporation of human rights arguments into the case for abolition. It will also include a consideration of some of the obstacles that have prevented the voices of abolitionists from being heard and how they have been gradually overcome. Section 3.3 will examine the content of some of the arguments for the abolition of mental health law. I argue that while the case for abolition can be partly explained by the history of abuse and oppression of people with mental illness in most societies, it is too simplistic to conclude that the call for abolition is simply an extreme 'reaction' to poor treatment. Rather, I argue that the case for abolition rests on a qualitatively different conceptual basis that challenges the assumptions that are traditionally used to justify mental health laws, including the concept of mental illness itself. In section 3.4 I conclude with how understanding the case for abolition is crucial to form a basis of a critique of it and the value of these arguments for future law and systemic reform.

3.2 The Emergence and Development of the Call for Abolition

Opposition to mental health law is probably as old as mental health law itself. As Nick Crossley writes:

> It is possible to identify acts of resistance and even resistance groups amongst those deemed insane for as far back into the historical record as one chooses to go (Crossley 1999a; Porter 1987). Wherever individuals are deemed insane, grouped as such and differentially treated, the potential for resistance exists and the actuality can be identified if one searches hard enough for it.[4]

The most vocal and persistent of all opposition groups have been former psychiatric patients. In the nineteenth and twentieth centuries many former patients in the United Kingdom and the United States such as Elizabeth Packard, Elizabeth Stone, and Clifford Beers sought to protest against their incarceration and treatment in asylums by publishing personal accounts of their experiences.[5] John Perceval, son of the English prime minister, published two volumes of his Narrative between 1838 and 1840, describing his experiences in various 'mad houses' as well as starting the first ever user-led advocacy service, the Alleged Lunatics' Friend Society, a forerunner of the modern user and survivor movement.[6]

It can, however, be difficult to distinguish between individual complaints, general criticisms of law and psychiatry, arguments for law and systemic reform, and those

[4] Crossley, 'Not Being Mentally Ill' (n 1) 164.

[5] Judith Cook and Jessica Jonikas, 'Self-Determination among Mental Health Consumers/Survivors: Using Lessons from the Past to Guide the Future' (2002) 13(2) J Disabil Policy Stud 87 (hereafter Cook and Jonikas, 'Self-Determination among Mental Health Consumers/Survivors').

[6] David Brandon, 'A Friend to Alleged Lunatics' (2007) (October) Mental Health Today 37, 37 (hereafter Brandon, 'A Friend to Alleged Lunatics').

arguments that demand the abolition of mental health law. This is because the aims of ex-patients and their early advocacy groups were unclear, intemperate, and 'liable to be discounted as the residual effects of mental illness'.[7] As Clive Unsworth asks:

> Were they opposed to the conceptualization and treatment of insanity as a *medical* condition? Did they accept this, but object to *coercive* psychiatry? Did they in fact wish the treatment of mental illness to be more assimilated to that of physical illness or less? The answers to these questions were not always clear, with the result that they tended to articulate a generalized suspicion and sense of grievance rather than to base their case upon systematic analysis of the deficiencies of the system and how they could be remedied.[8]

Clive Unsworth's three questions are still pertinent to the arguments for abolition today. The answers to these questions vary in radical politics, as discussed below. But, the case for abolition as it is currently articulated by the CRPD Committee, answers the first question in the positive by conceptualizing mental illness as a 'mental impairment' which medicine is unable to 'cure'. However, abolitionists also conceptualize mental impairment as a 'disability' that is created by and should be remedied by society. Abolitionists answer the second question in the negative, by objecting to coercive psychiatry, hence the call for the abolition of mental health law. However, abolitionists may not seek the abolition of psychiatry itself, because many accept that there is place for psychiatry in the treatment of mental impairment for those who choose it voluntarily. In answer to the third question, these bodies seek to make the treatment of people with mental illness the same as people with physical illness, but also with people without disability at all.

Many of the early opponents of mental health law were concerned with the reform of the law and mental health system, rather than the abolition of mental health law. The approach taken depended on how the problems with the mental health system were defined and what the underlying causes of those problems were considered to be. For some reformers those problems were systemic. For example, in nineteenth century England there was general disquiet about asylums and in 1859 and 1877 two Select Committees of the House of Commons demanded that Lord Shaftsbury defend the Lunacy Commission (as the body offering legal oversight of the mental health system was then called).[9] As Jacqueline Atkinson notes:

> Shaftsbury, along with many asylum doctors, argued, as many still do, that what was most important was not a change in the law, but greater public support, as well as better staff and staff training.[10]

[7] Clive Unsworth, *The Politics of Mental Health Legislation* (Claredon Press, 1987) 67 (hereafter Unsworth, *The Politics of Mental Health*).

[8] ibid 68.

[9] Jacqueline Atkinson, *Advance Directives in Mental Health: Theory, Practice and Ethics* (Jessica Kingsley 2007) 33 (hereafter Atkinson, *Advance Directives*).

[10] ibid.

Similarly, in the early twentieth Century, ex-patient and reformer Clifford Beers in the United States sought to 'upgrade, not abolish mental hospitals'.[11]

The late nineteenth and early twentieth centuries were also periods of mental health law reform, in which law and medicine in mental health were involved in what has been described by many commentators as a 'power struggle' between 'legalism' and 'clinical discretion'.[12] The tenor of that law reform has tended to reflect periods of optimism and pessimism about the power of psychiatry to cure mental illness, with periods of optimism giving enhanced power to clinical discretion, and pessimism stricter legal controls over involuntary admission and treatment.[13] For example, the reforms in the English 1890 Lunacy Act introduced strict legal reforms in an attempt to totally regulate psychiatric power and remove clinical discretion, until this became unworkable and was 'swept away' in 1959.[14] In the meantime, patient rights were protected by the Mental Treatment Act 1930 (England and Wales) which introduced voluntary admission and discharge and the treatment of people with mental illness in hospital on the same basis as physical illness.[15] The Mental Health Act 1959 (England and Wales) is reported to have had the effect of consolidating the divergent strands of mental health law based on public and private patients into one under the National Health Service. Ironically, it was at that point when the medical control of mental illness was at its highest point, that the 'revisionist legal view reasserted itself' in the anti-psychiatry movement.[16]

As Paul Appelbaum explains:

> From the formulation of the first statutes governing civil commitment to the new asylums in the early 19th century to roughly the mid-1960s, the focus of civil commitment law was unchanged and unchallenged: persons who were mentally ill and in need of treatment could be committed for that care. Moreover, although the degree of judicial oversight waxed and waned over time, the procedures by which commitment could be effected were often entrusted to medical hands.[17]

While the impact of the anti-psychiatry movement on the call for the abolition of mental health law is discussed further below, what is important to note is that opposition to mental health law, as an organized political movement, is a relatively new idea that has only emerged in the last fifty to sixty years.[18] Its emergence fitted in to the broader civil rights movement and a general scepticism and distrust of institutions.[19]

[11] Norman Dain, 'Critics and Dissenters: Reflections on "Anti-Psychiatry" in the United States' (1989) 25 J Hist Behav 3, 6 (hereafter Dain, 'Critics and Dissenters').

[12] Unsworth, *The Politics of Mental Health* (n 7) Ch 1; Peter Bartlett and Ralph Sandland, *Mental Health Law: Policy and Practice* (3rd edn, Oxford University Press 2007) 11–12 (hereafter Bartlett and Sandland, *Mental Health Law*).

[13] Dain, 'Critics and Dissenters' (n 11) 3.

[14] Atkinson, *Advance Directives* (n 9) 34.

[15] ibid.

[16] ibid 35.

[17] Paul S Appelbaum, 'Almost a Revolution: An International Perspective on the Law of Involuntary Commitment' (1997) 25(2) J Am Acad Psychiatry Law 135, 136 (hereafter Appelbaum, 'Almost a Revolution').

[18] Dain, 'Critics and Dissenters' (n 11) 8.

[19] ibid.

There are several reasons for this. The first is that the general civil rights movement in the 1960s made organizing politically seem like a 'normal' response for disempowered groups.[20] Second, the views of disempowered groups often need to be embedded within a social movement in order to be heard.[21] Third, disempowered groups often identified with and supported each other. For example, the psychiatric user and survivor movement and 'mad' activists (as they describe themselves) received a lot of support from the black community in the United States and vice versa because they could empathize with the loss of rights.[22] Fourthly, mad activists often belonged to more than one movement and this led to the 'cross-fertilisation' of ideas and methods between movements (for example, civil rights, feminism, disabilities rights, etc).[23] Finally, many mad activists believe that their struggle is really a small part of a much broader struggle for the recognition of human rights and human dignity.[24] This recognizes the 'mutually reinforcing' nature of mental health and human rights, as human rights violations play an important part in the development of, as well as the social response to, mental impairment.[25]

While 'grass-roots' opposition groups to mental health law eventually developed their own philosophies and agendas, it is not surprising that many of them initially adopted anti-psychiatry doctrines that were popular at the time (see Chapter 1 and discussion in part 2 below).[26] It is also not surprising that much of the flavour of anti-psychiatry persists in modern arguments for the abolition of mental health law, espoused by mental health and disability advocacy groups. Many of these groups still dispute the existence of mental illness as a medical condition,[27] have reclaimed 'madness' as a self-descriptor,[28] regard themselves as 'eccentric citizens who do not fit in the Great Modernisation'[29] and point-out the irrationality of modern society in denying the reality of our imminent environmental crisis.[30] When mental health law is viewed as a form of social control, 'madness' is the right to be different and mental health law is about suppressing the core of that identity.[31]

[20] David W Oaks, 'Whose Voices Should Be Heard? The Role of Mental Health Consumers, Psychiatric Survivors, and Families' in Michael Dudley and others (eds), *Mental Health and Human Rights: Vision, Praxis and Courage* (Oxford University Press 2012) 566, 569 (hereafter Oaks, 'Whose Voices Should Be Heard?').

[21] Judith Herman, *Trauma and Recovery: The Aftermath of Violence—from Domestic Abuse to Political Terror* (Basic Books 1992) 2 (hereafter Herman, *Trauma and Recovery*).

[22] Fred Pelka, *What We Have Done: An Oral History of the Disability Rights Movement* (University of Massachusetts Press 2012) 292, 296 (hereafter Pelka, *What We Have Done*).

[23] ibid Ch 15.

[24] ibid 284; Oaks, 'Whose Voices Should Be Heard' (n 20) 566.

[25] Lawrence Gostin and Lance Gamble, 'The Human Rights of Persons with Mental Disabilities: A Global Perspective on the Application of Human Rights Principles to Mental Health' (2004) Md Law Rev 20 (hereafter Gostin and Gamble, 'The Human Rights of Persons with Mental Disabilities').

[26] Crossley, 'Not Being Mentally Ill' (n 1) 167.

[27] Tina Minkowitz, 'The United Nations Convention on the Rights of Persons with Disabilities and the Right to Freedom from Nonconsensual Psychiatric Interventions' (2007) 34 SJILC 405 (hereafter Minkowitz, 'The Right to Freedom from Nonconsensual Psychiatric Interventions'); Oaks, 'Whose Voices Shall be Heard' (n 20) 566.

[28] Crossley, 'Not Being Mentally Ill' (n 1) 170.

[29] Oaks, 'Whose Voices Shall be Heard' (n 20) 569.

[30] ibid 568.

[31] Minkowitz, 'The Right to Freedom from Nonconsensual Psychiatric Interventions' (n 27).

Abolitionists often point to the known adverse short- and long-term side-effects of psychiatric drugs and electro-convulsive treatment. David W Oaks, for example, is concerned that psychiatric treatments cause irreversible brain damage, far beyond that which is disclosed to patients and their friends, family, and supporters, by psychiatrists and the pharmaceutical industry.[32] While most contemporary abolitionists stop short of calling for the abolition of psychiatry, they are concerned that involuntary detention and treatment means that people diagnosed with mental illness are not properly informed of non-conventional treatment alternatives and are unable to make a free choice for themselves.[33]

The evolution of various opposition groups to psychiatry and mental health law since the 1960s is complicated and tends to follow changes in the tactics used by other dissident groups at the time.[34] The origins of the modern user and survivor movement leading to the call for the abolition of mental health law can be found in the formation of the Mental Patients Union in 1971('MPU') and the successful 'strike' against the closure of Paddington Day Hospital, a democratic therapeutic community in London.[35] However, there were similar movements outside England at the time.[36] The strike led to the formation of a more permanent union of mental patients and the infamous 'Fish Manifesto' with a picture of a fish on a hook (symbolic of persons with mental impairment) which advocated the abolition of compulsory admissions and treatment and the creation of peer-run alternatives, among other things.[37] The MPU used the industrial Marxist model popular at the time.[38] At the same time, radical deinstitutionalization in Trieste Italy by Franco Basaglia inspired the creation of a number of other patient-led organizations in the 1980s known as the European Network for Alternatives to Psychiatry, the British Network for Alternatives to Psychiatry, the Campaign against Psychiatric Oppression and the Hearing Voices Network.[39] In the mid-1980s two new organizations, Survivors Speak Out and United Kingdom Advocacy Network, drew on the survivor politics of AIDs and child abuse survivors, moving away from Marxism and taking back the right to self-identification and the giving of subjective testimony.[40] During that time mental health services came to view survivors as 'consumers', incorporating their views into working committees and paying some survivors as consultants and 'lay professionals'.[41] In the 1997–2000s, the Mad Pride movement celebrating 'mad' culture and music reflected the Gay and Black Pride movements and anti-corporate activism, whereas the 750th anniversary of Bethlam Hospital inspired the Reclaim Bedlam Campaign.[42]

32 Oaks, 'Whose Voices Shall be Heard' (n 20) 573–74.
33 ibid 572.
34 Nick Crossley, *Contesting Psychiatry: Social Movements in Mental Health* (Routledge 2006) 171 (hereafter Crossley, *Contesting Psychiatry*).
35 ibid 129.
36 J Haafkens and others, 'Mental Health Care and the Opposition Movement in the Netherlands' (1986) 22(2) Soc Sci Med 185; Dain ('Critics and Dissenters') (n 11).
37 Crossley, *Contesting Psychiatry* (n 34) 133.
38 ibid 132.
39 ibid 142–43.
40 ibid 163.
41 Theo Stickley, 'Should Service User Involvement Be Consigned to History? A Critical Realist Perspective' (2006) J Psychiatr Ment Health Nurs 570, 573 (hereafter Stickley, 'Should Service User Involvement Be Consigned to History?').
42 Crossley, *Contesting Psychiatry* (n 34) 184.

In America, the call for the abolition of civil commitment, with exceptions for a brief 48 hours of detention where a person was on the verge of or in the process of engaging in suicidal behaviour, emerged in response to President Carter's Commission on Mental Health on 15 February 1978, along with a call for investigation into other approaches like a dangerousness (the current risk model) and safeguarded parternalism model where a limited course of treatment was warranted after a cost-benefit analysis.[43] Similarly, in 1982 Stephen Morse published a paper setting out the grounds justifying the abolition of civil commitment, drawing on many of the arguments set out in section 3.3 below, especially those based on non-discrimination, the sacred value of liberty in democracies, and the difficulties of assessing the risk of violence and self-harm (although without using the language of human rights).[44]

The 'mad' movement was late to join the disability movement. In part, this was because many 'mad' people did not consider themselves 'disabled' and many still do not identify as being disabled and see the disability movement as interfering with the user and survivor movement's emphasis on the right to self-define.[45] For example, 'Erick' explains:

> Like seriously, a lot of crazy people don't just think: "Oh my god, I just lost it. I couldn't believe it. It was so horrible." Many of them are saying "It was the most fantastic journey I've ever been on. Even though it had positives and negatives, I would own it without any doubt." So someone saying, "There's your disability", it's like, "no, it is me being me in a society that doesn't like that."[46]

The delay in the mad movement joining the disability movement was also because people with physical disabilities had the same social prejudices against 'mad' people as the rest of society and were concerned that they were unpredictable, irrational, and violent.[47] However, some early 'mad' activists, like Judi Chamberlain, author of the influential *On Our Own* (1978) which described her experiences of the mental health system, recognized the potential relationship between the psychiatric user and survivor movement and the wider disability movement.[48] Judi Chamberlain was instrumental in building bridges between the two movements in the 1980s in the United States.[49] The overlap between the user and survivor movement and the wider disability

[43] Mental Health and Human Rights: Report of the Task Panel on Legal and Ethical Issues Submitted to the President's Commission on Mental Health 15 February 1978, (1978) 20 Ariz L Rev 49, 117, recommendation 32 (hereafter, 'President Carter's Report').

[44] Stephen Morse, 'A Preference for Liberty: The Case Against Involuntary Commitment of the Mentally Disordered' (1982) 70 Cal L Rev 54 (hereafter Morse, 'A Preference for Liberty').

[45] Helen Spandler and Jill Anderson, 'Unreasonable Adjustments? Applying Disability Policy to Madness and Distress' in Helen Spandler and others (eds), *Madness, Distress and the Politics of Disablement* (Policy Press 2015) 13, 22–23 (hereafter, Spandler and Anderson, 'Unreasonable Adjustments?'); Jasna Russo and Debra Shulkes, 'What We Talk About When We Talk About Disability: Making Sense of Debates in the European User/Survivor Movement' in Helen Spandler and others (eds), *Madness, Distress and the Politics of Disablement* (Policy Press 2015) 27, 11–34 (hereafter Russo and Skulkes 'What We Talk About When We Talk About Disability').

[46] Essya M Nabbali, 'A "Mad" Critique of the Social Model of Disability' (2009) 9(4) Int J Divers Organ Communities Nations 1, 4 (hereafter, Nabbali, 'A "Mad" Critique').

[47] ibid.

[48] Pelka, *What We Have Done* (n 22) 285.

[49] ibid.

movement has further developed since the 1990s and has been informed by the emergence of the various social models of disability involving the overcoming of social barriers to equality for persons with disabilities. Hence, mental impairment has been placed within a disability rights framework for the purpose of advocating for greater rights.

However, it is unclear to what extent the concerns of persons with mental impairments fit within the disability rights movement. It should be noted that the disability rights movement and British Social Model of Disability were primarily concerned with persons with physical impairments, particularly wheel-chair users, and it may not be appropriate to extend disability rights to persons with mental impairments without accommodating the unique experiences of persons with mental impairments.[50] The disability rights movement has also been criticized for glossing over the heterogeneity of mental impairments in terms of type and severity, course and temporal trajectory, treatment experiences, and intersectionality with other personal characteristics.[51] As noted by Nev Jones and Timothy Kelly:

> Pronounced differences in the natural course and meaning of psychosis, ranging from a few limited (sometimes even productive) episodes to chronic, debilitating impairments of language and communication are rarely acknowledged.[52]

The history of opposition to mental health law has paralleled the development of international human rights law. While human rights law has its origins in the enlightenment and notions of 'natural' rights, the modern human rights movement emerged in the aftermath of the horrors of the Holocaust and Nuremberg Trials.[53] The forced sterilization, non-consensual medical experimentation, and systematic extermination of people with mental illness in Nazi Germany along with other 'burdensome' and long despised social groups,[54] highlighted the vulnerability of people with mental illness to state-sanctioned violence and discrimination. However, despite this common heritage, people with mental illness continued to be socially excluded and marginalized in most societies and only modest human rights gains were made. That is, as Amita Dhanda argues, the Universal Declaration of Human Rights (1948) was not 'universal' in its application to disempowered groups.[55] For example, while the jurisprudence of the European Court of Human Rights has increased procedural

[50] Anne Plumb, 'UN Convention on the Rights of Persons with Disabilities: Out of the Frying Pan into the Fire?' in Helen Splander and others (eds), *Madness, Distress and the Politics of Disablement* (Policy Press 2015) 184 (hereafter Plumb, 'Out of the Frying Pan into the Fire?').

[51] Nev Jones and Timothy Kelly, 'Inconvenient Complications: On the Heterogeneities of Madness and Their Relationship to Disability' in ibid 43, 44–45 (hereafter Jones and Kelly, 'Inconvenient Complications').

[52] ibid 45.

[53] 'Mental Health, Human Rights and Their Relationship: An Introduction' in Michael Dudley and others (eds), *Mental Health and Human Rights: Vision, Praxis, and Courage* (Oxford University Press 2012) 1, 9 (hereafter 'Mental Health, Human Rights and Their Relationship').

[54] Michael Dudley and Fran Gale, 'Through a Glass, Darkly: Nazi Era Illuminations of Psychiatry, Human Rights and Human Rights Violations' in ibid 211, 211 (hereafter Dudley and Gale, 'Through a Glass, Darkly').

[55] Amita Dhanda, 'Universal Legal Capacity as a Universal Human Right' in ibid 177 (hereafter Dhanda, 'Universal Legal Capacity').

protections and some minimum standards for people with mental illness, it has not resulted in substantive reform.[56] Similarly, the enquiry by a United Nations Human Rights Sub-Commission into whether there were grounds for the involuntary detention and treatment of people with mental illness in 1977, culminated in the much maligned United Nations Principles for the Protection of Persons with Mental Illness and for the Improvement of Mental Health Care (1991) (MI Principles).[57] Ironically, the MI Principles had the effect of galvanizing the user and survivor movement in opposition to them and compelling them to join the campaign for the Convention on the Rights of Persons with Disabilities in 2008.[58] A novel feature of the CRPD is that it is the first international human rights treaty in which civil society, particularly disability advocates, have played a major role in its negotiation.[59] The involvement of disability advocates was argued as necessary not only to 'underscore the reliability and accountability of what DPOs [Disabled Peoples Organisations] as affected beneficiaries had to say, but more importantly, to highlight the locus of their moral authority for saying it as the population most affected'.[60] However, the absence of medical and health organizations in the negotiation of the CRPD may impede its practical implementation.[61]

As noted in Chapter 1, the issue of involuntary psychiatric detention and treatment is 'barely grazed by the CRPD text'.[62] This is because disability advocates and states involved in the drafting process were unable to reach agreement on the abolition of mental health law.[63] This 'negotiated silence'[64] with respect to mental health laws has left a vacuum that is being filled by the UN Reports, General Comments, and an emerging literature trying to make sense of what the CRPD means for people with mental impairment. However, as discussed in Chapter 1 section 1.3.2, the CRPD Committee has repeatedly called for the abolition of mental health law, making the abolition of mental health law a pertinent human rights issue that can no longer be ignored. The creation of the CRPD Committee in Article 34 of the CRPD has given abolitionists something they have never had before: an institutional voice.

[56] Mary Donnelly, *Healthcare Decision-Making and the Law: Autonomy, Capacity and the Limits of Liberalism* (Cambridge Law, Medicine and Ethics 2010) 238 (hereafter Donnelly, *Healthcare Decision-Making and the Law*).

[57] 'Mental Health, Human Rights and Their Relationship' (n 53) 26.

[58] Janet E Lord, 'Shared Understanding or Consensus-Masked Disagreement? The Anti-Torture Framework in the Convention on the Rights of Persons with Disabilities' (2010) 33 Loy LA Int'l Comp L Rev 27, 39 (hereafter Lord, 'Shared Understanding or Consensus-Masked Disagreement?').

[59] Rosemary Kayess and Phillip French, 'Out of Darkness into Light? Introducing the Convention on the Rights of Persons with Disabilities' (2008) 8(1) Hum Rights Law Rev 1, 4 (hereafter Kayess and French, 'Out of Darkness').

[60] Janet Lord and others, 'Lessons from the Experience of UN Convention on the Rights of Persons with Disabilities: Addressing the Democratic Deficit in Global Health Governance' (2010) [Fall] J Law Med Ethics 564, 567–68 (hereafter Lord, 'Global Health Governance').

[61] Peter Bartlett, 'The United Nations Convention on the Rights of Persons with Disabilities and Mental Health Law' (2012) 75(5) MLR 752, 757 (hereafter Bartlett, 'CRPD and MHL').

[62] Kayess and French, 'Out of Darkness' (n 59) 34.

[63] Bartlett, 'CRPD and MHL' (n 61) 756.

[64] Annagret Kampf, 'Involuntary Treatment Decisions: Using Negotiated Silence to Facilitate Change?' in Bernadette McSherry and Penelope Weller (eds), *Rethinking Rights-Based Mental Health Laws* (Oxford Hart 2010) 129 (hereafter Kampf, 'Negotiated Silence').

3.3 The Arguments Supporting the Case for Abolition

This section will set out the content of eleven arguments supporting the case for the abolition of mental health law and explore its conceptual, legal, and moral basis. Whilst these arguments have sufficient substance to rest on their own merits, the case for abolition cannot be properly understood in isolation from the historical abuse and ill-treatment of people with mental illness, touched on in section 3.2 of this Chapter. As neatly summarized by Lawrence Gostin and Lance Gable:

> The litany of abuses perpetrated against persons with mental disabilities is long and sadly varied. Persons with mental disabilities have been involuntarily confined without due process or adequate cause, subjected to squalid living conditions, denied appropriate care and treatment both within and outside of institutions, and confronted with daunting physical and social barriers that prevent their full participation in society.[65]

In Australia, the mistreatment of psychiatric patients and whistle-blowers at Chelmsford private psychiatric hospital, between 1965 and 1979, with dangerous and unproven psychiatric treatments, like 'deep sleep' therapy, is a national scandal that still engenders public distrust of psychiatry.[66] It also reflects the legacy of involuntary psychiatric treatment in Nazi Germany[67] and Soviet Russia.[68]

As peer worker Charlene Sukel also observes:

> psychiatric facilities often look and function more like prisons than places of care ... in South Africa, persons refusing hospital treatment may be resistant not because of diminished legal or mental capacity (however perceived), but because of the knowledge of what happens in those facilities.[69]

Understandably, these experiences have created a deep and lingering sense of suspicion, powerlessness, grievance, and rejection by society amongst people with mental impairment that permeates the entire case for the abolition of mental health law. When viewed through the eyes of those who know themselves to be outcasts, mental health law is often seen as an embodiment of their lesser social status. At the same time, mental health law is also often seen as easier to abolish than the entrenched social attitudes and assumptions that are perceived to underpin it.

[65] Lawrence O Gostin and Lance Gamble, 'Global Mental Health: Changing Norms, Constant Rights' (2008) 9(1) Georget J Int 83 (hereafter Gostin and Gamble 'Global Mental Health').

[66] Terry Carney, 'Commentary: Regulatory Dividends of Scandal—the Chelmsford Legacy' (2013) 21(3) Australias Psychiatry 220 (Carney, 'Chelmsford Legacy').

[67] Dudley and Gale, 'Through a Glass, Darkly' (n 54) 211.

[68] Robert van Voren, 'The Abuse of Psychiatry for Political Purposes' in Michael Dudley and others (eds), *Mental Health and Human Rights: Vision, Praxis, and Courage* (Oxford University Press 2012) 237 (hereafter van Voren 'Abuse of Psychiatry').

[69] Charlene Sunkel, 'The UN Convention: A Service User Perspective' (2019) 18(1) World Psych 51, 52 (hereafter Sunkel 'A Service User Perspective').

3.3.1 Mental Health Law is a Form of Social Control of Non-Conformists

The idea that mental health law is a form of social control of non-conformists, asserted as part of the anti-psychiatry movement, has long been an important platform for calls for the abolition of mental health law. As discussed in Chapter 2 in section 2.4, the 'anti-psychiatry' movement loosely refers to the work of a group of intellectuals and radicals in the 1960s and 1970s that criticized coercive institutional psychiatry and the medical model. These included RD Laing, David Cooper, Thomas Szasz, Thomas Scheff, Erving Goffman, and Michel Foucault.[70] These authors often use the term 'madness' rather than 'mental illness', which they regard as the medicalization of socially deviant behaviour.

While their ideology, goals, and politics differed and they were often critical of each other,[71] they are famous for the following ideas. First, that 'mental illness' is a myth, some people may experience 'problems in living' but this is a social not a medical problem (Thomas Szasz). Second, madness is a rational response to 'social oppression' and the techniques of psychiatric treatment are unjustifiably painful and damaging (RD Laing). Third, madness occurs as a result of people being conditioned to behave in response to psychiatric 'labels', rather than a genuine 'illness' manifested by 'real' symptoms (Thomas Scheff). Fourth, the psychiatric hospital is a 'total institution' and the behaviour of inmates is a response to being in hospital rather than an underlying illness (Erving Goffman). Fifth, madness is a way of industrialized capitalist society dealing with those considered to be unproductive and who do not conform (Michel Foucault).

As summarized by Michael Cavadino:

> The message of anti-psychiatry seemed to run as follows: keep people away from psychiatrists at all costs; psychiatric treatment is bad for you; psychiatric hospitals are worse than prisons; and most definitely, on no account should anyone ever be subjected to compulsory psychiatric hospitalization and treatment—this is always and necessarily a 'crime against humanity'... [72]

While anti-psychiatry has never been a mainstream view, it has been very influential in sparking debate and scrutiny of the assumptions that underpin orthodox psychiatry. For example, looked at through the wide-angle lens of history, the medicalization of madness, as recognized by Michel Foucault, sits within the epoch of modernity where 'the emergence of a technological culture: a culture where the difficulties and contradictions of human life show up as technical problems to be solved rationally'.[73] In this way, the need for order and discipline in economic and in cultural life, can be

[70] Michael Cavadino, *Mental Health Law in Context: Doctor's Orders?* (Dartmouth Publishing Company 1989) (hereafter Cavadino, *Doctor's Orders?*).

[71] Ron Roberts and Theodor Itten, 'Laing and Szasz: Anti-Psychiatry, Capitalism and Therapy' (2006) 93(5) Psychoanal Rev 781 (hereafter Roberts and Itten, 'Laing and Szasz').

[72] Cavadino, *Doctor's Orders?* (n 70) 3–4.

[73] Pat Bracken and Philip Thomas, 'From Szasz to Foucault: On the Role of Critical Psychiatry' (2010) 17(3) Philos Psychiatry Psychol 219, 225 (hereafter Bracken and Thomas, 'From Szasz to Foucault').

contrasted to the irrationality, disorder, and 'mental distress' of 'madness'. This serves as a useful reminder that society has a vested interest in the diagnosis, detention, and treatment of people with mental impairment and that mental impairment is conceived within that social context. That is, what is seen as mental impairment is in part driven by the demands of what is needed by society at a particular time and measures that are justified by society as being benevolent, may be perceived and experienced as self-serving, coercive, and punishing.

The anti-psychiatry critique has also been enormously influential in drawing attention to the social determinants and effects of mental impairment and the limitations of the medical model. The critique of the 'total institution' paved the way for an earlier abolition—the abolition of the asylum and the introduction of deinstitutionalization and community treatment in the 1980s. However, deinstitutionalization brought an expansion in coercive powers in the community through the introduction of community treatment orders.[74] Therefore, the abolition of the asylum can be thought of as the 'first wave' of abolition, paving the way for the 'second wave'—the abolition of mental health law itself.

The anti-psychiatry critique fortifies the arguments for the abolition of mental health law. The case for abolition becomes much stronger if people are being forcibly detained, treated, and subjected to seclusion and restraint for a mental illness that does not exist, if psychiatric treatments are dangerous and offer patients no or minimal benefits, and mental health law is really the manifestation of an intolerant and misinformed society. It can be seen then, that the case for abolition rests on more than just a response to historical abuses, but a fundamentally different conception of 'madness' and the social response to it. From this perspective, it is not so much that people with mental illness need to be 'fixed', but that society needs to be 'fixed'. This is a core premise of the critique of the medical or charitable model of disability rejected by the CRPD.

The 'categorical' approach of the medical model which 'labels' people with a particular diagnosis can be contrasted with a human rights approach which conceptualizes mental impairments as being a 'normal' part of 'human diversity' which raises the concern that mental health laws can be used to require social conformity 'on an assimilationist basis'.[75]

3.3.2 Mental Health Law is Discriminatory

The argument that mental health law is discriminatory forms the basis of most calls for the abolition of mental health law. This objection rests on three main grounds. The first is an objection to the idea of mental health law itself. That is, having a separate

[74] Philip Fennell, 'Institutionalising the Community: The Codification of Clinical Authority and the Limits of Rights-Based Approaches' in Bernadette McSherry and Penelope Weller (eds), *Rethinking Rights-Based Mental Health Laws* (Hart Publishing 2010) 13 (hereafter Fennell, 'Institutionalising the Community').

[75] Committee on the Rights of Persons with Disabilities, *General Comment No 1 (2014) Article 12: Equal Recognition before the Law*, 11th Sess, UN Doc CRPD/C/GC/1 (11 April 2014) [29] (hereafter 'General Comment 1').

law that 'singles out' people with mental illness from the rest of the population is regarded as offensive and discriminatory. Second, the involuntary detention and treatment of people with mental illness on the basis of risk and capacity criteria contained in most mental health laws are argued to be discriminatory because they make certain assumptions that people with mental illness are 'dangerous' and 'incompetent'. Finally, any denial of legal capacity to persons with disabilities, including mental illness, is argued to deprive people with mental illness of equality before the law and is therefore discriminatory. This last basis is that which is most strongly and recently argued by the CRPD Committee.

At the core of all of these arguments for abolition is the complex concept of 'discrimination' or unequal or unfairly differential treatment on the basis of a personal characteristic, in this case mental illness, or disability. The meaning of 'discrimination' is different in domestic and international law[76] and in psychological research and will be explored in depth in Chapters 6 and 7. For the moment, however, I will use it without qualification according to how it is articulated in the arguments for each of these bases.

I will consider each of these bases in turn.

3.3.2.1 Having a Separate Mental Health Law is Discriminatory

Mental health law, according to this argument, must be abolished because it is discriminatory, as it only applies to people with mental impairment. This argument challenges the entire concept of 'mental health law'. As Tina Minkowitz remarks, 'mental health law' suggests the regulation of a profession or service industry, 'that is oriented towards the interests of clinicians and service providers, rather than service users'.[77] It does not necessarily evoke what it is, the power to detain and treat people with mental impairment on an involuntary basis.

At its most basic, this argument asserts that mental health law is discriminatory because people with mental impairment are treated under a 'different set of principles' to people with physical illness.[78] People with mental impairment, it is argued, can be detained in hospital and treated against their will even where they would otherwise have the mental capacity to lawfully refuse treatment.[79] When set against the changes in the doctor patient-relationship in general medical law and ethics since the 1950s, which have given greater respect to the decision-making autonomy and informed consent of patients in general healthcare,[80] the involuntary detention and treatment of people with mental illness is a clear anomaly. This is especially so, if mental impairment is conceptualized as a 'real' medical condition, the same as or 'on par' with physical illness. The argument that people with mental impairment are discriminated against

[76] Rowena Daw, 'The Case for a Fusion Law: Challenges and Issues' in Bernadette McSherry and Ian Freckelton (eds), *Coercive Care: Rights, Law and Policy* (Routledge 2013) 93, 101 (hereafter Daw 'The Case for a Fusion Law').

[77] Tina Minkowitz, 'Abolishing Mental Health Laws to Comply with the Convention on the Rights of Persons with Disabilities' in Bernadette McSherry and Penelope Weller (eds), *Rethinking Rights-Based Mental Health Laws* (Hart Publishing 2010) 149, 149 (hereafter, Minkowitz, 'Abolishing Mental Health Laws').

[78] Richardson, 'Principle and Pragmatism' (n 3) 418.

[79] Daw, 'The Case for a Fusion Law' (n 76) 93, 99.

[80] Richardson, 'Principle and Pragmatism' (n 3) 415.

compared to people with intellectual disability and physical illness, is often raised to support 'fusion proposals' between mental health and guardianship law, so that there is a single regime for all people who lack capacity in healthcare decision-making (see Chapter 8).[81]

Discrimination, in the mental health context, is complicated by the presence of negative social perceptions and stereotypes of people with mental impairment (see Chapter 7 section 7.5(a)). The social stigmatization of people with mental impairment is a feature of all societies.[82] Further, the presence of discrimination against and the social exclusion of people with mental impairment and all of those associated with them (family, friends, supporters, and mental health professionals) is well documented in psycho-social research.[83] Therefore, the very existence of mental health law is argued to represent the legal expression or embodiment of those negative social perceptions and stereotypes, especially that people with mental illness are violent, unpredictable and to be feared.[84] In this way, mental health law operates as a form of 'structural' or 'institutionalised' discrimination.[85] It is also argued that having a separate mental health law, especially one that is based on concepts of risk and capacity, can perpetuate those negative perceptions and stereotypes throughout the community.[86] Significantly, recent research has indicated that people surveyed about their perceptions of people with mental impairment in the United States have used the words of legal civil commitment criteria 'dangerous to themselves and others'.[87]

3.3.2.2 Risk Criteria are Discriminatory

Most mental health laws contain risk criteria which must be satisfied to authorize the involuntary detention and treatment of people with mental impairment. Risk criteria are argued to be discriminatory because psychological research has indicated that people with mental impairment are no more likely to be violent and aggressive than the rest of the population.[88] Other factors, such as alcohol and substance use are suggested to be better predictors of violence with or without mental impairment.[89] The number of people with mental impairment[90] who are violent is vastly exaggerated and

[81] Neil Rees, 'The Fusion Proposal: A Next Step?' in Bernadette McSherry and Penelope Weller (eds), *Rethinking Rights-Based Mental Health Laws* (Hart 2010) 71, 87–90 (hereafter Rees, 'The Fusion Proposal').

[82] Diana Rose and others, 'Service User and Carer Stakeholder Perspectives on the Public Health Aspects of Diagnosis and Classification of Mental Illness' in Shekhar Saxena and others (eds), *Public Health Aspects of Diagnosis and Classification of Mental and Behavioural Disorders* (American Psychiatric Association and World Health Organisation 2012) 1, 4–5 (hereafter Rose, 'Service User and Carer Stakeholder Perspectives').

[83] Patrick Corrigan and others, 'The Stigma of Mental Illness: Explanatory Models and Methods for Change' (2005) Appl Prev Psychol 179, 179 (hereafter, 'The Stigma of Mental Illness').

[84] Tom Campbell, 'Mental Health Law: Institutionalised Discrimination' (1994) 28 Aust NZ J Psychiatry 554 (Campbell, 'Mental Health Law').

[85] ibid.

[86] Daw, 'The Case for a Fusion Law' (n 76) 102.

[87] Bernice A Pescosolido, 'The Public Stigma of Mental Illness: What Do We Think; What Do We Know; What Can We Prove?' (2013) 54(1) J Health Soc Behav 1, 9 (hereafter, Pescosolido, 'The Public Stigma of Mental Illness').

[88] Donnelly, *Healthcare Decision-Making and the Law* (n 56) 243.

[89] Daw, 'The Case for a Fusion Law' (n 76) 101.

[90] Patrick Corrigan and others, 'The Effect of New Stories on the Stigma of Mental Illness' (2013) 201(3) J Nerv Ment Dis 179.

sensationalized by the media. Further, clinical opinion, psychological testing, and actuarial approaches are not sufficiently reliable or valid to be able to identify those individuals with a mental impairment who are likely to be a risk to themselves or others.[91]

The association between mental impairment and violence only applies to certain *sub-groups* of people with mental impairment.[92] For example, people with schizophrenia, mania, and organic mental disorders (such as dementia) are more likely to cause harm to others, especially where there are other factors such as concurrent alcohol, substance abuse, and personality disorders.[93] The magnitude of this effect in respect of the commitment of severe violent offences (other than homicide) has been estimated at around 5 per cent[94] to 11 per cent.[95] That is, people with schizophrenia have between four to five times the risk of being violent than the rest of the general population and have fourteen to twenty-five times the risk of committing a homicide.[96]

When mental health law is conceptualized as a preventive detention regime, it reflects the prejudices of a fearful and risk-averse society.[97] It is also at odds with the fundamental principle of the criminal law that people should be punished for those acts it can be proved they have a committed, rather than for who they are.[98] If preventive detention laws are to continue to exist, they should be based on predictable risk for all persons, not just those with a mental illness.[99] Anything less, it is argued, is discriminatory.

3.3.2.3 Denial of Legal Capacity is Discriminatory

The most recent argument that mental health law should be abolished on the ground that it is discriminatory is that it denies persons with mental disabilities legal capacity on an equal basis with others in contravention of Article 12 of the CRPD. While there are multiple definitions of legal capacity, it generally refers to the ability of a person to make his or her own decisions and to have those decisions respected and upheld by law.

[91] Bernadette McSherry, *Managing Fear: The Law and Ethics of Preventive Detention and Risk Assessment, International Perspectives on Forensic Mental Health* (Routledge 2014) Ch 3 (hereafter McSherry, *Managing Fear*).

[92] Paul E Mullen, 'Schizophrenia and Violence: From Correlations to Preventive Strategies' (2006) 12 Adv Psychiatr Treat 239 (hereafter Mullen, 'Schizophrenia and Violence').

[93] Monika Edlinger and others, 'Risk of Violence of Inpatients with Severe Mental Illness—Do Patients with Schizophrenia Pose Harm to Others?' (2014) 213(3) Psychiatry Res 450 (hereafter Edlinger 'Risk of Violence'); Nicola Swinson and Jenny Shaw, 'Homicides and Mental Disorders: The National Confidential Inquiry' (2007) 6(11) Psychiatry 452 (hereafter Swinson and Shaw 'Homicides and Mental Disorders').

[94] Sandra Flynn and others, 'Serious Violence by People with Mental Illness: National Clinical Survey' (2014) 29(8) J Interpers Violence 1438 (hereafter Flynn, 'Serious Violence by People with Mental Illness').

[95] Natalia Yee and others, 'Severe Non-Lethal Violence During Psychotic Illness' (2011) 45(6) Aust NZ J Psychiatry 466 (hereafter Yee, 'Severe Non-Lethal Violence').

[96] Paul E Mullen, 'Facing up to Unpalatable Evidence for the Sake of Our Patients' (2009) 6(8) PLoS Medicine 1,1 (hereafter Mullen, 'Facing up to Unpalatable Evidence'); Seena Fazel and others, 'Schizophrenia and Violence: Systematic Review and Meta-Analysis' (2009) 6(8) PLoS Medicine 2 (hereafter Fazel, 'Schizophrenia and Violence').

[97] ibid 15.

[98] ibid 29.

[99] Stephen Rosenman, 'Mental Health Law: An Idea Whose Time Has Passed' (1994) 28 Aust NZ J Psychiatry 560, 565 (hereafter Rosenman, 'Mental Health Law').

There are two kinds of legal capacity under the CRPD: legal standing (being recognized as a person before the law as a holder of rights) and legal agency (the ability to exercise those rights).[100] Mental health law, it is argued, is discriminatory because it does not recognize either type of legal capacity. People with mental impairment are not recognized as holding the right to consent to or refuse medical treatment, or exercising healthcare decision-making rights in relation to their mental impairment.

This perspective conceptualizes mental health law as a substitute decision-making regime, which it is argued is prohibited by Article 12 (equality before law) of the CRPD. Bernadette McSherry defines substitute decision-making under mental health law as being where a third party, usually the treating psychiatrist, 'substitutes her or his decision to provide treatment for that individual with a mental impairment'.[101] She observes that 'substituted decision-making also underpins guardianship and administration laws, with guardians and administrators being appointed to make decisions in the "best interests" of the person concerned'.[102] As outlined in Chapter 1 in section 1.3.2, the CRPD Committee has refined its interpretation of substitute decision-making as being where a third party makes a decision for an individual with a mental impairment that is in their objective 'best interests'.[103] From this perspective, substitute decision-making does not refer to *all* decisions that are made on behalf of a person by a third party. That is, it would not include the situation where 'significant efforts' have been made to ascertain the wishes of a person with a mental impairment using suitable supports and a decision is made by a third party in accordance with the 'best interpretation' of their subjective 'will and preferences'.[104] Therefore, more accurately, substitute decision-making involves the overriding of a person's autonomy and self-determination by a third party decision to impose involuntary detention and treatment, either without a person's express consent (where they have not objected), or actively against their express wishes, or the 'best interpretation' of their will and preferences.

In arguing that the denial of legal capacity is discriminatory, the CRPD Committee and many legal scholars draw on an analogy with the denial of legal capacity to other groups who have historically been denied their legal capacity, or who still are denied their legal capacity in some jurisdictions today, based on the 'status approach'.[105] These groups include women, indigenous people, or people from particular ethnic groups, people designated as 'idiots' and 'lunatics', people with a criminal conviction and children under the age of majority, all of whom have been denied legal capacity. The consequences of the denial of legal capacity, under the status approach, are

[100] Gerard Quinn and Abigail Rekas-Rosalbo, 'Civil Death: Rethinking the Foundations of Legal Personhood for Persons with Disability' (2016) 56 Irish Jurist 286, 288 (hereafter Quinn and Rekas-Rosablo, 'Civil Death'); Eilionoir Flynn and Anna Arstein-Kerslake, 'Legislating Personhood: Realising the Right to Support in Exercising Legal Capacity' (2014) 10(1) In J Law Context 81, 83 (hereafter Flynn and Arstein-Kerslake, 'Legislating Personhood').

[101] Bernadette McSherry, 'Legal Capacity under the Convention on the Rights of Persons with Disabilities' (2012) 20 JLME 22, 27 (hereafter McSherry, 'Legal Capacity').

[102] ibid.

[103] General Comment 1 (n 75) [18] and [18b].

[104] ibid.

[105] Flynn and Arstein-Kerslake, 'Legislating Personhood' (n 102); General Comment 1 (n 75); McSherry, 'Legal Capacity' (n 103).

severe: a complete stripping of rights that is 'permanent and plenary' that has often been described as 'civil death'.[106] Unfortunately, the 'status approach' usually reflects the assumptions and prejudices of the dominant social group about the rationality and cognitive ability of the class of person denied their legal capacity to exercise autonomy and self-determination.[107] As Eilionoir Flynn and Anna Arstein-Kerslake point out:

> In the past, those of a different race or gender to the dominant group were thought to be not only socially, but biologically and cognitively, inferior.[108]

Even though modern mental health and guardianship and administration laws in western countries are limited as they only apply to a smaller group of persons, for example not everyone with a mental impairment, and only in relation to specific decisions, for example consent to hospital admission and psychiatric treatment, these laws are still regarded as being discriminatory. In the context of other western civil rights struggles and social movements that have challenged entrenched structural discrimination, denial of the legal capacity of persons with disabilities remains one of the last frontiers.

The CRPD closely aligns autonomy, or the freedom to make one's own choices and independence, with the concept of human dignity (although I discuss this further in Chapters 4 and 5). The CRPD Committee argues that 'recognition of legal capacity restores autonomy and respects human dignity',[109] whereas denying legal capacity based on disability has the effect of 'lowering his or her status as a person before the law'.[110]

Mental health law, it is argued, is discriminatory not just because it treats people with mental illness differently from people with cognitive impairments and physical illness, but because it treats people with disabilities (especially mental and cognitive impairments) differently from those without disabilities. That is, equality before the law means equality with people with all types of disabilities *and* people without disabilities who have full legal capacity.[111] This approach is consistent with General Comment 2 in which the CRPD seeks to expand the concept of what is 'normal' to cater for people with most impairments as part of a 'universal design' that promotes equality, with the concept of 'reasonable adjustment' applying to those people who have very rare disabilities.[112] In this way, disability is conceptualized as part of a continuum of natural human diversity, rather than as the exception, or the abnormal, rather than using 'difference' to justify special treatment.

Further, the right to equality before the law is argued to be 'indispensable' to the enjoyment of most other CRPD rights, especially the rights to liberty, health, freedom from torture, housing, employment, and education.[113]

[106] Michael L Perlin, '"Striking for the Guardians and Protectors of the Mind": The Convention on the Rights of Persons with Mental Disabilities and the Future of Guardianship Law' (2013) 117(4) Penn St L Rev 1159, 1162–63 (hereafter Perlin, 'Guardianship').

[107] McSherry, 'Legal Capacity' (n 103).

[108] Flynn and Arstein-Kerslake, 'Legislating Personhood' (n 102) 81.

[109] General Comment 1 (n 75) [29].

[110] ibid [13].

[111] Dhanda, 'Universal Legal Capacity' (n 55) 178.

[112] Committee on the Rights of Persons with Disabilities, *General Comment No 2 (2014) Article 9: Accessibility*, 11th Sess, UN Doc CRPD/C/GC/2, (11 April 2014) (hereafter General Comment 2).

[113] General Comment 1 (n 75) [8].

Under the support model of legal capacity, no one is denied legal capacity, regardless of their impairment. As Michael Bach and Lara Kerzner assert, the CRPD requires:

> . . . a paradigm shift in the law of capacity so that the question is no longer: Does a person have the mental capacity to exercise legal capacity? The question is instead: What types of supports are required for the person to exercise his or her legal capacity?[114]

Legal capacity is also seen as recognition of individual identity and personhood.[115] It is, of course, first and foremost the ability to make autonomous and legally binding decisions for major life choices which have historically been restricted for persons with disabilities such as voting, consenting to medical treatment, marrying and having children. But, it also trickles down to greater participation and control in minor choices, like what to wear, what to eat, what hobbies and experiences to pursue, where in practice people with disabilities have been denied choice and self-expression on a daily basis. The literature is filled with stories of people who had dull, uniform, and institutionalized lives, who were considered unreachable, but once they were given support were able to communicate even in unconventional ways and were able to reconnect with family and friends, participate in new activities and reach their potential.[116] Therefore, legal capacity is also an important precursor to a fundamental change in social attitudes to persons with disabilities and their capacity to participate in life.

In this section I have outlined the arguments made by abolitionists that mental health laws, in providing for a substitute decision-making regime, are discriminatory and should be immediately abolished and replaced with a supported decision-making model. However, as my arguments oppose abolition, I will further examine and respond to these arguments in Chapters 4 to 7.

3.3.3 'Free and Informed Consent' is Integral to the 'Right to Health'

While the denial of the right to 'free and informed consent' to medical treatment for people with mental illness as a form of discrimination has been discussed above, it deserves further comment as a core component of the case for abolition in its own right. This is because the right to 'free and informed consent' is a fundamental principle of contemporary medical law and ethics. It is 'perhaps the most widely recognized ethical safeguard in clinical care and research'.[117]

The requirement that consent is 'free' refers to the absence of force, coercion, manipulation, or 'undue influence'. It is the legal recognition of the right of a patient to

[114] Michael Bach and Lana Kerzner, *A New Paradigm for Protecting Autonomy in the Right to Legal Capacity* (2010) http://www.lco-cdo.org/en/disabilities-call-for-papers-bach-kerzner accessed 8 October 2019 (hereafter Bach and Kerzner, *A New Paradigm*).

[115] Flynn and Arstein-Kerslake, 'Legislating Personhood' (n 102).

[116] Kristen Booth Glen, 'Changing Paradigms: Mental Capacity, Legal Capacity, Guardianship, and Beyond' (2012) 44 Colum Hum Rts L Rev 93, 166–9 (hereafter Booth Glen 'Changing Paradigms').

[117] Ahmed Bait Amer, 'Informed Consent in Adult Psychiatry' (2013) 28(4) Oman Med J 228, 228 (hereafter Amer, 'Informed Consent').

control access to his or her body and patient autonomy and self-determination in weighing the 'pros and cons' involved in healthcare decision-making.[118] In addition, the ability to make one's own healthcare decisions can be thought of as an expression of authenticity or individual values and identity.[119] Therefore, the denial of the right to 'free and informed consent' encapsulates the central objection of the abolitionists to being admitted to hospital and treated by force, which is certainly not 'free'.

Just as importantly, the requirement that consent to treatment is informed is a right to receive information about the nature, risks, and expected outcomes of a medical procedure. In Australia, a doctor must consider what information and advice to provide a patient from the perspective of what is material to the patient, rather than the body of medical opinion.[120] That is, doctors use their specialist knowledge to empower patients to make their own decisions. When used properly, informed consent has been described as a 'dynamic process' and 'educational tool' that can be used to 'enhance the therapeutic alliance'.[121]

The argument of the abolitionists that consent must be informed, also reflects the long-held concerns of the psychiatric user and survivor movement that people diagnosed with mental impairment are not properly informed of the serious side-effects of medication and electroconvulsive therapy, or of the range of alternatives to conventional psychiatric treatment.[122] This means that the term 'informed consent' has a much wider meaning from the perspective of people with mental illness, than what is understood by conventional medicine.

The right to informed consent in domestic law is expanded by international human rights law. The right to health in Article 25(d) of the CRPD provides that health care must be provided to persons with disabilities on an equal basis with others '*including* free and informed consent'. Therefore, a denial of the right to free and informed consent is regarded as not just discriminatory but also as an infringement of the right to the highest attainable standard of health. This reflects a concern that in realizing the right to health, persons with disabilities are disproportionately denied their right to free and informed consent compared with other groups. That said, Article 25(d) only says that healthcare must 'include' free and informed consent, presumably the article would not apply where a person is unable to give free and informed consent (see Chapter 1, section 1.4.1(c)). Also, there is an argument that confining mental healthcare to those who are only able to give *free* and *informed* consent could amount to a discriminatory denial of healthcare for some persons with mental impairment when compared to persons without disability.

The right to informed consent is also related to the right to integrity of the person. As Penelope Weller observes 'human rights principles require respect for the physical and mental integrity of the person, which in turn grants a privileged position to the views of the person'.[123] Further, a lack of informed consent is argued to lend weight

118 Wanda K Mohr and Michael A Nunno, 'Black Boxing Restraints: The Need for Full Disclosure and Consent' (2011) 20 J Child Fam Stud 38, 38 (hereafter Mohr and Nunno, 'Black Boxing Restraints').

119 ibid 40.

120 *Rogers v Whitaker* (1992) 109 ALR 625, 634 (hereafter *Rogers v Whitaker*).

121 Mohr and Nunno, 'Black Boxing Restraints' (n 120) 46.

122 Pelka, *What We Have Done* (n 22).

123 Penelope Weller, *New Law and Ethics in Mental Health Advance Directives* (Routledge 2013) 6 (hereafter Weller, *New Law and Ethics*).

to the proposition that the imposition of unwanted mental health treatment on non-consenting patients constitutes torture and therefore must be abolished. These arguments are discussed further in section 3.3.8 below.

3.3.4 Mental Health Law is an Unjustified Interference with Liberty

The right to liberty is a cornerstone of most democratic societies and most international human rights conventions. Mental health law deprives people with mental impairment of their liberty through involuntary detention in hospital and may also do so by permitting the use of seclusion and restraint. Involuntary detention can be conceptualized as either a form of preventive detention, or as a substitute-decision made by a third party that the person with mental illness will be admitted to hospital without consent. Hospital admission is, of course, a decision that is usually made on a voluntary basis by mental health and general patients themselves. The confinement of people with mental impairment in hospital can be viewed as a form of social control and exercise of tutelary authority.[124]

This deprivation of liberty has long been argued as being an unjustified response to the actual risk posed by people with mental impairment and as being discriminatory for the reasons set out above.

The right to liberty and security of the person in Article 14 of the CRPD provides that:

1. States Parties shall ensure that persons with disabilities, on an equal basis with others:
   a. Enjoy the right to liberty and security of person;
   b. Are not deprived of their liberty unlawfully or arbitrarily, and that any deprivation of liberty is in conformity with the law, and that the existence of a disability shall in no case justify a deprivation of liberty.
2. States Parties shall ensure that if persons with disabilities are deprived of their liberty through any process, they are, on an equal basis with others, entitled to guarantees in accordance with international human rights law and shall be treated in compliance with the objectives and principles of this Convention, including by provision of reasonable accommodation.

Even though the right to liberty does not expressly refer to the abolition of mental health law, the CRPD Committee has referred to Article 14 as necessitating or including:

> . . . The right to be free from involuntary detention in a mental health facility and not to be forced to undergo mental health treatment (art.14).[125]

[124] Fennell, 'Institutionalising the Community' (n 74) 13.
[125] General Comment 1 (n 75) [27].

It has also been argued that mental health law contravenes this Article because diagnosis with a mental illness cannot by itself be used to justify a deprivation of liberty.[126] This is the case even though mental health laws do not apply to all people with mental illness, only to those who are considered to be at risk of harming themselves or others.[127] Instead, it is argued that persons with mental impairments, like persons without disabilities, should only be detained if and when they breach the criminal law and subject to the legal protections of a criminal trial.[128]

Of course, relying on the criminal law to control persons with mental impairments who commit crimes raises a number of complex moral dilemmas about the purpose and operation of the criminal justice system. Persons with disabilities are already disproportionately represented in prisons and it is reasonable to assume that if mental health law were to be abolished, many more persons with mental impairment who might have otherwise been treated in hospital or the community may end up in prison. Therefore, while the criminal law is not directly discriminatory against persons with mental impairment in that the same laws apply to everyone, the application of the criminal law to persons with disabilities may not necessarily be 'disability neutral' and may arguably lead to a worse outcomes, or simply trade one form of loss of liberty for another. Nonetheless, Stephen Morse argues that:

> . . . as argued at great length elsewhere, it is fair to hold nearly all persons, including crazy persons, (sic) responsible for their behaviour. If this is correct, then there is no reason not to use the criminal law to control criminal deviance. People can be both mad and bad. And to the extent they are bad, they deserve to be punished, especially if it appears possible that treating people as responsible encourages them to take responsibility for themselves.[129]

Morse goes on to argue that prisons ought to be cleaned up and improved so that mental health treatment can occur within them and that minor crimes such as vagrancy should be abolished.[130]

The interpretation of Article 14 remains, however, unsettled within the international human rights system. For instance, the Office of the High Commissioner for Human Rights has stated that persons with disabilities can be involuntarily detained and treated where the restriction on liberty is 'de-linked' with disability and is 'neutrally defined so as to apply to all persons on an equal basis'.[131] There is a division between international human rights bodies between those who interpret Article 14

[126] Bernadette McSherry and Kay Wilson, 'Detention and Treatment Down Under: Human Rights and Mental Health Laws in Australia and New Zealand' (2011) 19 Med Law Rev 548, 574 (McSherry and Wilson, 'Detention and Treatment Down Under').

[127] ibid.

[128] Dhanda 'Universal Legal Capacity' (n 55) 184; Susan Doyle Guilloud, 'The Right to Liberty of Persons with Psychosocial Disabilities at the United Nations: A Tale of Two Interpretations' (2019) 66 Int J Law Psychiatry 101497, 4 (hereafter Doyle Guilloud 'The Right to Liberty').

[129] Morse, 'A Preference for Liberty' (n 44) 97.

[130] ibid 97–98.

[131] *Thematic Study by the Office of the United Nations High Commissioner for Human Rights on Enhancing Awareness and Understanding of the Convention on the Rights of Persons with Disabilities*, UN Doc A/HRC/10/48 (26 January 2009) [49] (hereafter, 'Thematic Study').

as permitting 'disability neutral' restrictions on liberty de-linked from disability such as the Human Rights Committee, Committee Against Torture and Committee on the Elimination of Discrimination Against Women, and those that do not such as the CRPD Committee, Human Rights Council, and Special Rapporteurs on the Right to Health and Rights of Persons with Disabilities.[132] Susan Doyle Guiloud and Arlene Kanter argue that preventive detention on a 'disability-neutral' basis such as dangerousness would probably apply disproportionately to persons with mental impairments and therefore constitute indirect discrimination contrary to Article 14.[133] However, as argued in Chapter 7, the meaning of the concepts of equality and non-discrimination in the CRPD are ambiguous.

3.3.5 Mental Health Law is an Unjustified Interference with the Integrity of the Person

Tina Minkowitz argues that mental health law should be abolished because it is an unjustified interference with the integrity of the person.[134] Abolitionists also argue that involuntary detention and treatment is by its nature violent and traumatizing[135] and can involve locked doors and holding people down to administer treatments.[136] Psychiatric treatments often come with negative side-effects such as weight gain, fatigue, and sedation, shaking, sexual dysfunction, memory loss, and increased risk of heart disease and diabetes.[137] Cath Roper explains 'the drugs took away sensation, slowed thinking and caused internal alienation which was horrifying, like missing myself, watching myself die'.[138] Fiona Anderson complains that lithium therapy administered to her in 1990 has caused her ongoing chronic pain and kidney dysfunction.[139] Once in hospital, persons are often exposed to other patients with a range of unusual and sometimes harmful behaviours and can be subject to restrictive practices such as seclusion and restraint.[140] That said, patients have had different perceptions of their seclusion and restraint experiences. For some they are negative and traumatizing, while others report finding them helpful if they need time away from others, especially if they are done in a way that is mindful of maintaining the therapeutic

[132] Doyle Guilloud, 'The Right to Liberty' (n 130).

[133] ibid; Arlene S Kanter, *The Development of Disability Rights Under International Law From Charity to Human Rights* (Routledge 2015) 144–45 (hereafter Kanter, *The Development of Disability Rights*).

[134] Minkowitz, 'The Right to Freedom from Nonconsensual Psychiatric Interventions' (n 27).

[135] Cath Roper and Piers Gooding, 'This is Not a Story: From Ethical Loneliness to Respect for Diverse Ways of Knowing, Thinking and Being' in Elionoir Flynn and others (eds), *Global Perspectives on Legal Capacity Reform: Our Voices, Our Stories* (Cambridge University Press 2019) (hereafter Roper and Gooding, 'This is Not a Story'); Anna Arstein- Kerslake, 'Challenging the Foundations of Mental Health Law' (2015) 128 Precedent 32 (hereafter, 'Challenging the Foundations').

[136] ibid 156.

[137] Minkowitz 'The Right to Freedom from Nonconsensual Psychiatric Interventions' (n 27) 419.

[138] Roper and Gooding, 'This is Not A Story' (n 137) 156.

[139] Fiona Anderson and Bo Chen, 'Consent is More than Just Yes or No' in Elionoir Flynn, *Global Perspectives on Legal Capacity Reform: Our Voices, Our Stories* (Cambridge University Press 2019) 174, 179 (hereafter, Anderson and Chen, 'Consent is More than Just Yes or No').

[140] Roper and Gooding, 'This is Not a Story' (n 137) 154.

alliance and the person's safety and comfort.[141] Psychiatric best practice also involves seclusion and restraint reduction (with a view to elimination) programmes.[142]

Article 17 of the CRPD provides that:

> Every person with disabilities has a right to respect for his or her physical and mental integrity on an equal basis with others.

This is the first time this right has appeared in an international human rights treaty, although integrity of the person is mentioned at the regional level.[143] While the scope of the right is unclear, it can be construed as applying to the direct physical interference with the person, such as involuntary treatment of people with mental illness and the use of physical, mechanical, and chemical restraint, as well as deprivation of liberty, such as involuntary detention and seclusion. There may also be some overlap between the right to the integrity of the person and the right to security of the person. This could extend to both the physical and psychological security of the person, including freedom from fear.[144]

Tina Minkowitz has even gone so far as to compare interference with the integrity of the person with rape in terms of '... objectification, domination of the body and will and violation of boundaries of the self...'[145] While both are non-consensual, it is hard to say that the character of the involuntary detention and treatment is *exactly* the same as rape in that rape is sexual, is done entirely for the gratification of the rapist and exposes the victim to the risk of infection and unwanted pregnancy. Rape is also not done for a therapeutic purpose and unlike involuntary detention and psychiatric treatment does not offer any potential health benefits where a person is at risk of harming themselves or others. The issue of rape is a complex and controversial one and it also brings up the idea that involuntary psychiatric treatment can be a traumatizing trigger to some people of past sexual abuse[146] (hence, the need for coercion reduction and trauma-informed care)[147] and that some persons with mental impairments have reported that they have been raped or sexually assaulted by staff or other

[141] Caroline Larue and others, 'The Experience of Seclusion and Restraint in Psychiatric Settings: Perspectives of Patients' (2013) 34(5) Issues Ment Health Nurs 317, 322 (hereafter Larue, 'The Experience of Seclusion and Restraint').

[142] Melbourne Social Equity Institute, *Seclusion and Restraint Project Report* (University of Melbourne 2014) (hereafter *Seclusion and Restraint Project Report*).

[143] African Charter on Human and Peoples' Rights, opened for signature 27 June 1981, 1520 UNTS 217 (entered into force 21 October 1986), Art 4 (hereafter, 'African Charter'); Charter of Fundamental Rights of the European Union (2000) OJ (C364) 1 (7 December 2000), Art 3 (hereafter, 'European Union Charter'); American Convention on Human Rights, opened for signature 22 November 1969, 1144 UNTS 143 (entered into force 21 October 1986), Art 5 (hereafter, 'American Charter').

[144] James Spigelman, 'The Forgotten Freedom: Freedom from Fear?' (2010) 59 Int Comp Law Q 543 (hereafter Spigelman 'The Forgotten Freedom').

[145] Tina Minkowitz, 'Submission for Joint CEDAW-CRC General Recommendation/General Comment on Harmful Practices' World Network of Users and Survivors of Psychiatry, 31 August 2011 https://www.ohchr.org/Documents/HRBodies/CEDAW/HarmfulPractices/WorldNetworkofUsersandSurvivorsofPsychiatry.pdf (hereafter Minkowitz, 'Submission on Harmful Practices').

[146] Diana Rose and others, 'Service User Perspectives on Coercion and Restraint in Mental Health' (2017) 14(3) Br J Psych Int 59 (hereafter Rose, 'Service User Perspectives').

[147] Sandy Watson and others, 'Care without Coercion—Mental Health Rights, Personal Recovery and Trauma-Informed Care' (2014) 49(4) Aust J Soc Issues 529 (hereafter Watson, 'Care without Coercion').

patients while in hospital[148] (which is, of course, a crime and should not happen). The health system should also be improved to minimize the risk of sexual violence, such as, the creation of gender segregated services.

While earlier drafts of this Article included provisions that expressly addressed the issue of involuntary treatment, these were rejected by disability advocates as being too permissive.[149] This is because these earlier drafts permitted involuntary detention and treatment, albeit in limited circumstances. Therefore, the Article is expressed broadly, without any specific reference to mental health law. Tina Minkowitz has argued that Article 17, in conjunction with the right to freedom from torture and cruel and degrading treatment or punishment (Article 15) support the abolition of mental health law.[150] However, as outlined in Chapter 1 section 1.4.3, Bernadette McSherry has argued that Article 17 entails a more limited prohibition on unbeneficial and overly intrusive treatment rather than a complete abolition of mental health law.[151]

3.3.6 Involuntary Detention and Treatment is Torture or Cruel, Inhuman, or Degrading Treatment or Punishment

The argument that the involuntary detention and treatment of persons with mental impairment constitutes 'torture' is the most serious criticism of mental health law. This is because 'torture' is absolutely prohibited by international human rights law and this prohibition has a special status that puts it above a 'normal' treaty obligation.[152] That is, it is a pre-emptory norm that is part of international customary law and applies regardless of whether a state has accepted a treaty obligation containing the torture prohibition.[153] Treatment that falls short of the threshold of 'torture' may fit within the definition of cruel, inhuman, or degrading treatment or punishment.[154] This is also regarded as a serious human rights concern as it may create the conditions that allow torture to occur. The prohibition against torture and cruel, inhuman, or degrading treatment or punishment is important because it sets a minimum standard of treatment for all humans in all circumstances. It also recognizes the physical and psychological damage that can be caused by torture and cruel, inhuman, or degrading treatment and punishment.[155] If the involuntary detention and treatment of people with mental impairment is classified as 'torture' or 'cruel, inhuman, or degrading treatment or punishment', then according to international human rights law mental health law must be abolished as there is no basis on which it can be justified.

148 Roper, and Gooding, 'This is Not a Story' (n 137) 154.

149 Bernadette McSherry, 'Protecting the Integrity of the Person: Developing Limitations on Involuntary Treatment' (2008) 26(2) Law in Cont 111 (hereafter McSherry, 'Protecting the Integrity of the Person').

150 Minkowitz, 'The Right to Freedom from Nonconsensual Psychiatric Interventions' (n 27) 412.

151 McSherry, 'Protecting the Integrity of the Person' (n 151).

152 Lord, 'Shared Understanding or Consensus-Masked Disagreement?' (n 58) 33–4.

153 ibid.

154 ibid.

155 Derrick Silove and others, 'Descent into the Dark Ages: Torture and Its Perceived Legitimacy in Contemporary Times' in Michael Dudley and others (eds), *Mental Health and Human Rights: Vision, Praxis, and Courage* (Oxford University Press 2012) 225, 256–58 (hereafter, Silove 'Descent into the Dark Ages').

The prohibition on torture is a feature of numerous conventions, including the Convention Against Torture and other Cruel, Inhuman or Degrading Treatment or Punishment (1984) ('CAT'). The prohibition against torture is included in Article 15 of the CRPD, which 'parallels' Article 7 of the International Covenant on Civil and Political Rights (ICCPR).[156] The CRPD anti-torture framework is also argued to include the right to be free from exploitation and abuse (Article 16), the right to integrity of the person (Article 17), and the right to equal recognition before the law (Article 12).

Whilst torture has a long history as a form of social control and interrogation, the recognition of torture taking place outside the police and prison context, including violence against women,[157] is relatively recent.[158] In 2008 the Special Rapporteur on Torture, Manfred Nowak, issued a report on the application of the CAT for persons with disabilities, noting that the recent entry into force of the CRPD was a 'timely opportunity to review the anti-torture framework for persons with disabilities'.[159] According to the report:

> By recognizing and reframing violence and abuse perpetrated against persons with disabilities as torture or other cruel, inhuman or degrading treatment or punishment, victims and advocates can be afforded stronger legal protection and redress for violations of human rights.[160]

Clearly, the torture framework has been adopted to take advantage of the special character of 'torture' in international human rights law and to increase protection for persons with disabilities. That said, given that many persons with disabilities are detained in hospitals and other prison-like institutions that are isolated from public scrutiny, it is not a great conceptual leap to recognize that conditions in these environments could amount to torture or other cruel, inhuman, and degrading treatment or punishment. Further, the torture framework can extend to include the treatment of persons with disabilities in the community, such as reported situations where families restrain or cage persons with disabilities.

It is not surprising then that the freedom from torture framework has been used to criticize the poor living conditions of persons with disabilities in institutions, the use and abuse of restrictive interventions (such as seclusion and restraint), violence and sexual abuse, and denial of reasonable accommodation of the needs of persons

[156] International Covenant on Civil and Political Rights, opened for signature 16 December 1966, UNTS 999 (entered into force 23 March 1976), Art 7 (hereafter 'ICCPR').

[157] Committee Against Torture, *General Comment 2: Implementation of Article 2 by State Parties*, 39th sess, UN Doc CAT/C/GC/2/CRP.1/Rev4 (5–23 November 2007) [21] (hereafter CAT 'General Comment 2'); Manfred Nowak, *Report of the Special Rapporteur on Torture and other Cruel, Inhuman or Degrading Treatment or Punishment*, 7th Sess, UN Doc A/HRC/7/3 (15 January 2008)(hereafter Nowak, 'Report of Special Rapporteur').

[158] Human Rights Council, *Report of the Special Rapporteur on Torture and other Cruel, Inhuman or Degrading Treatment or Punishment, Juan E. Méndez*, 22nd Sess, UN Doc A/HRC/22/53 (1 February 2013) [15] (hereafter Mendez, 'Report of Special Rapporteur').

[159] Manfred Nowak, 'Protecting Persons with Disabilities from Torture', Office of the UN High Commissioner for Human Rights, 63rd Sess, UN Doc A/63/150, (July 2008) [41] (hereafter Nowak, 'Protecting Persons with Disabilities from Torture').

[160] ibid [47].

with disabilities.[161] The involuntary detention and treatment of people with mental illness has also been classified as torture by the Special Rapporteurs on Torture, Manfred Nowak in 2008[162] and Juan Méndez in 2013.[163] They argue that the involuntary detention and treatment of people with mental illness fits the definition of torture under Article 1 of the CAT because it meets the 'four elements' of the torture definition: severe pain and suffering, intent, purpose, and state involvement.

Involuntary detention and treatment is argued to cause severe pain and suffering on the basis that:

> Assessing the level of suffering or pain, relative in its nature, requires considering the circumstances of the case, including the existence of a disability, as well as looking at the acquisition or deterioration of impairment as result of the treatment or conditions of detention in the victim. Whereas a fully justified medical treatment may lead to severe pain or suffering, medical treatments of an intrusive and irreversible nature, when they lack a therapeutic purpose, or aim at correcting or alleviating a disability, may constitute torture and ill-treatment if enforced or administered without the free and informed consent of the person concerned.[164]

There is no doubt that certain psychiatric interventions, such as unmodified electroconvulsive therapy (where treatment is conducted without the use of anaesthetic and muscle relaxants) cause severe pain and suffering to people with mental illness.[165] It is also argued that the unpleasant side effects of medication, such as apathy, numbness, and uncontrollable shaking, constitute severe pain and suffering.[166] However, the argument that involuntary detention and treatment of people with mental impairment is torture seems to go further than this, so that the detention and treatment of the person without free and informed consent itself is sufficient to give rise to severe pain and suffering. This recognizes the distress involved in the intrusion of bodily and mental integrity and the power imbalance between medical professionals and people with mental illness. It is, however, unclear from the reports of the Special Rapporteur, whether just because involuntary detention and treatment can be classified as torture that every instance of involuntary detention and treatment will amount to torture or cruel, inhuman, or degrading treatment or punishment (and in supporting the reform rather than the abolition of mental health law, I argue that it does not). That is, I argue that involuntary detention in hospital and psychiatric treatment per se, without other evidence of ill-treatment, aggravating circumstances like violence, abuse, or severe side-effects where prolonged treatment has negligible benefits would not necessarily meet the legal threshold of severe pain and suffering. However, I accept that individuals with mental impairment have described involuntary detention and treatment as being subjectively experienced as 'torture'.[167] There is also evidence that 'torture' can

[161] ibid [38].
[162] ibid [38].
[163] Mendez, 'Report of Special Rapporteur' (n 160) [64].
[164] Nowak, 'Protecting Persons with Disabilities from Torture' (n 161) [47].
[165] Minkowitz, 'The Right to Freedom from Nonconsensual Psychiatric Interventions' (n 27) 27, 420.
[166] ibid.
[167] Testimony from a psychiatric survivor during a question and answer session at an 'afternoon tea' hosted by the National Mental Health Commission, Rydges Hotel Melbourne, 11 October 2013.

have long-term psychological effects that are more severe than post-traumatic stress disorder.[168] Tina Minkowitz, a vocal proponent of abolition, takes the conception of torture beyond the CAT definition, to argue that the 'torture' pertaining to involuntary detention and treatment of people with mental illness involves the destruction of the individual personality, once again highlighting concerns about loss of identity or personhood.[169]

The Special Rapporteur argues that the separate elements of 'intent' and 'purpose' in the CAT definition of torture are satisfied because involuntary detention and treatment are administered as a result of discrimination (as I set out in section 3.3.2 above). Therefore, the intent or purpose of reducing the symptoms of managing, or even curing, a mental impairment will not prevent treatment from being regarded as torture, where it is administered without 'free and informed' consent. Juan E Méndez is particularly critical of earlier authority from the European Court of Human Rights in *Herczegfalvy v Austria*[170] that allowed involuntary detention and treatment (in that case, long-term restraint and force feeding) as a matter of 'medical necessity'. The doctrine of 'medical necessity', as noted by Janet Lord, sets a 'dubiously high'[171] standard for cruel, inhuman, and degrading treatment and punishment that allows virtually any treatment to be used provided it can be justified as being therapeutic and within accepted medical practice at the time. However, as noted in Chapter 1 section 1.3.2 Juan Méndez has later indicated that involuntary detention and psychiatric treatment may fall outside the torture framework where a person is at risk of causing harm to themselves or others.

The final requirement of 'state involvement' in the definition of 'torture' has been also interpreted broadly:

> In relation to the State involvement requirement, the Special Rapporteur notes that the prohibition against torture relates not only to public officials, such as law enforcement agents in the strictest sense, but may apply to doctors, health professionals and social workers, including those working in private hospitals, other institutions and detention centres. As underlined by the Committee against Torture in its general comment No. 2 (2008), the prohibition of torture must be enforced in all sorts of institutions and States have to exercise due diligence to prevent, investigate, prosecute and punish such non-State officials or private actors.[172]

Presumably, laws passed by the state which permit the involuntary detention and treatment of people with mental illness would qualify as 'state involvement' if the definition of torture was otherwise satisfied. It would also include public and private hospitals and the use of 'torture' or cruel, inhuman, and degrading treatment and punishment by individuals, families, and carers in the community.

[168] Silove, 'Descent into the Dark Ages' (n 157) 225, 256.

[169] Minkowitz, 'The Right to Freedom from Nonconsensual Psychiatric Interventions' (n 27) 416.

[170] European Court of Human Rights, App no 10533/83, 24 September 1992 (hereafter, *Herczegfalvy v Austria*).

[171] Lord, 'Shared Understanding or Consensus-Masked Disagreement?' (n 58) 62.

[172] Nowak, 'Protecting Persons with Disabilities from Torture' (n 161) [51].

The prohibition against torture in Article 15 of the CRPD also prohibits the use of medical experimentation without free and informed consent. This is a modern recognition of the horrors of Nazi medical experimentation conducted on persons with disabilities during the Holocaust.[173] While most conventional psychiatric treatments permitted by mental health law would not be regarded as being 'experimental' (despite the limits of medical knowledge about how they work), Janet Lord observes that this prohibition could 'cover compulsory treatment that is non-standard and therefore experimental in nature, either of a medical drug or drug regimen, device, or procedure'.[174]

It can be seen then that the characterization of the involuntary detention and treatment of people with mental illness as 'torture' or other 'cruel, inhuman, degrading treatment and punishment', extends and amplifies other human rights arguments for the abolition of mental health law, particularly those relating to discrimination and lack of free and informed consent. It also draws attention to the historical and continuing human rights abuses of people with mental illness and persons with disabilities more generally.

While I accept that involuntary detention and psychiatric treatment can amount to torture and cruel, inhuman, and degrading treatment and punishment in certain circumstances which would also be an affront to a person's inherent dignity (Chapter 4 in section 4.2.5), I argue that the abolitionist interpretation that it is always so, is an extreme interpretation of the CRPD anti-torture framework (see Chapter 1, section 1.4.1(c)). It gives no weight to the intentions of the perpetrator, which while some doctors may be lacking in bedside manner, is likely to be the prevention of harm and restoration of health, or the possibility that denying medical treatment to a person who is in distress or liable to harm themselves or others, but who by reason of their illness is unable to consent, might also amount to torture or cruel, inhuman, and degrading treatment and punishment. The abolitionist interpretation also relies on the conceptualization of involuntary detention and psychiatric treatment as a form of discrimination. Although, as I argue in Chapters 6 and 7, this categorization is not certainly straightforward and may ignore the need to treat differently placed persons differently in order to achieve substantive and transformative equality. That said, where limited involuntarily detention and treatment is permissible, it ought to be implemented in a way that respects the inherent dignity of persons with disabilities (see Chapters 4 and 5 especially section 5.1).

3.3.7 Mental Health Law is Inconsistent with the Right to Independent Living

Some abolitionists argue that involuntary detention and treatment is inconsistent with the right to live independently and be included in the community.

The right to independent living (Article 19) has three components. First, it is the ability to choose where and with whom to live on an equal basis with others and not be forced to live in a particular situation. Second, it involves access to a range of services

[173] ibid 69–70.
[174] ibid 71.

to support living and inclusion in the community and third ensuring that community services which are available to the general population are equally available to persons with disabilities. More importantly, the right to independent living applies to everyone, even those who require very high levels of support and services to live in the community.[175] 'Independence' does not necessarily mean living on one's own and the obligation also includes the provision of supports to families to assist them in ensuring that persons with disabilities are included in the community.[176]

While it does not expressly mention institutionalization, there is no doubt that Article 19 is aimed at moving persons with disabilities out of institutions and into the community. The definition of an institution is not dependent on its size and can include everything from large hospitals to small group homes.[177] It is more the manner of living which is imposed on the person rather than a place such as isolation and segregation from the community; loss of control, rigid routines, uniformity, and lack of tailoring services to the individual, a paternalistic approach, and a large number of persons with disabilities living in the same environment all sharing the same assistants and support services.[178] However, Article 19 is not just aimed at preventing the physical segregation of persons with disabilities by forcing them to live in institutions. It also extends to ending the emotional segregation of people who are physically located in the community but are essentially still isolated.[179] That is, it aims to separate the provision of accommodation from the provision of disability services and turn persons with disabilities into active employers rather than the passive recipients of care determined by others. Arlene Kanter argues that supported housing is the key to the implementation of Article 19.[180] Supported housing is housing which is:

> secured from the regular housing market, which the person with a disability may choose to rent or own, and live alone or with others, of his or her choice. While living there, the person can choose to arrange for his own services, support and personal assistance.[181]

Article 19 also involves reforming mainstream community services from accessible buildings and transport to health and education services that meet the needs of persons with disabilities. Therefore, Article 19 is a welcome and significant change in the living circumstances of persons with disabilities in giving them far more day-to-day control over their lives. The right of persons with disabilities to live independently became quite relevant during the COVID-19 pandemic, as some people had services

[175] General Comment 5: Article 19: Living Independently and Being Included in the Community, 14–31 August 2017 CRPD C/18/1, [20] (hereafter General Comment 5).

[176] ibid [16(a)] and [55].

[177] ibid [16(c)].

[178] Giuseppe Palmisano 'Article 19 [Living Independently and Being Included in the Community]' in V Della Fina and others (eds), *The United Nations Convention on the Rights of Persons with Disabilities* (Springer 2017) 365 (hereafter Palmisano, 'Article 19').

[179] Tirza Leibowitz, 'Living in the Community, Access to Justice: Having the Right Makes All the Difference' in Maya Sabatello and Marrianne Schulze (eds), *Human Rights and Disability Advocacy* (University of Pennsylvania Press 2014) 45, 46 (hereafter Leibowitz, 'Living in the Community').

[180] Kanter, *The Development of Disability Rights* (n 135) 98.

[181] ibid.

withdrawn due to their failure to observe lockdown rules and were instead confined in their homes or transferred to institutional care in a nursing home (where there have been a number of outbreaks) supposedly for their 'safety'.[182]

Article 19 is also an example of a 'hybrid' right. The right to choose and not be forced is argued to be a civil and political right which is immediately realizable, while the provision of individualized disability support and the adjustment of mainstream community services requires significant resources which being a socio-economic right may be progressively realized.[183] The right to independent living raises many issues around resourcing and costs, although some savings may be made through the closure of institutions.[184] Oliver Lewis and Genevra Richardson observe that the right to independent living is enormously ambitious and would involve wide-ranging changes the scale of which the CRPD Committee has failed to understand.[185]

The right to independent living has been used as a ground by some Abolitionists to support the abolition of mental health law, although exactly how it applies is less clear. In General Comment 5 on Article 19 the CRPD Committee asserts that the 'physical and regulatory institutionalization, including of children and forced treatment in all its forms' is a barrier to the implementation of Article 19 (cl 15(d)). It also asserts that Article 19 'entails the obligation to release all individuals who are confined against their will in mental health services or other disability-specific forms of deprivation of liberty' (cl 48). However, the theoretical basis for the link between mental health law and independent living is not spelled out. Temporarily being admitted to hospital for medical treatment (as happens with most people without disabilities who need acute care) does not necessarily inhibit independent living in the community and could potentially support it. According to the Australian Institute of Health and Welfare in 2017–2018 the average length of hospital stay for persons with mental impairment in Australia was fifteen days, which would hardly constitute 'living' in a hospital.[186] That is, the right to independent living appears to be more indirectly related to the abolition of mental health law compared with other CRPD provisions like the right to legal capacity (Article 12) or the right to liberty (Article 14). But, Article 19 would be relevant in states where persons with mental impairments are still routinely treated in long-stay hospitals and institutions. Problems related to independent living tend to be the most pronounced for persons with disabilities in middle income countries which tend to still deliver mental health care in institutions, whereas higher income countries have had deinstitution programmes in place for many years and low income countries did not have any institutions in the first place.[187] Nevertheless compliance by States

[182] Kay Wilson, 'The COVID-19 Pandemic and the Human Rights of Persons with Mental and Cognitive Impairments Subject to Coercive Powers in Australia' (2020) Int J Law Psychiatry (in press).

[183] Oliver Lewis and Genevra Richardson, 'The Right to Live Independently and be included in the Community' (2020) 69 Int J Law Psychiatry 101499 9 (hereafter Lewis and Richardson, 'The Right to Live Independently'); General Comment 5 (n 177) [39].

[184] Kanter, *The Development of Disability Rights* (n 135) 102–3.

[185] ibid.

[186] Australian Institute of Health and Welfare 'Mental Health Services in Australia' (13 October 2020) https://www.aihw.gov.au/reports/mental-health-services/mental-health-services-in-australia/report-contents/overnight-admitted-mental-health-related-care/specialised-overnight-admitted-patient-mental-health-care accessed 16 November 2020 (hereafter, AIHW 'Mental Health Services 2020').

[187] Kanter, *The Development of Disability Rights* (n 135) 66.

Parties with Article 19 may prevent involuntary detention and psychiatric treatment where the reason for that treatment is caused by a lack of appropriate community supports.[188] There is no doubt that community treatment options are widely underfunded and require further development in all countries. The General Comment does not make any explicit comments about community treatment orders and their role in helping people to live in the community.

The implementation of independent living in Article 19 raises similar issues as for legal capacity in Article 12 in that it relies on being able to determine the will and preferences of a person with mental impairment about their desired living arrangements. Article 19 assumes that persons with disabilities will always understand what supports they need to live independently and be included in the community and will have some capacity to manage them (even with support). There is also no discussion of what happens if a person with mental impairment refuses some or all community supports even if they are needed for them to live in the community safely and be included in the community in any meaningful way. What happens if a person with mental impairment endangers their life, health, and property while living independently and refusing assistance? What if it is difficult to find people who will want to provide them with support without psychiatric treatment (eg because they are violent or abusive, or just very difficult)? While Article 19 would certainly improve the lives of many persons with disabilities by removing them from impersonal and restrictive institutions to a place with a sense of home and belonging which cannot be underestimated, the implementation in the 'hard cases' still raises some difficult questions which have not yet been engaged with by the CRPD Committee and the abolitionist literature.

3.3.8 Mental Health Law is Ineffective and Un-therapeutic

Not only is the involuntary detention and treatment of people with mental illness a violation of human rights (as discussed above), but according to the abolitionists it is ineffective and damaging to the therapeutic alliance. As set out above, the CRPD Committee has asserted that there is no empirical evidence of the effectiveness of involuntary detention and treatment of mental illness.[189] Advocates from the user and survivor movement also point out that while some individuals have found psychiatric treatment helpful, 'the overall results of the mental health system's over-reliance on powerful psychiatric drugs have been profoundly and disturbingly negative'.[190] In some countries 'detention is often tantamount to treatment'.[191] Involuntary detention and treatment and coercion have been linked to lower levels of treatment satisfaction,

[188] General Comment 5 (n 177) [82].

[189] General Comment 1 (n 75) [38].

[190] Pelka, *What We Have Done* (n 22) 567.

[191] Jasna Russo and Diana Rose, '"But What if Nobody's Going to Sit Down and Have a Real Conversation with You?" Service user/Survivor Perspectives on Human Rights' (2013) 12(4) J Public Ment Health 184, 188 (hereafter Russo and Rose, 'But What if Nobody's Going to Sit Down and Have a Real Conversation with You?').

less therapeutic alliance between health professionals and people with mental impairment, and poorer treatment outcomes.[192]

However, not all persons with mental impairments report that involuntary detention and psychiatric treatment is ineffective and as outlined in Chapter 1 section 1.2, it has been estimated that between 40–80 per cent are grateful for intervention in retrospect. For example, research by Katsakou and colleagues into why psychiatric patients considered their hospitalization right or wrong found that the over 50 per cent of people were very positive about their involuntary detention and treatment and another 33 per cent were ambivalent in that they agreed that intervention was required, but would have preferred less coercion (eg better communication and community care).[193] Only 27 per cent of patients believed their involuntary detention and treatment was wrong and resented the disruption in their lives.[194] As observed by Graham Morgan, who was diagnosed with schizophrenia:

> . . . for me, compulsory treatment in the community probably keeps me alive and yet I am aware there is limited evidence that this form of intervention is effective. However, I think there is ample evidence that detention in hospital when desperate, when you cannot bear another day, when the television is beaming horrific messages and instructions into your brain is needed . . . if left to exercise my legal capacity, I would have died and no peer support, no compassionate friend or loving professional, no aspect of Open Dialogue or eCPR would have made any difference . . .[195]

Randomized controlled trials, the gold standard in medical testing, involve a number of ethical difficulties and tend to be inconclusive about the effectiveness of coercion.[196] However, while the effectiveness of involuntary detention and psychiatric treatment has been relatively under-studied, a review of the research by Mario Luciano found that there is some evidence to support clinical improvement among patients who undergo involuntary detention and psychiatric treatment (to the same level as voluntary patients), but that persons treated without their consent had a more negative patient-therapist relationship and reduced satisfaction with and engagement in their treatment.[197] In essence, that involuntary detention and psychiatric treatment was medically effective, but persons with mental impairment were unhappy about it.

[192] Damian Smith and others, 'Satisfaction with Services Following Voluntary and Involuntary Admission' (2014) 23(1) J Ment Health 38 (hereafter Smith, 'Satisfaction with Services').

[193] Christina Katsakou and others, 'Psychiatric Patients' Views on why their Involuntary Hospitalisation was Right or Wrong: A Qualitative Study' (2012) 47 Soc Psychiatry Psychiatr Epidemiol 1169, 1172 (hereafter Katsakou, 'Hospitalisation was Right or Wrong').

[194] ibid 1172, 1174.

[195] Jillian Craigie and others, 'Legal Capacity, Mental Capacity and Supported Decision-Making: Report from a Panel Event' (2019) 62 Int J Law Psych 160, 163 (hereafter Craigie, 'Panel Event').

[196] John Dawson, 'Randomised Controlled Trials of Mental Health Legislation' (2002) 10 Med Law Rev 308, 319–21 (hereafter Dawson, 'Randomised Controlled Trials').

[197] Mario Luciano and others, 'Use of Coercive Measures in Mental Health Practice and Its Impact on Outcome: A Critical Review' (2014) 14(2) Expert Rev of Neurother 131, 133 (hereafter Luciano, 'Use of Coercive Measures').

3.3.9 There are Other Better Non-Coercive Alternatives

As discussed above in section 3.3.2.3, some advocates and scholars have argued that the Abolition with Support model offers a better alternative to substitute decision-making in mental health and guardianship and administration law. This is because a person is offered support to make their own decisions, rather than having a decision made for them by a third party or a decision imposed upon them which is inconsistent with their will and preferences.

Significantly, the support model allows people to refuse all support and the ability to make legally binding decisions, regardless of whether other people such as their friends, family, or other professionals believe that they require support.[198] In this regard, it offers people with mental illness unprecedented autonomy and self-determination.

Supported decision-making is what Piers Gooding describes as 'an emerging concept'[199] that has its origins in the disability sector (see also Chapter 7 section 7.5.2). The CRPD Committee has stated that 'support' is a broad term that encompasses both informal and formal support arrangements of varying types and intensity.[200] It can include choosing one or more trusted persons to assist in exercising their legal capacity for certain types of decisions, peer support, advocacy (including self-advocacy support), assistance with communication, universal design and accessibility, development and recognition of diverse non-conventional methods of communication, and the ability to plan in advance using advance statements.[201] The amount and type of support a person requires to make a decision will vary between people and tests of mental ability should not be used to assess the eligibility of a person for support.[202] Unlike substitute decision-making, the aim of support should be to build the capacity of the person to make their own decisions so that they can become less dependent on support in the long-term.[203]

In addition, the psychiatric user and survivor movement has not only lobbied for the abolition of mental health law, but has also historically offered people with mental impairment peer-run alternatives to conventional psychiatry including safe houses, peer support, and coping skills.[204] These offer people with mental impairment an 'alternative' non-coercive mental health system, where a much wider range of behaviours and emotional responses are tolerated. Abolitionists point to the existence of a range of alternative approaches like the 'open dialogue' program in Finland in which everyone involved shares their perspectives to increase understanding and the 'hearing voices network' in which people learn to explore, understand, and carry on with life despite hearing voices.[205] While there is some dispute as to whether these

198 General Comment 1 (n 75) [17].

199 Piers Gooding, 'Supported Decision-Making: A Rights-Based Disability Concept and Its Implications for Mental Health Law' (2013) 20(3) Psychiatry Psychol & L 431, 431 (hereafter, Gooding, 'Supported Decision-Making').

200 General Comment 1 (n 75) [15].

201 ibid.

202 ibid [16].

203 ibid [20].

204 Dain, 'Critics and Dissenters' (n 11) 13.

205 Minkowitz, 'Abolishing Mental Health Laws' (n 77) 163–4.

approaches are sufficiently 'evidence-based' in the traditional sense, there is certainly evidence that many individuals have found them helpful. The post-psychiatry movement argues that conventional psychiatry should not ignore this evidence, but find new and creative ways to incorporate this knowledge to provide more responsive and individually tailored mental health services.[206]

Similarly, the recovery movement represents a relatively new response to mental illness. While the recovery model is very broad and has several definitions and variations,[207] in essence it reconceptualizes the notion of recovery away from a narrow clinical definition where:

> a person should no longer display any clinical symptoms or any limitations that may be related to such symptoms, and should be in a position to function independently of the help of others.[208]

Rather, it recognizes that recovery itself can be a 'journey' or process rather than a rigidly defined outcome.[209] It envisages a wider concept of recovery that is related to living a meaningful and 'contributing life'.[210] That is,

> all symptoms of an illness do not need to disappear for a person to have control over his/her life, deal constructively with individual propensities and idiosyncracies and enjoy self-reliance and freedom of choice.[211]

A person is able to incorporate mental illness into their personal identity, in which he or she accepts their mental illness as part of themselves, but not the centre of their whole life.[212] It gives optimism and hope, rather than a limited and negative prognosis.[213] From this perspective, the coercive mental health system is seen as disempowering and a barrier to recovery.[214] Coercion is also argued to be vicariously traumatic for family members and create difficulties in seeking help in times of crisis.[215] A completely voluntary mental health system, it is argued, would empower

[206] Pat Bracken and others, 'Psychiatry Beyond the Current Paradigm' (2012) 201 Br J Psych 430 (hereafter Bracken, 'Psychiatry Beyond the Current Paradigm').

[207] Mary O'Hagan and others, 'Recovery in New Zealand: An Evolving Concept?' (2012) 24(1) Int Rev Psych 56 (hereafter O'Hagan, 'Recovery in New Zealand').

[208] Michaela Amering and Margit Schmolke, *Recovery in Mental Health: Reshaping Scientific and Clinical Responsibilities* (Peter Stastny tr, Wiley 2009) 45 (hereafter Amering and Schmolke, *Recovery in Mental Health*).

[209] Patrick Corrigan and Ruth Ralph, 'Introduction: Recovery as Consumer Vision and Research Paradigm' in Patrick Corrigan and Ruth Ralph (eds), *Recovery in Mental Illness: Broadening Our Understanding of Wellness* (American Psychological Association 2005) 3, 5 (hereafter Corrigan and Ralph, 'Recovery as a Consumer Vision').

[210] National Mental Health Commission, 'A Contributing Life: The 2013 National Report Card on Mental Health and Suicide Prevention' (2013) <http://www.mentalhealthcommission.gov.au/our-report-card/reporting-back-and-looking-forward.aspx> (hereafter, 'A Contributing Life').

[211] Amering and Schmolke, *Recovery in Mental Health* (n 208) 11.

[212] ibid.

[213] Mike Slade and others, 'Recovery Grows Up' (2012) 21(2) J Ment Health 99, 101 (hereafter Slade 'Recovery Grows Up').

[214] Corrigan and Ralph, 'Recovery as a Consumer Vision' (n 212) 12.

[215] Watson, 'Care without Coercion' (n 149) 541.

people with mental illness to take responsibility for choosing the right mix of treatments and supports to manage their illness in the context of their whole life. While the recovery model has been influential in mental health law reform worldwide, there are concerns that its implementation has stagnated more recently and it is still often seen as being inapplicable to inpatient psychiatric treatment.[216] Purists would argue that mental health law is incompatible with the level of personal control envisaged by the recovery model, and for this reason, must be abolished. However, I argue that reforming mental health law is compatible with expanding the range of non-coercive alternatives available to persons with mental impairment (see Chapter 8, sections 8.2 and 8.5).

3.3.10 The 'Dignity of Risk'

Piers Gooding points out that persons with disabilities are entitled to take risks, make mistakes, and live with the consequences, the same way as persons without disabilities.[217] This is discussed further in Chapter 5, section 5.2.2. Paternalistic substitute decision-making regimes, like mental health law, deprive people with mental impairment of an important learning and self-discovery opportunity.[218] Further, as Michaela Amering and Margit Schmolke argue:

> . . . we must be careful to distinguish between a person making (from our perspective) a dumb or self-defeating choice, and a person who is truly at risk in order to embrace the all important concept of the 'dignity of risk' and the 'right to failure' (Degan 1996).[219]

Piers Gooding argues that supported decision-making can support the 'dignity of risk' by making a person aware of their responsibilities and the likely consequences of their proposed course of action, as well as making institutions less risk averse as more responsibility is shifted back to the individual.[220] Sandy Watson and colleagues also argue that denial of dignity of risk and personal control can also cause harm.[221]

3.3.11 Mental Health Law is 'Too Easy' and Creates a Culture of Coercion throughout the Entire Mental Health System

Many abolitionists argue that the existence of mental health law makes involuntary detention and treatment the 'easy option' in responding to people with mental impairment. As psychiatrists have compulsory powers at their disposal, they do not need to

216 Sean Kidd and others, 'Mental Health Reform at a Systems Level: Widening the Lens on Recovery Oriented Care' (2014) 59(5) Can J Psychiatry 243 (hereafter Kidd, 'Mental Health Reform').
217 Gooding, 'Supported Decision-Making' (n 202) 436.
218 ibid.
219 Amering and Schmolke, *Recovery in Mental Health* (n 211) 55.
220 Gooding, 'Supported Decision-Making' (n 202).
221 Watson, 'Care without Coercion' (n 149) 535.

explain their proposed course of treatment, persuade a person to consent, or negotiate with people with mental impairment. The effect of the power to involuntarily detain and treat makes the whole mental health system coercive, as even voluntary patients may not be truly 'voluntary', but agree to hospital admission and treatment to avoid the 'stigma' of being sectioned.[222] In any event, 'voluntary' patients may not be permitted to discharge themselves from hospital if they are considered to fall within the civil commitment criteria.[223] Compulsory powers to detain and treat mean that there is no incentive for psychiatrists to better develop their communication and interpersonal skills. It is also consistent with the experience of people who have been denied their legal capacity who report a sense of powerlessness and 'a lack of explanation or an opportunity to challenge the process'.[224] More and better communication can reduce the need for seclusion and restraint and the consequent loss of trust, fear, and suspicion of staff and avoidance of services among persons with mental impairments who have had bad experiences.[225] From this perspective, mental health law must be abolished because it is feared that as long as they exist, they will be used. As Amita Dhanda argues:

> Persons arguing for the retention of the model of selective legal capacity with substitution, constantly assert that this model would only apply in the rarest of rare cases, after all alternatives of recognising capacity with support have been exhausted. This remedy of compromise is suggested without realizing how the exception could swallow the rule. Once the law permits the argument of incompetence to be raised against persons with disabilities then it cannot prevent the levelling of the allegation of incompetence to be raised against all persons with disabilities.[226]

Therefore, there can be no exceptions, abolition is the only solution.

The abolitionists are also wary that law reform to narrow the scope of civil commitment criteria may not have the desired effect in practice. Historically, changes to mental health law have had little change on who gets involuntarily detained and treated.[227] This is because in practice, mental health law may be manipulated by mental health professionals and tribunals 'at the margins' and is moulded to reflect 'widely held moral sentiments'.[228] There is also concern that 'mild reform can be a trap' because what is required is more than 'new slogans, tokenism and a few model programmes'.[229] Accordingly, it is argued that the only 'safe path' to implement real change is to abolish, rather than reform mental health law.

222 Donnelly, *Healthcare Decision-Making and the Law* (n 56) 227.
223 ibid.
224 European Agency for Fundamental Rights, 'Equality: Legal Capacity of Persons with Intellectual Disabilities and Persons with Mental Health Problems' (2013) <http://fra.europa.eu/en/publications-and-resources>(accessed 8 October 2019) 7 (hereafter, 'European Agency for Fundamental Rights Report').
225 Rose, 'Service User Perspectives' (n 146) 60.
226 Dhanda, 'Universal Legal Capacity' (n 55) 182.
227 Appelbaum, 'Almost a Revolution' (n 17).
228 ibid 144.
229 Oaks, 'Whose Voices Shall be Heard' (n 20) 571.

3.4 Conclusion

It is evident from this chapter that the case for the abolition of mental health law has evolved from general opposition into a sophisticated package of inter-linked arguments that provide both a powerful critique of mental health law and a new vision for the social response to mental impairment.

It has been argued in this chapter that it is necessary for the arguments in favour of the abolition of mental health law not just to be heard, but to be properly understood. This is first as a matter of respect and inclusion of those who have long been silenced and excluded, but also to be able to critically evaluate its strengths and weaknesses, and to use the valuable insights gained from understanding the case for abolition to provide a new direction for legal and systemic reform. This understanding will inform my arguments set out in Chapters 4 to 8.

The case for the abolition of mental health law is certainly fuelled by a deep-seated sense of injustice and has come to be increasingly articulated in the 'language of rights'. By firmly placing persons with mental impairment within human rights discourse, the CRPD has enabled long-held criticisms about mental health law to be expressed with unprecedented accuracy and to harness the legal and moral authority of international human rights law. The CRPD has also given the abolitionists a conceptual framework from which to 'reframe' and lift the profile of key issues. Most dramatically, the involuntary detention and treatment of people with mental impairment has been 'reframed' within the torture framework as a form of legalized and prohibited violence. The call for the abolition of mental health law by the CPRD Committee and Special Rapporteur on Torture has given the case for abolition unprecedented exposure.

However, when broken down into its core components the case for abolition reveals a number of basic concerns. First, there is a suspicion that mental health law is more motivated by the desire to maintain social control and conformity, than with the rights, well-being, and recovery of people with mental illness. Second, that mental health law creates a distinction where there is none. Mental health law incorrectly views human diversity as mental and legal incapacity. Therefore, it unfairly 'singles-out' and discriminates against people with mental illness, who are denied the ability to make legally binding healthcare decisions enjoyed by those without mental illness. Third, the rights to equality before the law (Article 12), free and informed consent (Article 25(d)), liberty (Article 14), personal integrity (Article 17), independent living (Article 19), and the anti-torture framework (Article 15), can all be seen as expressions of a single desire: for full autonomy, self-determination and control of their own body and mind, in all circumstances. This is seen as full recognition of legal personhood and the preservation of individual identity, but also as the only remedy to the abuses historically suffered by persons with mental impairments. However, the abolitionist interpretation of the CRPD, also highlights the selective and limited list of rights abolitionists rely on compared with the entire suite of rights contained in the convention and covered by the object and purpose of the CRPD, and that the abolitionist interpretation of some rights tends to be the most extreme interpretation of that right. Finally, there is the anxiety that in a reform-resistant mental health system, abolition is the only option because in the words of Amita Dhanda any 'exception could swallow the rule'.

These claims are set within a socio-historical context in which people with mental illness have good reason to feel misunderstood, stigmatized, and discriminated against, disliked by society for being themselves, ignored, and under-valued. This deep-seated sense of injustice contributes to an 'environment of distrust' that makes law reform very difficult as the law must try to anticipate and legislate to prevent what are perceived as and feared to be potential abuses. It also indicates that the abolitionists are looking to use legal change as more than an increase in legal rights and protections, but as an instrument of broader social change.

4
The 'Interpretive Compass' of the CRPD: The Theory of Dignity

4.1 Introduction

The principles of dignity, equality, and participation are the core human rights principles that permeate the CRPD and form what I have called the 'interpretive compass' of the CRPD. These principles underlie each of the articles of the CRPD and are necessary to understand its legal and moral direction. According to Oliver Lewis 'the principles represent the moral basis of the CRPD, explaining the reasons for its existence, and providing guidance for national authorities, courts and the treaty monitoring body on how to interpret the CRPD'.[1] As foreshadowed in Chapter 1, it is impossible to interpret the CRPD without a grasp of the meaning of dignity (including autonomy), equality, and participation as those terms are repeated throughout it. It is my contention that a more in depth understanding of the interpretive compass can provide important insights into answering the larger question of how the CRPD should be interpreted and whether mental health law should be abolished or reformed.

The principles of dignity, equality, and participation are also found in the eight guiding principles of the CRPD in Article 3, which were intended to guide the interpretation of the CRPD in accordance with the *Vienna Convention on the Law of Treaties*,[2] discussed in section 1.4.1. More broadly, the principles of dignity, equality, and participation underpin all international human rights treaties. However, there is some overlap and duplication between the principles in Article 3. For example, non-discrimination (Article 3(b)), equality of opportunity (Article 3(e)), and equality between men and women (Article 3(g)) all relate to the principle of equality. Similarly, respect for difference and acceptance of persons with disabilities as part of human diversity and humanity (Article 3(d)) is related to all three principles of dignity, equality, and participation.

The Australian Law Reform Commission referred to 'autonomy' and 'accountability' as 'framing principles' of the CRPD in its report on *Equality Capacity and Disability* interpreting the CRPD in the Australian context. I will include autonomy as an aspect of dignity as both often appear together in the CRPD and, as I explain in Chapter 5 section 5.2.2, have a close conceptual and at times conflicting relationship.

[1] Oliver Lewis, 'The Expressive, Educational and Proactive Roles of Human Rights: A Analysis of the United Nations Convention on the Rights of Persons with Disabilities' in Bernadette McSherry and Penelope Weller (eds), *Rethinking Rights-Based Mental Health Laws* (Hart Publishing 2010) 97, 102 (hereafter Lewis, 'Expressive, Educational and Proactive').

[2] Negotiation Archives, Notes of Fourth Session of CRPD Negotiation, 23 August–3 September 2004, Volume 5 #2 24 August 2004, Mexico (hereafter, 'Negotation Archives Fourth Session').

Mental Health Law. Kay Wilson, Oxford University Press. © Kay Wilson 2021. DOI: 10.1093/oso/9780192843258.003.0004

I have decided not to include individual 'accountability' because it is not really a separate 'principle' in the text of the CRPD and the accountability of persons with disabilities for their own decisions is an aspect of autonomy. I have also chosen to focus on the aspects of the principles most relevant to the issue of the abolition and reform of mental health law.

While the principles of dignity, equality, and participation are intricately interrelated, I deal with each of them in turn in Chapters 4 to 7, but point out the relationships between them where relevant.

In this chapter I focus on the theoretical basis of dignity because it is often regarded as the foundational human rights concept and moral basis of international human right law. Also, equality and non-discrimination and participation in decision-making, which I discuss in Chapters 6 and 7, are often regarded as aspects of dignity. I deal with the application of the concept of dignity to the Abolition with Support model in Chapter 5. The concepts of equality, non-discrimination, and participation are covered in Chapter 6 and problems with the application of equality, non-discrimination, and participation in relation to the Abolition with Support model in Chapter 7.

I begin this chapter by considering the use of the concept of 'inherent dignity' in the CRPD and its importance in the disability context. I then consider the meaning of 'inherent dignity' in international human rights law drawing on history, philosophy, and bioethics and some of the controversies surrounding the concept in the general and disability context. I argue that dignity is relevant to the mental health context in two ways. First, it relates to the loss of dignity that persons with mental impairment may experience by reason of their impairment itself and secondly, it relates to the way persons with mental impairment have historically been treated by the mental health system and society more generally. Within this context, I argue that the meaning of dignity is wider than the legal recognition of autonomy. On a balanced and holistic reading of the CRPD which gives effect to all human rights, dignity may at times be given priority over autonomy, which could provide a human rights justification for limited detention and psychiatric treatment, rather than the abolition of mental health law (see Chapter 5). Nonetheless, loss of dignity that is caused by the mental health system must also be addressed and provides a strong basis for significant systemic and legal reform.

4.2 Inherent Dignity in the CRPD

There is no doubt that the concept of inherent dignity is as central to the CRPD as it is to all human rights treaties since the term first entered into human rights discourse at the end of the Second World War. In fact, 'it would simply be impossible today to adopt a new international human rights document without human dignity as its basis'.[3] In many western societies, the concept of inherent dignity also functions as the theoretical basis for egalitarianism, a principle of legal theory and a ground of judicial

[3] Philippe-Andre Rodriguez, 'Human Dignity as an Essentially Contested Concept' (2015) 28(4) Camb Rev Int Aff 743, 743 (hereafter Rodriguez, 'Human Dignity').

reasoning. The concept also appears in many political manifestos, constitutions, and legislation, including mental health laws.[4] Inherent dignity is also often regarded as informing the meaning of each specific human right particularly: the right to life,[5] the right to social security, education, and other social, economic, and cultural rights that enable the free development of the personality and a dignified life,[6] anti-slavery, and the right to fair compensation[7], the right of all persons deprived of their liberty to be treated with inherent dignity[8] and, as discussed below, the prohibition on torture and cruel, inhuman, or degrading treatment. In the words of Deryck Beyleveld and Roger Brownsword: 'human dignity is the rock on which the superstructure of human rights is built.'[9]

As noted in Chapter 3, the concept of inherent dignity is especially powerful in the disability context as persons with disability have historically not been recognized as having dignity or as being fully human,[10] their dignity has frequently not been protected, and many human rights claims by persons with disabilities are related to the loss of dignity.[11] For persons with disabilities human dignity shifts the focus from a person's deficiencies to the recognition of his or her inherent worth.[12] As Lee Ann Basser observes, 'the promise of human rights is that all people are of equal worth and the implication of human dignity provides the basis for people with disabilities to reconstruct themselves as ordinary people.'[13] Human dignity is an analytical tool to understand social structures, shed light on how people are viewed and policies are implemented, and to educate society on the inherent worth of persons with disabilities.[14]

The term inherent dignity appears repeatedly in the text of the CRPD in a variety of different contexts, more often than in any other previous human rights treaty.[15] The preamble echoes the importance of inherent dignity in the *Universal Declaration on Human Rights* and establishes the relationship between the CRPD and international human rights law.[16] It also specifically links inherent dignity and equality by pointing out that 'discrimination against any person on the basis of disability is a violation of

[4] Remy Debes, 'Introduction' in Remy Debes (ed), *Dignity: A History* (Oxford University Press 2017) 1, 8 (hereafter Debes, 'Introduction').

[5] Elizabeth Wicks, 'The Meaning of "Life": Dignity and Rights to Life in International Human Rights Treaties' (2012) 12(2) Hum Rights Law Rev 199 (hereafter Wicks, 'The Meaning of Life').

[6] *Universal Declaration of Human Rights*, GA Res 217A (III) UN GAOR, 3rd Sess, 185th plen mtg, UN Doc A/810 (10 December 1948), Art 22 (hereafter 'UNHDR').

[7] ibid Art 23(3).

[8] *International Covenant on Civil and Political Rights*, opened for signature 16 December 1966, 999 UNTS 171 (entry into force 23 March 1976), Art 10(1) (hereafter 'ICCPR').

[9] Deryck Beyleveld and Roger Brownsword, *Human Dignity in Bioethics and Biolaw* (Oxford University Press 2001) 13 (hereafter Beyleveld and Brownsword, *Human Dignity in Bioethics*).

[10] Frederic Megret, 'The Disabilities Convention: Human Rights of Persons with Disabilities or Disability Rights?' (2008) 30(2) Hum Rights Q 494, 501 (hereafter Megret, 'The Disabilities Convention').

[11] Lee Ann Basser, 'Human Dignity' in Marcia H Rioux and others (eds), *Critical Perspectives on Human Rights and Disability Law* (Martinus Nijhoff Publishers 2011) 17, 36 (hereafter Basser, 'Human Dignity').

[12] ibid 18.

[13] ibid.

[14] ibid 18–19.

[15] Annagret Kampf, 'Involuntary Treatment Decisions: Using Negotiated Silence to Facilitate Change?' in Bernadette McSherry and Penelope Weller (eds), *Rethinking Rights-Based Mental Health Laws* (Oxford Hart 2010) 129, 137 (hereafter Kampf, 'Negotiated Silence').

[16] CRPD, Preamble (a).

the inherent dignity and worth of the human person'.[17] Even more significantly, promoting respect for the inherent dignity of persons with disabilities forms the object and purpose of the CRPD,[18] and appears as the first interpretive principle in Article 3(a) along with individual autonomy including the freedom to make one's own choices, and the independence of persons.[19] In its substantive provisions, the CRPD requires States Parties to raise awareness of and 'foster respect for the rights and dignity of persons with disabilities'[20] and to recognize the 'full development of human potential and sense of dignity and self-worth' provided by education.[21] The CRPD also requires services to be provided to persons with disabilities in a way which is respectful of their dignity, such as healthcare[22] and recovery and reintegration following an experience of violence, exploitation or abuse.[23]

However, despite the importance of inherent dignity in the CRPD, the text alone provides little normative content beyond its association with recognition, autonomy, equality, and service provision. It is therefore difficult to ascertain the 'ordinary meaning' and the true richness of the concept of inherent dignity as 'the heart of human rights protection'[24] in the CRPD, without moving beyond a purely textual analysis. Unfortunately, considering the object and purpose of the CRPD, to understand the meaning of inherent dignity is circular (as the object and purpose is to promote inherent dignity) and, as already noted above, looking to the intentions of the parties negotiating the CRPD with respect to the future of mental health law is unhelpful, as they are in conflict.

It is certainly true that the CRPD is designed to create a 'paradigm shift' and disability re-orientation of mainstream human rights law, but exactly how far the shift goes and precisely what it entails is still a matter of debate. While human rights treaties should be interpreted for the benefit of the person they are intended to protect, in respect of the abolition or reform of mental health law it is uncertain what that benefit is: abolition may confer some benefits such as the ability to refuse unwanted treatment and decision-making support, but may also come with some costs with respect to deterioration in health, potential loss of life, and other negative life consequences. Further, the text of the CRPD does not shed light on the tension between the principles of dignity and autonomy.[25] For example, what if a person's autonomous acts are inconsistent with his or her inherent dignity? This is discussed in Chapter 5 section 5.2.2 below.

The value of *travaux preparatoires* to treaty interpretation can be overstated, especially where the parties cannot be said to have a common intention because they

[17] CRPD, Preamble (h).
[18] CRPD, Art 1.
[19] CRPD, Art 3(a).
[20] CRPD, Art 8.
[21] CRPD, Art 24(a).
[22] CRPD, Art 25(d).
[23] CRPD, Art 16.
[24] Kampf, 'Negotiated Silence' (n 15) 134.
[25] Richard M Duffy and Brendan D Kelly, 'Rights, Laws and Tensions: A Comparative Analysis of the Convention on the Rights of Persons with Disabilities and the Who Resource Book on Mental Health, Human Rights and Legislation' (2017) 54 Int J Law Psychiatry 26, 33 (hereafter Duffy and Kelly, 'Rights, Laws and Tensions').

did not reach agreement on a key issue. The views of one party (or group) cannot unilaterally determine the meaning of a multilateral treaty. However, the *travaux preparatoires* provide some indications of the intention of the drafters in including inherent dignity in the CRPD which was first mentioned as an underlying principle guiding the convention in Mexico in 2002.[26] The first is that discrimination was considered a violation of inherent dignity[27] as discussed in section 4.2.2 below. The second is that the word 'inherent' was included to make dignity consistent with other human rights treaties and the inclusion of 'inherent dignity' was intended to give the CRPD broader reach to include resident non-citizens.[28] While the CRPD refers to 'dignity', 'human dignity', and 'inherent dignity' interchangeably throughout the convention, it will be interesting to see if the CRPD Committee makes a distinction between them.[29] The third is that dignity was taken from the original title of the treaty the 'International Convention on Protection and Promotion of the Rights and Dignity of Persons with Disabilities' to make it shorter and it was decided that dignity should instead be put in Article 1 (purpose) and Article 3 (principles).[30] The fourth is that dignity was understood as something that all persons are born with and that existed separately from human rights and that a person is entitled to inherent dignity even if they are unable to enjoy their human rights fully. Several States Parties made statements which indicated that human rights need to respect and enhance inherent dignity, but that human rights alone may not be enough to ensure persons with disabilities receive inherent dignity. As noted by Sarah Arduin, the comments of States Parties evidenced an intention that 'none of the rights laid down in the Convention may be used to harm the dignity of persons with disabilities',[31] a view which is consistent with my interpretation of the CRPD that inherent dignity has a wider meaning than autonomy and that none of the rights in the CRPD should be interpreted to require the abolition of mental health law where that may harm the inherent dignity of persons with mental impairments. For example, in the second session 16 to 27 June 2003, Thailand stated that 'self-determination and autonomy can only be realized with people who have already had self-determination. Persons with Disability who cannot express their own self-determination are still entitled to live in dignity'.[32] In the fourth session, 23 August to 3 September 2004, Persons with Disability Association supported the working group formulation of the purpose in Article 1 'but encouraged the incorporation of the concept of dignity as the recognition of rights alone will not necessarily ensure that persons with disability are treated with dignity'.[33]

[26] Informal briefing on the Ad Hoc Committee 26 June 2002, United Nations, New York, Executive Summary of the Discussions of the Extert Meeting (hereafter, 'Informal Briefing').

[27] CRPD Negotiation Archives, Second Session, 16 June to 27 June 2003 (hereafter 'Negotiation Archives, Second Session').

[28] ibid Landmine Survivors Network.

[29] Sarah Arduin, 'Article 3 General Principles' in Ilias Bantekas, Michael Stein, and Dimitris Anastasiou (eds), *The UN Convention on the Rights of Persons with Disabilities: A Commentary* (OUP 2018) 92 (hereafter Arduin, 'Article 3').

[30] CRPD Negotiation Archives, Seventh Session, 16 January to 3 February 2006 (hereafter Negotiation Archives, Seventh Session').

[31] Arduin, 'Article 3' (n 29) 92.

[32] Negotiation Archives, Second Session (n 27).

[33] CRPD Negotiation Archives, Fourth Session, 23 August to 3 September 2004 (hereafter 'Negotiation Archives, Fourth Session').

In the fifth session 24 January to 3 February 2006 Lichenstein made the point that governments can confer rights but not dignity which is inherent to everyone and must not be framed as something that must be promoted or conferred, Jordan observed that dignity needed to be treated carefully as it is present in all humans and is greater than human rights, and Mauritious noted that dignity comes before human rights law and that the enhancement of dignity can only be manifested by the expression of rights.[34]

Unfortunately, the concept of inherent dignity has attracted little attention in the CRPD literature.[35] While the *Handbook on the Human Rights of Persons with Disabilities* written by Marriane Schultz, who was present at the negotiations also provides some insights into the CRPD's drafting history, it is of limited assistance.

According to the *Handbook* the reference to inherent dignity in Article 1 of the CRPD was described as 'somewhat troublesome, as dignity as such cannot be guaranteed'.[36] With respect to the principles in Article 3 (a), it is noted that:

> as is highlighted under ... Article 1, dignity is not a right or enforceable principle as such, but rather a state of being to be aimed for. Subsequently, the principle that is enshrined is "respect" for the dignity of an individual ...

The use of the term 'inherent dignity' in the *Handbook* as something that cannot be guaranteed and that is aspirational in nature, seems to be at odds with the text of the CRPD which uses the word 'inherent' linked to the meaning of human dignity in international human rights law as being intrinsic, inviolable, and inalienable.

It is also unclear what the role of inherent dignity is in the CRPD. The *Handbook* claims that inherent dignity 'is not a right or an enforceable principle but a state of being'.[37] On the other hand, Sigrid Graumann claims that inherent dignity in the CRPD is:

> the founding moral principle of an adequate human rights framework that is truly inclusive and universal and hence recognizes the particular needs and living conditions of people with diverse impairments. What follows is that, by stating that 'someone has dignity,' what is expressed is that she or he has to be recognized as a bearer of human rights. And saying 'her dignity has been violated' indicates a systematic disregard of human rights.[38]

[34] Negotiation Archives, Seventh Session (n 31) 30 January 2006.

[35] The four papers are Sigrid Graumann, 'Human Dignity and People with Disabilities' in Marcus Duwell and others (eds), *The Cambridge Handbook of Human Dignity* (Cambridge University Press 2014) 484 (hereafter Graumann, 'Human Dignity'); Ragnfrid Eline Kogstad, 'Protecting Mental Health Clients' Dignity—the Importance of Legal Control' (2009) 32 Int J Law Psychiatry 383 (hereafter Kogstad, 'Protecting Mental Health Clients' Dignity'); Elif Celik, 'The Role of the CRPD in Rethinking the Subject of Human Rights' (2017) 21(7) Int J Hum Rights 933 (hereafter Celik, 'The Role of the CRPD'); Kampf, 'Negotiated Silence' (n 15) 129.

[36] Marianne Schulze, *Understanding the UN Convention on the Rights of Persons with Disabilities* (Handicap International 2009) 22 (hereafter Schulze, Understanding the UN Convention).

[37] ibid.

[38] Graumann, 'Human Dignity' (n 35) 484.

That is, inherent dignity in the CRPD could be understood as the underlying justification for human rights. It could also be akin to the 'right to have rights' and be included in the social order, or it may refer to particularly bad breaches of rights which go to the heart of what it means to be human. However, it is notable that a framework which respects inherent dignity is intended to be *both* truly inclusive and universal and to cater to diverse needs and conditions of persons with different impairments. Therefore, respecting the inherent dignity of persons with mental impairments may mean something different when compared with persons who have other impairments and is consistent with a discretionary approach which distinguishes between the needs of individuals on a case-by-case basis.

It can be seen then that the concept of inherent dignity is significantly undertheorized in the CRPD. However, inherent dignity does have a more established meaning in international human rights law, which is useful in developing a deeper understanding of both inherent dignity, autonomy and the relationship between the two. Inherent dignity also appears in different disciplines, including religion, history,[39] law,[40] philosophy,[41] psychology,[42] and bioethics,[43] and it has been framed as both a moral and a legal concept.[44] It is reasonable to infer that the pre-existing meaning of 'inherent dignity' in international human rights law is relevant, especially where the drafting committee was not permitted to create new rights.[45] While the CPRD certainly emphasizes the importance of autonomy and equality as aspects of the inherent dignity of persons with disabilities, the concept of inherent dignity in the CRPD is a different concept and I argue that it should be given its own independent meaning.

Of course, the meaning of inherent dignity in international human rights law is not straightforward. It has certainly has its sceptics who have criticized its vagueness, its usefulness compared with other concepts,[46] and has raised concerns that as a supervening human rights norm it can be illiberal (in terms of restricting freedom of thought and behaviour) and it can be used to justify legal moralism and paternalism.[47] Alternatively, dignity has been described as a 'placeholder' which carries an enormous amount of content but different content for different people.[48] Notwithstanding these concerns, the concept of inherent dignity also has many supporters who regard dignity as crucial for explaining the theoretical basis of human rights law, understanding

[39] Debes, 'Introduction' (n 4) 1.

[40] Christopher McCrudden, 'Human Dignity and Judicial Interpretation of Human Rights' (2008) 19(4) EUR J Int Law 655 (hereafter McCrudden, 'Human Dignity').

[41] Ronald Dworkin, *Justice for Hedgehogs* (Harvard University Press 2011) (hereafter Dworkin, *Justice for Hedgehogs*).

[42] Donna Hicks and Archbishop Emeritus Desmond Tutu, *Dignity: The Essential Role It Plays in Resolving Conflict in Our Lives and Relationships* (Yale University Press 2011) (hereafter Hicks and Tutu, *Dignity*).

[43] Ruth Macklin, 'Dignity Is a Useless Concept' (2003) 327(20–27) Br Med J 1419 (hereafter Macklin, 'Dignity Is a Useless Concept').

[44] Jeremy Waldron, 'Dignity and Rank' in Jeremy Waldron and Meir Dan-Cohen (eds), *Dignity, Rank, and Rights* (Oxford University Press 2012) 13 (hereafter Waldron 'Dignity and Rank').

[45] Andrea Broderick, *The Long and Winding Road to Equality and Inclusion for Persons with Disabilities: The United Nations Convention on the Rights of Persons with Disabilities* (Intersentia 2015) 66 (hereafter Broderick, The Long and Winding Road to Equality).

[46] Macklin, 'Dignity Is a Useless Concept' (n 43) 1419.

[47] Tarunabh Khaitan, 'Dignity as an Expressive Norm: Neither Vacuous nor a Panacea' (2012) 32(1) Oxf J Leg Stud 1, 2–3 (hereafter Khaitan, 'Dignity as an Expressive Norm').

[48] McCrudden, 'Human Dignity' (n 40) 678.

what it means to be human and mediating conflicts between rights.[49] Understood as a complex and 'multivocal'[50] concept, inherent dignity is able to garner a much wider meaning than the sum of its parts, while still being responsive to a variety of contexts. Tarunabh Khaitan has observed that inherent dignity can also be conceptualized as an important expressive human rights norm, which is unique in that it protects the person from acts which express disrespect for them as a person or involve insult or humiliation.[51]

It is also necessary to acknowledge that the concept of dignity has undergone considerable historical evolution, traces of which still survive in the contemporary human rights understanding of its meaning. The original meaning of dignity can be traced back to ancient Rome, where the linguistic roots of the word can be found in the Latin word 'dignatas' meaning 'status' or 'value' and 'worth'[52] which was originally limited to persons of high social status and rank. Not only were persons of high rank treated with respect, they were also expected to behave with a noble bearing worthy of their status.[53] The concept of human dignity also features in Christian thought and the work of Thomas Aquinas, where humans are believed to derive their dignity as a reflection of their likeness to god. The Christian version of dignity is the opposite from the Roman, as it involves the rejection of high social status and the acceptance of unworthiness.[54] However, it was not until the humanists of the Renaissance and most famously the philosophy of Immanuel Kant that a secular understanding of human dignity, as the inherent, inalienable, equal moral worth of the human person, independent of rank and social status, emerged. Jeremy Waldron argues that the process of transition from dignity as rank to inherent dignity involved a kind of 'levelling up'[55] (which Michael Rosen has also described as the 'expanding circle theory'[56]) whereby all humans were given the high status that was previously reserved for the nobility. Jeremy Waldron argues that the content of contemporary human dignity can be inferred by expanding the privileges once held by persons of rank to the rest of the population.

However, despite the debate and ambiguity which surrounds the concept of inherent dignity there are a number of core claims about inherent dignity for which there is wide consensus, even if its meaning is unsettled at the margins.[57] In trying to distil a workable concept of inherent dignity in international human rights law and the CRPD, I will explore what I regard as its seven key features, along with some of the conceptual conundrums, in turn. These key characteristics are that: inherent dignity requires recognition of inalienable intrinsic human worth; inherent dignity must be

[49] Khaitan, 'Dignity as an Expressive Norm' (n 47) 1.

[50] Mika LaVaque-Manty, 'Universalizing Dignity in the Nineteenth Century' in Remy Debes (ed), *Dignity: A History* (Oxford University Press 2017) 301, 308 (hereafter LaVaque-Manty 'Universalizing Dignity').

[51] Khaitan, 'Dignity as an Expressive Norm' (n 47) 4.

[52] Donna J Perry and others, 'The Right to Life in Peace: An Essential Condition for Realizing the Right to Health' (2015) 17(1) Health Hum Rights 148, 152 (hereafter Perry, 'The Right to Life').

[53] Doris Schroeder, 'Dignity: Two Riddles and Four Concepts' (2008) 17 Camb Q Healthc Ethics 230, 234 (hereafter Schroeder, 'Two Riddles').

[54] Michael Rosen, *Dignity: Its History and Meaning* (Harvard University Press 2012) 14 (Rosen, Dignity).

[55] Jeremy Waldron, 'Dignity, Rights, and Responsibilities' (2011) 43(1) Ariz St L J 1107, 1119 (hereafter Waldron, 'Dignity Rights and Responsibilities').

[56] Rosen, *Dignity* (n 55) 9.

[57] McCrudden, 'Human Dignity' (n 40) 711.

equal; persons must behave and be treated with inherent dignity; the state should be organized to support inherent dignity; and inherent dignity requires respect for autonomy, where a person is autonomous.

4.2.1 Inherent Dignity Requires Recognition of Inalienable Intrinsic Human Worth

The overriding feature of inherent dignity as a human rights concept is its recognition of the inalienable intrinsic human worth of every person, which is widely attributed to Kant's philosophy. When discussing Kant I think it wise to adopt Christopher McCrudden's caution that:

> it would be rash, indeed, for a non-Kantian scholar to purport to get fully to grips with Kant's use of the idea, since it is notoriously contested territory, but several aspects of Kant's use of the term seem clear.[58]

To this I would add that Kant's conception of dignity needs to be interpreted within the context of his wider moral theory where it is the moral law, rather than the person him or herself, that requires respect for dignity.[59] I also agree with those scholars who regard Kant as providing the inspiration and imagination for the contemporary concept of human dignity, rather than being its only author.[60]

The Kantian aspects of human dignity I focus on here are Kant's distinction between things which have a price (things which are capable of being substituted for one another) and the inalienable inner worth of the moral law (which is incomparable and has immeasurable dignity).[61] According to Kant, respect for human dignity prohibits treating persons as a means rather than as an end.[62] While it is not easy to determine what treating someone as an end involves,[63] there is general consensus that Kant meant that persons should not be treated as an instrument or tool to achieve the goals of others without regard to their own interests or well-being.[64] Kant himself uses the example of completing suicide as an example of persons treating themselves as a means rather than as an end.[65] I will temporarily put to one side the other claim about dignity for which Kant is famous, that human dignity is grounded in moral autonomy, (which is problematic because it excludes some persons with disabilities from having human dignity) which I discuss in section 4.2.7 below.

[58] ibid 659–60.

[59] Oliver Sensen, 'Dignity: Kant's Revolutionary Conception' in Remy Debes (ed), *Dignity: A History* (Oxford University Press 2017) 237, 242 (hereafter Sensen 'Dignity').

[60] For example, ibid 261; Dworkin, *Justice for Hedgehogs* (n 41) 264.

[61] Allen Wood and others, *Immanuel Kant, Groundwork for the Metaphysics of Morals* (Yale University Press 2002), 52 (hereafter Wood, *Immanuel Kant*).

[62] ibid 51.

[63] Rosen, *Dignity* (n 55) 86.

[64] Schroeder, 'Two Riddles' (n 54) 232; Beyleveld and Brownsword, Human Dignity *in Bioethics* (n 9) 16–17.

[65] Wood, *Immanuel Kant* (n 62) 47.

Some theorists conceptualize human dignity as having a 'thick' meaning which expresses what it means to treat persons in accordance with their inner moral worth in a positive sense, and a 'thin' meaning which reflects the meaning of human dignity in the negative, that is, as a prohibition on torture and inhuman and degrading treatment.[66] The 'thick' meaning of the concept of human dignity as equal, inalienable, inner moral worth, gives everyone an unconditional respect-worthy status, regardless of their achievements or desert.[67] That is, dignity is regarded as an unearned status that reflects the inestimable worth of the human person.[68] To this extent, human dignity encapsulates the personalist philosophy (which underpins human rights) that the difference between being *something* and being *someone* is so radical it does not admit of degrees.[69]

While everyone has inalienable inner moral worth as a birthright that is never diminished, one of the paradoxes of human dignity is that in certain situations dignity can be said to be 'lost'. Thus, the 'thin' meaning of human dignity encapsulates when persons are treated, or treat themselves, in a way which is inconsistent with their inner moral worth, so that they are treated as being less than human: like an animal, an object, or a non-entity. Loss of inherent dignity includes torture and cruel, inhuman, and degrading treatment or punishment (see also Chapter 3, section 3.3.6). In the health context, persons often complain of being treated like an object to which things can be done without consultation, rather than being a subject with an individual personality, sense of themselves, and their own views.[70]

Lee Ann Basser argues that in the disability context respecting dignity requires that the needs of the whole person are recognized. She writes:

> While it is important to acknowledge the structural barriers which disable many people, it is impossible to accord dignity to a person with disability without looking internally as well as externally. People are disabled, their lives are made more challenging and difficult by their impairments and functional limitations of body and mind as well as by external systemic disadvantage. It is the requirement of dignity that ensures that "whole" people are seen and responded to.[71]

The paradox that human dignity is inherent and inviolable, but can sometimes be lost, has caused some theorists to explain it by referring to different 'types' of dignity. For example, Doris Schroeder refers to aristocratic dignity (high rank), comportment dignity (having a well-mannered demeanour), and meritorious dignity (being

[66] Doron Shultziner, 'Human Dignity—Functions and Meanings' (2003) 3(3) Global Jurist Topics 1, 6 (hereafter Shultziner, 'Human Dignity'); McCrudden, 'Human Dignity' (n 40) 681.

[67] Paul Formosa and Catriona Mackenzie, 'Nussbaum, Kant, and the Capabilities Approach to Dignity' (2014) 17 Ethical Theory Moral Pract 875, 877 (hereafter Formosa and Mackenzie, 'Nussbaum and Kant').

[68] Remy Debes, 'Human Dignity before Kant' in Remy Debes (ed), *Dignity: A History* (Oxford University Press 2017) 210 (hereafter Debes, 'Human Dignity before Kant').

[69] Thomas D Williams and Jan Olof Bengtsson, 'Personalism' in Edward N Zalta (ed), *The Stanford Encyclopedia of Philosophy* (Spring 2014 ed, 2014) (hereafter Williams and Bengtsson, 'Personalism').

[70] Emily Jackson, 'From "Doctor Knows Best" to Dignity: Placing Adults Whole Lack Capacity at the Centre of Decisions About Their Medical Treatment' (2018) 81(2) MLR 247, 264 (hereafter Jackson, 'From "Doctor Knows Best" to Dignity').

[71] Basser, 'Human Dignity' (n 11) 22.

honourable and morally praiseworthy).[72] Similarly, Lennart Nordenfelt identifies four types of dignity being: basic human dignity (belonging to everyone), dignity as merit (high rank), dignity as moral stature (having a dignified character), and dignity of identity (as an integrated and autonomous person which can be lost through illness and aging).[73] In a similar vein, Donna Hicks distinguishes between dignity and respect: persons always have dignity which must be honoured no matter what they do, but their actions may not be deserving of respect which must be earned.[74]

However, of these explanations of the dignity paradox, the work of Simon Coghlan on exploring the 'moral depth' of human dignity is the most applicable to this book.[75] He distinguishes between two forms of dignity: alienable (or small d-dignity) which involves the giving of honour and respect as well as preventing degrading and demeaning treatment, and inalienable (or Capital D- Dignity) which refers to inherent human worth.[76] While these two forms of dignity are conceptually separate, they are also highly interdependent: small d-dignity violations are considered a subset of the different kinds of attack that can be made on Capital D-Dignity (inherent dignity).[77] Small d-dignity violations link 'the profound worth of humans to their vulnerability to misfortune, to the rightness of showing them love and to the wonderfulness of taking a keen interest in their lives and moral growth'.[78] That is, humans as bearers of Capital-D Dignity can be degraded and honoured in a range of distinctive ways as a function of their small-d dignity.[79]

4.2.2 Inherent Dignity must be Equal

While I will discuss the meaning of 'equality' in Chapters 6 and 7, I acknowledge that equality is important to the meaning of inherent dignity which belongs to every person, especially where inequality creates significant disadvantage and marks social inferiority. The CRPD Committee has also reinforced the association between inherent dignity and equality in General Comment 6 on Equality and Non-Discrimination, in which it notes that discrimination, lack of attention to intersectionality, failure to recognize diversity, and harassment are all linked with violations of inherent dignity.

4.2.3 Behaving with Dignity

Deriving from the concept of dignity as high rank, dignity has long been associated with the idea of a person's noble bearing and comportment and of presenting oneself

[72] Schroeder, 'Two Riddles' (n 54) 234.
[73] Lennart Nordenfelt, 'The Varieties of Dignity' (2004) 12(2) Health Care Anal 69, 72–74 (hereafter Nordenfelt, 'The Varieties of Dignity').
[74] Hicks and Tutu, *Dignity* (n 43) 5.
[75] Simon Coghlan, 'The Moral Depth of Human Dignity' (2018) 41(1) Philos Investig 71 (hereafter Coghlan, 'The Moral Depth of Human Dignity').
[76] ibid 76, 87.
[77] ibid.
[78] ibid 75.
[79] ibid 86.

to others in ways which conform to social standards of worthy behaviour. It is an aspect of dignity which coheres with the notion of personal accountability. That is, to use the language of Simon Coghlan (above) it is a kind of small-d dignity or indignity which can have an impact on a person's Capital-D Dignity.

However, exactly how the requirement to behave in a dignified manner fits within the contemporary concept of human dignity is less clear and is somewhat controversial. It reflects the Kantian view that even though human beings have intrinsic value, that worth also requires them to behave with dignity.[80] Therefore, inherent dignity involves a certain amount of self-respect and an imperative not to engage in conduct unbecoming of a human being.[81] The duty to preserve one's dignity takes priority over one's inclinations and preferences.[82] As Jeremy Waldron describes it:

> when we hear the claim that someone has dignity, what comes to mind are ideas such as: having a certain sort of presence, uprightness of bearing; self-possession and self-control; self-presentation of someone to be reckoned with; not being abject, pitiable, distressed, or overly submissive in circumstances of adversity.[83]

Ronald Dworkin argues that dignity comes with an obligation to take one's life seriously and to adopt an attitude of trying to live it well.[84] By the same token, selling oneself into slavery is widely regarded as being degrading and beneath human dignity, even if one chooses or relishes it.[85] It is also widely accepted that persons who violate another person's dignity, are acting in an undignified manner.

While Deryck Beyleveld and Roger Brownsword have some reservations about the need for dignified behaviour where it is equated to matters of etiquette as being too flimsy a basis for constraining inherent dignity, they see it as a matter of degree and are nonetheless reluctant to dismiss the duty to act in a dignified manner completely.[86] Instead, they explain the importance of dignified behaviour as a kind of 'virtue' that humans should seek to attain:

> The virtue of dignity is one in which humans, confronted with adversity (whether social or natural) and the limitations of human finitude, seek to balance the will to resist (to overcome) with the will to submit (to accept); in such a context, those whose character is attuned to the virtue of human dignity will find an appropriate balance.[87]

John Vorhaus observes that dignified behaviour may be particularly challenging for persons with disabilities and may be an unrealistic expectation in those

[80] Rosen, *Dignity* (n 55) 30; Beyleveld and Brownsword, *Human Dignity in Bioethics* (n 9) 55.

[81] John Kleinig, 'Paternalism and Human Dignity' (2017) 11 Crim Law Philos 19, 25 (Kleinig 'Paternalism and Human Dignity').

[82] Beyleveld and Brownsword, *Human Dignity in Bioethics* (n 9) 56.

[83] Waldron, 'Dignity Rights and Responsibilities' (n 56) 22; Kleinig 'Paternalism and Human Dignity' (n 82) 27.

[84] Dworkin, *Justice for Hedgehogs* (n 41) 205.

[85] Shultziner, 'Human Dignity' (n 67) 13.

[86] Beyleveld and Brownsword, *Human Dignity in Bioethics* (n 9) 44.

[87] ibid 50.

circumstances.[88] That said, the concept of behaving in a dignified manner still has some relevance in the disability context. In the health context, Linda Barclay notes that maintaining personal appearance, in the sense of being clean and tidy is important to the inherent dignity of persons who are ill, and preventing a person from presenting themselves in a dignified manner is a dignity violation.[89] Dignified behaviour also recognizes those persons who maintain their dignity by resisting the humiliating circumstances in which they find themselves, including disability rights activists.[90] Further, the loss of self-control and comportment caused by ageing, serious illness, pain and disability which are often considered to be undignified and sit behind calls for 'death with dignity' reflect the notion of dignified comportment may be in tension with the Kantian concept of inalienable dignity.[91]

4.2.4 Inherent Dignity Requires a Person to be Treated with Dignity

The implication that all persons deserve to be treated with dignity is fairly self-explanatory and has been discussed above. However, I include a further discussion here to underline its importance to the overall concept of inherent dignity and reinforce that being treated by others in way which is consistent with dignity is part of a relational understanding of inherent dignity.[92]

I also want to discuss a quote from Lee Ann Basser that what it means for persons with disabilities to be treated with inherent dignity:

> Adopting these elements of human dignity allows for an understanding of what it means in fact to be treated consistently with dignity. First is the absolutely crucial requirement that a person's physical integrity is respected. This has consequences both in every day interactions and in "extraordinary" situations such as those involving medical treatment, unwanted sexual advances and punitive measures. Secondly, human dignity means that every person has the inherent right to be treated as an individual with a personality. This means that the right to freedom of opinion and belief, (including religion), inherent in the values of a liberal state are accorded to everyone. Thirdly, human dignity means that a person must be given voice about any issues which affect their lives and must have the ability wherever possible to exercise choice. Finally, inherent dignity of any individual requires that he or she has access to a fair share of the goods of society. This means that the availability of resources to any individual is dependent on the socio-economic environment in which they live, but dignity dictates that there is a fair distribution of those goods between members of the society.[93]

[88] John Vorhaus, 'Dignity, Capability, and Profound Disability' (2015) 46(3) Metaphilosophy 462, 472 (hereafter Vorhaus, 'Dignity').

[89] Linda Barclay, 'In Sickness and in Dignity: A Philosophical Account of the Meaning of Dignity in Health Care' (2016) 61 Int J Nurs Stud 136, 139 (hereafter Barclay, 'In Sickness and in Dignity').

[90] Vorhaus, 'Dignity' (n 89) 468.

[91] Schroeder, 'Two Riddles' (n 54) 236.

[92] Jennifer Nedelsky, *Laws Relations: A Relational Theory of Self, Autonomy, and Law* (Oxford University Press 2011) 41 (hereafter Nedelsky, *Laws Relations*).

[93] Basser, 'Human Dignity' (n 11) 17.

While this is a very useful quotation about what it means to be treated with dignity for persons with disabilities, I would argue that some of these examples, especially about bodily integrity and medical treatment, might be modified in the specific situation of persons with mental impairments. While Lee Ann Basser does not address the issues surrounding the abolition and reform of mental health law for persons with mental impairment directly, she does, as noted above, acknowledge the importance of seeing the needs of the whole person in order to respect inherent dignity. She also remarks:

> For people with disabilities this means asking the question about whether the treatment or interaction is predicated on preserving and protecting the moral worth of the individual, not on some idea about the person's disability. On the other hand, denying the importance of the disability and the needs arising as a result of the disability would itself be an affront to human dignity. The principle of dignity requires that the whole person is taken into account.[94]

That is, how to treat persons with mental impairment who are refusing treatment with dignity is not straightforward. While involuntary detention and treatment may violate dignity by overriding a person's wishes, not intervening where a person is in distress could also be an affront to dignity.

It is also important to understand that people are very sensitive to threats to their inherent dignity and that research suggests that people respond to threats to their dignity in the same way as to a physical threat.[95] It is perhaps this sensitivity that may underlie some of the tensions surrounding the issue of whether to abolish or reform mental health law.

4.2.5 The State should be Organized to Support Inherent Dignity

Inherent dignity as a human rights concept contains within it a moral claim and legal requirement that the state is organized so that its institutions respect and support dignity.[96] This is a requirement that the state and community must take positive measures to uphold dignity, rather than just give formal passive respect for dignity,[97] such as ratifying and implementing the CRPD.

4.2.6 Inherent Dignity Involves Respect for Autonomy

The concept of inherent dignity has long been intertwined with autonomy, but the nature of the relationship is complex and contested. On the one hand, bioethicist Ruth

[94] ibid 36.
[95] Hicks and Tutu, *Dignity* (n 43) 7.
[96] Marcus Duwell, 'Human Dignity: Concepts, Discussions, Philosophical Perspectives' in Marcus Duwell and others (eds), *The Cambridge Handbook of Human Dignity* (Cambridge University Press 2014) 32 (hereafter Duwell, 'Human Dignity').
[97] Rhoda E Howard and Jack Donnelly, 'Human Dignity, Human Rights and Political Systems' (1986) 80(3) Am Polit Sci Rev 801, 803 (hereafter, Howard and Donnelly, 'Human Dignity and Political Systems').

Macklin has claimed that 'dignity is a useless concept, it means no more than respect for persons and their autonomy'.[98] This statement has been widely criticized as being driven by her frustration with the use of dignity by opponents of certain kinds of cutting-edge medical research, rather than any real concern to theorize dignity.[99] On the other hand, whether respect for autonomy is an essential component of dignity at all is disputed and rejected by many religions, including Catholicism (in which there is inherent dignity in unspoken affection, relationships and dependence),[100] and states, such as Germany (in which autonomy is limited by community needs).[101] In relation to these two conceptions of human dignity Deryck Beyleveld and Roger Brownsword argue that human dignity can be conceptualized as empowerment where autonomy prevails, and as a form of constraint where paternalism and social deference prevail.[102] A moderate view is that autonomy is a component of human dignity, but is not synonymous with it. What I argue in this book is that inherent dignity has a wider meaning than autonomy and that, in some situations, inherent dignity limits autonomy (especially, as discussed in Chapter 5 section 5.2.1 below, where 'autonomy' is very broadly defined by abolitionists).

The relationship between inherent dignity and autonomy stems from the Kantian claim that inherent dignity is based on the ability of humans to make rational decisions for themselves as moral agents, which it is argued, distinguishes humans from animals, objects, and from God. The Kantian approach is, to some extent, in accordance with the work of Pico della Mirandola who also claims that human dignity is based on the human ability to choose what one wants to be according to one's will.[103] Martha Nussbaum also requires persons with dignity to have at least minimal capacities for agency, which while at a lower level than Kant's rationality, still requires some amount of active striving.[104] For Ronald Dworkin, dignity requires self-respect which, as described above, is an attitude that people believe it is important to live well. It also requires authenticity (which is wider than autonomy), in that people must live in accordance with their values and goals within their own situation even if it means defying social norms.[105]

Traditionally, the view that inherent dignity is grounded in autonomy has been problematic for persons with disabilities. This is because only rational agents capable of moral decision-making were regarded as being human and as requiring respect for their inherent dignity, thereby excluding certain persons such as infants and some persons with disabilities from respect for their inherent dignity and certain human rights.[106] The irony is that it is perhaps those very persons who are arguably the most

[98] Macklin, 'Dignity Is a Useless Concept' (n 43) 1419.

[99] Waldron, 'Dignity Rights and Responsibilities' (n 56) 30.

[100] ibid 28–29.

[101] Sandra Fredman, *Human Rights Transformed: Positive Rights and Positive Duties* (Oxford University Press 2008) 700 (hereafter Fredman, *Human Rights Transformed*).

[102] Beyleveld and Brownsword, *Human Dignity in Bioethics* (n 9) 12.

[103] McCrudden, 'Human Dignity' (n 40) 659.

[104] Formosa and Mackenzie, 'Nussbaum and Kant' (n 68) 875, 879.

[105] Dworkin, *Justice for Hedgehogs* (n 41).

[106] For example, Janet E Lord and Michael Ashely Stein, 'Contingent Participation and Coercive Care: Feminist and Communitarian Theories of Disability and Legal Capacity' in Bernadette McSherry and Ian Freckelton (eds), *Coercive Care: Rights, Law and Policy* (Routledge 2013) 31, 31 (hereafter, Lord and Stein, 'Contingent Participation'); Waldron, 'Dignity Rights and Responsibilities' (n 56) 29.

dependent on others who are in the most need of having their human dignity and humanity respected. The exclusionary nature of dignity based on rational autonomy has often been addressed by explaining it on the basis that it is the human potential for rational autonomy as a species which is important, rather than the individual manifestations of it. As Sigrid Graumann explains:

> A realistic understanding instead considers autonomy as a developmental concept realised to different degrees in certain periods of life. On this understanding, it is not the developed capacity of autonomy of a particular person, but the potential for autonomy of the human being—regardless of the degree of individual development of this capacity—should be considered as the basis of human dignity.[107]

That is, since humans typically have the potential for autonomy, whether it is realized for a particular person or not, then all humans should be taken to have inherent dignity. Or in the words of Daniel Sulmasy 'it is not being black or white, male or female, able or disabled that grounds arguments for dignity. Rather all that counts is being human.'[108]

Alternatively, Remy Debes argues that the normative ground for human dignity may not be rationality.[109] Rather, following a second strand of reasoning in the philosophy of Rousseau, Pufendorf, and Diderot,[110] human dignity may also be grounded within the interpersonal context of humans as passionate agents, capable of feeling, emotion, and sentiment.[111] Such an account of human dignity provides a broader more inclusive understanding of human dignity, independent of autonomy. That said, conceptions of inherent dignity which de-emphasize rationality and moral autonomy, lessen the distinction between humans, animals, and other living things and the conception of dignity as being species-specific.

However, if autonomy is regarded as a uniquely human characteristic which grounds inherent dignity, then the failure of others to recognize what a person with mental impairments perceives as their autonomy may be experienced by the person as a lessening of their self-worth and to this extent as a dignity violation.[112] That is, some people (usually those who do not see their involuntary detention or treatment as justified) will see that weight was not given to their views as a form of what Stephen Darwall calls 'recognition respect':[113] the respect

107 Graumann, 'Human Dignity' (n 36) 487.

108 Daniel P Sulmasy, 'Dignity, Disability, Difference and Rights' in DC Ralston and J Ho (eds), *Philosophical Reflections on Disability* (Springer 2010) 183, 191 (hereafter Sulmasy, 'Dignity, Disability, Difference and Rights').

109 Debes, 'Human Dignity before Kant'.

110 ibid. Debes argues that these three thinkers developed the concept of human dignity before Kant using a non-rational basis.

111 ibid 219.

112 Alasdair Maclean, *Autonomy, Informed Consent and Medical Law: A Relational Challenge* (Cambridge University Press 2009) 24 (hereafter Maclean, *Autonomy, Informed Consent, and Medical Law*) (while Maclean makes the point that preventing a person from making a decision based on the idea that others know better smacks of inequality, he expressly does not include persons who lack mental capacity of which may include many persons with mental impairments).

113 Stephen Darwall, 'Respect and the Second-Person Standpoint' (2004) 78(2) Proc Add Am Phil Assoc 43, 44 (hereafter Darwall, 'Respect and the Second-Person Standpoint').

people automatically demand from each other as moral equals, independent of merit.[114]

That said, the provision of psychiatric treatment, even involuntarily, may not reflect a lack of respect for inherent dignity, but rather the opposite, a concern for the moral worth of persons with mental impairment and their well-being.[115] That is, respect for persons with mental impairment includes respect for their autonomy *and* their well-being.[116] As I discuss further below, it may also reflect a society in which individual autonomy is over-valued as an attribute of personhood and human worth, at the expense of other more passive and more caring ways of being.[117] Another difficulty with grounding inherent dignity in autonomy is that all human capabilities, including autonomy are contingent, whereas dignity is inherent and inalienable.[118] That is, loss of autonomy can only ever be a feature of small d-dignity, rather than Capital D-Dignity.[119]

4.3 Conclusion

Inherent dignity is an important concept for persons with disabilities (for whom recognition of inherent dignity has often been denied). While respect for inherent dignity is an underlying principle of the CRPD and directly informs some of the rights of persons with disabilities in the CRPD, the meaning of inherent dignity in the CRPD is under-theorized. However, human dignity has long been a cornerstone of international human rights law as a justification for human rights, an interpretive tool, and a 'source' of human rights, as well as having expressive value.

While the meaning of inherent dignity is unsettled and has evolved over time (it is no longer limited to persons of high rank), it has a number of different components. First, inherent dignity requires the recognition of intrinsic human worth. It is both inherent and inalienable (referred to by Simon Coghlan as Capital-D Dignity), but is also alienable and contingent as demonstrated by the many ways it can be violated and honoured (small-d dignity). Second, everyone has inherent dignity by simply being human regardless of age, sex, race, wealth, health, ability, and social station: human dignity thus requires equality. Third, while it is controversial, it is also arguable that as beings with inherent dignity, humans have an obligation to behave in a way in which they respect their own dignity and that such an obligation can act as a constraint on their behaviour. Fourth, what is less controversial is that inherent dignity requires that persons be treated in a way that is consistent with their intrinsic worth, although exactly what that means may be unclear as both respecting autonomy and the need of a

[114] Matthew Burch, 'Autonomy, Respect, and the Rights of Persons with Disabilities in Crisis' (2017) 34(3) J Appl Philos 390, 398 (hereafter Burch, 'the Rights of Persons with Disabilities in Crisis').

[115] Sulmasy, 'Dignity, Disability, Difference and Rights' (n 109) 192.

[116] Maclean, *Autonomy, Informed Consent and Medical Law* (n 113) 13.

[117] David Bilchitz, 'Dignity, Fundamental Rights and Legal Capacity: Moving Beyond the Paradigm Set by the General Comment on Article 12 of the Convention on the Rights of Persons with Disabilities' (2016) 32(3) SAJHR 410 (hereafter Bilchitz, 'Dignity, Fundamental Rights and Legal Capacity').

[118] Beyleveld and Brownsword, *Human Dignity in Bioethics* (n 9) 23.

[119] Coghlan, 'The Moral Depth of Human Dignity' (n 76) 73.

person for medical treatment could be construed as treating them with dignity. Fifth, inherent dignity is such a core human rights value, the state should exist to serve individuals (rather than vice versa) and should be organized to support inherent dignity. Finally, while it is controversial, inherent dignity probably involves respect for autonomy, but is a concept which is wider than autonomy and includes other values that recognize the intrinsic worth of persons, such as caring for a person's health and well-being.

5

Application of Inherent Dignity to the Abolition with Support Model

5.1 Introduction

In Chapter 4, I have set out the theoretical understanding of 'inherent dignity' in the CRPD and international human rights law. However, in this Chapter I apply the concept of 'inherent dignity' to the situation of persons with mental impairments and to the Abolition with Support model, where I specifically explore the tensions that can occur between inherent dignity and autonomy (broadly defined). I argue that mental health law should be reformed rather than abolished and that the CRPD does not require the abolition of mental health law because inherent dignity is broader than autonomy, permitting limited involuntary detention and psychiatric treatment in order to preserve the inherent dignity of persons with mental impairments.

I begin by demonstrating that the concept of inherent dignity is not completely abstract, but also needs to be understood in the particular social and cultural contexts in which it is used. For instance, in western societies, failure to follow certain social practices, such as wearing clothes in public, eating with cutlery, and defecating in private would be widely regarded as undignified.[1] Further, in certain social contexts markers of lower status, such as being forced to ride in the back of the bus, is undignified.[2] Similarly, enormous inequality in wealth and education along with severe material deprivation is undignified as it undermines the capacity to see poor people as human beings, or to lead a dignified life.[3]

It is also important to note that there are specific instances in the general and mental health contexts where inherent dignity is threatened by the nature of the illness or impairment itself and by the way care is delivered including through healthcare settings and the behaviour of others.[4] In the general health context, symptom control (especially pain relief), lack of privacy, and staff behaviour (talking down to the patient and acting as though they are inconvenienced by the patient) are the most common themes in dignity research.[5] Other dignity-related issues include: too much focus on surgery

[1] John Vorhaus, 'Dignity, Capability, and Profound Disability' (2015) 46(3) Metaphilosophy 462, 467 (hereafter Vorhaus, 'Dignity, Capability and Profound Disability'.

[2] Martha Nussbaum, 'The Capabilities of People with Cognitive Disabilities' (2009) 40(3–4) ibid 331, 336 (hereafter Nussbaum, 'Capabilities'); Alicia Ely Yamin, *Power, Suffering and the Struggle for Dignity: Human Rights Frameworks for Health and Why They Matter* (University of Pennsylvania Press 2016) (hereafter Yamin, *Power, Suffering and the Struggle for Dignity*).

[3] Yamin, *Power, Suffering and the Struggle for Dignity* (n 2) 152.

[4] Linda Barclay, 'In Sickness and in Dignity: A Philosophical Account of the Meaning of Dignity in Health Care' (2016) 61 Int J Nurs Stud 136, 137 (hereafter Barclay, 'In Sickness and Dignity').

[5] ibid 139.

Mental Health Law. Kay Wilson, Oxford University Press. © Kay Wilson 2021. DOI: 10.1093/oso/9780192843258.003.0005

without any emotional support, the need for the patient to assume an active role to be viewed as an equal co-player in care and treatment, wearing de-individuating hospital clothes, and disruptions to daily rhythm as part of being in a hospital.[6] Conversely, when patients are given too much autonomy by staff and they are expected to do more for themselves than they are capable of (and believing that they should be independent, are too ashamed to ask for help) also involves a loss of dignity.[7]

Loss of dignity in mental healthcare is also reported to include three categories of experiences: miscommunication (where staff and patients are unable to establish a rapport); rejection (where patients receive no or inadequate treatment); and humiliation/punishment (bad experiences such as removal of cigarettes and trauma imposed by the system, such as forced treatment and seclusion and restraint).[8] Ragnfrid Kogstad also identifies 'otherness' or the belief that some persons are not worth communicating with and a focus on purely medical rather than economic and social factors which contribute to mental impairment as undignified.[9] Other barriers to dignity include: not being 'heard' or involved in decision-making; not being offered alternatives to coercive interventions (such as counselling and time out); lack of privacy (constant supervision); physical characteristics of the setting (such as overcrowding, poor staffing levels and quality, impoverished or unclean environments);[10] feeling stigmatized and labelled and being judged for bizarre behaviour;[11] and being treated as if patients are on a conveyor belt or as if staff were following a recipe.[12]

Patients have generally reported feeling that their dignity has been respected when staff are polite, friendly, helpful, empathetic, respectful,[13] treat them as individuals and acknowledge them as a person, make patients feel accepted, appreciated, and encouraged[14] and take time for 'the little things'.[15] Hiding away in the nurses' station is antithetical to dignity and reinforces staff superiority, whereas continuous and regular interaction, being asked how you are, and playing cards with you, supports dignity and human rights.[16]

[6] Tina Seidelin Rasmussen and Charlotte Delmar, 'Dignity as an Empirical Lifeworld Construction—in the Field of Surgery in Denmark' (2014) 9 Int J Qual Stud Health Well-being 1 (hereafter Rasmussen and Delmar, 'Dignity as an Empirical Lifeworld Construction').

[7] Charlotte Delmar, 'The Interplay between Autonomy and Dignity: Summarizing Patients Voices' (2013) (16) Med Health Care Philos 975, 977 (hereafter Delmar, 'Interplay between Autonomy and Dignity').

[8] Ragnfrid Eline Kogstad, 'Protecting Mental Health Clients' Dignity—the Importance of Legal Control' (2009) 32 Int J Law Psychiatry 383, 385 (hereafter Kogstad, 'Protecting Mental Health Clients' Dignity').

[9] ibid 384.

[10] Mary Chambers and others, 'The Experiences of Detained Mental Health Service Users: Issues of Dignity in Care' (2014) 15 BMC Medical Ethics 50, 53–55 (hereafter Chambers, 'Detained Mental Health Service Users').

[11] Darlene Robinson, 'Dignity in Older Adults with Schizophrenia Residing in Assisted Living Facilities' (2018) 56(2) J Psychosoc Nurs 20, 24–25 (hereafter Robinson, 'Dignity in Older Adults with Schizophrenia').

[12] Frode Skorpen and others, 'Views Concerning Patient Dignity Among Relatives to Patients Experiencing Psychosis' (2016) 30 Scand J Caring Sci 117, 125 (hereafter Skorpen, 'Patient Dignity Among Relatives').

[13] Rasmussen and Delmar, 'Dignity as an Empirical Lifeworld Construction' (n 6) 2.

[14] Robinson, 'Dignity in Older Adults with Schizophrenia' (n 11) 23–24.

[15] Veronika Williams and others, '"It's the Little Things That Count": Healthcare Professionals' Views on Delivering Dignified Care: A Qualitative Study' (2016) J Adv Nurs 782, 785–6 (hereafter Williams, 'It's the Little Things That Count').

[16] Jasna Russo and Diana Rose "But What if Nobody's Going to Sit Down and Have a Real Conversation with You?" Service user/Survivor Perspectives on Human Rights' (2013) 12(4) J Public Ment Health 184,190

It can be seen then that there is some overlap between the loss of dignity by general and mental health patients, indicating that there is something about being a patient and staff attitudes that most people potentially find demeaning. Other aspects of having an undignified environment and undignified treatment by the healthcare system can and should be addressed separately from mental health law by systemic reform.

5.2 Can Inherent Dignity Act as a Limit on Autonomy?

My discussion of the meaning of inherent dignity indicates that it is wider than the concept of autonomy and that there may be situations in which the two concepts may clash. The purpose of this section is to explore the relationship between inherent dignity and autonomy further, including when inherent dignity may act as a limit on autonomy.

However, before I do so, it is necessary to look more closely at the meaning of autonomy and how it has been incorporated into the CRPD. That is, it is necessary to consider whether certain acts by persons with mental impairments, such as the refusal of hospital admission and psychiatric treatment, can or should always be regarded as being autonomous in the first place.

5.2.1 The Concept of Autonomy

There can be no doubt that autonomy is regarded as particularly precious by persons with disabilities as it has been historically denied and promoting it is a key objective of the CRPD.[17] In addition, agency, freedom from paternalistic institutions and controlling professionals, self-reliance, independence, and the ability to live a full life in the community has long been one of the 'projects' that has served the political purpose of unifying the diverse disability rights movement and gaining support from conservatives.[18] For some, autonomy and equality are the keys to all human rights protection, to inherent dignity, and to being able to claim and exercise rights.[19] Further, as David Bilchitz points out, if one is using an autonomy-based interpretation of inherent dignity, without giving dignity a wider meaning, the dire consequences of not recognizing the autonomy of some persons with disabilities (whether it is present or not) would be to exclude them as rights-holders.[20]

(hereafter, Russo and Rose, 'But What If Nobody's Going to Sit Down and Have a Real Conversation with You?').

[17] CRPD Preamble, [140]; Art 3(a).

[18] Samuel R Bagenstos, *Law and the Contradictions of the Disability Rights Movement* (Yale University Press 2009) 25–26 (hereafter Bagenstos, *Contradictions of the Disability Rights Movement*).

[19] Rhoda E Howard and Jack Donnelly, 'Human Dignity, Human Rights and Political Systems' (1986) 80(3) The Am Polit Sci Rev 801, 803 (hereafter Howard and Donnelly, 'Human Dignity'); James Griffin, *On Human Rights* (Oxford University Press 2008) (hereafter Griffin, *On Human Rights*).

[20] David Bilchitz, 'Dignity, Fundamental Rights and Legal Capacity: Moving Beyond the Paradigm Set by the General Comment on Article 12 of the Convention on the Rights of Persons with Disabilities' (2016) 32(3) SAJHR 410, 424 (hereafter Bilchitz, 'Dignity, Fundamental Rights and Legal Capacity').

While there are many human rights which are designed to protect autonomy albeit not without limitations (such as legal capacity, freedom of speech, and religion), there is no distinct 'right to autonomy' in international human rights law or in the CRPD.[21] The right of self-determination in Article 1 of the ICCPR applies to 'peoples', especially tribal and indigenous groups post-colonization and peoples within areas occupied by foreign powers, not individuals, which is why the CRPD drafters were told that 'self-determination' was a 'no-go' even though many preferred the concept of 'self-determination' to autonomy.[22] For instance, the European Disability Forum notes that 'whichever word is finally used (individual autonomy or self-determination) it has to be made clear that its meaning includes the right to make one's own choices and decisions which is a key principal'.[23] In the fourth session, Chile made the point that self-determination means personal self-determination.[24] That said, in the seventh session Canada changed its position by stating that it preferred autonomy over self-determination as self-determination had other connotations in international law and autonomy was concerned with the individual.[25] Australia agreed with Canada but argued (unsuccessfully) that Article 3(a) was problematic as there was no existing unfettered right of autonomy in international or domestic law and that references to autonomy would be better in the preamble.[26] Sarah Arduin has reviewed all the *travaux preparatoires* for the general principles (Article 3) in detail and she agrees that how the principle of autonomy applies to persons with no or limited autonomy remains very challenging and unclear.[27]

Frederic Megret observes that the absence of a right to autonomy in the CRPD could be based on:

> ... the idea that one might hesitate to describe autonomy as a right because it is in the nature of autonomy that it can be recognised or impeded, but not granted as such to individuals who are not, in essence, autonomous.[28]

[21] Frederic Megret, 'The Disabilities Convention: Human Rights of Persons with Disabilities or Disability Rights?' (2008) 30(2) Hum Rights Q 494, 512 (hereafter Megret, 'The Disabilities Convention'); Cf Piers Gooding, *A New Era for Mental Health Law and Policy: Supported Decision-Making and the UN Convention on the Rights of Persons with Disabilities* (Cambridge University Press 2017) 123 (hereafter Gooding, *A New Era*) (Gooding claims that there is a long history of a right to autonomy in human rights law, I believe this is incorrect).

[22] It is not stated who from the UN told the CRPD drafters to use 'autonomy' rather than 'self determination': Marianne Schulze, *Understanding the UN Convention on the Rights of Persons with Disabilities* (Handicap International 2009) 30 (hereafter Schulze, *Understanding the* UN *Convention*).

[23] CRPD Negotiation Archive, Second Session, 16 June 2003 to 21 June 2003 (hereafter Negotiation Archive, Second Session).

[24] CRPD Negotiation Archive, Fourth Session, 23 August to 3 September 2004 (hereafter Negotiation Archive, Fourth Session).

[25] CRPD Negotiation Archive, Seventh Session, 16 January to 3 February 2006, 30 January 2006 (hereafter Negotiation Archive, Seventh Session).

[26] ibid.

[27] Sarah Arduin 'Article 3 General Principles' in Ilias Bantekas, Michael Stein, and Dimitris Anastasiou (eds), *The UN Convention on the Rights of Persons with Disabilities: A Commentary* (Oxford University Press 2018) 94 (hereafter Arduin, 'Article 3').

[28] Megret, 'The Disabilities Convention' (n 20) 512.

Other theorists are also of the view that autonomy cannot be conceived of as a right or at best only as a highly qualified right. For example, Jennifer Nedlesky comments:

> I think it is most helpful not to designate it as a right as such—as indeed most constitutions do not. This is because of its strong internal dimension and the role of the individual work to develop it.[29]

Similarly, Alasdair Maclean observes that 'if conceived as a right then it is logically impossible for it to be absolute ... Thus, ignoring the problem of ability, any right to autonomy cannot be the freedom to do what one wants.'[30]

I will refer to the distinction between the legal recognition of autonomy (whether it is recognized or impeded) and the existence of autonomy in the following discussion of the concept of autonomy and the problem of whether certain acts by persons with mental impairments really are (or should be regarded as) autonomous. At this point, it is important to make clear that I agree with the concept of organizing society to maximize the autonomy of all persons, including persons with mental impairments, even if I have concerns about assuming that all acts are autonomous, especially in the so-called 'hard-cases'.[31]

The linguistic roots of the concept of autonomy can be found in the concepts of 'self-governance' or 'self-legislation' (auto-nomia).[32] That is, rather than to obey god, humans have the autonomy to make decisions for themselves.[33] There are many different theories of autonomy, such that autonomy can probably be best conceptualized as occurring on a continuum with different 'levels' of autonomy. Alasdair Maclean divides the autonomy continuum into three broad categories which he calls the libertarian approach, the liberal view and the communitarian approach.[34] The libertarian approach sees autonomy as simply self-determination.[35] It is pure freedom which regards persons rather than individual acts as autonomous, makes no demand for rationality, or any requirement for the person to be capable of acting morally.[36] As I discuss below, the libertarian approach is similar to the position of abolitionists. The liberal view requires rationality and focuses on autonomous acts rather than autonomous persons, whereas the communitarian view is the most onerous as it requires autonomous acts to be rational and have substantive moral content.[37]

Thus, the first requirement for all categories of autonomy is liberty, that is, freedom from interference by the state or others (which is the only requirement from a

[29] Jennifer Nedelsky, *Laws Relations: A Relational Theory of Self, Autonomy, and Law* (Oxford University Press 2011) 75 (hereafter Nedelsky, *Laws Relations*).

[30] Alasdair Maclean, *Autonomy, Informed Consent and Medical Law: A Relational Challenge* (Cambridge University Press 2009) 29 (hereafter Maclean, *Autonomy, Informed Consent and Medical Law*).

[31] Ronald Dworkin, *Justice for Hedgehogs* (Harvard University Press 2011) (hereafter Dworkin, *Justice for Hedgehogs*).

[32] Y Michael Barilan, 'Respect for Personal Autonomy, Human Dignity, and the Problems of Self-Directedness and Botched Autonomy' (2011) 36 J Med Philos 496, 497 (hereafter Barilan 'Botched Autonomy').

[33] Griffin, *On Human Rights* (n 19) 150.

[34] Maclean, *Autonomy, Informed Consent and Medical Law* (n 30) 11.

[35] ibid.

[36] ibid 13.

[37] ibid 11.

libertarian approach). That is, 'freedom to make one's own choices' is only one aspect of autonomy. Another external requirement of autonomy, argued by Mary Donnelly (drawing on the philosophy of Joseph Raz), is that a person has adequate choices and the development of autonomy-building measures to give persons more decision-making power.[38] However, it is also widely accepted (taking a liberal or communitarian view) that the freedom to make one's own decisions alone is not sufficient for autonomy.[39] The idea of 'self-governance' does not only refer to constraints on others, it also implies freedom from 'internal limitations that impede meaningful choice'[40] and some measure of control over oneself, not mere license. However, how rationality is determined and what level of rationality is required for a person to be regarded as autonomous is less clear. There are likely to be times where it is hard to distinguish between a decision that is difficult to comprehend and a decision which is truly irrational.[41] As noted by Genevra Richardson, the bar can be set higher or lower, but there is probably some point where a person is not autonomous.[42]

Many philosophers, like Kant, tend to imagine persons with a high level of autonomy who are able to fully appreciate all of the facts (without being swayed by emotion), make faultless inferences, and explain their decisions to others.[43] While Kant could be considered communitarian in the sense that his view of autonomy requires persons to act morally, it does not specify what that morality is other than that it be universal.

Michael Y Barilan also refers to a high level of autonomy:

> In addition to sincerity and related subjective states of mind, an autonomous position must stand the tests of coherence (logical structure of reasoning), of ontology (reasoning is not based on delusions or deceit), and of plasticity (absence of overtly rigid adherence to one's own beliefs). It may be said that the autonomous person acts out of a conscientious stance. However, this stance is not only action-oriented self-reflection, but is also open to reflections coming from other people. The person is open to deliberation, to "reason-giving", and to persuasion, not self-governance as such, but self-governance that is sincerely interactive with some other people and which targets substantial questions of value and personal choice.[44]

Conversely, informed consent, albeit the stalwart of medical ethics, is regarded as requiring a low level of autonomy or mere voluntariness.[45] At the other end of the

[38] Mary Donnelly, *Healthcare Decision-Making and the Law: Autonomy, Capacity and the Limits of Liberalism* (Cambridge Law, Medicine and Ethics 2010) 257 (hereafter Donnelly, *Healthcare Decision-Making and the Law*).

[39] Jillian Craigie, 'A Fine Balance: Reconsidering Patient Autonomy in Light of the UN Convention on the Rights of Persons with Disabilities' (2015) 29(6) Bioethics 398 (hereafter Craigie, 'A Fine Balance').

[40] Lawrence O Gostin, *Public Health Law: Power, Duty, Restraint* (2nd edn, University of California Press 2008) 49 (hereafter Gostin, *Public Health Law*).

[41] Maclean, *Autonomy, Informed Consent and Medical Law* (n 30) 52.

[42] Genevra Richardson, 'Mental Capacity in the Shadow of Suicide: What Can the Law Do?' (2013) 9 Int J Law Context 87, 96 (hereafter Richardson, 'Mental Capacity in the Shadow of Suicide').

[43] Griffin, *On Human Rights* (n 19).

[44] Barilan 'Botched Autonomy' (n 32) 500.

[45] ibid 497;Catriona Mackenzie and Wendy Rogers, 'Autonomy, Vulnerability and Capacity: A Philosophical Appraisal of the Mental Capacity Act' (2013) 9(1) Int J Law Context 37, 43 (Mackenzie and Rogers, 'Autonomy, Vulnerability and Capacity').

spectrum, he also refers to minimal levels of autonomy as 'natural self-directedness' a quality shared with animals.[46]

Similarly, Catriona Mackenzie and Wendy Rogers claim that autonomy requires freedom conditions, competence conditions, authenticity conditions, and accountability conditions.[47] Freedom conditions relate to a lack of external interference. Competence conditions are those minimal internal conditions and cognitive and emotional capabilities to be able to process information to make a decision, usually considered by the law to be informed consent.[48] Authenticity conditions are the extent to which persons regard a decision to be their own that is, the extent to which it expresses their practical identity, values, beliefs, and commitments.[49] It involves some level of reflective endorsement by the person.[50] Accountability conditions are a requirement that autonomous persons are prepared to be accountable for their decisions, by explaining the reasons for decisions to others and taking responsibility for the outcomes, however negative.[51]

Jennifer Nedelsky argues for a relational approach to autonomy. That is, she rejects conceptions of autonomy that equate it with independence and argues that autonomy needs to be understood within the social context of individuals' relationships with those around them and with wider social institutions, the state, the world, and the ways in which those relationships foster and impede their autonomy.[52] However, she also considers the importance of the internal aspects of autonomy, which she regards as the process of 'finding one's own law' where 'the word "finding" captures the importance of discernment in the exercise of the capacity for autonomy, and "law" points to the importance of commitments to oneself'.[53] To exercise autonomy requires effort. An autonomous person must exercise his or her judgment and deep self-reflection to decide which influences to accept and reject beyond personal preferences.[54] Nedelsky also acknowledges that there are internal forces (which fall well short of mental impairment) which are not always conducive to autonomy such as, 'fears and anxieties, and even a sense of duty'.[55] The process of exercising autonomy is cognitive, but it can involve tuning into one's body, learning from dreams, attending and following what gives one joy, playfulness, and humour.[56] It also involves consulting with and reflecting on the perspectives of others.[57] From this point of view then, autonomy is more than agency (or reflexive thoughtless actions),[58] it is not simply doing whatever one wants or thinks one wants, and not all decisions are autonomous.

46 Barilan 'Botched Autonomy' (n 32) 504.
47 Mackenzie and Rogers, 'Autonomy, Vulnerability and Capacity' (n 45) 41.
48 ibid 42.
49 ibid 43.
50 ibid.
51 ibid 45.
52 Nedelsky, *Laws Relations* (n 29) 118.
53 ibid 50.
54 ibid 58.
55 ibid 61.
56 ibid 50.
57 ibid 59–60.
58 Jaime Lindsey, 'Developing Vulnerability: A Situational Response to the Abuse of Women with Mental Disabilities' (2016) 24 Fem Leg Stud 295, 299 (hereafter Lindsey, 'Developing Vulnerability').

On an abolitionist interpretation, however, autonomy involves the removal of external barriers and the granting of decision-making freedom by the repeal of mental health law and the offering of decision-making support to assist those with mental impairments to make their own decisions. In the words of Elif Celik, autonomy is conceptualized by abolitionists as an 'achievable and valuable target through the guarantee of rights, rather than being a starting point to be granted rights'.[59] That is, there is no internal issue of autonomy that exists beyond a person's social and political environment.[60] The issue is not whether autonomy is present or absent, but rather trying to ascertain what persons want in accordance with their non-cognitive 'will' and 'preferences' and when all reasonable efforts have been made, 'the best interpretation of their will and preferences'.[61] Such an interpretation may not even be made by persons themselves, but rather by a facilitator who analyses what is known about the person and tries to determine what the person would have wanted.[62] Therefore, the abolitionist approach to autonomy seeks to work around any requirement for an internal capacity for autonomy such as being able to process and weigh information, exercising judgment, or engaging in self-conscious reflection. However, it does encourage consultation with others with respect to the offering of decision-making support, although this is not mandatory as a person is entitled to reject some or all types of support.[63] The focus is on the authenticity requirement in that the point of trying to determine a person's will and preferences is on reaching a decision which is consistent with a person's values, beliefs, and life goals. Jillian Craigie argues that autonomy in the CRPD requires a fine balance between achieving autonomy and facilitating authenticity and self-expression.[64]

However, despite the emphasis on authenticity in the abolitionist approach, in the 'hard cases' a person's will and preference may be difficult to determine: persons may not express any will or preference in the present or the past, his or her will and preferences could be unclear or confusing, and a person's 'will' and 'preference' may even be contradictory. The primacy given to autonomy assumes that humans are decision-makers who always know what we want.[65] In perhaps the most difficult cases a person's 'will' and 'preference' is clear but it may appear to be a symptom of the person's mental impairment, rather than their actual 'will' and 'preference'. In fact, the sudden and extreme break between a person's current expressed preferences and their diachronic identity is characteristic of many serious types of mental impairment.[66] For instance,

[59] Elif Celik, 'The Role of the CRPD in Rethinking the Subject of Human Rights' (2017) 21(7) Int J Hum Rights 933, 941 (hereafter Celik, 'Rethinking the Subject of Human Rights').

[60] Craigie, 'A Fine Balance' (n 39) 401.

[61] Committee on the Rights of Persons with Disabilities 'General Comment No 1 (2014) Article 12: Equal Recognition before the Law' (11 April 2014) UN Doc CRPD/C/GC/1, [21] (hereafter General Comment 1).

[62] Anna Arstein-Kerslake and Eilionoir Flynn, 'The General Comment on Article 12 of the Convention on the Rights of Persons with Disabilities: A Roadmap for Equality before the Law' (2016) 20 Int J Hum Rights 484 (hereafter Arstein-Kerslake and Flynn, 'The General Comment on Article 12').

[63] General Comment 1 (n 62) [19].

[64] Craigie, 'A Fine Balance' (n 39) 402.

[65] Meredith Stone and others, 'Estranged Relations: Coercion and Care in Narratives of Supported Decision-Making in Mental Healthcare' (2020) 46 Med Humanit 62, 69 (hereafter Stone, 'Estranged Relations').

[66] Jillian Craigie, 'Capacity, Value Neutrality and the Ability to Consider the Future' (2013) 9(1) Int J Law Context 4, 6 (hereafter Craigie, 'Capacity, Value Neutrality'); Craig Edwards, 'Beyond Mental Competence' (2010) 27(3) J Appl Philos 273, 277 (hereafter Edwards, 'Beyond Mental Competence').

persons with bipolar disorder may have clear preferences in the manic phase of their illness, which may be at odds with their usual long-term motivating commitments. Persons with anorexia nervosa may have strong preferences to refuse or restrict food that are incompatible with their desire not to die.[67] In situations where a person's 'will' conflicts with their 'preferences', George Szmukler has proposed that priority should be given to respecting a person's 'will' as it is likely to be closer to representing their stable, long-held beliefs and life goals (or authenticity), rather than their more fleeting preferences.[68] That said, it may be difficult to distinguish between a person's will and their preferences[69] and it is also unclear whether having one's 'preferences' overridden to respect one's 'will' would be experienced as any less forced or be less traumatic than any other substitute decision. Nevertheless, it is hard to see how essentially guessing a person's will and preference makes him or her autonomous or honours his or her authenticity, not to mention being a process which lacks transparency.[70] In short, taking an expansive view of autonomy may be inclusive, but it may also make the concept of autonomy meaningless.

Supports, however, may not be sufficient for all persons with mental impairments regardless of the adequacy of that support, or severity of their impairments or the complexity of the decision, see discussion in Chapter 7 section 7.5.2 below. Persons may refuse all support potentially leaving them perilously close to abandonment. As pointed out by Eva Kittay 'an ethic of care requires that what is offered can be taken up by the person cared for. Unless the provisions are appropriate they are not care'.[71] Therefore, even taking the abolitionist interpretation of the CRPD, there are still likely to be some decisions by some persons with mental impairment which are not autonomous, despite being recognized as such by the abolitionist approach.

Of course, the effect of my argument is that there may be some persons, who by reason of their impairments, are permanently 'locked out' of the benefits of autonomy. In my view legal recognition of autonomy is not enough to make a decision autonomous in practice where autonomy may not actually exist (see observations of Frederic Megret, Jennifer Nedlesky, and Alistair MacClean about the nonsensical concept of a right to autonomy in section 5.2.1 above). However, it does not by extension mean that persons with mental impairment lack inherent dignity, or human rights protection, access to support, or the ability to participate in shaping their life at all.

[67] Craigie, 'Capacity, Value Neutrality' (n 66) 4; Edwards, 'Beyond Mental Competence' (n 66) 279.

[68] George Szmukler, 'The UN Convention on the Rights of Persons with Disabilities: "Rights, Will and Preferences" in Relation to Mental Health Disabilities' (2017) 54 Int J Law Psychiatry 90, 94 (hereafter Szmukler, 'Rights, Will and Preferences'); George Szmukler, '"Capacity", "Best Interests", "Will and Preferences" and the UN Convention on the Rights of Persons with Disabilities' (2019) 18(1) World Psychiatry 34 (hereafter Szmukler, 'Capacity, Best Interests and Will and Preferences').

[69] Tilman Steinert, 'The UN Committee's Interpretation of "Will and Preferences" Can Violate Human Rights' ibid 45 (hereafter Steinert, 'UN Committee's Interpretation of "Will and Preferences"').

[70] Emily Jackson, 'From 'Doctor Knows Best' to Dignity: Placing Adults Whole Lack Capacity at the Centre of Decisions About Their Medical Treatment' (2018) 81(2) MLR 247, 274 (hereafter Jackson, 'From 'Doctor Knows Best' to Dignity'); Matthew Burch, 'Autonomy, Respect, and the Rights of Persons with Disabilities in Crisis' (2017) 34(3) J Appl Philos 396–97 (hereafter Burch, 'The Rights of Persons with Disabilities in Crisis').

[71] Eva Feder Kittay, 'The Ethics of Care, Dependence, and Disability' (2011) 24(1) Ratio Juris 49, 56 (hereafter Kittay, 'The Ethics of Care').

5.2.2 The Limitation of Autonomy by Inherent Dignity

Assuming that persons with mental impairments have autonomy for certain acts, including refusing psychiatric treatment, it is possible for that autonomy to conflict with a person's inherent dignity. Such conflicts are more likely to occur where autonomy is given a very expansive meaning as it is by the abolitionists. Such conflicts are a vexed issue not just in the disability context, but in general international human rights law.

For a conflict between inherent dignity and autonomy to occur, inherent dignity must have an objective rather than subjective meaning and a meaning that is wider and different from autonomy (as I have argued). That is, there must be certain autonomous acts which can be regarded as impugning the inherent dignity, not just of the individual, but of humanity as a collective.[72] The effect of a collective concept of inherent dignity in setting a standard for what it means to be human can be illiberal, and where those standards are aimed at protecting the person, paternalistic and, at worst, moralistic. It also follows that individuals would not be able to use their autonomy to waive their inherent dignity as the inherent dignity of the human species is not theirs to waive.[73] Further by definition, something which is inherent cannot be waived. To use the distinction of Dereck Beyleveld and Roger Brownsword, inherent dignity as a collective term, is being used in a way which is constraining, rather than empowering individual choice.[74]

The conflict between autonomy and dignity can be seen in prohibitions on the grounds of protecting one's inherent dignity with respect to: enslaving oneself, voluntary cannibalism, and peep shows.[75] However, probably the most widely discussed example in the literature is the case of *Wackenheim v France* or 'the dwarf-throwing case', in which Mr Wackenheim argued unsuccessfully before the ICPPR Committee, that he ought to be able to choose his work and that respect for his autonomy, together with the dignity of having a job (as opposed to being unemployed), should outweigh what others regard as the indignity of being thrown.[76] On the one hand, there are those commentators who are sympathetic to Mr Wackenheim and prefer a more individualistic concept of inherent dignity. For example, Michael Rosen argues that the strong obligation of states to respect inherent dignity, does not apply in the same way to individuals who ought to be entitled to behave in an undignified way provided that they do so willingly, with full awareness of the consequences and where no one is harmed.[77]

[72] Marcus Duwell, 'Human Dignity: Concepts, Discussions, Philosophical Perspectives' in Marcus Duwell and others (eds), *The Cambridge Handbook of Human Dignity* (Cambridge University Press 2014) 36 (hereafter Duwell, 'Human Dignity').

[73] Christopher McCrudden, 'Human Dignity and Judicial Interpretation of Human Rights' (2008) 19(4) EUR J Int Law 655, 705 (hereafter McCrudden, 'Human Dignity').

[74] Deryck Beyleveld and Roger Brownsword, *Human Dignity in Bioethics and Biolaw* (Oxford University Press 2001) 34 (hereafter Beyleveld and Brownsword, *Human Dignity in Bioethics*); Genevra Richardson, 'Involuntary Treatment, Human Dignity and Human Rights' in Marcia H Rioux and others (eds), *Critical Perspectives on Human Rights and Disability Law* (Martinus Nijhoff Publishers 2011) 137, 139 (hereafter Richardson, 'Involuntary Treatment, Human Dignity and Human Rights').

[75] John Kleinig, 'Paternalism and Human Dignity' (2017) 11 Crim Law Philos 19 (hereafter Kleinig, 'Paternalism').

[76] *Wackenheim v France*, Communication No 854/1999, 15 July 2002 CCPR/C/75/854/1999 (hereafter *Wackenheim v France*).

[77] Michael Rosen, *Dignity: Its History and Meaning* (Harvard University Press 2012), 69 (hereafter, Rosen, *Dignity*).

Marcus Duwell is concerned that the prohibition on dwarf-tossing is an example of where some societal groups impose their ideals of human value on others.[78] Similarly, he has argued that the ICCPR Committee did not give enough weight to the dignity of choosing one's own work, having a job, and being self-supporting.

On the other hand, there are those who argue that ICCPR Committee was correct and that inherent dignity ought to be understood in a collective-sense and as requiring a duty to oneself. That is, allowing one person to compromise their dignity by allowing themselves to be treated as an object, or to use Kantian language to give oneself away for a price, is degrading for all dwarves and humanity as a whole. As Deryck Beyleveld and Roger Brownsword argue, the idea that people with dwarfism may recover a sense of self-esteem must be a form of 'false consciousness' as it is incompatible with the indignity of being thrown.[79] Similarly, Jeremy Waldron argues for the importance of giving effect to inherent dignity as its own value and taking into account the surrounding context in understanding why individuals ought not to be able to choose to act in an undignified manner.[80] Simon Coghlan also observes:

> Michael Rosen submits that Monsieur Wackenheim, a man with dwarfism who insisted that his dignity was offended by a ban on dwarf-tossing, got a "raw deal." Rosen regards dwarf-tossing as on the same moral level as undignified drunken behaviour. This overlooks the importance of the fact that dwarfs have historically been treated as something like circus freaks.[81]

The state has always had a role in regulating the labour market and restricting the free choice of individuals exposing themselves to various kinds of harm. To this extent all labour law in insisting on occupational health and safety is paternalistic, even if it is not usually thought of as being so. However, I would add that a state which takes human dignity so seriously as to prohibit a person from gaining income from dwarf-tossing also has an obligation to prevent discrimination against people with dwarfism in all aspects of life and to ensure that people with dwarfism are able to access other meaningful occupations to enable them to live a dignified life.

While there is always some danger that if a concept like 'inherent dignity' is defined too broadly that it may become what Marcus Duwell fears will be a 'trojan horse' which undermines human rights,[82] I argue that with respect to the context of the debate about the future of mental health law, such concerns are exaggerated. While 'inherent dignity' as a collective norm may be to some degree 'illiberal', human rights are not the same as liberalism (even if western interpretations have always taken a liberal slant and given more weight to civil and political rights), and it is in the nature of human rights in setting universal standards of acceptable conduct that it will of necessity be illiberal in the sense of limiting individual liberty at the edges.

[78] Duwell, 'Human Dignity' (n 72) 29.
[79] Beyleveld and Brownsword, *Human Dignity in Bioethics* (n 74) 27.
[80] Waldron, 'Dignity Rights and Responsibilities' (n 56) 1107, 1133.
[81] Coghlan, 'The Moral Depth of Human Dignity' (n 76) 71, 79.
[82] Duwell, 'Human Dignity' (n 72) 29.

The issue then becomes when and to what extent does inherent dignity place limits on the autonomy of persons with mental impairments and what are those limits? In the disability context, Brendan Kelly argues that in some circumstances respecting the inherent dignity of persons with mental impairments may justify coercive interventions.[83] He also argues that inherent dignity should become the new civil commitment criteria.[84] However, the contested and amorphous meaning of inherent dignity makes it too unclear to act as an effective and easy to apply criterion and it should instead be used as a general human rights principle as it currently is. As I argue in Chapter 8, there may be times where inherent dignity may justify limited involuntary detention and psychiatric treatment. At a minimum, such acts would include those which are self-destructive and possibly those which offend widely accepted norms of dignified behaviour. Greater weight ought to be given to preserving inherent dignity where a person may have diminished autonomy. Such an approach would permit limited paternalism.

Of course, in western societies, where the autonomous liberal subject is the 'norm' and independence is highly celebrated, there are those who strongly object to any limitations on autonomy and see almost all state interference, whatever the degree or justification, as over-reach. Hence, the word 'paternalism' generally has negative and pejorative connotations, and the often-used description that something 'smacks of paternalism' is usually enough to automatically dismiss it (usually without further analysis). However, the idea that autonomy for its own sake can be over-valued is starting to attract interest with respect to persons *without* disabilities.[85] The ideal of the autonomous liberal subject has also been criticized as being unrealistic and as failing to recognize the nature of embodied human vulnerability, reinforcing inequality and injustice.[86] Even James Griffin accepts that autonomy is not an unalloyed good: if it is too exaggerated it may undermine justified deference to authority or trust in others.[87] Further, the autonomy-paternalism binary may not accurately or completely capture caring human relations in the disability context. As observed by Eva Kittay:

> ... paternalism is the only alternative to autonomy when autonomy is the norm of all human interaction. Cooperative, respectful, attentive relations are, I suggest, better alternatives than paternalistic responses toward those who depend on us in times of need.[88]

Recent research by Meredith Stone and colleagues also indicates that for some persons with mental impairment 'having agency in making decisions was not their biggest concern; that what worried them most was "*not that others boss you about, but*

[83] Brendan Kelly, 'Dignity, Human Rights and the Limits of Mental Health Legislation' (2014) 31 Ir J Psychol 75, 75 (hereafter Kelly, 'Dignity').

[84] ibid.

[85] Sarah Conly, *Against Autonomy: Justifying Coercive Paternalism* (Cambridge University Press 2012) (hereafter Conly, *Against Autonomy*); Cass Sunstein, *Why Nudge?: The Politics of Libertarian Paternalism* (Yale University Press 2014) (hereafter Sunstein, *Why Nudge?*).

[86] Martha Albertson Fineman, 'The Vulnerable Subject and the Responsive State' (2010) 60 Emory Law J 251 (hereafter Fineman, 'The Vulnerable Subject').

[87] Griffin, *On Human Rights* (n 19) 153.

[88] Kittay, 'The Ethics of Care' (n 71) 55.

that nobody cares'".[89] Stepping back and allowing a person with mental impairment to make their own decisions without coercion when what they really need is 'somebody to give you a kick up the pants' can be perceived by some persons with mental impairment as a lack of caring, buck-passing, and refusing to take responsibility on the part of clinicians and family members.[90] Put simply there may be times where non-coercion is not consistent with good care,[91] that what a person *wants* is not what they *need*. Therefore, the question which needs to be asked is to what extent are abolitionists complaints really about lack of recognition for autonomy even for acts which are arguably not autonomous, or just about services which are underfunded and leave people feeling unimportant and uncared for?

The most famous opponent of paternalism is widely regarded as John Stuart Mill who claimed that, 'the only purpose for which power can be rightfully exercised over any member of a civilised community, against his will, is to prevent harm to others'.[92] However, as discussed in Chapter 2 section 2.3, even Mill did not extend his anti-paternalism to persons who did not have sufficient maturity and experience and ordinary cognitive abilities.[93] While such a qualification is necessarily exclusionary of some persons, the liberty advocated was not without boundaries: it was expected that external regulation was unnecessary as common sense, experience, rationality, and self-interest would act as self-imposed controls on behaviour, especially destructive, degrading, or senseless behaviour. Further, the liberty advanced was intended not just to be an individual, but a social good. While it did not prohibit certain self-regarding behaviour such as drunkenness where it did not obstruct a person's social responsibilities,[94] it was assumed that most people would not be drinking themselves into the gutter and that the real purpose of defending liberty was to promote continuous self-improvement and to release individuals from the bonds of social convention and mediocrity.[95] In the words of John Kleinig, 'a liberal society is grounded in a conception of human dignity that eschews degradation and debasement, whether or not they are self-chosen'.[96]

Further, even dignity theorists who adopt an autonomy-based account of dignity, such as Kant, Pico della Mirandola, and Ronald Dworkin (mentioned above) anticipate that people will use their autonomy to act morally, to choose an 'angelic' life, or to exercise their self-respect and authenticity responsibly. Michael Barilan would even go so far to say that those whose life seems like a random series of self-injurious and self-degrading acts with no consistent pattern of aiming at some good, create the problem of 'botched autonomy'.[97] The problem, of course, with taking too expansive a view of autonomy, to the point in which it includes any indicators of 'will' or 'preference' no matter how irrational, is that those self-imposed boundaries on destructive

89 Stone, 'Estranged Relations' (n 65) 69.
90 ibid.
91 ibid.
92 John Stewart Mill, in David Bronwich and George Kateb (eds), *On Liberty* (Yale University Press 2003) 80 (hereafter Mill, *On Liberty*).
93 ibid 132.
94 ibid 160.
95 ibid 129.
96 Kleinig, 'Paternalism' (n 75) 36.
97 Barilan, 'Botched Autonomy' (n 32) 497.

and degrading behaviour may not exist and the results may have serious consequences which the person may not anticipate or want.

Thus, while mental health care can be delivered in a way in which it does not respect a person's inherent dignity discussed above, there are times where a mental impairment and the absence of intervention itself may result in a loss of dignity. It is not (as noted above in Chapter 4 section 4.2.3) unheard of for people to regard loss of functioning and those things that make us uniquely human due to illness and old age, as humiliating and undignified, and in the most extreme situations such concerns undergird cries for 'death with dignity'. Brendan Kelly refers to the example of persons with mental impairment who are living in filth and squalor that is a danger to their physical health and is at a standard which would be generally regarded as below what is fit for a human being.[98] He also points out that for the majority of persons with mental impairment, it is not involuntary detention and treatment which is undignified, but lack of access to any treatment at all.[99] With respect to persons with mental impairment who may lack 'insight' into their condition he argues:

> an individual with psychosis, who is untreated, homeless, and singing aloud or undressing in the street is, by most objective standards, in an undignified position, but the individual may not perceive this indignity subjectively owing to the effects of illness. An individual without such a mental disorder in a similar position is more likely to perceive their situation differently, experience subjective indignity, and take corrective action.[100]

That is, such behaviour may not only be regarded as undignified in an objective sense in violating widely accepted social norms, but also subjectively, in that persons concerned may well cringe if they saw a video recording of themselves when they are well. Some of these indignities are undoubtedly contributed to by social causes: a person could (and arguably should) be offered housing, and a person could be asked to tone it down and be offered clothes. One would also hope that a compassionate society would make allowances for persons behaving in such a manner by reason of their mental impairment. This example, however, is of course mild compared to other arguably autonomous, but undignified acts, with more serious and irreversible consequences, such as self-harm or suicide. For example, a woman who tries to cut off her healthy right arm to quiet the voices in her head,[101] a person who is starving to death who refuses to eat for fear of becoming obese,[102] a woman who believed she would reach an enlightened state if she jumped off a building and landed with her head in the right place,[103] or

[98] Kelly, 'Dignity' (n 83) 75; Richard M Duffy and Brendan D Kelly, 'Rights, Laws and Tensions: A Comparative Analysis of the Convention on the Rights of Persons with Disabilities and the Who Resource Book on Mental Health, Human Rights and Legislation' (2017) 54 Int J Law Psychiatry 26, 33 (hereafter Duffy and Kelly, 'Rights, Laws and Tensions').

[99] Kelly, 'Dignity' (n 83) 75.

[100] ibid.

[101] Kate Richards, *Madness: A Memoir* (Penguin Group 2013), 1 (hereafter Richards, *Madness*).

[102] *Re E (Medical Treatment Anorexia)* [2012] EWHC 1639 (COP) (hereafter *Re E (Medical Treatment Anorexia)*).

[103] Piers Gooding, 'Navigating the 'Flashing Amber Lights' of the Right to Legal Capacity in the United Nations Convention on the Rights of Persons with Disabilities: Responding to Major Concerns' (2015) 15 Hum Rights Law Rev 45, 61–62 (hereafter Gooding, 'Navigating the 'Flashing Amber Lights').

persons who harm themselves as a distraction or outlet for their immediate psychological distress and pain, without thinking of the consequences.[104]

Similarly, Anne Plumb gives a number of examples of risky actions by persons with mental impairment:

> a survivor who wrote on an on-line forum about lighting candles to keep evil influences at bay (her house burned down); a friend of mine who thought he could stop buses by standing ahead of them with his arms outstretched; and I very nearly stepped into a bath of boiling water in the belief that I needed to demonstrate faith in God (aka mystics running over hot coals). Authorities have responded to these risks in ways totally unacceptable to many of us, but should this mean that no-one should intervene?[105]

Of course, even if an act is undignified it does not necessarily follow that it justifies coercion or legal intervention. John Kleinig, for example, has argued that even though loss of dignity can justify limited paternalism, there are a range of responses to it.[106] Legal intervention, he argues, should be reserved only for the most serious, irreversible, and self-destructive indignities (for example, enslavement, cannibalism, and paid gladiatorial contests).[107] Other less coercive responses include licensing, restricting certain activities to the private realm (eg extreme sadomasochism), giving information and warnings, and using social work instead of law.[108] Such an approach requires a certain amount of subjective line-drawing and Kleinig is a bit too permissive, especially with respect to how the state should respond to undignified matters involving women like humiliating pornography or demeaning peep shows and women's 'choices' in a patriarchal society. But, Kleinig's work is nonetheless valuable in demonstrating that there are multiple responses to preserving a person's dignity and ways of balancing autonomy, dignity, and limited paternalism, an argument which forms the basis of Chapter 8. It is also akin to the 'least restrictive alternative' principle of mental health law.

One of the concerns of disability activists is that the medical discretion given to psychiatrists under mental health law creates tension between the competing knowledges of the doctor and the patient, empowering the doctor to 'judge' the patient.[109] This structure creates a power imbalance between doctor and patient and it is argued that this is degrading to the patient's inherent dignity. A further concern is the same as that long held by anti-paternalists, such as Mill, that mental health law overrides the presumption that the patient knows their body and situation best and it thereby permits

[104] *Nottinghamshire Healthcare NHS Trust (Applicant) v RC (Respondent)* [2014] EWHC 1317 (COP), 7 and 37 (in that case the court held that RC sometimes lacked capacity when he cut himself, but that he still had capacity to make an advance decision under the Mental Capacity Act 2005 (England and Wales) to refuse a blood transfusion on religious grounds that were unrelated to his mental disorder) (hereafter *Nottinghamshire Healthcare NHS Trust (Applicant) v RC*).

[105] Jillian Craigie and others, 'Legal Capacity, Mental Capacity and Supported Decision-Making: Report from a Panel Event' (2019) 62 Int J Law Psychiatry 160, 190 (hereafter Craigie, 'Panel Event').

[106] Kleinig, 'Paternalism' (n 75) 33.

[107] ibid 33–35.

[108] ibid.

[109] Kogstad, 'Protecting Mental Health Clients' Dignity' (n 8) 384.

the doctor to interfere wrongly. This is what Cass Sunstein refers to as the Epistemic Argument or objection to paternalism.[110] However, there are two responses to this issue: the first is that there may actually be times where persons are not the best judge of their situation or of how to maintain their dignity, and the second is that having others decide does not necessarily mean that the decision cannot be informed by the person's knowledge of themselves and their situation. This is discussed in Chapter 8, especially sections 8.3 and 8.4.2.

Paternalists have drawn on research in psychology and behavioural economics which indicates that the reasoning ability of all humans is far more flawed than philosophers like Mill assumed and that people frequently make choices which undermine their overall life goals, often with drastic consequences.[111] While the effect of mental impairment on decision-making is unknown and depends on the type and severity of the impairment, as well as fluctuations over-time, there is also reason to believe that persons with mental impairments may not always be good decision-makers or 'know better' than others. Psychiatrists are not the only authorities on mental impairment or its effects on a particular person, but they do have extensive training and can contribute knowledge drawn from their clinical experience of treating other persons with similar problems.

Further, many persons with mental impairment themselves admit that their mental impairment can distort their reasoning and their decision-making ability. For example, many persons with anorexia nervosa report that their impairment is controlling and that compulsion can assist them in temporarily removing responsibility for their recovery.[112] Similarly in *Cambridge University Hospitals NHS Foundation Trust v BF*[113] a woman suffering from severe ovarian cancer and paranoid schizophrenia withdrew the consent she originally gave to a total abdominal hysterectomy that was necessary to save her life when she was well, because 'bad voices' and 'bad machines' were controlling her mind.[114]

Involuntary detention and psychiatric treatment has been viewed as depriving the person with mental impairment of the so-called 'dignity of risk' a term that was coined by Robert Perske in 1972 after comparing American and Scandinavian approaches in providing care to persons with cognitive impairments.[115] This is also discussed in Chapter 3, section 3.3.10. It is based on his observation that if persons with cognitive impairments are too overprotected and emotionally smothered, they essentially end up living in a gilded cage: completely safe, but without the freedom that gives life excitement and allows people to grow and develop.[116] However, the 'dignity of risk' was never intended to promote recklessness; rather it was emphasized to allow a person to experience fair and prudent risk-taking involved in 'normal' life experiences like using public transport, having a romantic relationship, living in one's own apartment, and

[110] Sunstein, *Why Nudge?* (n 85) 7.
[111] ibid; Conly, *Against Autonomy* (n 85).
[112] Jackson, 'From 'Doctor Knows Best' to Dignity' (n 70) 271–72.
[113] [2016] EWCOP 26.
[114] ibid.
[115] Robert Perske, 'The Dignity of Risk and the Mentally Retarded' (1972) 10(1) Ment Retard 1 (hereafter Perske 'The Dignity of Risk').
[116] ibid.

working on normal machinery.[117] It is also an issue in which what applies to persons with cognitive impairments may not apply in the same way to persons with mental impairments, who are more unpredictable, may deteriorate over time and involve impulses to harm oneself or others. As Piers Gooding observes 'critics could reasonably point out that some types of risk, whether during mental health crises or otherwise, carry no dignity whatsoever'.[118]

There may also be times where involuntary detention and psychiatric treatment will restore autonomy to a person with mental impairment and refusal would be to accept a future where all of a person's decisions are tainted by compromised autonomy. There is a parallel here with persons losing their autonomy by agreeing to enslave themselves. Piers Gooding argues, drawing on the philosophy of John Rawls, that respect for diversity means that people ought to be able to reject autonomy and freedom as central tenets of the good life, even if that means enslaving themselves.[119] However, there is also an argument here that voluntarily giving up a person's autonomy (such as through agreeing to slavery), involves a violation of inherent dignity and should be prohibited on that basis. As Jeremy Waldron observes, to conceive of slavery as a matter of personal choice is to weaken inherent dignity and to turn it into something that is no longer conceptualized as inalienable.[120] He warns that if people 'do that they should be aware of how much of a hard-fought heritage of natural rights ideas they are giving up and how bad a bargain that has proved in the past'.[121]

5.3 Conclusion

In this chapter I have explored how the concept of inherent dignity in the CRPD and human rights literature might apply in the mental health context. I have also explored the meaning and scope of the concept of autonomy and which concept should prevail where autonomy and inherent dignity are in tension. I have argued, contrary to the broad definition propounded by abolitionists, that autonomy is a matter of fact rather than a right which may not always be present even with the use of support. However, where autonomy does exist, I have argued for a moderate position that autonomy is part of but not superior to the concept of inherent dignity. I have argued that in situations where a person's autonomous acts are degrading, violate widely accepted norms, and are likely to be irreversible, inherent dignity may override autonomy. The priority given to inherent dignity is stronger where autonomy is likely to be seriously compromised. However, not all violations of inherent dignity justify involuntary detention and psychiatric treatment, other less invasive intervention may need to be tried first.

[117] ibid.
[118] Gooding, *A New Era* (n 21) 129.
[119] ibid 141–43.
[120] Waldron, 'Dignity Rights and Responsibilities' (n 56) 1129.
[121] ibid.

6
The Interpretive Compass Part 2: Theories of Equality and Non-Discrimination

6.1 Introduction

In Chapters 4 and 5 I have explored the first part of the 'interpretive compass' which I am using as my conceptual framework to interpret the CRPD (see Chapter 1 section 1.4.1) being the concept and application of 'inherent dignity' to the call for the abolition of mental health law. In this Chapter and Chapter 7, I consider the second part of the 'interpretive compass' being the concepts of equality and non-discrimination and participation. Participation is an element of equality and non-discrimination, but it is also an important CRPD human rights principle in its own right, although it is more straightforward and has a somewhat smaller literature, so I cover it less extensively, than the more contested and difficult concepts of equality and non-discrimination. As I did for inherent dignity, in this chapter I examine the meaning and scope of the concepts of equality and non-discrimination in the CRPD and international human rights law, and in Chapter 7, I set out the difficulties of applying the concepts of equality, non-discrimination, and participation to the Abolition with Support model and the context of persons with mental impairment.

Equality and non-discrimination are often described as being 'at the heart of the CRPD',[1] and there is no doubt that the CRPD is a group-specific equality and non-discrimination convention in the mould of the Convention on the Elimination of Racial Discrimination (CERD) and the Convention on the Elimination of Discrimination Against Women (CEDAW). The CRPD text is peppered with the terms 'equality' and 'non-discrimination' in the preamble, the general principles (Article 3) and two specific clauses within the main body of the convention (Articles 4 and 5). The phrase 'on an equal basis with others' appears in the text of almost every right. Indeed, equal[ity] forms the 'liet motif of the CRPD'[2] and is repeated at least thirty-one times throughout the Convention.[3]

[1] Jenny E Goldschmidt, 'New Perspectives on Equality: Towards Transformative Justice through the Disability Convention?' (2017) 35(1) Nord J Hum Rights 1, 7 (hereafter Goldschmidt, 'New Perspectives on Equality'); Theresia Degener, 'Disability in a Human Rights Context' (2016) 5 Laws 5 (Degener, 'Disability in a Human Rights Context').

[2] Oddny Mjoll Arnardottir, 'A Future of Multidimensional Disadvantage Equality?' in Oddny Mjoll Arnardottir and Gerard Quinn (eds), *The UN Convention on the Rights of Persons with Disabilities: European and Scandinavian Perspectives* (Martinus Nijhoff Publishers 2009) 65 (hereafter Arnardottir, 'Multidimensional Disadvantage').

[3] Frederic Megret and Dianah Msipa, 'Global Reasonable Accommodation: How the Convention on the Rights of Persons with Disabilities Changes the Way We Think About Equality' (2014) 30 SAJHR 253, 253 (hereafter Megret and Msipa, 'Global Reasonable Accommodation').

Mental Health Law. Kay Wilson, Oxford University Press. © Kay Wilson 2021. DOI: 10.1093/oso/9780192843258.003.0006

Equality and non-discrimination have assumed importance in the CRPD for two specific reasons. The first is the United Nations General Assembly saw the CRPD purely as an 'implementation treaty' in which existing human rights were to be applied to the lived experiences of persons with disabilities.[4] That is, the drafters were not supposed to create any new rights.[5] Therefore, the concepts of equality and non-discrimination were often used as a proxy to expand the scope of the CRPD, while still keeping the CRPD within the ambit of the pre-existing rights known to human rights law.[6] Secondly, under the British version of the social model of disability, which dominated the approach of civil society groups during the treaty negotiations (although, I have argued in favour of the *interactive* model of social disability see Chapter 1, section 1.4.1.2 and 1.4.1.3), the phenomenon of disability itself is conceptualized as socially constructed discrimination and inequality, rather than as having only a medical basis in impairment.[7] Therefore, it is the goal of the CRPD to eliminate the inferior social status of persons with disability so that persons with disability are recognized as being different but equal.

However, despite the strong and repeated commitment to equality and non-discrimination in the CRPD, what this actually means is far from clear. Unfortunately, the term 'equality' and the key phrase 'on an equal basis with others' (originally, 'on an equal footing')[8] are not defined anywhere in the text of the CRPD, including the definition of discrimination in Article 2. Like dignity and autonomy, equality is a highly contested concept in law, politics, and philosophy which has been criticized as being both an empty concept,[9] and for evoking too many different meanings.[10] While the CRPD Committee's General Comment 6 on Equality and Non-discrimination[11] offers some further elaboration on the meanings of equality and non-discrimination in the CRPD, as argued in section 6.2 and Chapter 7 below, it has probably only scratched the surface of the issues about equality and non-discrimination with respect to the abolition of mental health law.

Oddny Mojoll Arnadottir has argued that the significance of the meaning of equality in the CRPD is not static, but is evolving and must be understood within the wider context of human rights law.[12] According to General Comment No 6:

[4] Andrea Broderick, *The Long and Winding Road to Equality and Inclusion for Persons with Disabilities: The United Nations Convention on the Rights of Persons with Disabilities* (Intersentia 2015) 65 (Broderick, *The Long and Winding Road to Equality*).

[5] Arnardottir 'Multidimensional Disadvantage' (n 2) 44.

[6] ibid.

[7] ibid.

[8] CRPD Negotiation Archives, Fourth Session, 23 August to 3 September 2004, Volume 5 # 2, 24 August 2004 (hereafter Negotiation Archives, Fourth Session).

[9] Peter Westen, 'The Empty Idea of Equality' (1982) 95(3) Harv L Rev 537, 547–51 (hereafter Westen, 'Empty Idea of Equality').

[10] George Rutherglen, 'Disparate Impact, Discrimination and the Essentially Contested Concept of Equality' (2006) 74(4) Fordham L Rev 2313, 2324 (hereafter Rutherglen, 'Disparate Impact').

[11] CRPD Committee, General Comment No 6 (2018): Equality and Non-discrimination, 26 April 2018, [5] (hereafter 'General Comment 6').

[12] Arnardottir, 'Multidimensional Disadvantage' (n 2) 41.

> the Convention on the Rights of Persons with Disabilities has taken into account the experiences offered by the other conventions and its equality and non-discrimination principles represent the evolution of the United Nations tradition and approach.[13]

The CRPD contains a number of advances in the human rights understanding of equality and non-discrimination. For example, the CEDAW and the CERD are the product of an era which still focussed on negative state obligations and the equal treatment principle, whereas the CRPD is more concerned with asymmetrical disadvantage experienced by individuals and groups in society.[14] The CRPD includes a duty to accommodate to ensure individualized application of the equality paradigm, seeks to expand the universal equality norm to include the experiences of persons with disabilities, and expressly takes into account multidimensional and intersectional approaches to non-discrimination by recognizing that people have layers of identity apart from their disability such as gender, race, and age.[15]

However, more recently there has been a suggestion from some disability rights activists and scholars, such as Theresia Degener,[16] Jenny E Goldschmidt,[17] and Bronagh Byrne,[18] that the understanding of the terms 'equality' and 'non-discrimination' in the CRPD may be different from their meaning in pre-existing human rights norms (despite the prohibition on creating new rights). It is this new meaning of equality which apparently explains the failure of states to grasp the 'true' meaning of the CRPD,[19] rather than the concepts being retrospectively stretched by the CRPD Committee to try to mandate a specific outcome, such as the abolition of mental health law, which was expressly rejected by States Parties. Such interpretations are usually based on a strong minority rights approach, in which the pre-existing understanding of the concepts of 'equality' and 'non-discrimination' themselves are seen as suspect, having being developed by the majoritarian non-disabled 'oppressors' without input from persons with disabilities.[20] The danger of such an approach, of course, is that the meaning of 'equality' and 'non-discrimination' become completely subjective. From there, it can be claimed that 'equality' and 'non-discrimination' mean whatever certain persons with disabilities say they mean, regardless of their ordinary meaning and the limits of their semantic carrying capacity, the purpose of the CRPD, and the intentions of the parties at the time the CRPD was negotiated as set out in Chapter 1 section 1.4.1. As noted by Andrea Broderick, 'it is also important to bear in mind that the interpretation of the CRPD should not be overly dynamic, in the sense that it should not be based on wishful thinking'.[21] Despite their critique, these disability rights

[13] General Comment 6 (n 11) [5].
[14] Broderick, *The Long and Winding Road to Equality* (n 4) 146.
[15] ibid.
[16] Theresia Degener, 'Establishing Equality and Non-discrimination: The United Nations Committee on the Rights of Persons with Disabilities' New Model of Inclusive Equality' Melbourne Social Equity Institute, University of Melbourne, 11 January 2018, 6 (hereafter Degener, 'New Model of Inclusive Equality').
[17] Goldschmidt, 'New Perspectives on Equality' (n 1).
[18] Bronagh Byrne, 'Dis-Equality: Exploring the Juxtaposition of Disability and Equality' (2018) 6(1) Soc Incl 9, 10–11 (hereafter Byrne, 'Dis-Equality').
[19] Degener, 'Disability in a Human Rights Context' (n 1) 19–20.
[20] Byrne, 'Dis-Equality' (n 18) 10–11; Goldschmidt, 'New Perspectives on Equality' (n 1) 2–3.
[21] Broderick, *The Long and Winding Road to Equality* (n 4) 9.

activists and scholars have not proposed a disability specific meaning of equality and non-discrimination.

The definition of 'discrimination on the basis of disability' in Article 2 of the CRPD is defined as being:

> any distinction, exclusion or restriction on the basis of disability which has the purpose or effect of impairing or nullifying the recognition, enjoyment or exercise, on an equal basis with others, of all human rights and fundamental freedoms in the political, economic, social, cultural, civil or any other field. It includes all forms of discrimination, including denial of reasonable accommodation.

The definition of discrimination in Article 2 of the CRPD follows other non-discrimination conventions such as the CEDAW and CERD, although it does not expressly refer to direct and indirect discrimination and the 'denial of reasonable accommodation' as a form of discrimination is new to the CRPD.

While the CRPD text and literature tends to assume that equality and non-discrimination are simply the positive and negative versions of the same concept,[22] the theoretical literature about equality and non-discrimination is more nuanced.[23] That is, the concept of discrimination is narrower than the concept of equality, referring to specific instances where persons have not been treated with equal concern or respect due to some personal characteristic such as race, sex, or disability, with respect to the exercise of certain rights, including those associated with employment, or access to particular goods or services.[24] While it is often assumed that non-discrimination measures will create equality, this is not necessarily so, as non-discrimination tends to be limited to ensuring that certain traits do not taint the enjoyment of rights or distribution of goods and services, rather than in securing a substantively equal opportunity or outcome. The distinction between equality and non-discrimination was noted by Mexico during the CRPD negotiations in which equality was regarded as the social goal.[25] In this book, I will treat non-discrimination and equality as closely related but not necessarily synonymous concepts, the result being that at times the two may be in tension.

There is consensus in the CRPD literature that there is scant explanation of and significant gaps in the understanding of the meaning of 'equality' and 'discrimination' in the text of the CRPD and concern about how these concepts might apply in real life situations. For example, Bronagh Byrne observes 'equality theorising in the context of disability remains in its infancy'.[26] Further, as noted by Maria H Roux and Christopher Riddle:

[22] For example, Arnardottir, 'Multidimensional Disadvantage' (n 2) 43.

[23] Tarunabh Khaitan, *A Theory of Discrimination* (Oxford University Press 2015) 7 (hereafter Khaitan, A Theory of Discrimination).

[24] Elisa Holmes, 'Anti-Discrimination Rights without Equality' (2005) 68(2) MLR 175, 194 (hereafter Holmes, 'Anti-Discrimination Rights').

[25] Marianne Schulze, *Understanding the UN Convention on the Rights of Persons with Disabilities* (Handicap International 2009) 41 (hereafter Schulze, *Understanding the UN Convention*).

[26] Byrne, 'Dis-Equality' (n 18) 9.

> In 2007, the UN Convention on the Rights of Persons with Disabilities was ratified. While it mentions equality of opportunity as well as practices of non-discrimination, it fails to make explicit how we should conceptualize and apply the notion of equality.[27]

Similarly, Jenny Goldschmidt remarks that 'the concretisation of equality as a principle in legal practice is a very complex and demanding exercise'.[28] John Dawson is concerned that the concept of discrimination especially as interpreted by the CRPD Committee is 'ambiguous' and is more complex than acknowledged in General Comment No 1.[29] Paul Skowron also argues for caution and humility with respect to the prospect of achieving disability equality despite the hope that has been generated by the CRPD:

> Nowhere in the world is on even the most generous interpretation, close to the sort of equality that the Convention promises. Accordingly, there is not yet a single example of how to achieve this equality or any concrete details of how it might work in any given society. In these circumstances, rhetoric about implementing a new paradigm too easily implies that the Convention has the answers . . .[30]

However, the same might be said with respect to all international human rights conventions: the promise of equality and non-discrimination remains elusive.

The *travaux preparatoires* provide some guidance as to the meaning of equality and non-discrimination in the CRPD, although as noted above in section 4.1, there are limitations on how much *travaux preparatoires* can assist in the interpretation of a convention where there are many parties and much disagreement. Further, during the CRPD negotiations the delegates were not necessarily thinking about how every aspect of the agreement would apply to the issue of the abolition of mental health law, the deep theoretical meanings of each term, or the nuances of how each principle and article would interact with all the others. However, the *trauvaux preparatoires* reinforce the importance of equality and non-discrimination in the CRPD and that the drafters envisaged substantive rather than merely formal equality. For instance, Canada stated in the Fourth Session:

> The concept of substantive equality has been developed in a number of domestic systems including Canada's which recognises that persons with disabilities may require different treatment, namely accommodation of their needs and circumstances and thus positive action by States in order to enjoy the same opportunities as others.[31]

[27] Marcia H Rioux and Christopher A Riddle, 'Values in Disability Policy and Law: Equality' in Marcia H Rioux and others (eds), *Critical Perspectives on Human Rights and Disability Law* (Martinus Nijhoff Publishers 2011) 37, 53 (hereafter Rioux and Riddle, 'Values in Disability Policy and Law').

[28] Goldschmidt, 'New Perspectives on Equality' (n 1) 7.

[29] John Dawson, 'A Realistic Approach to Assessing Mental Health Laws Compliance with the UNCRPD' (2015) 40 Int J Law Psychiatry 70 (hereafter Dawson, 'A Realistic Approach').

[30] Paul Skowron, 'Humility When Responding to the Abuse of Adults with Mental Disabilities' (2017) 53 ibid 102, 108 (hereafter Skowron, 'Humility').

[31] Negotiation Archives, Fourth Session (n 8).

In response the International Disability Caucus stated that:

> . . . it would support a separate paragraph on preferential measures as long as it was understood that measures for preferential treatment do not mean separate or unequal standards and they would not be imposed on persons with disabilities.[32]

Access to 'crisis hostels' for persons with mental impairments (see also section 8.5), was argued to be part of substantive equality rather than specific measures or preferential treatment or affirmative action.[33]

There was also much discussion about whether the CRPD should expressly prohibit direct and indirect discrimination (being disproportionate disadvantage in relation to an apparently neutral requirement) and 'hidden' discrimination, as persons with disability more frequently encounter indirect discrimination. However, there was concern from some parties that an express reference to indirect discrimination may mean that the Human Rights Committee's exception that differential treatment which is objective, reasonable, and proportionate and made with a legitimate aim would not constitute indirect discrimination would apply.[34] On the other hand, Canada argued in light of jurisprudence from its Supreme Court that the distinction between direct and indirect discrimination was not necessary as the two were not conceptually different.[35] The Ad Hoc Committee drafting the CRPD removed the reference to the Human Rights Committee's exception to indirect discrimination avoiding the difficulty of having to list legitimate aims or qualifying the definition of indirect discrimination,[36] although it did not explicitly prohibit the Human Right's Committee's exception. The issue of whether and to what extent the exception which has been widely accepted in international human rights law, including by the CERD and CEDAW Committee's, might apply to the CRPD remains unknown. Jessica Lynn Corsi suggests it might at least apply in the case of specific measures.[37] Sandor Gurbai argues that whether the CRPD includes the Human Rights Committee's exception is ambiguous under the principles of interpretation of the VCLT, but that the CRPD Committee has avoided the issue in General Comment 6 and has sent mixed messages in its jurisprudence as to whether the exception might apply with respect to indirect discrimination.[38] The issue is to what extent can the CRPD Committee indirectly exclude otherwise well accepted principles of international human rights law?

However, the term 'systemic' discrimination was rejected during the drafting of the CRPD because it was considered too imprecise and not well known,[39] even though

[32] ibid.
[33] ibid.
[34] ibid.
[35] ibid.
[36] Jessica Lynn Corsi, 'Art 5 Equality and Non-discrimination' in Ilias Batekaz and others (eds), *The UN Convention on the Rights of Persons with Disabilities: A Commentary* (Oxford University Press 2018) 151 (hereafter Corsi, 'Art 5 Equality and Non-discrimination').
[37] ibid 168.
[38] Sandor Gurbai, 'Beyond the Pragmatic Definition? The Right to Non-discrimination of Persons with Disabilities in the Context of Coercive Interventions' (2020) Health Hum Rights Journal (in press) (hereafter Gurbai, 'Beyond the Pragmatic Definition?).
[39] Negotiation Archives, Fourth Session (n 8).

subsequent references to 'transformative' equality (discussed below) seem to touch on this concept.

Accordingly, in this Chapter, I argue that the text of the CRPD is based on a wide-ranging, eclectic, and under-developed conception of equality and discrimination which is prone to inherent tensions, especially in relation to the proposed abolition of mental health law. This is consistent with the nature of the CRPD as a negotiated text and 'incompletely theorised agreement' as explained in Chapter 1, section 1.4.1. I begin by describing all of the different types of equality and non-discrimination which underpin the model of equality and non-discrimination in the CRPD. In Chapter 7, I then point out some of the difficulties in deriving the meaning of equality and discrimination (such as a narrow 'equality of what', finding appropriate comparators and the problem of 'levelling down', reconciling the demands of different rights, equal treatment and 'the dilemma of difference', conflict between different types of equality and non-discrimination, distinguishing between unfair stereotypes and actual differences, and the limits of relativism for securing rights).In applying the concepts of equality and non-discrimination to the situation of persons with mental impairment. I argue in accordance with my overarching contention that a meaning of equality and non-discrimination which is consistent with the overall purpose of the CRPD to ensure the enjoyment of *all* of the rights of persons with mental impairments is to be preferred. That is, in accordance with international human rights law, all rights are seen as 'universal, indivisible, interdependent and interrelated'.[40] I propose a holistic vision of equality in which persons with disabilities are able to live a meaningful life with housing, education, employment, family, and leisure taking into account their impairments and where realization of one right should not be at the cost of sacrificing others. That said it would be incorrect to see the CRPD *only* as an equality and non-discrimination treaty.

6.2 The Eclectic Model of Equality and Non-discrimination in the CRPD

The CRPD takes an all-encompassing approach to the meaning of 'equality' and 'non-discrimination'. As noted by Theresia Degener 'the CRPD encompasses all concepts of equality and thus implicates formal, substantive and transformative duties on State Parties ...'[41] By the same token, the definition of discrimination in Article 2 also applies to '*all* forms of discrimination' (emphasis added). However, the CRPD provides no explanation of how these different types of inequality and discrimination interact, or how to resolve any conflicts between them.

As Amartya Sen has observed, the most momentous and central question posed by the promise of equality in all social theories is 'equality of what'?[42] This is because most

[40] Vienna Declaration and Programme of Action Adopted by the World Conference on Human Rights in Vienna on 25 June 1993 (hereafter, 'Vienna Declaration').

[41] Degener, 'Disability in a Human Rights Context' (n 1) 19.

[42] Amartya Sen, *Inequality Reexamined* (Oxford University Press 1995) 12, 21 (hereafter Sen, *Inequality Reexamined*).

social theories mandate equality in certain respects but permit inequality in others.[43] The issue of 'equality of what' is also useful to distinguish between different types of equality and non-discrimination.

Most accounts of equality begin with the Aristotelian approach that like is treated alike and differences are treated differently in proportion to their unlikeness.[44] The first limb, that 'like is to be treated alike', is the most straightforward and can be understood as 'formal equality'. That is, the law should treat everyone the same regardless of their social context.[45] As Camilla Kong puts it 'equal treatment in this respect requires abstracting from an individual's defining characteristics, focusing instead on universal, value-neutral features we all share, such as our common humanity'.[46] For formal equality, the 'equality of what' is the same treatment. The principle of formal equality is probably the oldest (originating in the first phase of equality law known as 'universal sameness' from 1950s–1970s)[47] and is probably the most widely accepted equality principle. It is also claimed to combat negative stereotyping[48] and direct discrimination. That is, treating similarly situated persons less favourably on certain grounds, such as race, gender, sexual orientation, and disability.[49]

However, treating people the same as a matter of formal equality, without taking into account their differences, pre-existing social disadvantage, and lack of opportunities, (that is, ignoring the second limb), tends to exacerbate rather than challenge inequality in the broader sense.[50] Therefore, most contemporary models of equality usually seek to achieve some sort of 'substantive equality' that accommodates differences and looks at the equality of opportunities and/or outcomes.[51] For substantive equality, the 'equality of what' is not equal treatment, but the result of the equal distribution of rights, opportunities, goods, and services. The acknowledgment that people are situated differently (due to corporeal and socio-historical differences) means that formal equality is not enough to combat indirect discrimination. That is, some policies or practices may appear to be neutral but in fact have a disproportionately negative impact on the person with disability or have the effect of social exclusion.[52] Substantive equality emerged in the 1970s in the context of women's equality with men and is often called the substantive difference model.[53]

The words 'recognition, enjoyment or exercise' in the definition of discrimination in Article 2 of the CRPD suggests that the CRPD is concerned with both formal

[43] ibid 19.

[44] Stefan Gosepath, 'Equality' in Edward N Zalta (ed), *The Stanford Encyclopedia of Philosophy* (Spring 2011 ed, 2011) https://plato.stanford.edu/archives/spr2011/entries/equality/ accessed 10 October 2019, [2.1] and [2.2] (hereafter Gosepath, 'Equality').

[45] ibid [2.3].

[46] Camillia Kong, 'The Convention for the Rights of Persons with Disabilities and Article 12: Prospective Feminist Lessons against the "Will and Preferences" Paradigm' (2015) 4 Laws 709, 711 (hereafter Kong, 'Prospective Feminist Lessons').

[47] Arnardottir, 'Multidimensional Disadvantage' (n 2) 48.

[48] General Comment 6 (n 11) [10].

[49] ibid [18(a)].

[50] Sandra Fredman, *Human Rights Transformed: Positive Rights and Positive Duties* (Oxford University Press 2008) 178 (hereafter Fredman, *Human Rights Transformed*).

[51] ibid.

[52] General Comment 6 (n 11) [18(b)].

[53] Arnardottir, 'Multidimensional Disadvantage' (n 2) 54.

and substantive equality, whereas the words 'purpose or effect' connotes direct and indirect discrimination (without explicitly using direct and indirect, for the reasons set out above). Formal equality is also called *de jure* equality (as only occurring in law), whereas substantive equality is referred to as *de facto* equality (being equal in fact or real life). As noted by the CRPD Committee the phrase 'on an equal basis with others' means:

> on the one hand, that persons with disabilities shall not be granted more rights or benefits than the general population. On the other hand, the term requires that States parties take positive action to achieve *de facto* equality for persons with disabilities to ensure that they can actually enjoy all human rights and fundamental freedoms.[54]

Andrea Broderick argues that based on the ordinary meaning and purpose of the CRPD the phrase 'on an equal basis with others' recognizes that persons with disabilities are in a position of pre-existing historical disadvantage, which ought to be remedied with specific measures designed to put persons with disabilities on par with the mainstream population.[55]

More recently, from mid 1990s to date[56] the concept of 'transformative equality' has emerged in the CRPD literature, which goes beyond formal and substantive equality, by trying to redress the socio-historical causes of inequality through changes in social structures and power relations.[57] While there is considerable overlap between substantive and transformative equality, substantive equality focuses on stamping out discriminatory behaviour, structures, and systems, whereas transformative equality seeks to use positive measures to change the discriminatory behaviour, structures, and systems themselves.[58] With respect to transformative equality, the meaning of 'equality of what' is the equality of power relations. As explained by Andrea Broderick:

> a model which seeks to ensure equality as transformation would require a redistribution of power and resources to nurture the innate capabilities of persons with disabilities and it would also involve the participation of persons with disabilities in every aspect of the reform agenda.[59]

Transformative equality is probably the most amorphous of the different types of equality as well as the most difficult to codify in law and to apply to concrete situations.[60] Jessica Lynn Corsi defines it as 'obliging states parties too make both structural and individually tailored adjustments in order to achieve full inclusion of persons with disabilities'.[61]

[54] General Comment 6 (n 11) [19].
[55] Broderick, *The Long and Winding Road to Equality* (n 4) 95.
[56] Arnardottir, 'Multidimensional Disadvantage' (n 2) 54.
[57] Tina Minkowitz, 'CRPD and Transformative Equality' (2017) 13(1) Int J Law Context 77, 77 (hereafter Minkowitz, 'Transformative Equality'); Goldschmidt, 'New Perspectives on Equality' (n 1) 5.
[58] Degener, 'Disability in a Human Rights Context' (n 1) 17.
[59] Broderick, *The Long and Winding Road to Equality* (n 4) 37.
[60] Arnardottir, 'Multidimensional Disadvantage' (n 2) 65.
[61] Corsi, 'Art 5 Equality and Non-discrimination' (n 36) 141.

With respect to transformative equality, the CRPD permits 'specific measures' to ensure de facto equality.[62]

While Theresia Degener aligns formal equality with the medical model of disability, substantive equality with the social model, and transformative equality with what she calls the human rights model (being a somewhat further developed version of the social model of disability based on the CRPD which I discuss in Chapter 1, section 1.4.1.2),[63] in my view this classification is too simplistic as the different models of disability do not accurately correspond with the different types of equality. For instance, the CRPD Committee completely rejects the medical model, but at the same time insists on the formal equality of persons with mental impairments with those without disability by abolishing mental health law. Similarly, the social model of disability does not account for substantive inequality which may be caused by the nature of a person's impairment independently from the way his or her disability may be socially constructed.

The CRPD also mentions 'equality of opportunity' in Article 3(e). According to General Comment No 6, the equalization of opportunities moves the CRPD from a model of formal equality to substantive equality.[64] However, 'equality of opportunity' is controversial in the disability context. On the one hand, it is said to permit the preferential treatment of persons who suffer from discrimination by removing barriers to the enjoyment of rights and social inclusion.[65] It also involves developing the innate potential of persons with disabilities.[66] On the other hand, it is often regarded as a very weak form of substantive equality, as it only considers the effect of the removal of barriers which hinder free competition between individuals, without being concerned with the equality of results or outcomes.[67] For this reason, equal opportunity rarely clashes with formal equality.[68] However, equality of opportunity has been criticized in the disability context because it assumes that fair competition can exist[69] and it does not address the fundamental differences faced by persons with disabilities which have caused their disentitlement.[70] As Marcia Rioux and Christopher Riddle observe:

> ... an equality of opportunity perspective nonetheless fails to recognize that social marginalization and devaluation occur as a result of ranking individuals in a competitive framework.[71]

[62] CRPD, Art 5.

[63] Degener, 'Disability in a Human Rights Context' (n 1) 18.

[64] General Comment 6 (n 11) [10].

[65] Valentina Della Fina, 'Article 3 [General Principles]' in V Della Fina and others (eds), *The United Nations Convention on the Rights of Persons with Disabilities* (Springer International Publishing 2017) 128–29 (hereafter Della Fina, 'Article 3').

[66] Broderick, *The Long and Winding Road to Equality* (n 4) 41.

[67] Hugh Collins, 'Discrimination, Equality and Social Inclusion' (2003) 66(1) MLR 16, 18 (hereafter Collins, 'Discrimination, Equality and Social Inclusion').

[68] ibid.

[69] Byrne, 'Dis-Equality' (n 18) 15.

[70] Rioux and Riddle, 'Values in Disability Policy and Law' (n 27) 45.

[71] ibid.

The CRPD outlaws four different types of discrimination being: direct discrimination, indirect discrimination, denial of reasonable accommodation and harassment.[72] Direct and indirect discrimination are discussed above and harassment is probably not relevant to the situation of persons with mental impairments with respect to the abolition of mental health law. Reasonable accommodation is another approach for taking into account the differences which are experienced by persons with disabilities. It is defined in Article 2 as:

> necessary and appropriate modification and adjustments not imposing a disproportionate or undue burden, where needed in a particular case, to ensure to persons with disabilities the enjoyment or exercise on an equal basis with others of all human rights and fundamental freedoms.

General Comment 6, only discusses reasonable accommodation with respect to equal access, in which it limits reasonable accommodation as a remedy for individuals rather than groups with similar problems.[73] The individual nature of reasonable accommodation is also reflected in the words of Article 2 'where needed in a particular case'. However, mental health law could arguably be broadly conceptualized as a form of 'reasonable accommodation' in the sense that it creates a structure to assess and respond to the individual differences of persons with mental impairments and to make adjustments (that is, providing access to treatment) for those persons who are the most severe and meet the civil commitment criteria. The limitation of 'disproportionate or undue burden' in the definition of reasonable accommodation stops short of creating an absolute right to participate in society, but the absence of any obligation of employers and service providers to justify discrimination which is proportionate and relates to a legitimate social aim means that the definition of discrimination in the CRPD is significantly wider than in domestic legislation.[74]

According to General Comment No 6, the phrase 'equality under the law' is different from 'equality before the law' (being formal equality, that is, sameness or consistency of treatment)[75] and is apparently unique to the CRPD. Instead, according to the CRPD Committee, equality under the law means 'that there should be no laws that allow for specific denial, restriction or limitation of the rights of persons with disabilities, and that disability should be mainstreamed in all legislation and policies'.[76] However, there is no recorded discussion of this meaning of 'equality under the law' during the CRPD negotiations[77] and such a distinction or definition does not appear in the text of the CRPD itself. Andrea Broderick argues that the ordinary meaning of 'equality under the law' is that laws should be as wide and inclusive as possible and apply fairly to all groups.[78] However, if the concept of 'equality under the law' is construed too broadly

[72] General Comment 6 (n 11) [18].
[73] ibid [23–24].
[74] Sarah Fraser Butlin, 'The UN Convention on the Rights of Persons with Disabilities: Does the Equality Act 2010 Measure up to UK International Commitments?' (2011) 40(4) Ind Law J 428, 437 (hereafter Butlin, 'Equality Act 2010').
[75] Corsi, 'Art 5 Equality and Non-discrimination' (n 36) 157.
[76] General Comment 6 (n 11) [14].
[77] Broderick, *The Long and Winding Road to Equality* (n 4) 87.
[78] ibid.

it would contradict many of the other provisions of the CRPD specifically designed to address difference. For example, this interpretation would prevent specific measures to rectify historical discrimination as a result of social or corporeal differences, including use of quotas, targeted recruitment, redistribution of resources, and preferential treatment, undertaken with the participation of disabled person's organizations.[79] While the text of the CRPD regards specific measures as optional, Andrea Broderick argues that on a purposive reading of the treaty, specific measures could in some circumstances be a mandatory obligation of states and should even be permanent (as opposed to temporary) where they are designed to redress entrenched disadvantage caused by the biological differences of certain impairments (such as mental and cognitive disabilities).[80]

A preference for mainstreaming, which is to incorporate the principle of disability equality and non-discrimination into all laws, policies, programmes, and practices, is also mentioned in the CRPD preamble. Mainstreaming is a way of trying to universalize disability rights. It involves expanding the underlying conception of what a human being is, on which human rights law is based, to include persons with mental impairments.[81] However, mainstreaming is not a panacea as it is impossible to incorporate every kind of difference into the norm as some differences may conflict with others and it has been described as a practical and less radical or controversial solution than affirmative action.[82] Theresia Degener has also noted that the CRPD needs to apply to all persons with disabilities, including those with higher support needs, not just those who are 'fit' for mainstreaming.[83] Further, mainstreaming does not preclude different treatment due to the use of specific measures, reasonable accommodation, or addressing intersectionality or discrimination on multiple grounds. The CRPD is also the first human rights treaty to refer to intersectionality and multiple discrimination, that is, the idea that persons can have different experiences of discrimination depending on their other identities, although it has been criticized for doing so in a superficial and cumulative way and for giving insufficient regard to race.[84]

The state obligation of equality applies to states to respect the equality of persons with disabilities by refraining from discrimination and unequal treatment, to protect persons with mental impairments from discrimination and inequality by non-state actors in the private sphere and to fulfil equality and non-discrimination where persons with mental impairments cannot do so themselves (such as, through provision of support services).[85]

[79] ibid 128–29; CRPD, Art 5(4).

[80] ibid 128 and 132.

[81] Frederic Megret, 'The Disabilities Convention: Towards a Holistic Concept of Rights' (2008) 12(2) Int J Hum Rights 261, 262–63 (hereafter Megret, 'Towards a Holistic Concept of Rights'); Elif Celik, 'The Role of the CRPD in Rethinking the Subject of Human Rights' (2017) 21(7) ibid 933, 936–38 (hereafter Celik, 'Rethinking the Subject of Human Rights').

[82] Arnardottir, 'Multidimensional Disadvantage' (n 2) 62.

[83] Degener, 'Disability in a Human Rights Context' (n 1).

[84] Beth Ribet, 'Emergent Disability and the Limits of Equality: A Critical Reading of the UN Convention on the Rights of Persons with Disabilities' (2011) 14 YHRDLJ 155, 171, 178 (hereafter Ribet, 'Emergent Disability').

[85] Broderick, *The Long and Winding Road to Equality* (n 4) 81.

It can be seen then that trying to encompass all forms of inequality and non-discrimination is rather complex. It is, therefore, not surprising that several multi-dimensional approaches to conceptualizing equality and non-discrimination have emerged. Such models are more holistic and cover more than one 'equality of what'. A well-known example is Sandra Fredman's four dimensions of substantive equality.[86] These are (i) redressing disadvantage (the redistributive dimension); (ii) addressing stigma, stereotyping, prejudice, and violence (the recognition dimension); (iii) facilitating participation (the participatory dimension); and (iv) accommodating difference, including through structural change (the transformative dimension).[87] The different dimensions are intended to mediate each other, with no one dimension overriding the others.[88] Similarly, John Baker and colleagues propose five dimensions of inequality across different aspects of life: (i) respect and recognition; (ii) resources; (iii) love, care, and solidarity; (iv) power; and (v) working and learning.[89] The CRPD Committee in General Comment No 6 has also introduced a new multi-dimensional model which it calls 'inclusive equality'. This is very similar to Sandra Fredman's model, except for the mention of intersectionality and the last dimension about making space for difference. Apparently, inclusive equality:

> . . . embraces a substantive model of equality and extends and elaborates on the content of equality in: (a) a fair redistributive dimension to address socio-economic disadvantages; (b) a recognition dimension to combat stigma stereotyping, prejudice and violence and to recognize the dignity of human beings and their intersectionality; (c) a participative dimension to reaffirm the social nature of people as members of social groups and the full recognition of humanity through inclusion in society; and (d) an accommodating dimension to make space for difference as a matter of human dignity.[90]

The mention of human dignity introduces the dignitarian account of equality and non-discrimination which prohibits conduct which is demeaning and does not treat people with equal concern and respect as outlined in Chapter 4.[91] Andrea Broderick observes that the dignitarian focus of the CRPD reflects Nussbaum's capabilities approach that 'the inherent capabilities, the innate potential and the equal moral worth of each disabled individual is valued and taken into account in the formulation of appropriate measures to counteract disadvantage'.[92] The focus on social inclusion as a form of equality accords with the work of Hugh Collins who argues that English non-discrimination law can be best understood as being motivated by equality tempered

[86] Sandra Fredman, 'Emerging from the Shadows: Substantive Equality and Article 14 of the European Convention on Human Rights' (2016) 16 Hum Rights Law Rev 273, 282 (hereafter Fredman, 'Emerging from the Shadows').

[87] ibid.

[88] Fredman, 'Emerging from the Shadows' (n 86) 283.

[89] John Baker and others, *Equality: From Theory to Action* (Palgrave MacMillian 2004) 22–25 (hereafter Baker, *Equality: From Theory to Action*).

[90] General Comment 6 (n 11) [11].

[91] Deborah Hellman, *When Is Discrimination Wrong?* (Harvard University Press 2008) 6, 29 (hereafter Hellman, *When Is Discrimination Wrong?*).

[92] Broderick, *The Long and Winding Road to Equality* (n 4) 142.

by social inclusion.[93] As will be discussed below, the principle of social inclusion adds a 'perfectionist' and 'paternalist' dimension to the principle of equality, in that the concern is not equal distribution of rights and material goods, but the distribution of non-material goods, such as, being employed, building a social network, and participating in civil society, which are thought to be 'good' for both personal well-being and social cohesion.[94] The principle of participation and social inclusion is also a key value of the CRPD and the interpretive compass[95] which is discussed in detail in Chapter 7 section 7.6 below.

6.3 Conclusion

In this chapter, I argue that the CRPD contains an eclectic and incoherent concept of equality and non-discrimination even though both concepts permeate the Convention. In trying to protect persons with mental impairments from inequality and discrimination of every description, the CRPD provides little guidance about how to deal with whether to prioritize formal, substantive, or transformative equality when they are inconsistent with each other. I explore the implications of all of these different approaches to equality and non-discrimination with respect to the call for the abolition of mental health law in the next chapter.

[93] Collins, 'Discrimination, Equality and Social Inclusion' (n 67) 40.
[94] ibid 24.
[95] CRPD Article 3; Goldschmidt, 'New Perspectives on Equality' (n 1) 9–10.

7

Difficulties with the Meaning of Equality, Non-Discrimination and Participation in the CRPD, and their Application to the Abolition with Support Model

7.1 Introduction

Given that the CRPD seeks to address inequality and discrimination of every possible type for every person with every kind of disability, it is difficult to arrive at a coherent approach which addresses the inequality of and discrimination against persons with mental impairment in every sense (as I argue in Chapter 6 above). While abolitionists claim that the abolition of mental health law is the most equal approach as it incorporates all types of equality and non-discrimination, in reality abolitionists are quite selective in emphasizing some types of equality over others. There is no doubt that the abolition of mental health law ensures formal equality with respect to the right to legal capacity and prevents direct discrimination so that persons with and without mental impairment are treated 'the same' by the law. Differences in decision-making ability, which must be accommodated to achieve substantive equality for persons with mental impairments, are not recognized by abolitionists through mental health law, but through the offering of support, which persons with mental impairments are entitled to refuse.[1] As mental health law is conceptualized by abolitionists as a structural barrier to equality and therefore is regarded as the cause of inequality, abolition of it and the introduction of support is argued to satisfy the requirements of transformative equality.[2] The question is whether this focus on achieving formal equality, eliminating direct discrimination, and the offering of decision-making support is sufficient to achieve the comprehensive and ambitious vision of equality and non-discrimination in the CRPD? I argue that it is not.

7.2 Equality of What?

The call for the abolition of mental health law is centred on equality with respect to legal capacity under Article 12 of the CRPD between persons with and without

[1] Committee on the Rights of Persons with Disabilities 'General Comment No 1 (2014) Article 12: Equal Recognition before the Law' (11 April 2014) UN Doc CRPD/C/GC/1, [28] and [29] (hereafter 'General Comment 1).

[2] Tina Minkowitz, 'CRPD and Transformative Equality' (2017) 13(1) Int J Law Context 77, 84–85 (hereafter Minkowitz, 'Transformative Equality').

Mental Health Law. Kay Wilson, Oxford University Press. © Kay Wilson 2021. DOI: 10.1093/oso/9780192843258.003.0007

mental impairment. It is also claimed that equal legal capacity is necessary for the enjoyment of liberty and security of the person, personal integrity, freedom from torture, violence, exploitation and abuse, and independent living.[3] Of course, treating persons with and without mental impairment 'the same' with respect to legal capacity (even if support is offered), may perpetuate inequality with respect to other CRPD rights such as access to health care and rehabilitation, being able to participate effectively in education, obtaining and continuing employment, living independently, and participating in and being included in the community. It would also limit the ability of the state to redress the effects of significant and pre-existing poverty and social exclusion suffered by persons with mental impairments. Joel Anderson points out that western societies presuppose that most persons have a high capacity for autonomy and that where this is misaligned with a person's actual ability, it can lead to further vulnerability, including a sense of shame and humiliation for the person, and a situation where a person permanently 'falls behind' which compounds social inequality.[4]

For instance, if a person with mental impairment were to refuse psychiatric treatment and commit a crime, it could result in a term of imprisonment and deprivation of liberty, bearing in mind that persons with mental impairment are already over-represented in prisons and are a socially disadvantaged group.[5] As Peter Bartlett points out, prisons are not a particularly humane place for persons with mental impairment and a criminal record could make it harder for persons with mental impairment to rent a property and achieve full social participation and independent living on release.[6]

While it could be argued that going to prison where a person with mental impairment has committed a crime makes them 'equal' to persons without impairment who commit crimes, it is an argument which raises complex issues. For instance, what level of criminal responsibility should persons bear for refusing psychiatric treatment based on their will and preferences if they were unable to recognize the effect of their mental impairment on their decision-making and behaviour?[7] Further, recent research indicates that it is possible for a person to be generally aware that they have problems with decision-making, while still being unable to avoid falling into those very pitfalls when actually making a decision in practice.[8]

More importantly, as I argue elsewhere, abolishing mental health law may create equality with respect to legal capacity, but may not give persons with mental

[3] General Comment 1 (n 1) [40], [42], [44]–[45].

[4] Joel Anderson, 'Vulnerability, Autonomy Gaps and Social Exclusion' in Christine Straehle (ed), *Vulnerability, Autonomy and Applied Ethics* (Routledge 2016) 62 (hereafter Anderson, 'Vulnerability, Autonomy Gaps and Social Exclusion').

[5] Vijaya Murali and Femi Oyebode, 'Poverty, Social Inequality and Mental Health' (2004) 10 Adv Psychiatr Treat 216 (hereafter Murali and Oyebode, 'Poverty, Social Inequality and Mental Health').

[6] Peter Bartlett, 'The United Nations Convention on the Rights of Persons with Disabilities and Mental Health Law' (2012) 75(5) MLR 752, 774 (hereafter Bartlett, CRPD, and MHL).

[7] Meron Wondemaghen, 'Testing Equality: Insanity, Treatment Refusal and the CRPD' (2018) 25(4) Psychiatry Psychol & L 174, 179 (hereafter Wondemaghen, 'Testing Equality').

[8] Barton Palmer, 'Executive Dysfunction as a Barrier to Authenticity in Decision Making' (2018) 25(1) Philos Psychiatry Psychol 21, 22 (hereafter Palmer, 'Executive Dysfunction').

impairment who are at risk of suicide or accident, equal protection of their right to life.[9] It is true that most persons with mental impairment do not complete suicide or experience suicidal ideation, planning or attempts and not all persons who complete suicide or are involved in avoidable accidental death have a mental impairment. However, of those who do complete suicide (roughly 5,000 per year or around 10.2 per 100,000 in the United Kingdom),[10] the results of psychological autopsies, in which investigators create a psychological profile of the person before their death, indicate that the overwhelming majority of suicides (90 per cent) are completed by persons with mental impairment.[11] In Victoria, analysis of coronial reports have indicated that approximately 50 per cent of persons who complete suicide had a diagnosed mental impairment, with other stressors such as drug and alcohol problems, trouble with the police, and relationship breakdown contributing factors (although the results of that study were dependent on the accuracy of coronial records and may have been higher if undiagnosed mental impairments were included).[12] Persons with mental impairments have also been found to have around three to six times the rates of accidental death, including from alcohol and drug misuse, than the general population.[13] In fact, respecting the legal capacity of persons with mental impairment who take their own lives may actually result in a loss of human diversity to society (as there may be fewer persons with mental impairment who are alive) and undermine the participation and social inclusion of persons with mental impairment which underpins the CRPD (death being the ultimate form of social exclusion).[14] It may also further disadvantage those persons with mental impairment who are the most severely impaired, especially if they reject or do not obtain decision-making support.[15]

Equality with respect to legal capacity could also expose persons with mental impairment to acquiring further impairments, such as physical or cognitive damage caused through self-harm, avoidable accident, or unsuccessful suicide attempts. While abolitionists and disability rights advocates try to avoid saying anything negative about impairment,[16] it seems nonsensical to deny that additional impairments can further

[9] Kay Wilson, 'The Call for the Abolition of Mental Health Law: The Challenges of Suicide, Accidental Death and the Equal Enjoyment of the Right to Life' (2018) 18 Hum Rights Law Rev 651 (hereafter Wilson, 'Right to Life').

[10] Kirsten Windfuhr and Navneet Kapur, 'Suicide and Mental Illness: A Clinical Review of 15 Years of Findings from the UK Confidential Inquiry into Suicide' (2011) 100 Br Med Bull 101, 103 (hereafter Windfuhr and Kapur, 'Suicide and Mental Illness').

[11] JTO Cavanagh and others, 'Psychological Autopsy Studies of Suicide: A Systematic Review' (2003) 33 Psychol Med 395, 399 (hereafter Cavanagh, 'Psychological Autopsy Studies').

[12] Angela Clapperton and others, 'Relative Risk of Suicide Following Exposure to Recent Stressors, Victoria, Australia' (2019) 43(3) Aust N Z J Public Health 254, 254 (hereafter Clapperton, 'Suicide Following Exposure to Recent Stressors').

[13] Urara Hiroeh and others, 'Death by Homicide, Suicide, and Other Unnatural Causes in People with Mental Illness: A Population-Based Study' (2001) 358 The Lancet 2110, 2111 (hereafter Hiroeh, 'Death by Homicide'); 'People with Mental Illness Six Times More Likely to Die in an Accident' (2013) September/October Mental Health Today 6 (hereafter, 'Accident'); SS Gau and AT Cheng, 'Mental Illness and Accidental Death: Case Control Psychological Autopsy Study' (2004) 175 Br J Psychiatry 422 (hereafter Gau and Cheng, 'Mental Illness and Accidental Death').

[14] Wilson, 'Right to Life' (n 9) 670.

[15] ibid 685–6.

[16] Theresia Degener, 'Disability in a Human Rights Context' (2016) 5 Laws 35 (Degener, hereafter 'Disability in a Human Rights Context').

complicate, limit, increase pain and suffering, and disadvantage persons with mental impairments, even in the most equal and inclusive society. Further, acknowledging that it is desirable to prevent further impairments (where it is possible to do so) does not mean that people with multiple impairments are less worthy, but is no more than a simple recognition of the realities of impairment. The narrow focus of the CRPD only on the rights of persons once they have impairments rather than on the social inequalities which cause particular persons to become impaired in the first place is a weakness of the CRPD.[17] While Theresia Degener argues that the obligation on states to prevent further impairments is an obligation that arises from other human rights treaties[18] (perhaps in the same way that disability rights have always been part of state obligations in general human rights treaties), its conspicuous absence in the CRPD still seems like a missed opportunity to clarify and amplify the right in what would seem to be its natural home. It also limits the ability of the CRPD in achieving transformative equality.

While the inequality flowing from the legal recognition of legal capacity with respect to the enjoyment of other CRPD rights could and should be addressed through the removal of social and environmental barriers and greater social acceptance of human diversity (such as, reasonable accommodation and support for decision-making), some inequality arising from the effects of the impairment itself may be unavoidable. For instance, if persons are preoccupied by or fixated with their own internal idiosyncratic concerns springing from their mental impairment (such as, delusions, paranoia, anxiety, mania, depression, self-harm, or suicidal thoughts) it may inhibit their ability to recognize and protect their own interests (including accessing support for decision-making, medical treatment, or other assistance). Kate Richards explains how her psychosis and severe depression interfere with her decision-making:

> when I'm sick I believe the delusional stuff to the same degree that you might know and believe the sky is above and the earth is below. And if someone were to say to me that the delusional thinking is, in fact, delusional, well that's the same as if I assure you now that we walk on the sky. Of course you wouldn't believe me, and that's why it's sometimes so hard for people who are sick like this to accept treatment—to know that they even need treatment.[19]

Healthcare is not just about improving well-being, it is of instrumental value because it assists in following and implementing life plans.[20] As noted by Amartya Sen, 'problems of social injustice and inequity between different classes and groups relate strongly to extensive disparities in well-being . . .'[21]

[17] Beth Ribet, 'Emergent Disability and the Limits of Equality: A Critical Reading of the UN Convention on the Rights of Persons with Disabilities' (2011) 14 YHRDLJ 155, 159 (hereafter Ribet, 'Emergent Disability).

[18] Theresia Degener, *Establishing Equality and Non-Discrimination: The United Nations Committee on the Rights of Persons with Disabilities' New Model of Inclusive Equality*, 11 January 2018, Melbourne Social Equity Institute, University of Melbourne, 5 (hereafter Degener, *Establishing Equality and Non-Discrimination*).

[19] Kate Richards, *Madness: A Memoir* (Penguin Group 2013) 174 (hereafter Richards, *Madness*).

[20] Alasdair Maclean, *Autonomy, Informed Consent and Medical Law: A Relational Challenge* (Cambridge University Press 2009) 28 (hereafter Maclean, *Autonomy, Informed Consent and Medical Law*).

[21] Amartya Sen, *Inequality Reexamined* (Oxford University Press 1995) 72 (hereafter Sen, Inequality Reexamined).

An inward focus on the symptoms of a person's mental impairment may also inhibit the ability of a person to participate meaningfully and be included in society (such as, by being able to do a job). As Tom Shakespeare observes, disability discrimination can only partly explain the high unemployment rates among persons with disabilities, some of the lack of participation must be attributed to the impact of the impairment itself.[22] For instance, some persons with mental impairment simply struggle with regular, stressful work.[23] Further, it may even be dangerous for persons with a different perception of reality to try to do certain types of work.

In short, formal equality with respect to legal capacity and the ability to refuse involuntary detention and psychiatric treatment may create or entrench inequality with respect to the enjoyment of many other CRPD rights and reinforce the powerlessness and poverty of persons with disability in society. It may also undermine substantive and transformative equality with respect to the benefits and power of persons with mental impairments in society.

7.3 Equality with Respect to Whom? The Problem of Finding an Appropriate Comparator

While it is possible for inequality and discrimination to occur without using a comparator on the basis that some conduct is just unfair and demeaning in and of itself,[24] the concepts of equality and discrimination are inherently comparative and the CRPD explicitly incorporates the notion of comparison in the key phrase 'on an equal basis with others'. The 'others' (at least from the abolitionist perspective) are persons without disabilities, with parallels being drawn to the legal treatment of victims of domestic violence and human trafficking as being an appropriate point of comparison in determining 'equality'.[25] Of course, this assumes that persons with mental impairment and victims of domestic violence and human trafficking are comparable in a meaningful way. While some persons suffering from domestic violence or human trafficking, may also have mental impairments, for the comparison to work it is necessary to assume that they do not. It is true that both groups can be thought of as having had their will overborne, but the loss of autonomy in each case is very different. Persons suffering from domestic violence or human trafficking have lost autonomy by having their will overborne by another person (where their reasoning skills are still presumably intact), whereas some persons with a mental impairment have lost autonomy by reason of their mental impairment which may interfere with how they receive, understand, and appreciate information and make decisions. Further, the state may be reluctant to use coercion to force a person to leave a domestic violence or human trafficking situation for

[22] Tom Shakespeare, *Disability Rights and Wrongs Revisited* (Routledge 2013) 31 (hereafter Shakespeare, Disability Rights and Wrongs Revisited).

[23] ibid.

[24] Sophia Reibetanz Moreau, 'Equality Rights and the Relevance of Comparator Groups' (2006) 5(1) JLE 81, 82 (hereafter Moreau, 'Equality Rights and the Relevance of Comparator Groups').

[25] Eilionoir Flynn and Anna Arstein-Kerslake, 'State Intervention in the Lives of People with Disabilities: The Case for a Disability-Neutral Framework' (2017) 13(1) Int J Law Context 39, 43 (hereafter Flynn and Arstein-Kerslake, 'State Intervention in the Lives of People with Disabilities').

reasons other than respecting the victim's autonomy. For instance, a domestic violence victim may legitimately fear leaving (statistically the most dangerous time for a victim is threatening to leave or immediately after leaving an abusive partner) in circumstances where the state can never completely guarantee their safety.[26] Alternatively, leaving may cause a victim significant financial detriment and the state does not want to take more than a minimal responsibility for supporting a victim and any children in a relationship it still considers private. Further, it may also be thought that the appropriate course of action is to punish the perpetrators, rather than to coerce the victim to leave (an option which is obviously not available with respect to restoring the autonomy of persons with mental impairments).[27] Alternatively, using the same analogy between persons with mental impairments and victims of domestic violence, Camilla Kong argues that the state *should* intervene to remove women from violent situations and that failure of the state to do so means that the state has abrogated its positive obligations to support individual autonomy instead of preserving the public/private distinction.[28] Therefore, it seems that the comparison between persons with mental impairments and victims of domestic violence and human trafficking may not be a fair or valid one. Nor does it necessarily support the notion that the state ought to refrain from intervening to respect the autonomy of persons with mental impairments in the interests of equality between persons with and without disability.

The other issue is what sort of equality are abolitionists trying to achieve by giving persons with mental impairments the same rights as victims of domestic violence and human trafficking (being two of the most downtrodden and 'vulnerable' groups in society)? It is unclear who is similarly situated with persons with mental impairment. Does the unique fluctuating, diverse, and deteriorating nature of mental impairment which can be associated with self-harm and suicide make it completely different from all other human experiences? Or, is the appropriate comparator anyone who lacks mental capacity for whatever reason? Or, is the appropriate comparator an average person with 'normal' autonomy (as opposed to a victim of domestic violence or human trafficking) without mental impairment?

Further, comparisons between persons with and without disabilities highlight the problems with the relativity of equality. That is, the rights of persons with disabilities are dependent on the rights of persons without disabilities which form the 'norm' on which all rights are based.[29] For instance, if persons without disabilities do not have rights to universal healthcare (as in the United States) then neither do persons with disabilities, even though persons with disabilities have far greater healthcare needs.[30] Further, why should persons with disabilities live up to the non-disabled norm? As

[26] Fiona Brookman and Mike Maguire, 'Reducing Homicide: A Review of the Possibilities' (2004) 42 Crime, L & Soc Change 325, 339 (hereafter Brookman and Maguire, 'Reducing Homicide').

[27] Jaime Lindsey, 'Developing Vulnerability: A Situational Response to the Abuse of Women with Mental Disabilities' (2016) 24 Fem Leg Stud 295, 304 (hereafter Lindsey, 'Developing Vulnerability').

[28] Camillia Kong, 'The Convention for the Rights of Persons with Disabilities and Article 12: Prospective Feminist Lessons against the "Will and Preferences" Paradigm' (2015) 4 Laws 709, 718 (hereafter Kong, 'Prospective Feminist Lessons').

[29] Bronagh Byrne, 'Dis-Equality: Exploring the Juxtaposition of Disability and Equality' (2018) 6(1) Soc Incl 9, 15 (hereafter Byrne, 'Dis-Equality').

[30] Ribet, 'Emergent Disability (n 17) 155.

Tom Shakespeare and colleagues point out, persons with disabilities may not need equality with non-disabled persons, but rather to have the specific needs associated with their impairments met.[31] For example, access to appropriate rehabilitation can be empowering and necessary for some persons to enjoy equality in social participation, inclusion, education, and employment.[32]

Finally, the distinction between persons with mental impairment and persons without mental impairment, by way of clear comparison, is not particularly clear-cut or can be conceived as binary. While it is certainly true that persons without mental impairments also make risky and impulsive decisions, those decisions are not necessarily the same quality as those made by persons with mental impairment. For example, if persons without mental impairment start suddenly acting unpredictably, erratically, out of character, and in violation of certain social norms associated with rationality (such as based on a perception of reality that is contrary to widely accepted facts, does not consider future consequences, misjudges self-interest by giving away all their wealth to a complete stranger without an appropriate explanation, or becomes unusually passive),[33] it is likely that the people around them will question whether they are mentally well and at least try to seek a psychiatric assessment. In fact, a sudden, inexplicable and marked change in a person's behaviour is often thought to be characteristic of the onset of mental impairment.[34] That is, persons without a diagnosed mental impairment would still be treated as if they *might* have a mental impairment based on their behaviour.

In summary, the purposes of understanding equality and non-discrimination with respect to persons with mental impairment the meaning of the phrase 'on an equal basis with others' begs the question of 'which others' and invites the difficulty of determining exactly who is an appropriate comparator. Non-disabled persons are a broad group and some sub-groups such as victims of domestic violence and human trafficking are equally if not more disadvantaged than persons with disabilities. Comparisons between those who are not similarly situated is a form of false equivalence which is at best questionable and at worst unfair and can only lead to a denial of substantive equality and indirect discrimination likely to reinforce and compound social disadvantage. Equality which only involves the same treatment between the disabled with the non-disabled may simply reinforce the non-disabled norm without giving proper respect to the needs and differences of persons with disabilities.

[31] Tom Shakespeare and others, 'Rehabilitation as a Disability Equality Issue: A Conceptual Shift for Disability Studies?' (2018) 6(1) Soc Incl 61, 64 (hereafter Shakespeare, 'Rehabilitation as a Disability Equality Issue').

[32] ibid.

[33] Marie Failinger, 'The Paradox in Madness: Vulnerability Confronts the Law' (2012) 1 Ment Health Law and Pol J 127, 130–31 (hereafter Failinger, 'Paradox in Madness').

[34] Craig Edwards, 'Beyond Mental Competence' (2010) 27(3) J Appl Philos 273 (hereafter Edwards, 'Beyond Mental Competence'); Katrine Del Villar, 'Should Supported Decision-Making Replace Substituted Decision-Making? The Convention on the Rights of Persons with Disabilities and Coercive Treatment Under Queensland's Mental Health Act 2000' (2015) 4 Laws 173, 182 (hereafter Del Villar, Should Supported Decision-Making Replace Substituted Decision-Making?').

7.4 Is Involuntary Detention and Psychiatric Treatment a Detriment or a Benefit?

The definition of discrimination on the basis of disability in Article 2 applies where a measure has the effect 'of *impairing* or *nullifying* the recognition, enjoyment or exercise, on an equal basis with others, of *all* human rights' (emphasis added). Discrimination does not apply where differential treatment might confer a benefit for persons with mental impairments. Anna Nilsson and Lucy Series observe that the issue of whether involuntary detention and psychiatric treatment actually constitutes a disadvantage is where 'the real heat of debates concerning article 12 of the CRPD lies, rather than in technical questions of statistical comparisons.'[35] As noted by John Dawson, 'involuntary psychiatric treatment, for instance, could both limit a person's autonomy and promote their social inclusion, health and standard of living'[36] so that involuntary detention and psychiatric treatment can be conceptualized not just as a detriment, but as an advantage with respect to the realization of other human rights. I would add, to this observation, the protection of life and the enjoyment of all other human rights for which life is a necessary precondition and empowering the person to participate more effectively in society and to partake of a universal right to mental health, well-being, and flourishing.[37] While abolitionists may dismiss concerns about access to healthcare as being irrelevant and as belonging to the medical model,[38] as pointed out by epidemiologists, access to healthcare and the distribution of goods, services, and opportunities within a society is also very much a social matter which can significantly impact health and lifespan.[39]

However, while involuntary detention for the purposes of psychiatric treatment in very limited circumstances, as discussed in Chapter 8, may be a benefit or advantage for persons with mental impairment, it is not something which gives persons with mental impairment more rights than those without mental impairment, contrary to the definition of 'on an equal basis with others' in General Comment 6. Rather, it simply aims to redress a pre-existing (social or corporeal) disadvantage and probably only partially at that, as even with medical intervention persons with mental impairments usually require many other types of social support to function in society.

Therefore, to the extent that limited involuntary detention for the purposes of psychiatric treatment confers a benefit or is used to redress a pre-existing disadvantage, then it does not fit within the definition of discrimination in the CRPD.

35 Anna Nilsson and Lucy Series 'Art 12 CRPD Recognition Before the Law' in Ilias Bantekas and others, *The UN Convention on the Rights of Persons with Disabilities: A Commentary* (Oxford University Press 2018) 342 (hereafter Nilsson and Series, 'Art 12').

36 John Dawson, 'A Realistic Approach to Assessing Mental Health Laws Compliance with the UNCRPD' (2015) 40 Int J Law Psychiatry 70, 71 (hereafter Dawson, 'A Realistic Approach').

37 Andrew Molas, 'Defending the CRPD: Dignity, Flourishing and the Universal Right to Mental Health' (2016) 20(8) Int J Hum Rights 1264 (hereafter Molas, 'Defending the CRPD').

38 CRPD Committee, General Comment No 6 (2018): Equality and Non-discrimination, 26 April 2018, [2] (hereafter, 'General Comment 6').

39 Michael Marmot, 'Social Justice, Epidemiology and Health Inequalities' (2017) 32 Eur J Epidemiol 537, 543–44 (hereafter Marmot, 'Social Justice'); Shawn Currie and others, 'Health Surveillance Data to Examine the Relationship of Depression Prevalence to Social Determinants of Health and Access to Mental Health Services' (2013) 32(1) Can J Commun Ment Health 43, 54 (hereafter Currie, 'Health Surveillance Data').

7.5 Addressing the Sameness and Difference of Persons with Mental Impairment

While there are a number of difficulties in conceptualizing and applying the concepts of equality and non-discrimination in the CRPD, most of them stem from how the sameness and difference of persons with mental impairment are understood. As Megan Conway observes, persons with disabilities are caught in a paradox: they must identify themselves as 'different' from the mainstream to have their disability-specific injustices addressed (such as by creating a disability-specific convention like the CRPD), while at the same time demand to be seen as 'the same' to stamp out stigma and discrimination.[40] Unfortunately, the law struggles to deal with the sameness and difference of persons without using categories to classify,[41] and categories can at once amplify, while also simplifying and flattening difference. In the words of Mark Brandon:

> in short, ... [it is claimed] ... that disabled persons should be able to lay claim to the benefits of law, while not being prisoners to law's categories. That's a tall order, and in my more sceptical moments, I wonder whether it is achievable.[42]

In judging sameness and difference of persons with mental impairment then there are two issues. The first is whether persons with mental impairment really are sufficiently 'the same' as those without mental impairment that the law should ignore their differences. That is, whether any perceived difference is 'imaginary' being only a matter of social stigma, stereotyping, and discrimination. The second is whether supported decision-making is sufficient to respond to such differences. I will deal with each of them in turn.

7.5.1 Is the Difference Between Persons With and Without Mental Impairment Real?

The first point to make here is that, contrary to what is often asserted by abolitionists, different treatment in and of itself is not necessarily discriminatory or unequal. In fact, making distinctions between groups is an unavoidable part of public policy and regulation,[43] and may be necessary to recognize and respond appropriately to difference, human diversity, and identity to achieve substantive equality. Similarly, stereotyping is probably a mental short-cut which is unavoidable whenever attention is given to group

[40] Megan Conway, 'Embodying the Law: Negotiating Disability Identity and Civil Rights' in Austin Sarat (ed), *Law and the Imagining of Difference* (Emerald Publishing Limited 2018) 43, 44 (hereafter Conway, 'Embodying the Law').

[41] Mark Brandon, 'Comment: Differences and (in)Equalities' in ibid 135–36 (hereafter Brandon, 'Differences and (in)Equalities').

[42] ibid 142.

[43] Deborah Hellman, *When Is Discrimination Wrong?* (Harvard University Press 2008) 2–3 (hereafter Hellman, *When is Discrimination Wrong?*).

rather than individual traits.[44] Given that groups are an important part of society it may be undesirable for states to ignore group traits in policy-making altogether.[45]

The issue of the sameness and difference of persons with mental impairments is a particularly difficult one. Part of the problem is that even within the group of persons with disability and mental impairment there is considerable heterogeneity in the type and combination of impairments, in severity of the symptoms, whether symptoms are chronic or episodic and the length of time a person has been mentally impaired and their treatment history which make it difficult to generalize. On the other hand, ignoring differences and treating everyone 'the same' using formal equality is also a generalization and not recognizing legitimate differences can also be unequal and amount to indirect discrimination.[46]

While 'dangerousness' and 'incapacity' are common stereotypes of persons with mental impairment, they are stereotypes which are at least partially accurate. Most persons with mental impairment are not dangerous and mental health law has never been intended to apply to those who are not sufficiently seriously ill to require treatment, or who seek medical assistance themselves. There are, however, a small proportion of persons with mental impairments who do cause harm to themselves or others associated with their mental impairment, as discussed above and in Chapter 3, section 3.3.2.2. The difficulty lies in trying to accurately predict who they are. As for incapacity, there is considerable medical evidence that serious mental impairments can reduce cognitive functioning,[47] especially when making 'hot' decisions which involve uncertain outcomes and strong emotions.[48] There is also evidence that mental impairments can create an altered sense of self-experience in which some patients have reported concerns about losing control or been 'taken over', having a strong external locus of control (with a focus on medication), and concerns about mental chaos and disorganization.[49] Persons with schizophrenia often jump to conclusions and use markedly less information in making decisions than persons without psychosis.[50]

[44] Luke A Boso, 'Dignity, Equality and Stereotypes' (2017) 92 Wash Law Rev 1119 (hereafter Boso, 'Dignity, Equality and Stereotypes').

[45] ibid.

[46] Aron Dhir, 'Human Rights Treaty Drafting through the Lens of Mental Disability: The Proposed International Convention on Protection and Promotion of the Rights and Dignity of Persons with Disabilities' (2005) 41 Stan J Int'l L 181, 190 (hereafter Dhir, 'Human Rights Treaty Drafting through the Lens of Mental Disability').

[47] Lisa M McTeague and others, 'Transdiagnostic Impairment of Cognitive Control in Mental Illness' (2016) 83 J Psychiatr Res 37, 44 (hereafter, McTeague, 'Transdiagnostic Impairment'); Maria Dorofeikova and others, 'Cognitive Deficit in Patients with Paranoid Schizophrenia: Its Clinical and Laboratory Correlates' (2018) 262 Psychiatry Res 542, 546 (hereafter Dorofeikova, 'Cognitive Deficit'); Donald M Linhorst and others, 'Opportunities and Barriers to Empowering People with Severe Mental Illness through Participation in Treatment Planning' (2002) 47(4) Soc Work 425, 426 (hereafter Linhorst, 'Participation in Treatment Planning').

[48] LE MacKenzie and others, 'Hot and Cold Executive Functions in Youth with Psychotic Symptoms' (2017) 47 Psychol Med 2844, 2850 (hereafter MacKenzie, 'Hot and Cold Executive Functions').

[49] Alan B McGuire and others, 'Altered Self-Experience and Goal Setting in Severe Mental Illness' (2015) 18 Am J Psychiatr Rehabil 333 (hereafter McGuire, 'Altered Self-Experience').

[50] Karrie Shogren and others, 'Supported Decision Making: A Synthesis of the Literature across Intellectual Disability, Mental Health, and Aging' (2017) 52(2) Educ Train Autism Dev Disabil 144, 150 (hereafter Shogren, 'Supported Decision Making'); Jose Luis Rubio, 'Jumping to Conclusions in Psychosis: A Faulty Appraisal' (2011) 133 Schizophr Res 199, 199 (hereafter Rubio, 'Jumping to Conclusions in Psychosis').

Further, even common disorders such as anxiety and depression can seriously interfere with decision-making. For example, it is difficult for a person to make important decisions if they feel like the following:

> Because of my anxiety, when I'm in a real high state of anxiety . . . I am sweating. I can't talk. I'm shaking. It's like I want to break out of the building.[51]

While this is a situation where perhaps taking a break and getting access to support may help, if the stress cannot be reduced, it is doubtful that a person who is overwhelmed by such feelings can make a decision.

While the MacArthur Treatment Competence Study has indicated that some persons admitted to hospital retain mental capacity (that is, the ability to understand, retain, and weigh information and communicate a decision[52]), there were also subgroups of persons (especially with schizophrenia and to a lesser degree depression) who lacked mental capacity.[53] It should also be noted that the MacArthur Study excluded those most seriously affected by mental health conditions and that all participants were on psychoactive medications at the time they participated in the study, so that there may have been some treatment effects (although this is denied by the authors).[54] While incapacity should not be assessed without taking into account the social context of a particular decision or whether sufficient information was provided to the person in an appropriate way,[55] it indicates that the law should be structured to deal with the incapacity of persons with mental impairments, in those individual cases where incapacity is relevant. This is further explored in Chapter 8. The claim by abolitionists that capacity testing constitutes indirect discrimination because it applies more so to persons with mental impairments than other groups, seems incorrect if it is actually measuring a genuine difference between persons who are not similarly situated.

However, it is not whether a stereotype is false or true so much as how the government uses the stereotype that is important, especially where it has the purpose or effect of subordinating the group or denying the ability of an individual to form and express identity.[56] Abolitionists often make comparisons between persons with disability and other oppressed and stereotyped social groups, such as those discriminated against on the basis of race and sex. However, discrimination is on the basis of race and sex, is usually a matter of supposition rather than actual difference, which is why persons

[51] Rosie Harding and Ezgi Tascioglu, 'Supported Decision-Making from Theory to Practice: Implementing the Right to Enjoy Legal Capacity' (2018) 8 Societies 25, 29 (Harding and Tascioglu, 'Supported Decision-Making').

[52] This is the usual form of the mental capacity test taken from Mental Capacity Act 2005 (Eng & Wales) s 3 (hereafter, MCA).

[53] Thomas Grisso and Paul S Appelbaum, 'The Macarthur Treatment Competence Study III' (1995) 19(2) Law Hum Behav 149, 169 (hereafter Grisso and Appelbaum 'Macarthur Treatment Competence'); Gabrielle Manderelli and others, 'Mental Capacity in Patients Involuntarily or Voluntarily Receiving Psychiatric Treatment for Acute Mental Disorder' (2014) 59(4) JFS 1002 (Manderelli, 'Mental Capacity in Patients Involuntarily').

[54] Grisso and Appelbaum, 'Macarthur Treatment Competence' (n 53) 151–52.

[55] Penelope Weller, 'Legal Capacity and Access to Justice: The Right to Participation in the CRPD' (2016) 5 Laws 43, 52 (hereafter Weller, 'Legal Capacity and Access to Justice').

[56] Boso, 'Dignity, Equality and Stereotypes' (n 44) 1125.

with disabilities may face far greater social barriers and have made less progress than other groups.[57] As observed by Gerard Quinn, 'the main conceptual problem in the disability context is that persons with disabilities are not always similarly situated with others. Though often exaggerated through stereotypes, the difference of disability can be real.'[58] As already noted, where a stereotype is used for the purposes of assisting persons with mental impairments to obtain access to much needed treatment, it is not necessarily an act of subordination by the state, but care and assistance in helping persons to live and improve their lives (at least compared to what their lives would be like with mental impairment and without treatment). More consideration needs to be given to whether treatment actually has that effect in an individual case and should be carefully weighed against the 'price' of compulsion, in terms of benefit and trauma to the particular person. This is explored in Chapter 8.

Of course, abolitionists and disability rights activists claim that persons with disabilities should not be required to obtain medical treatment to 'cure' them or be 'fixed' in order to obtain equality. For example, Simona Giordano writes 'equality is not served by rendering people equal: equality is served by them being treated with equal concern and respect, whether or not they are different.'[59] That is, disability is an expression of human diversity as an aspect of identity. However, as noted above, for persons with serious mental impairments, medical treatment alone is usually insufficient to render them 'equal' without a whole raft of other kinds of social support and accommodations. First, many persons with mental impairment, such as activist Patricia Deegan, use hospitalization and medications along with therapy, self-help, mutual support, friends, religion, work, exercise, and spending time with nature, as an important part of managing their own recovery.[60] That is, the diversity remains, but medical treatment assists persons in coping with it. Second, persons with mental impairments, as compared with persons with other kinds of impairments, are in the unusual position of having to decide which identity to develop. In fact, a disruption of identity may be a feature of a mental impairment, in that persons may believe that they are god or Jesus Christ, a vampire, or that an MI5 agent is trying to poison them,[61] or there may simply be a division between the mentally ill and mentally well self. As Elyn Saks explains:

> the question of identity for a person with mental illness, particularly episodic mental illness is fraught ... except those who are chronically ill, people with mental illness have their mentally ill self and their mentally healthy self. If you are in this situation, who is the real you?[62]

[57] Conway, 'Embodying the Law' (n 40) 44, 60–61, 64; Shakespeare, *Disability Rights and Wrongs Revisited* (n 22) 29–30.

[58] Gerard Quinn and Oddny Mjoll Arnardottir, 'Introduction' in Oddny Mjoll Arnardottir and Gerard Quinn (eds), *The UN Convention on the Rights of Persons with Disabilities: European and Scandinavian Perspectives* (Martinus Nijoff Publishers 2009) xx (hereafter Quinn and Arnardottir, 'Introduction').

[59] Simona Giordano, 'A Heaven without Giants or Dwarfs: Equality, Gender and Disabilities' (2014) 23 Camb Q Healthc Ethics 22, 28 (hereafter Giordano 'A Heaven without Giants or Dwarfs').

[60] Patricia Deegan, 'Recovering Our Sense of Value after Being Labeled Mentally Ill' (1993) 31(4) J Psychosoc Nurs Ment Health Serv 7 (hereafter Deegan, 'Recovering Our Sense of Value').

[61] Del Villar, 'Should Supported Decision-Making Replace Substituted Decision-Making?' (n 34) 187.

[62] Elyn R Saks, 'Psychosis and Identity' (2017) 68(4) Ala L Rev 923, 928 (hereafter Saks, 'Psychosis and Identity').

And

> with chronic mental illness we must say either that the person has been transformed into a different person—the ill person—or that the person's real self is being hidden and is still there. The mentally ill self may then be inauthentic even though it is most often present.[63]

The abolitionist approach is to privilege the person's mentally impaired identity, over their mentally well identity, at whatever stage of illness. This question has troubled the courts which have recognized that in some persons with long-term disability their mental impairment may have become so conflated with their personality, it may not be meaningful to distinguish between the autonomous wishes of the person and the impact of their impairments.[64] However, there are situations, particularly around the onset or early episodes of mental impairment, in which there is still a clear distinction between a person's mentally well identity and their mentally impaired identity. In such situations not intervening would seem to significantly disadvantage a person with mental impairment for whom their mentally well identity is still the most authentic expression of the self, and who may be able to achieve greater equality and long term quality of life with psychiatric treatment. The issue of which identity is more 'authentic' is something that ought to be assessed on a case-by-case basis, perhaps using a mental capacity approach, as explored in Chapter 8, rather than for a blanket law to recognize one or the other.

7.5.2 Can Supported Decision-Making Make Persons with Mental Impairment Equal with Persons without Mental Impairment?

Supported decision-making is perhaps the most exciting and promising aspect of the proposed abolition of mental health law and is a key component of most other law reform proposals as well. This is explored further in Chapter 8. There is no doubt that persons with mental impairments are often not consulted and are not provided with any or sufficient medical information in an accessible form and that the information gap is a significant type of inequality. For example, persons with mental impairments receive less counselling on their psychiatric medications compared with patients taking medications for cardiovascular conditions, despite the majority of pharmacists believing that persons with mental impairments did not have all the necessary drug information from their physician or pharmacist to manage care.[65] Persons with mental impairment can certainly benefit from greater clinical engagement and participation in decision-making, and studies have consistently indicated that building relationships of trust and respect is important for the recovery process, greater ownership

[63] ibid 929.

[64] *X NHS Trust v Mr B* [2015] EWCOP 60 [13] (hereafter, *X NHS Trust v Mr B*).

[65] Scott Wakeham and Cheryl A Sadoski, 'Beyond Equality: Providing Equitable Care for Persons with Disabilities' (2017) 150(4) CPJ/RPC 251, 253 (hereafter Wakeham and Sadoski, 'Beyond Equality').

of treatment plans by persons with mental impairment, and reduction in compulsory admissions.[66]

Crucially, supported decision-making performs a vital role in the abolition with support model in ensuring the substantive equality of persons with mental impairments in exercising their legal capacity in decisions about healthcare. While the abolition of mental health law treats everyone 'the same', supported decision-making is intended to accommodate differences in the actual decision-making abilities of persons with mental impairments. The key issue, of course, is whether supported decision-making is capable of securing substantive equality, promoting autonomy, and assisting persons with mental impairments to make healthcare decisions on an equal basis with others. I argue that while supported decision-making is a useful tool, which should be further developed through research, it is not sufficient at this stage to secure the substantive equality of persons with mental impairments on its own.

The concept of supported decision-making was brought into the CRPD negotiations by Inclusion International (an international organization, representing persons with cognitive impairments and their families, with 200 national member organizations from 115 countries) with support from its Canadian member, the Canadian Association for Community Living.[67] While most persons with disabilities involved in negotiating the CRPD were articulate verbal communicators, Inclusion International was especially concerned to ensure that the CRPD included the perspective of persons with severe cognitive impairments and very high support needs.[68] For such persons, the role of families and friends in providing support was 'an essential bridge' for them to communicate and to have any capacity to act at all.[69] Many other disability organizations were suspicious of the role of families, fearing interference and the undermining of autonomy, but the attendance of two persons with very high support needs and their families during the negotiations convinced other disability organizations of the need for a right to supported decision-making.[70] Thus, supported decision-making as a CRPD concept was born, based on the notion of supported decision-making developed in Canada in the late 1980s and early 1990s which recognized that persons with cognitive impairments could still make their own decisions even with the use of support.[71] Supported decision-making then is a cognitive disability concept which has been expanded to the mental health context.[72]

While the CRPD literature often makes a distinction between 'supported decision-making' and 'support for legal capacity', for convenience I will simply use the term 'supported decision-making' to apply to both. The concept of supported decision-making

[66] Shogren, 'Supported Decision Making' (n 50) 152.

[67] Anna MacQuarrie and Connie Laurin-Bowie, 'Our Lives, Our Voices: People with Intellectual Disabilities and Their Families' in Maya Sabatello and Marriane Schulze (eds), *Human Rights and Disability Advocacy* (University of Pennsylvania Press 2013) 25, 27 (hereafter MacQuarrie and Laurin-Bowie, 'Our Lives, Our Voices).

[68] ibid 32.

[69] ibid.

[70] ibid 37.

[71] ibid 36.

[72] Piers Gooding, 'Supported Decision-Making: A Rights-Based Disability Concept and Its Implications for Mental Health Law' (2013) 20(3) Psychiatry Psychol & L 431, 431 (hereafter Gooding, 'Supported Decision-Making').

is still evolving and according to Joanne Watson and colleagues can 'appear circular due to its infancy'.[73] In essence supported decision-making refers to a broad range of formal and informal assistance aimed at helping a person to make decisions between good options.[74] One of the most widely used and accepted descriptions of supported decision-making is by Michael Bach and Lana Kerzner who have identified three broad types of support. First, support in formulating an individual's purposes, exploring a range of choices with them and making decisions. Second, support in communicating with and making arrangements with others and third, support in managing an individual's obligations under any agreements made.[75] It can involve life planning to help individuals identify their values and life purpose to guide decision-making, independent advocacy and representation supports to deal with third parties and overcome attitudinal barriers that presume the person is incapable of making a decision, relationship building to find and develop supporters with sufficient knowledge of the person, and administrative support in entering into and carrying out agreements.[76] It can also include legal frameworks which create formalized structures for supported decision-making, such as recognizing the supported person as the decision-maker and regulating the appointment, duties, powers, and legal status of supporters.[77] Supports are social or technological in nature and can include advance decisions in which a person sets out their will and preferences with respect to hospital admission and treatment when they are well in advance of an episode of illness.[78] Within the CRPD model, health interventions, such as medications are not counted as supports, even if some persons with mental impairments use them as a form of support for their recovery.

However, it should be remembered that supported decision-making is more than just giving persons assistance to make their own decisions. In situations where a person requires very high levels of support, however, the onus on the supporter to 'interpret' the will and preferences of the person with disability becomes increasingly high so that the distinction between supported and substitute decision-making becomes blurred. Where a person is unable to make a decision, or a sufficiently clear decision, then a facilitator will look for evidence of the person's will and preferences and try to make a decision that best reflects their diachronic identity, that is, what gives persons their long-term and enduring identities,[79] and their life story. Yet, the decision

[73] Joanne Watson and others, 'Supporting End of Life Decision Making: Case Studies of Relational Closeness in Supported Decision Making for People with Severe or Profound Intellectual Disability' (2017) 30 J Appl Res Intellect Disabil 1022, 1023 (hereafter Watson, 'Supporting End of Life Decision Making').

[74] Piers Gooding, *A New Era for Mental Health Law and Policy: Supported Decision-Making and the UN Convention on the Rights of Persons with Disabilities* (Cambridge University Press 2017) 118 (hereafter Gooding, *A New Era*).

[75] Michael Bach and Lana Kerzner, 'A New Paradigm for Protecting Autonomy in the Right to Legal Capacity' (2010) (hereafter Bach and Kerzner, 'A New Paradigm').

[76] ibid.

[77] For example, *Representation Agreement Act (Revised Statues of British Columbia)* 1996 c405 (hereafter RAA, BC).

[78] Hui Yun Chan, 'Refusing Treatment Prior to Becoming Incapacitated: Supported Decision-Making as an Approach in Advance Directives' (2018) 24 Eur J Health Law 24 (hereafter, Chan, 'Supported Decision-Making as an Approach in Advance Directives').

[79] Alexander Pruss, 'A Deflationary Theory of Diachronic Identity' (2012) 90(1) Australas J Philos 19, 19 (hereafter Pruss, 'Diachronic Identity').

will still be regarded as belonging to the supported person. Support is also not compulsory, and persons with mental impairment can control how much support they wish to receive and can reject all support.

The idea that a person with mental impairment can use support to effectively 'close the gap' in decision-making autonomy and legal capacity with persons without mental impairment, and thereby put themselves on an equal footing, has strong appeal. As Terry Carney asks 'what's not to like?'[80] It is, unfortunately, on the journey from the abstract to the reality, where the drawbacks of supported decision-making become apparent and its ability to create substantive equality for persons with mental impairment (following the abolition of mental health law) becomes doubtful. While some of the difficulties arise from a widely acknowledged dearth of research, many are conceptual flaws which are not easily overcome.

The first and probably most important issue is whether supported decision-making can be expanded as a technique from persons with cognitive impairments to persons with mental impairments. While Terry Carney alludes to the idea that persons with mental impairment, unlike persons with cognitive impairments, may not need supported decision-making in addition to the abolition of substitute decision-making, he provides no explanation or authority for this statement.[81] In response to this I argue that the idea that persons with mental impairment, except perhaps those who are only mildly affected, do not need support in decision-making seems ambitious given that mental impairments can severely distort a person's thinking and even more so if he or she is in emotional distress (including feeling stressed, unsure of the best decision, or fearful of being judged),[82] even if he or she is able to communicate a decision. In fact, some persons with mental impairment themselves have wondered if any amount of support would be sufficient to assist them when they are in crisis.[83] For example Loree Cook-Daniels states:

> The proposals made for supporting decision-making simply cannot be applied to people with volatile and unstable desires over time (and whilst I dislike emphasizing my disability politics I have personal experience with epilepsy and psychosis) and am genuinely confused as to how the [U.N.] Committee thinks anyone could support my decisions at times when my own will was unknowable to me.[84]

While there are the so-called 'hard cases' where a person makes no decision, or expresses contradictory desires, there is also the situation where a person has no trouble expressing a clear decision which seems to contradict the person's diachronic identity

[80] Terry Carney, 'Supported Decision-Making in Australia: Meeting the Challenge of Moving from Capacity to Capacity-Building?' (2017) 35(2) Law in Cont 44, 45 (hereafter Carney, 'Supported Decision-Making in Australia').

[81] Terry Carney, 'Prioritising Supported Decision-Making: Running on Empty or a Basis for Glacial-to-Steady Progress?' (2017) 6 Laws 24 (hereafter Carney, 'Prioritising Supported Decision-Making').

[82] Shogren, 'Supported Decision Making' (n 50) 151.

[83] Dilip Jeste, 'Supported Decision Making in Serious Mental Illness' (2018) 81(1) Psychiatry: Interpers and Biol Proc 28, 35 (hereafter Jeste, 'Supported Decision Making').

[84] Loree Cook-Daniels, 'Supported Decision-Making: Pathway to More Rights or More Wrongs?' (2015) (May/June) Victimization of the Elderly and Disabled 5, 15 (hereafter, Cook-Daniels, 'Supported Decision-Making').

and because of the nature of their impairment it does not seem to be an autonomous or authentic decision. For example, where a person with paranoia rejects certain family members he trusted before the onset of his illness and suddenly turns to a family member he had previously fallen out with who takes the money he had formerly carefully saved and isolates him from the rest of the family.[85] Or, where a person refuses treatment because they believe their clinician is an assassin.[86] Ironically, if a person was unable to express a decision, their facilitators would try to make a decision which was consistent with their diachronic identity prior to the onset of illness. As Terry Carney observes 'ethically it is surely not enough to create the *conditions* for an autonomous decision without asking if the decision is *in fact* autonomous'.[87]

At present, empirical research on supported decision-making is still emerging and so far the extent to which support can assist persons with mental impairment is equivocal at best.[88] While there is some indication that simplifying information, including giving verbal information while a person followed it on an information sheet and getting persons to paraphrase it, was the most effective strategy for persons with mental impairment compared with persons with cognitive impairment and dementia, the improvement was only modest.[89] There was only a shift in decision-making ability using this type of support for 9 out of 82 people.[90] There is some evidence in a study by Rosie Harding and Ezgi Tascioglu that among persons with cognitive disability, supported decision-making is being used with respect to 'everyday' decisions about what to eat, wear, or do, but less so for more complex life decisions, including healthcare, which are still dominated by substitute decisions.[91] The authors blame the mental capacity legal framework for skewing supported decision-making towards everyday decisions, stating that the 'functional assessment of capacity allows and indeed facilitates the drive towards substitute decision-making for more complex matters'.[92] However, the same study indicated that many persons with cognitive disability (for example, the person to whose standard answer to every direct question about what he wanted was 'no') struggled in making even the most basic everyday decisions, such as taking a shower, and that care-workers often had to resort to various kinds of 'nudges', persuasion, and manipulation to 'support' them to make decisions.[93] An alternative explanation, not explored in the study, is that if persons with severe impairments cannot make even the most basic concrete decisions with support, then it is likely they will battle even more so with decisions which are abstract and involve wider and longer term considerations.

[85] Failinger, 'Paradox in Madness' (n 33) 128.

[86] Ad Hoc Committee on the Mental Capacity Bill, *Report on the Mental Capacity Bill*, (Northern Ireland Assembly, 25 January 2016) NIA 252/11-16, para 32 (hereafter, 'Report on MCA NI Bill').

[87] Carney, 'Supported Decision-Making in Australia' (n 80) 45–46.

[88] For example, Shogren, 'Supported Decision Making' (n 50); Davidson and others, 'Supported Decision Making: A Review of the International Literature' (2015) 38 Int J Law Psychiatry 61 (hereafter Davidson, 'Supported Decision Making').

[89] Davidson, 'Supported Decision Making' (n 88) 65.

[90] ibid.

[91] Harding and Tascioglu, 'Supported Decision-Making' (n 51) 26.

[92] ibid 39.

[93] ibid 29.

Decisions made with 'support' where persons are severely impaired and require high levels of facilitation, also often involve far less rigorous consideration of the relevant issues. For instance, in a recent study Joanne Watson and colleagues claim that a person with severe cognitive impairment was 'supported' to refuse life-saving treatment by his family and members of a 'circle of support' who decided that he would not have wanted a tracheotomy, simply because he did not like it in the past.[94] The study gave no information about his long-term prognosis (that is, whether he was likely to recover from the surgery), or his level of pain and discomfort caused by foregoing the surgery. It is hard to see how such a decision could be considered to be 'equal' or even comparable with the decision-making process of a person without disabilities, who would not make a decision based solely on whether they *liked* having a tracheotomy or not, without counterbalancing it against their likely death, any suffering that may result from refusing the surgery, and possible recovery and quality of life post-surgery.

Further, the use of supported decision-making with mental health specific issues such as the effects of episodic illness, delusions, self-harm, suicide, or how to deal with persons in acute crises have not been investigated or considered in depth in the literature.[95] The possibility of a person who expresses a will and preference for self-harm or suicide or other highly risky or damaging actions raises particular ethical concerns.[96] While there are few details about what providing support for a person in suicidal state actually entails, it seems to involve trying to create a safe and comfortable space to assist them to understand what is happening and to facilitate their making a decision about whether or not to end their lives which reflects their will and preferences, whatever the result.[97] As explained, by Tina Minkowitz:

> there is a great deal of evidence to suggest that ordinary kindness and acceptance meets people's needs for practical support and emotional support during such an experience without violating their rights and while carrying much lower risk of lifelong trauma and lifelong dependency on services.[98]

It may also include the offering of various group healthcare decision-making processes, involving the person's family, friends, and mental health professionals.[99] Jillian Craigie argues that the giving of support may even 'endorse helping the person make a "good" decision in a specific sense: part of the aim of support is to make a self-expressive decision'.[100]

[94] Watson, 'Supporting End of Life Decision Making' (n 73) 1031.

[95] Davidson, 'Supported Decision Making' (n 88) 66; Jeste, 'Supported Decision Making' (n 83) 37; Shogren, 'Supported Decision Making' (n 50) 150.

[96] Carney, 'Supported Decision-Making in Australia' (n 80) 59.

[97] Submission of CDLP Galway quoted in Australian Law Reform Commission, *Equality, Capacity and Disability in Commonwealth Laws* (Australian Government 2014) [3.86]–[3.88] (hereafter 'ALRC Report').

[98] 'Advancing the Rights of Users and Survivors of Psychiatry Using the UN Convention on the Rights of Persons with Disabilities—an Interview with Tina Minkowitz' in Helen Spander and Jill Anderson (eds), *Madness, Distress and the Politics of Disablement* (Policy Press 2016) 179 ('Interview with Tina Minkowitz').

[99] Flynn and Arstein-Kerslake, 'State Intervention in the Lives of People with Disabilities' (n 25) 52.

[100] Jillian Craigie, 'A Fine Balance: Reconsidering Patient Autonomy in Light of the UN Convention on the Rights of Persons with Disabilities' (2015) 29(6) Bioethics 398, 403 (hereafter Craigie, 'A Fine Balance').

However, it may be extremely difficult for supporters to provide support to a person who is in a fragile and desperate state of mind. The recent United States case in which Michelle Carter was convicted of involuntary manslaughter for being too encouraging in supporting her friend Conrad Roy III to complete suicide, even though she genuinely believed it was in accordance with his will and preferences, is illustrative.[101] It raises the issue of whether a supporter is always required to try to talk a person out of suicide or high risk behaviours or to go along with the possibility that death may be what a person wants. It also demonstrates the fine line between 'support' and 'coercion' and giving someone the courage of their convictions and recognizing that they may have changed their mind. Further, as pointed out above, respecting a person's legal capacity may involve sacrificing their right to life. The right to make one's own mistakes seems less compelling when the results are likely to be irreversible or fatal or to limit future autonomy.[102]

As support needs to be individually tailored, it may be difficult to determine what type of support and how much support a person needs, 'calibrating the level and quality of support to match and assist realization of a person's will and preferences and rights is not a simple matter of *presuming* that unaided information or other support is adequate to the task.'[103] That is, genuine supported decision-making is not a 'one-size-fits-all' or 'tick the box' exercise.[104] Obviously, the effectiveness and quality of support is very dependent on the availability, skills, and integrity of the relevant supporters and their knowledge of the particular person, which are likely to be very uneven across different situations. Studies indicate that the most effective support is given by those supporters who are in intimate and very close relationships with the person who is being supported, although new supporters may be able to increase their knowledge of the person by relying on stories about the person from others.[105] Unfortunately, many persons with disabilities who require support are socially isolated and in government trials finding appropriate supporters has been a recurring difficulty. Supported decision-making has also proven very time-consuming and expensive with modest rewards.[106] The down-side of course is that resources for all governments are finite and that the resources directed to supported decision-making may reduce funding for other valuable programs and treatments.[107]

Related to this is the further difficulty of trying to ensure that the support that is provided is not coercive, overly paternalistic or manipulative so that the support offered actually yields a person's authentic decision, rather than undermining the equal autonomy supported decision-making aims to foster. For instance, Anna Arstein-Kerslake is concerned that supported decision-making has the very real potential of being co-opted by service providers and used to subordinate the will and

[101] Katharine Seelye and Jess Bidgood 'Guilty Verdict for Young Woman Who Urged Friend to Kill Himself' *The New York Times* (16 June 2017): http://nyti.ms/2sxl1XR (hereafter Seelye and Bidgood, 'Guilty Verdict').

[102] Maclean, *Autonomy, Informed Consent and Medical Law* (n 20) 28.

[103] Carney, 'Supported Decision-Making in Australia' (n 80) 52.

[104] Anna Arstein-Kerslake, 'Future Directions in Supported Decision-Making' (2017) 37(1) Disabil Stud Q 5 (hereafter, Arstein-Kerslake, 'Future Directions in Supported Decision-Making').

[105] Watson, 'Supporting End of Life Decision Making' (n 73) 1029, 1032.

[106] Carney, 'Prioritising Supported Decision-Making' (n 81).

[107] Maclean, *Autonomy, Informed Consent and Medical Law* (n 20) 49.

preferences of persons with disabilities to the interests of service providers.[108] Terry Carney also warns that supported decision-making itself could easily become just another disability service under the National Disability Insurance Scheme (NDIS) that is controlled by others.[109] Conversely, Piers Gooding argues that issues of undue influence, coercion, manipulation, and wanting to please others are exaggerated and are characteristic of all adult relationships and of conceptualizing autonomy in a relational way.[110] However, I think he underestimates the asymmetry of the power relationship between the supporters and the supported, which is far more imbalanced and dependent than the usual relationships between most adults without mental impairments. In fact, persons with mental impairments may even find benign attempts by supporters to give information and to present different options that are outside their own thinking deeply troubling, a situation that can be amplified where a person has less decision-making experience.[111] It also misunderstands the concept of 'relational autonomy' described above, as it is not the provision of support by one's relations which makes autonomy 'relational' but rather how a person's relations in a wider sense with other people, the state, law, and the world, support or hinder an individual's autonomy and how law structures and nurtures those relationships.[112] In fact, Katrine Del Villar argues the opposite, that is, involuntary detention and psychiatric treatment is often a last resort where the relationship between persons with mental impairment and their supporters is at breaking point and treatment is necessary to restore the person's identity so that the person can return to and resume the relationship.[113] Piers Gooding also makes the point that issues of coercion, paternalism, and manipulation in supported decision-making are probably just as serious for substitute decision-making.[114] However, as set out in Chapter 8, substitute decision-making is more transparent with respect to the trade-offs made in decision-making and more subject to judicial oversight than supported decision-making.[115]

The provision of support is intended under the CRPD to be subject to 'safeguards' to ensure that the person with mental impairment is not unduly influenced and to prevent conflict of interest and abuse.[116] As persons with disabilities often receive the majority of their assistance from friends and family, it is important that States Parties take care to protect persons with disabilities from discrimination and inequality by non-state actors in the private realm.[117] However, the exact 'safeguards' required by

[108] Arstein-Kerslake, 'Future Directions in Supported Decision-Making' (n 104).

[109] Carney, 'Prioritising Supported Decision-Making' (n 81).

[110] Piers Gooding, 'Navigating the "Flashing Amber Lights" of the Right to Legal Capacity in the United Nations Convention on the Rights of Persons with Disabilities: Responding to Major Concerns' (2015) 15 Hum Rights Law Rev 45, 56 (hereafter Gooding, 'Navigating the Flashing Amber Lights').

[111] Craigie, 'A Fine Balance' (n 100); Carney, 'Supported Decision-Making in Australia' (n 80) 58–59.

[112] Jennifer Nedelsky, *Laws Relations: A Relational Theory of Self, Autonomy, and Law* (Oxford University Press 2011) 19 (hereafter Nedelsky, *Laws Relations*); Del Villar, Should Supported Decision-Making Replace Substituted Decision-Making? (n 34) 188–89.

[113] Del Villar, Should Supported Decision-Making Replace Substituted Decision-Making? (n 34) 188.

[114] Gooding, 'Navigating the Flashing Amber Lights' (n 110) 57.

[115] Matthew Burch, 'Autonomy, Respect, and the Rights of Persons with Disabilities in Crisis' (2017) 34(3) J Appl Philos 391 (hereafter Burch 'Autonomy, Respect').

[116] CRPD, Article 12(4).

[117] Andrea Broderick, *The Long and Winding Road to Equality and Inclusion for Persons with Disabilities: The United Nations Convention on the Rights of Persons with Disabilities* (Intersentia 2015) 99 (hereafter Broderick, The Long and *Winding Road to Equality*).

the CRPD and how they operate are yet to be determined. Anna Arstein-Kerslake has suggested that for persons with cognitive impairments the supporter should be required to act like a 'cognitive prosthesis' so that they essentially 'act merely as a tool for the expression of the individual's personalized conception of the good'.[118] The 'cognitive prosthesis' model sets out four principles for safeguarding the relationship of supported decision-making being: (1) recognition of legal capacity, (2) ensuring inequality of power is not abused and turned into domination, (3) decisions made are an expression of the will and preferences of the person and not the supporter, and (4) that any supported decision-making system is not over-regulating.[119] However, while this model is a good start, it stops short of giving supporters concrete guidance, or a legislative framework of safeguards that sets out the responsibilities of supporters and those supported against which people can be held accountable, which is important for those who are less trusting of the competence, motives, and integrity of individuals in positions of power. The privatization of decision-making appears inherently difficult to police and it may be impossible for a sufficiently comprehensive structure to be developed. In addition, it may be unrealistic to expect supporters, especially those who are close to the person with mental impairment, such as a parent, to put their feelings to one side, and to pretend they have no personal stake in the decisions of the person with mental impairment.[120] The supported decision-making model constructs the supporter as an altruistic, self-displacing, relationship-suspending advocate for the person with mental impairment but empirical research indicates this aspiration is too simplistic and unrealistic.[121]

No matter how respectful, socially inclusive, and useful decision-making support and social support services are, persons with mental impairments may either not seek decision-making support, or may actively reject all offers of support. Further, some models, such as guardianship in Peru, expect persons with disabilities to be able to arrange their own supports (see section 1.3.2), which while reducing the risk that persons with disabilities may be pushed to accept support they do not want, increases the risk that they may slip through the cracks and have no support because they cannot arrange the support that they need. The failure to obtain support may be associated with their impairment, their past experiences with and general distrust of services, lack of suitable supporters, or pure inertia. A person may also reject services and support because they are being abused and their abusers want to avoid detection.[122] The ability to not seek or to reject support based only on a person's subjective judgment of his or her own needs is a core tenet of the abolitionist interpretation of the CRPD,[123] which to this extent enshrines a right to be left alone. The ability to reject support is also claimed

[118] Anna Arstein-Kerslake, 'An Empowering Dependency: Exploring Support for the Exercise of Legal Capacity' (2016) 18(1) Scand J Disabil Res 77, 78 (hereafter Arstein-Kerslake, 'An Empowering Dependency').

[119] ibid.

[120] Wilson, 'Right to Life' (n 9) 685.

[121] Meredith Stone and others, 'Estranged Relations: Coercion and Care in Narratives of Supported Decision-Making in Mental Healthcare' (2020) 46 Med Humanit 62, 66 (hereafter Stone, 'Estranged Relations').

[122] Kirsty Keywood, 'The Vulnerable Adult Experiment: Situating Vulnerability in Adult Safeguarding Law' (2017) 53 Int J Law Psychiatry 88, 91 (hereafter Keywood, 'The Vulnerable Adult Experiment').

[123] General Comment 1 (n 1) [19].

to protect a person from inappropriate or low quality support. Pushing persons with mental impairment to accept support because others believe that they need it could be experienced as harassment and as an affront to their dignity. However, in insisting on the right to reject support, abolitionists may go beyond classical liberal theory which permits attempts to warn, advise, persuade, and reason with persons, provided they are not forced.[124] The ability to reject support may also create inequity between persons with disabilities as the most seriously impaired persons may be the most disadvantaged. That is, by not seeking or rejecting support, the most seriously impaired persons may be in the worst position to evaluate the costs and benefits of psychiatric or other treatment or support options and to use the support that is on offer to reflect on what their will and preferences are.

However, a use of supported decision-making in the mental health context which may be promising is with respect to the creation of advance decisions. Advance decisions have been defined as a form of support, in allowing persons to make their will and preferences known before an episode of illness, but also as a tool which can itself be created using supports.[125] Unfortunately, advance decisions are plagued with a raft of difficulties surrounding low uptake, whether a person had mental capacity and was acting autonomously at the time it was made, vagueness and lack of clarity, whether there have been subsequent changes which may affect the persons prior wishes, and whether the relevant people are aware of the advance decisions existence. However, the possibility of using supported decision-making to create an advance decision may alleviate some of these concerns, especially if a clinician is involved in providing information.[126] That is, an independent clinician can do a capacity assessment, ensure the advance decision is expressed properly, ensure that the person is properly informed about what he or she is refusing, pick up any undue influence, and explain possible changes and ensure attention is given to the advance decision at the time of crisis.[127] This is further discussed in Chapter 8, section 8.4.2.

The other matter to bear in mind is that maintaining control or autonomy is not important to everyone and that contrary to the assumptions underlying the CPRD, some persons with mental impairment do not wish to make their own decisions about medical care in order to obtain 'equality'.[128] For example, recent research by Fauzia Knight and colleagues indicates that persons with mental impairments have four types of narrative positions describing the type of support for decision-making they preferred.[129] These were: the 'Inward Expert' who wanted their clinicians to recognize their personal expertise in understanding their condition;[130] the 'Outward Entrustor' who was more interested in developing a caring and trusting relationship with their clinician

[124] John Stuart Mill, in David Bronwich and George Kateb (eds), *On Liberty* (Yale University Press 2003) 156, 159 (hereafter Mill, *On Liberty*).
[125] Chan, 'Supported Decision-Making as an Approach in Advance Directives' (n 78).
[126] ibid 36–38.
[127] ibid.
[128] Davidson, 'Supported Decision Making' (n 88) 63.
[129] Fauzia Knight and others, 'Supported Decision-Making: The Expectations Held by People with Experience of Mental Illness' (2018) 28(6) Qual Health Res 1002 (hereafter Knight, 'Supported Decision-Making').
[130] ibid 1005.

than in exercising control;[131] the 'Self-Aware Observer' who sought help to manage their unwell identity and who sought collaborative relationships with clinicians;[132] and 'Social Integrators' who were concerned with acquiring support through medical advice, peer and social support and community participation.[133] These positions were fluid so that some Inward Experts became Outward Entrustors when they were more acutely unwell.[134] This study presents a nuanced account of the kinds of support that are necessary to achieve the equality of persons with mental impairments and their participation in decision-making.

7.6 Participation

As already touched on above, full and equal participation is a central principle of the CRPD, underpinning dignity, autonomy, and equality, as well as being a key plank of the disability rights movement encapsulated by the motto 'nothing about us without us'. While participation is a procedural rather than substantive right,[135] it plays an important role in structuring power relations within the human rights framework. In particular, it subverts top-down (imposed from above) in favour of bottom-up (or grass-roots) decision-making, it promotes human dignity by treating individuals as subjects rather than objects who are capable of having a say about their destiny, and it permits pluralist approaches to policy and programme development.[136] In democratic societies, participation is a way in which persons can protect and exercise their rights in the bureaucratic state.[137] As Jennifer Nedelsky observes:

> Participation means more than a chance to convey the particularities of one's situation; it means participation in determining norms that will govern the decision ... but it is not enough to follow a participatory procedure if the substance of the decision ignores the participation.[138]

As well as making people feel included, participation is also intended to improve the quality, transparency, and legitimacy of decision-making as greater knowledge and wider perspectives are taken into account and to promote compliance.[139]

Historically, the largest barrier to full social participation for persons with mental impairments has been institutionalization.[140] A denial of participation and the ability

131 ibid 1007.
132 ibid 1008.
133 ibid 1009.
134 ibid 1009.
135 Weller, 'Legal Capacity and Access to Justice' (n 55) 44.
136 Alicia Ely Yamin, 'Suffering and Powerlessness: The Significance of Promoting Participation in Rights-Based Approaches to Health' (2009) 11(1) Health Hum Rights 6, 6–7 (hereafter Yamin, 'Suffering and Powerlessness').
137 Nedelsky, *Laws Relations* (n 112) 147–48.
138 ibid 147.
139 Sandra Fredman, *Human Rights Transformed: Positive Rights and Positive Duties* (Oxford University Press 2008) 198 (hereafter Fredman, *Human Rights Transformed*).
140 Conway, 'Embodying the Law' (n 40) 48.

to be heard is often claimed to lead to abuses[141] and a loss of personhood. Further, as pointed out by Hugh Collins, 'the goal of social inclusion does emphasise the contribution of participation in public life as a contribution to "well-being"'.[142]

With respect to decision-making regarding mental health care, participation occurs at the individual as well as at the collective level. At the individual level, it occurs through processes, such as supported decision-making, shared decision-making and involvement in treatment planning,[143] which allow individuals to express their views about their healthcare, ascertain their will and preferences and be involved in decision-making (discussed in section 7.5.2 above). It also includes building a person's capacity for participation,[144] including the provision of reasonable accommodation.[145] At a collective level, participation occurs through processes such as CRPD implementation and the development of policies and programmes. In fact, the CRPD is unique as a human rights instrument because not only was it developed with civil society participation, but it requires that disabled persons organizations (DPOs) be involved in the development of legislation, policies, and programmes[146] and in the monitoring and implementation of the CRPD.[147] Further, breaking down barriers to participation is one of the purposes of the CRPD[148] which is seen as being necessary for the recognition of all civil and political and socio-economic rights. The requirements for collective participation are elaborated on by the CRPD Committee in draft General Comment No 7, with a view to creating a tool for transformative equality and social change.[149] A key feature of the General Comment is that persons with disabilities need to be involved in decision-making which relates to them at all levels of government as well as various ad hoc committees.[150]

The value of participation is relatively uncontroversial. I have no difficulty with the idea that persons should be involved in and participate in decision-making about their lives at an individual or collective level to the maximum extent possible. Practices by States Parties, such as not consulting persons with disabilities at all, or only doing so as 'illusory participation' to affirm a decision which has essentially already been made[151] clearly amount to bad faith and are in breach of the CRPD.

However, it is my argument that participation means that persons are consulted about and have their views taken seriously in decision-making processes.[152] In

141 Christopher H Maylea, 'A Rejection of Involuntary Treatment in Mental Health Social Work' (2017) 11(4) Ethics Soc Welf 336, 338 (hereafter Maylea, 'A Rejection of Involuntary Treatment').

142 Hugh Collins, 'Discrimination, Equality and Social Inclusion' (2003) 66(1) MLR 16, 40 (hereafter Collins, 'Discrimination, Equality and Social Inclusion').

143 Linhorst, 'Participation in Treatment Planning' (n 47) 425.

144 Fredman, *Human Rights Transformed*) (n 139).

145 Janet E Lord and Rebecca Brown, 'The Role of Reasonable Accommodation in Securing Substantive Equality for Persons with Disabilities: The UN Convention on the Rights of Persons with Disabilities' in Marcia H Rioux (ed), *Critical Perspectives on Human Rights and Disability Law* (Martinus Nijhoff 2011) 273, 277 (hereafter Lord and Brown, 'The Role of Reasonable Accommodation').

146 CRPD, Art 4.3.

147 CRPD, Art 33.3.

148 CRPD, Art 1.

149 CRPD Committee, *General Comment on article 4.3 and 33.3 of the convention on the participation with persons with disabilities in the implementation and monitoring of the convention*, 16 March 2018, (hereafter 'General Comment 7').

150 ibid [24].

151 Shakespeare, Disability Rights and *Wrongs Revisited* (n 22).

152 See CRPD, Art 4.

accordance with the CRPD Committee, the views of persons with disabilities should be given due weight and should only be departed from with good reason.[153] To this extent, participation should be defined by persons with disabilities themselves.[154] However, participation does not mean that States Parties have to do what persons with disabilities say no matter what, nor do they have a power of veto. Rather, participation involves consultation in good faith and not dictation. It is a right as well as a responsibility.[155] The result of my definition of participation is that the decision-making process will often involve compromise between different interests, including interests that are wider than those of persons with disabilities (such as friends and families and the community). Further, as pointed out by Andrea Broderick, the type of participation a person with disability may be able to enjoy may vary according to the nature of their impairments.[156]

The other issue I wish to discuss with respect to participation is to point out the difficulties involved in ensuring that participation is in fact representative of all persons with disabilities and whether such representation is even possible (an issue which is not considered in the CRPD itself). First, it should be noted that a great many people with impairments are unaware of the disability rights movement and probably do not even identify as being disabled.[157] Therefore, DPOs will not be representative of them. Participation favours well organized, committed and knowledgeable groups and may inadvertently further marginalize more disorganized groups.[158] Even during the negotiation of the CRPD, representatives had to be reminded of the large number of disabled persons who were not in the room especially those with very high support needs.[159] As noted in Chapter 1 section 1.4.1.2, activists like Anne Plumb are concerned that the views of abolitionists during the CRPD negotiations were not representative of all persons with mental impairments. Anna Nilsson and Lucy Series also point out that the DPOs may not have represented more 'moderate' user groups and that the role in the CRPD negotiations of a key group directly affected by Article 12—persons with dementia - was limited.[160] While abolitionists often complain that persons without direct lived experience of involuntary detention and treatment are 'unqualified' to have an opinion in the debate about the future of mental health law,[161] the same question can be asked of abolitionists. Namely, how is it that they are qualified to 'speak for' *all* other persons with mental impairments who may have a variety of views and experiences? Second, disability groups have different constituencies and goals and that more established 'peak' organizations with a wider base, often have less opportunities to consult with their members and may need to take positions which

[153] General Comment 7 (n 149) [21].
[154] hereafter Broderick, The Long and *Winding Road to Equality* (n 117) 70.
[155] ibid 70.
[156] ibid 69.
[157] Shakespeare, Disability Rights and *Wrongs Revisited* (n 22) 72.
[158] Fredman, *Human Rights Transformed*) (n 139) 201.
[159] MacQuarrie and Laurin-Bowie, 'Our Lives, Our Voices (n 67) 25.
[160] Nilsson and Series, 'Art 12' (n 35) 343.
[161] For example, Liz Brosnan, 'Who's Talking About Us Without Us? A Survivor Research Interjection into an Academic Psychiatry Debate on Compulsory Community Treatment Orders in Ireland' (2018) 7 Laws 33 (hereafter Brosnan, 'Who's Talking About Us Without Us?').

reflect the diversity of their memberships.[162] By contrast, smaller advocacy-focussed organizations are driven more directly by their members and are able to take more radical positions,[163] although given their small membership are by definition less representative. Third, the CRPD Committee also maintains that there needs to be a distinction between organizations for families, supporters and service providers, and organizations made up of persons with disabilities, so that persons with disabilities remain the dominant voice.[164] Fourth, the role for civil society in CRPD implementation and monitoring has the potential to fundamentally change the priorities of grassroots disability organizations from satisfying the material and more immediate needs of their members, in favour of national or international initiatives.[165] Fifth, it is also important that persons who sit at the intersections of multiple identities have their specific interests represented.[166] However, in trying to do so participation could become quite unwieldy as it may involve a large number of DPOs who are representative of persons with different impairments and social groups who are inclusive of age, sex, nationality, sexual orientations, and so on.[167]

7.7 Conclusion

In this Chapter I have delved into difficult questions of how to apply equality and non-discrimination in the CRPD and whether involuntary detention and treatment really is a form of unequal treatment and discrimination. In particular, I argue that there are difficulties in determining the 'equality of what' or which type of equality should prevail as equality claims rarely apply across the board. Other issues include determining equality with whom (or whether persons with and without mental impairment are comparable), whether involuntary detention and psychiatric treatment is a detriment or benefit, addressing the sameness and difference of persons with mental impairment and whether supported-decision making is enough to make the persons without mental impairment 'equal'. I argue that achieving substantive and transformative equality and non-discrimination for persons with mental impairments is far more complex than abolishing mental health law and to treat persons with and without mental impairments as 'the same' with respect to legal capacity in a formal sense. Not intervening, despite achieving formal equality, may actually further entrench inequality and discrimination against persons with mental impairments with respect to their ability to enjoy other CRPD rights and to live in and participate in the community on an equal basis with others.

Another form of equality within the CRPD is that involved in participating in decision-making, as well as a being an important CRPD principle in its own right.

[162] Laufey Love and others, 'Achieving Disability Equality: Empowering Disabled People to Take the Lead' (2018) 6(1) Soc Incl 1, 3 (hereafter Love, 'Achieving Disability Equality').

[163] ibid.

[164] General Comment 7 (n 149) [15].

[165] Stephen Meyers, 'NGO-ization and Human Rights Law: The CRPD's Civil Society Mandate' (2016) 5 Laws 147 (hereafter Meyers, 'NGO-ization').

[166] Fredman, *Human Rights Transformed* (n 139) 202.

[167] General Comment 7 (n 149) [36].

Implementing participation means that the views of persons with mental impairments and their organizations should be sought and accorded a high value in the decision-making process and States Parties should not depart from those views without good reason. However, ensuring equality in decision-making participation can have its difficulties especially in ensuring that those who participate are representative of all persons with disabilities. The claim that the abolitionists only represent the most radical elements of the disability rights movement has been used to criticize the call for the abolition of mental health law.

8
The Interpretive Framework and the Reform (as opposed to the Abolition) of Mental Health Law

8.1 Introduction

As outlined in Chapter 3, abolitionists argue that the abolition of mental health law is the only option for CRPD compliance and that it is needed to improve the lives of persons with mental impairment, mainly by reducing the trauma of involuntary interventions, preventing abuse, and increasing individual control and sense of personhood. However, it is my contention that the reform, as opposed to the abolition, of mental health law is the preferable direction for the future. It is also my position that contrary to the arguments of abolitionists, there is more than one possible interpretation of the CRPD, and that in applying the interpretive compass (described in Chapters 4 to 7) the reform of mental health law is just as, if not more, compatible with the CRPD taken as a whole than the abolition of mental health law. In accordance with my entire argument, in this chapter I also seek to address many of the concerns which underlie the position of abolitionists (outlined in Chapter 3) particularly in promoting individual autonomy where possible, in addition to concerns which the abolitionists have given less attention to such as the right to life and the prevention of suicide.[1]

However, rejecting the abolition of mental health law as either being required or desirable raises a number of questions. First, what are the options for the reform of mental health law? Second, why is reform better and more compatible with the object and purpose of the CRPD than abolition? Third, how does the interpretive compass of 'inherent dignity, equality and participation' assist in reaching that conclusion?

The purpose of this chapter is to address these questions. In the course of doing so I argue that it is important to keep an open mind to a variety of approaches to implementing the CRPD, rather than simply be fixed on one strategy: abolition. I argue that in order to maximize all of the rights of persons with mental impairments, the focus should be pragmatic rather than ideological. Combining the best ideas regarding the implementation of the CRPD will help ensure the inherent dignity, equality, and participation of persons with mental impairments. It will also enable individual differences in the type and severity of mental impairments to be accommodated. As set out in Chapter 1, I conceptualize disability as an *interaction* between the person with mental impairment and social and environmental barriers. Therefore,

[1] Kay Wilson, 'The Call for the Abolition of Mental Health Law: The Challenges of Suicide, Accidental Death and the Equal Enjoyment of the Right to Life' (2018) 18 Hum Rights Law Rev 651 (hereafter Wilson, 'The Right to Life').

Mental Health Law. Kay Wilson, Oxford University Press. © Kay Wilson 2021. DOI: 10.1093/oso/9780192843258.003.0008

I give weight to the effect of mental impairment on the person as well as to the removal of social and environmental barriers.

While I have already discussed the abolition of mental health law at length in Chapter 3 and in my discussion of the interpretive compass of the CRPD in Chapters 4 to 7, I have not as yet considered the alternatives to abolition. While there are many possible approaches, I will focus on two particular models (and variations of them) which have come to the fore in the literature: what I call the Mental Capacity with Support and the Support Except Where There is Harm models. These two models give primacy to supporting persons with mental impairments to make their own decisions, but permit limited involuntary detention and psychiatric treatment in certain circumstances as a last resort. Mental Capacity with Support is the more widely discussed model and has the most support in the literature. It also seems to have more political support than abolition,[2] especially in the United Kingdom (probably because of the existence of various Mental Capacity Acts),[3] although capacity approaches now feature in most Australian mental health laws in post-CRPD reforms,[4] and recent reforms to European legislation.[5]

However, choosing between reform options is difficult because the details involved in each model are still being debated within the literature, which as Paul Skowron notes can make comparisons premature.[6] Of the two, I argue that the Mental Capacity with Support model, which while not perfect is the best model for respecting dignity (including autonomy), equality, and participation. That said, the Support Except Where There is Harm model could potentially offer quite wide scope for individual decision-making depending on how it is interpreted and implemented (although the model seems somewhat under-developed). The amendments to the Mental Health Act 1983 (UK), proposed by Simon Wessely in a recent Independent Review, with their emphasis on providing support, increasing participation and choice, and reducing coercion, could also fit within the Support Except Where There is Harm Approach.[7] There is overlap between the two approaches. It is wrong to think that the prevention of harm plays no part in the Mental Capacity with Support model,[8] or that the assumption that

[2] Renu Barton-Hansen, 'Reforming Best Interests: The Road Towards Supported Decision-Making' (2018) 40(3) J Soc Wel & Fam L 277, 284 (hereafter Barton-Hansen 'Reforming Best Interests'); Genevra Richardson, 'Mental Capacity in the Shadow of Suicide: What Can the Law Do?' (2013) 9(1) In J Law Context 87, 93 (hereafter Richardson, 'Mental Capacity in the Shadow of Suicide').

[3] For example, *Mental Capacity Act* 2005 (UK) (hereafter MCA UK) and *Mental Capacity Act* 2016 (Northern Ireland) (hereafter MCA NI).

[4] Bernadette McSherry and Kay Wilson, 'The Concept of Capacity in Australian Mental Health Law Reform: Going in the Wrong Direction?' (2015) 40 Int J Law Psychiatry 60 (hereafter McSherry and Wilson 'The Concept of Capacity'); Sascha Callaghan and Christopher Ryan, 'An Evolving Revolution: Evaluating Australia's Compliance with the Convention on the Rights of Persons with Disabilities in Mental Health Law' (2016) 39(2) UNSWLJ 596 (hereafter, Callaghan and Ryan 'An Evolving Revolution').

[5] Marie Fallon-Kund and Jerome E Bickenbach, 'New Legal Capacity Laws and the United Nations Convention on the Rights of Persons with Disabilities: An Overview of Five Countries in Europe' (2017) 24 Eur J Health Law 285, 290 (hereafter, Fallon-Kund and Bickenbach 'New Legal Capacity Laws').

[6] Paul Skowron, 'Giving Substance to "the Best Interpretation of Will and Preferences"' (2019) 62 Int J Law Psychiatry 125, 125 (hereafter Skowron, 'Giving Substance to 'the Best Interpretation of Will and Preferences').

[7] Independent Review of the MHA 1983, 'Modernising the Mental Health Act: Increasing Choice, Reducing Compulsion' (UK Government, Final Report, December 2018) (hereafter 'Wellesley Report').

[8] John Fanning, 'Continuities of Risk in the Era of the Mental Capacity Act' (2016) 24(3) Med Law Rev 415 (hereafter Fanning, 'Continuities of Risk').

persons with mental impairments lack mental capacity plays no part in mental health law or the Support Except Where There is Harm model. The difference is one of emphasis and degree and to this extent, intervention to prevent harm could be thought of as respecting inherent dignity where it involves the restraint of autonomous acts that are degrading, violate widely accepted norms, and are likely to be irreversible (as argued in Chapter 5, section 5.2).

This chapter is organized into four parts. In section 8.2, I make some general comments about the abolition of mental health law and the Mental Capacity with Support and Support Except Where There is Harm models. In section 8.3, I define the Mental Capacity with Support model and consider the pros and cons of the model with respect to the principles of dignity (including autonomy), equality, and participation in the CRPD. In that discussion I also consider how the Mental Capacity with Support model might be further developed to address some of the concerns of abolitionists and to maximize its transparency, which is one of its key advantages over the 'best interpretation of will and preferences' approach articulated by the abolitionists. In section 8.4, I will do the same for the Support Except Where There is Harm model, bearing in mind that this approach is less developed and has far less literature on it than Mental Capacity With Support (so my discussion will be far less extensive). In section 8.5, I briefly discuss other alternatives to coercion and other systemic and social reforms that could form part of the broader reform 'package'.

8.2 General Comments about the Different Approaches

As set out in Chapter 2, mental health law has traditionally involved tension between legalism (where outcomes are dictated by rigid application of the law that is consistent across individuals) and flexibility and discretion.[9] However, in the debate about the future of mental health law, that tension is somewhat recast. It is now the abolitionists who favour legalism by arguing in favour of outlawing involuntary detention and psychiatric treatment in all cases in order to create legal certainty, whereas proponents of the Mental Capacity with Support and Support Except Where There is Harm models seek to create a legal structure for flexibility and discretion that allows for individualized responses to meet different needs.

While the call for the abolition of mental health law does not necessarily go so far as to call for the abolition of psychiatry and seeks to frame the debate on the recognition of individual choice, the issue of whether psychiatry is actually beneficial for persons with mental impairment lingers in the background. Abolitionists assume that psychiatry cannot provide persons with mental impairment any benefits, or at least that the negative effects of involuntary detention and treatment, outweigh any benefits (see Chapter 3, especially section 3.3.8). The Mental Capacity with Support and Support Except Where There is Harm models, by contrast, accept that psychiatric care can be beneficial and at times life-saving, even if it is given without consent, while at the same time trying to maximize the space for individual autonomy and choice. These

[9] Jennifer Brown, 'The Changing Purpose of Mental Health Law: From Medicalism to Legalism to New Legalism' (2016) 47 Int J Law Psychiatry 1 (hereafter Brown, 'The Changing Purpose of Mental Health Law')

two theoretical positions with respect to the benefits (or not) of psychiatry are important because they determine whether in situations of uncertainty, usually referred to as the 'hard cases', the law should favour intervention or restraint. While the Mental Capacity with Support and Support Except Where There is Harm models would not be sufficient to satisfy Abolitionists, they give individuals far more say in their treatment than existing mental health law.

It is also important to note that all sides of the debate about the future of mental health law agree involuntary detention and psychiatric treatment is over-used and that a reduction in coercion in psychiatry is desirable.[10] Contrary to Amita Dhanda, I see no inconsistency between considering substituted decision-making as 'a necessary evil' in some cases, but also seeing it as suboptimal and to be avoided if possible.[11] There is also general agreement that the CRPD provides little practical guidance as to how it applies in the 'hard cases' or situations of emergency.[12] All proposals involve the offering of support to assist persons with mental impairment with decision-making with all the advantages and disadvantages that the giving of support entails (set out in Chapter 7, section 7.5.2).[13] Moreover, all proposals, to work properly, will involve a significant injection of resources along with patience, trust and good will.[14]

While several alternatives to involuntary detention and psychiatric treatment exist and are discussed below, it is important to note that none of those alternatives have involved a complete abolition of mental health law. For example, in Germany the constitutional bans on coercion in 2011–2012 still permitted involuntary psychiatric treatment in emergencies and while rates of involuntary treatment dropped, there were reported increases in the use of restraints.[15] In Trieste in Italy which has a system focused on complete deinstitutionalization and community care, involuntary psychiatric treatment is still permitted based on the seriousness of a person's mental impairment, even though rates are significantly lower than other European countries (see Chapter 3, section 3.2).[16] While studies of peer respite services have indicated that they can reduce hospital admissions by up to 70 per cent, those who had longer respite (and presumably more serious and complicated issues) still ended up in hospital.[17] Further, in middle and low income countries, the provision of more psychiatric services is seen as ultimately reducing the coercion experienced by persons with mental impairments who are otherwise caged and restrained by their families (see Chapter 1, section 1.5).[18]

[10] Faraaz Mahomed and others, 'Involuntary Mental Health Treatment in the Era of the United Nations Convention on the Rights of Persons with Disabilities' (2018) PLoS Medicine 1 3 (hereafter Mahomed, 'Involuntary Mental Health Treatment').

[11] Amita Dhanda, 'From Duality to Indivisibility: Mental Health Care and Human Rights' (2016) 32(3) SAJHR 438, 452 (hereafter Dhanda, 'From Duality to Indivisibility')

[12] Mahomed, 'Involuntary Mental Health Treatment' (n 10) 5.

[13] Lucy Series, 'Relationships, Autonomy and Legal Capacity: Mental Capacity and Support Paradigms' (2015) 40 Int J Law Psychiatry 80, 83–84 (hereafter Series, 'Relationships, Autonomy and Legal Capacity').

[14] Mahomed, 'Involuntary Mental Health Treatment' (n 10) 3.

[15] Piers Gooding and others, *Alternatives to Coercion in Mental Health Settings: A Literature Review* (Melbourne Social Equity Institute, University of Melbourne 2018) 37 (hereafter Gooding, *Alternatives to Coercion in Mental Health Settings*).

[16] R Mezzina, 'Forty Years of the Law 180: The Aspirations of a Great Reform, Its Successes and Continuing Need' (2018) 27(4) Epidemiol Psychiatr Sci 336 (hereafter Mezzina, 'Forty Years of the Law 180').

[17] Gooding, *Alternatives to Coercion in Mental Health Settings* (n 15) 42.

[18] ibid 10.

Greater variety of non-coercive alternatives to psychiatry to address 'unmet need' may have the side-effect of reducing overall coercion.[19] However, hospital-based psychiatric support is still likely to be needed in situations of psychiatric crisis, even if it is supplemented with general community support aimed at preventing emergencies and helping persons with mental impairments live more fulfilling lives.[20]

8.3 The Mental Capacity with Support Model

8.3.1 What is the Mental Capacity with Support Model?

As explored in Chapter 2, in most western societies, contemporary mental health law reflects the harm model where involuntary detention and psychiatric treatment is based on whether a person with mental impairment is assessed to be at risk of harming themselves or others, regardless of whether that person has mental capacity to make healthcare decisions. Advocates of the Mental Capacity with Support model propose that mental health law should be reformed to reflect a mental capacity model, or alternatively that mental health law should be abolished and fused with guardianship and general medical laws which are based on a mental capacity model.[21] The mental capacity model recognizes that differences in mental functioning can be relevant to a person's ability to make different types of decisions and ties mental capacity to legal capacity. It creates what Genevra Richardson calls a 'binary-divide'[22] between persons who are assessed to have mental capacity to make a particular decision (based on a functional test of person's ability to understand, appreciate, weigh, and communicate relevant information)[23] for whom the law permits to make even life-threatening medical decisions, and those who lack mental capacity for whom the law authorizes a third party decision-maker to make a decision in their 'best interests'.[24] Thus, the Mental Capacity with Support model has two limbs: the first involves determining a person's mental capacity (where there is reason to believe that the presumption of capacity may be rebutted) and the second, where a person is assessed to lack mental capacity, is to determine his or her best interests. That said, in Australia there may be a shift away

[19] ibid.

[20] ibid 117.

[21] For example, George Szmukler and Brendan Kelly, 'We Should Replace Conventional Mental Health Law with Capacity-Based Law' (2016) 209 Br J Psychiatry 449 (hereafter Szmulker and Kelly 'We Should Replace Conventional Mental Health Law with Capacity-Based Law'); Sascha Callaghan and Christopher Ryan, 'Is There a Future for Involuntary Treatment in Rights-Based Mental Health Law?' (2014) 21(5) Psychiatry Psychol & L 747 (hereafter Callaghan and Ryan 'Is There a Future for Involuntary Treatment'); John Dawson, 'A Realistic Approach to Assessing Mental Health Laws Compliance with the UNCRPD' (2015) 40 Int J Law Psychiatry 70 (hereafter, Dawson, 'A Realistic Approach'); Rowena Daw, 'The Case for a Fusion Law: Challenges and Issues' in Bernadette McSherry and Ian Freckelton (eds), *Coercive Care: Rights, Law and Policy* (Routledge 2013) 93 (hereafter Daw, 'The Case for a Fusion Law'); Mental Capacity Act 2016 (Northern Ireland); George Szmukler and others, 'Mental Health Law and the UN Convention on the Rights of Persons with Disabilities' (2014) 37 Int J Law Psychiatry 245 (hereafter Szmukler, 'Mental Health Law').

[22] Richardson, 'Mental Capacity in the Shadow of Suicide' (n 2) 90.

[23] MCA UK, s 3.

[24] Genevra Richardson, 'Mental Disabilities and the Law: From Substitute to Supported Decision-Making' (2012) 65 Curr Leg Probl 333, 337, 339 (hereafter Richardson, 'Mental Disabilities and the Law').

from an explicit 'best interests' test in the mental health sector towards a focus on determining the 'least restrictive alternative' treatment when a person has been found to lack mental capacity. This is discussed further in this section below.

There are also different variations of the Mental Capacity with Support model. For example, there are approaches where diagnosis is important such as in the *Mental Capacity Act* 2005 (England and Wales) and various Australian Mental Health Acts[25] and those where it is not important such as the *Mental Capacity Act* 2016 (Northern Ireland) and *Assisted Decision-making Capacity Act* 2015 (Ireland);[26] different conceptualizations and measures of mental capacity;[27] different approaches to the risk of harm to others (such as involuntary detention without treatment for persons with mental impairments who lack mental capacity in some American states and Canadian provinces);[28] and different approaches to the weight a person's wishes and feelings should be given if he or she is assessed to lack mental capacity.

Brian Murray argues that there are in fact several different models of mental capacity.[29] The first is mental health law in which he argues diagnosis with a mental impairment (or a status test) acts as a proxy for mental incapacity,[30] although I would add that at present, evidence of risk of harm beyond diagnosis is required by the law as well, even if this may not always happen in practice. The next 'crudest form' of the mental capacity test he calls 'evidencing choice', which only involves the ability to indicate a preference for an option without any reasoning or justification.[31] 'Evidencing choice' is the core of the abolitionist approach and the incorporation of the persons subjective 'wishes and feelings' into an assessment of their 'best interests'. While it still leaves the fate of the person with mental impairment in the hands of an external decision-maker,[32] the new emphasis on wishes and feelings in the 'best interests' test has been widely regarded as a way of 'softening the capacity cliff-edge'[33] in which mental capacity was an 'all-or-nothing' test.[34] The use of 'wishes and feelings' has been argued to be preferable to 'will and preferences' as it explicitly recognizes the

[25] Such as the *Mental Health Act* 2014 (Vic) (hereafter, MHA Vic); *Mental Health Act* 2013 (Tas) (hereafter, MHA Tas); *Mental Health Act* 2014 (WA) (hereafter, MHA WA); McSherry and Wilson 'The Concept of Capacity' (n 4) 62.

[26] Alex Ruck Keene, 'Is Mental Capacity in the Eye of the Beholder?' (2017) 11(2) Adv Ment Health Intellect Disabil 30, 32–33 (hereafter Ruck Keene, 'Is Mental Capacity in the Eye of the Beholder?').

[27] Brian Joseph Murray, 'Mental Capacity: Different Models and Their Controversies' (2017) 23 Br J Psychiatry 366 (hereafter Murray, 'Mental Capacity').

[28] Mary Donnelly, 'From Autonomy to Dignity: Treatment for Mental Disorders and the Focus for Patient Rights' (2008) 26(2) Law in Cont 37, 42 (hereafter Donnelly, 'From Autonomy to Dignity'); *Mental Health Act*, RSO 1990, c M.7, s 15 (1.1) (e); *Health Care Consent* Act 1996 (Ontario) (hereafter, MHA and HCCA Ontario).

[29] Murray, 'Mental Capacity' (n 27).

[30] ibid 366.

[31] ibid 367

[32] Lucy Series, 'The Place of Wishes and Feelings in Best Interests Decisions: Wye Valley NHS Trust v Mr B' (2016) 79(6) MLR 1101 (hereafter Series, 'The Place of Wishes and Feelings').

[33] Emily Jackson, 'From "Doctor Knows Best" to Dignity: Placing Adults Whole Lack Capacity at the Centre of Decisions About Their Medical Treatment' (2018) 81(2) ibid 247, 248 (hereafter Jackson, 'From Doctor Knows Best to Dignity').

[34] Malcolm Parker, 'Getting the Balance Right: Conceptual Considerations Concerning Legal Capacity and Supported Decision-Making' (2016) 13 Bio Inq 381, 388 (Parker, 'Getting the Balance Right').

emotive aspects of decision-making.[35] The next model involves demonstrating actual understanding of all information relevant to a decision (which Murray regards as too high a bar as information is infinite), and demonstrating a potential to understand (which is dependent on the information presented to a person and undue influence).[36] Finally, Murray argues there is the 'rationality test' which courts often use as part of the functional test. Under the rationality test, persons with mental impairment must demonstrate that they have considered the information rationally and explain their reasons so that another person is able to logically follow them.[37] The decision-maker will then attempt to determine if the mental impairment is influencing the decision, or if the decision might reflect the person's reasoning when he or she was well.[38] The problem with this approach is that the analysis can be contaminated by the values of the decision-maker.[39] These issues with respect to the different types of mental capacity will be discussed further below.

Similarly, Mary Donnelly argues that the law conceptualizes mental capacity as involving three components of autonomy: understanding (what the decision involves); authenticity (how the well the decision reflects a person's subjective values and sense of self); and rationality (whether a person's reasons are objectively rational or reflect a process of rational decision-making).[40] Of these, the abolitionist approach really only focusses on authenticity and even then the authenticity of a decision can be unclear where a person's will and preferences conflict, or very little is known of the person. It is also difficult to see how a decision that a person does not understand can be authentic or further a person's autonomy. The mental capacity model has a long history which pre-dates the CRPD.[41] However, since the CRPD, variations on the mental capacity model incorporate supported decision-making as a way of assisting persons to make a decision that would be legally regarded as being made with mental capacity. Where persons fall short of achieving mental capacity, supported decision-making can be used to ascertain their wishes and feelings for the purposes of determining their best interests.[42] The provision of support is designed to reduce the risk that individuals are deprived of making their own decisions by professionals who do not bother to consult them, present information in a cursory or inappropriate way, and do not give sufficient time for persons to respond or seek advice from those they trust. That is, the Mental Capacity with Support model takes into account contextual social

[35] Mary Donnelly, 'Best Interests in the Mental Capacity Act: Time to Say Goodbye?' (2016) 24(3) Med Law Rev 318, 328 (hereafter Donnelly, 'Best Interests in the Mental Capacity Act').

[36] Murray, 'Mental Capacity' (n 27) 368–69.

[37] ibid 369.

[38] ibid 370.

[39] ibid.

[40] Mary Donnelly, *Healthcare Decision-Making and the Law: Autonomy, Capacity and the Limits of Liberalism* (Cambridge Law, Medicine and Ethics 2010) 94–100 (hereafter Donnelly, *Healthcare Decision-Making and the Law*).

[41] See for example, Report of the Expert Committee, *Review of the Mental Health Act 1983* (November 1999) (hereafter 'Richardson Report').

[42] George Szmukler and Michael Bach, 'Mental Health Disabilities and Human Rights Protections' (2015) 2 Glob Ment Health 1 (hereafter Szmukler and Bach 'Mental Health Disabilities'); Callaghan and Ryan 'An Evolving Revolution' (n 4) 610.

and environmental factors in decision-making.[43] Unlike the abolitionist approach, the Mental Capacity with Support model provides a 'success criterion' for the effectiveness of support: it is successful when a person can demonstrate functional capacity,[44] as opposed to whenever a will and preference is expressed or determined by a facilitator regardless of the extent to which that determination may or may not reflect the person's actual will and preferences after considering all of the information relevant to the decision and the likely consequences of the decision. Accordingly, the use of support to assist a person to pass a mental capacity assessment is the least controversial approach to the provision of support.[45] While the provision of support may not always be sufficient to assist a person to make a capacious decision, recent studies suggest that most persons with mental impairment who are assessed to lack mental capacity, still retain at least partial mental capacity.[46] Even though research is ongoing it is reasonable to expect that many of the borderline cases might be able to demonstrate mental capacity with support.[47]

The right to receive decision-making support is already included in the *Mental Capacity Act* 2005, and a finding of incapacity cannot be made without all reasonable support being provided.[48] However, as discussed in section 8.5.1 below, this provision has been described as an 'orphan principle' which could be further bolstered in law and practice.[49] Other measures include giving persons with mental impairments the ability to nominate their own supporters and the availability of independent advocates to assist the person in making their voice heard.[50] Where a person has an on-going mental impairment it is possible to discuss a patient's preferences when he or she is in recovery and to fine tune them over time:[51] possibly through the use of advance statements, directives or some kind of joint crisis planning. These mechanisms are discussed further in this section below. To the extent it involves supporters, rather than considering the decision-making abilities of the person with mental impairment in isolation, the Mental Capacity with Support model incorporates a relational approach to autonomy.[52]

Where a person is assessed to lack mental capacity and a substitute decision needs to be made, recent English cases have applied the 'best interests' test so as to give greater weight to a person's subjective will, preferences, values, and beliefs, over their objective medical best interests.[53] That is, 'best interests' is not necessarily synonymous with

[43] Matthe Scholten and Jakov Gather, 'Adverse Consequences of Article 12 of the UN Convention on the Rights of Persons with Disabilities for Persons with Mental Disabilities and an Alternative Way Forward' (2017) J Med Ethics 1, 6 (hereafter Scholten and Gather, 'Adverse Consequences of Article 13').
[44] ibid 5.
[45] Jillian Craigie, 'A Fine Balance: Reconsidering Patient Autonomy in Light of the UN Convention on the Rights of Persons with Disabilities' (2015) 29(6) Bioethics 398, 401 (hereafter Craigie, 'A Fine Balance').
[46] Aoife Curley and others, 'Categorical Mental Capacity for Treatment Decisions among Psychiatry Inpatients in Ireland' (2019) 64 Int J Law Psychiatry 53 (hereafter Curley, 'Categorical Mental Capacity').
[47] ibid 57–58.
[48] MCA UK s 1(3).
[49] Ruck Keene, 'Is Mental Capacity in the Eye of the Beholder?' (n 26) 36.
[50] Szmukler, 'Mental Health Law' (n 21) 249.
[51] ibid 249.
[52] Richardson, 'Mental Disabilities and the Law' (n 24) 342.
[53] For example, *Aintree University Hospitals Foundation Trust v James* [2013] UKSC 67 (hereafter, *Aintree University Hospitals Foundation Trust v James*); *X NHS Trust v B* [2015] EWCOP 60 (hereafter, *University Hospitals Foundation Trust v James*).

whatever treatment is medically indicated, but will include broader consideration of social and psychological factors. The creation of a legal presumption that substitute decision-makers should respect the wishes and feelings of persons with mental impairment who lack mental capacity, unless there is good reason to depart from them, is also gathering momentum.[54]

In Victoria, the Mental Health Act 2014 provides for a mental capacity assessment which allows a person with mental capacity to consent to and refuse electroconvulsive therapy ('ECT') which is similar to other jurisdictions such as England and Wales. However, under the Victorian Act, where a person lacks mental capacity, the case will turn on whether there is a less restrictive alternative to ECT, rather than general consideration of whether involuntary treatment is in the person's best interests. In a recent appeal from the Mental Health Tribunal to the Supreme Court of Victoria in *PBU & NJE v Mental Health Tribunal* ('the ECT case')[55] Justice Bell indicated that 'the compulsory treatment regime represents a paradigm shift from best-interests paternalism to the least-restrictive kind of treatment'.[56] In his Honour's view, best-interests paternalism involves too great a focus on the outcome of a decision, whereas the least restrictive alternative test gives more power to the patient by recognizing self-determination, freedom from non-consensual treatment, personal inviolability, and supported decision-making.[57] However, the insistence of the value neutrality of the least restrictive alternative test may be no more than His Honour's rhetoric. Instead, I argue that the better interpretation is that the Victorian legislators simply assumed that if a person with a mental impairment has been assessed to lack mental capacity then ECT will always be in their best interests (without requiring a separate consideration of the question of best interests), unless a less restrictive alternative treatment exists.

While the CRPD Committee has rejected the Mental Capacity with Support model as being CRPD compliant, the text of the CRPD itself does not expressly criticize functional tests of mental capacity,[58] or require the abolition of substitute decision-making or the best interests approach.[59] Proponents argue that the Mental Capacity with Support model is actually CRPD compliant, because their interpretation of equal recognition before the law in Article 12(4) of the CRPD permits substitute decision-making in limited circumstances provided it is for the shortest possible time and subject to safeguards such as external judicial review.[60] As John Dawson argues, mental capacity is seen as a way of mediating between conflicting negative rights to non-interference by the state and positive rights to social benefits and inclusion.[61] That

[54] Jackson, 'From Doctor Knows Best to Dignity' (n 33); Barton-Hansen 'Reforming Best Interests' (n 2) 277; Ruck Keene, 'Is Mental Capacity in the Eye of the Beholder?' (n 26) 36.

[55] [2018] VSC 564.

[56] ibid [101].

[57] ibid [252].

[58] Murray, 'Mental Capacity' (n 27) 372.

[59] Wayne Martin and others, *Achieving CRPD Compliance: Is the Mental Capacity Act of England and Wales Compatible with the UN Convention on the Rights of Persons with Disabilities? If Not, What Next?* (University of Essex, Essex Autonomy Project 2014) 13 (hereafter Martin, *Achieving CRPD Compliance*); Donnelly, 'Best Interests in the Mental Capacity Act' (n 35) 321.

[60] Dawson, 'A Realistic Approach' (n 21) 74; Richardson, 'Mental Disabilities and the Law' (n 24) 346.

[61] Dawson, 'A Realistic Approach' (n 21) 71.

is, the Mental Capacity with Support model balances the rights to liberty, equality, and bodily integrity with other important rights protected by the CRPD including the rights to life, health, education, employment, and social inclusion.[62] Within the Mental Capacity with Support model, real-life outcomes, not just abstract principles, are important.[63] There is support for interpretations of the CRPD as requiring the maximizing of autonomy, but also providing protection for 'vulnerable' individuals.[64] The Mental Capacity with Support model could also harmonize the CRPD and ECHR approaches to the right to life of persons with mental impairments.[65] Others believe that giving the wishes and feelings of the person who lacks capacity precedence, unless there is a good reason to depart from them, would go a long way towards exercising legal capacity on an equal basis and therefore CRPD compliance.[66]

The greatest strength of Mental Capacity with Support over the best interpretation of will and preferences paradigm is that Mental Capacity with Support is more transparent and avoids the hidden exercise of power.[67] It treats 100 per cent support as a legal fiction and where a person is assessed to lack mental capacity, the Mental Capacity with Support model is more open in describing best interests assessment as a form of substitute decision-making by a third party, as opposed to trying to interpret their will and preferences no matter how unclear the knowledge of their will and preferences are.[68] There is also a problem where there is no indication of what a person's will and preferences might be.[69] In those situations, it can be assumed that people want to be treated in accordance with their best interests—to be 'warm, comfortable, well-nourished, cared for and treated with respect'.[70] The Mental Capacity with Support model means that there is a distinction between the interests of the person with mental impairment and the decision-maker, whereas for the abolition paradigm the supporter and the person with mental impairment's views are collapsed into each other, making it difficult to monitor or object to in court.[71] By giving responsibility entirely to the person with mental impairment, supporters are left unaccountable.[72] False beliefs that persons with mental impairment are exercising their legal capacity with support may mean it takes longer to pick up exploitation or abuse (a key justification for abolishing mental health law).[73]

62 Martin, *Achieving CRPD Compliance* (n 59) 30; Brendan Kelly, 'Mental Health, Mental Illness, and Human Rights in India and Elsewhere: What Are We Aiming For?' (2016) 58(2) Ind J Psych 168, 174 (hereafter Kelly 'Human Rights in India').

63 Kelly, 'Human Rights in India' (n 62) 174.

64 Murray, 'Mental Capacity' (n 27) 372; Martha Albertson Fineman, 'Equality, Autonomy and the Vulnerable Subject in Law and Politics' in Martha Fineman and Anna Greer (eds), *Vulnerability: Reflections on a New Ethical Foundation for Law and Politics* (Taylor and Francis 2013) 13 (herafter Fineman, 'Equality, Autonomy and the Vulnerable Subject'.

65 Wilson, 'Right to Life' (n 1) 664.

66 Ruck Keene, 'Is Mental Capacity in the Eye of the Beholder?' (n 26) 36.

67 Donnelly, 'Best Interests in the Mental Capacity Act' (n 35) 326; Parker, 'Getting the Balance Right' (n 34) 391.

68 Series, 'Relationships, Autonomy and Legal Capacity (n 13) 86.

69 Donnelly, 'Best Interests in the Mental Capacity Act' (n 35) 326.

70 ibid.

71 Scholten and Gather, 'Adverse Consequences of Article 12' (n 43) 4.

72 ibid 5.

73 Parker, 'Getting the Balance Right' (n 34) 389; Mahomed, 'Involuntary Mental Health Treatment' (n 10).

There is also a 'hybrid' model which combines the Mental Capacity with Support model with the Support Except Where There is Harm model. That is, mental capacity can only be a ground for involuntary detention and psychiatric treatment where persons make a decision which is likely to put them at risk of harm, rather than allowing a mental capacity assessment to permeate all of their decisions.[74] Therefore, persons who lack mental capacity would be entitled to refuse psychiatric treatment where they are not at risk of harm. However, John Dawson argues that the mental capacity model should extend beyond situations where treatment refusal by persons who lack mental capacity entails a risk of physical harm to other situations which may involve financial and relationship loss, or result in persons not meeting their own goals, or a loss of stability and control over a person's own life, in the interests of furthering their 'positive' liberty.[75] At the very least, intervention could be justified in situations where it is necessary to preserve a person's inherent dignity, especially where his or her conduct seriously violates widely accepted social norms, and is likely to be irreversible (see Chapter 5, section 5.2.2). Involuntary detention and psychiatric treatment without having to demonstrate harm, also promotes early intervention and treatment success.[76]

It is often argued by abolitionists that those persons with mental impairments who are in favour of involuntary detention and psychiatric treatment could state their preferences in advance in an advance directive (see also Chapter 7, section 7.5.2). However, this would be of no assistance to persons who experience their first episode of psychiatric impairment. Advance directives are also a way that a person could express their 'will and preferences' to refuse all treatment or particular interventions when they are well. In this sense advance directives are more theoretically compatible with the Mental Capacity with Support model, than the Abolition with Support model. That is because advance directives depend on competence—a person's decision when competent overrides their preferences when incompetent.[77] The practical use of advance directives can be enhanced by health professionals providing supported decision-making including information and advice on pitfalls and burdens of relevant treatments at the time they are created.[78] However, advance directives still have a number of pitfalls. As Renu Barton-Hansen argues that the CRPD is premised on the idea that current preferences should be given primacy as people may change their minds after different life experiences.[79] Brian Murray and Lucy Series also have concerns about not having enough information about past wishes and relying too much on past wishes so that people lose the right to have their present wishes recognized or to change their minds.[80]

It should also be noted that harm has long been part of the application of the mental capacity test. For example, in *Re T*, often referenced for its protection of the right of a

74 Series, 'Relationships, Autonomy and Legal Capacity' (n 13) 87.
75 John Dawson, 'Concepts of Liberty in Mental Health Law' (2009) 12(1) Otago LR 23, 23 and 32–33 (hereafter Dawson, 'Concepts of Liberty').
76 ibid.
77 Scholten and Gather, 'Adverse Consequences of Article 12' (n 43) 5.
78 ibid 6.
79 Barton-Hansen 'Reforming Best Interests' (n 2) 291.
80 Murray, 'Mental Capacity' (n 27) 372; Series, 'Relationships, Autonomy and Legal Capacity (n 13) 86.

person with mental capacity to reject medical treatment for any reason or none at all, also notes that the capacity test should be applied more stringently where the risk of harm is higher.[81] As Genevra Richardson notes 'the competence required to consent to taking an aspirin may be judged in practice by identical standards to those used to judge refusal, but in relation to life-saving surgery competence to refuse is likely to be tested with much greater rigour than competence to consent'.[82] Most mental capacity models also contain powers to involuntarily detain and treat those who are at risk of harming others. Such coercion is justified as being in their best interests.[83] The issue of the prevention of self-harm is more controversial than harm to others, although a Mental Capacity with Support model that is designed to honour autonomy and self-determination would permit persons with mental capacity to make decisions that may include the risk of self-harm.[84] Mental capacity legislation would also need to incorporate the safeguards from mental health legislation such as restrictions on the length of detention and review processes and safeguards around the use of force to avoid the loss of hard won rights.[85]

8.3.2 Dignity including Autonomy

The Mental Capacity with Support model is argued by me and others to respect both the autonomy and dignity of persons with mental impairments.[86] From this perspective autonomy is intrinsically related to decision-making ability as well as having some capability of self-reflection and self-governance.[87] It involves respecting individuals as they are, as opposed to insisting on giving them legal recognition for abilities they do not have.[88] As Alex Ruck-Keene observes:

> without a person either at the material time or in advance having had a very basic level of understanding of a situation or decision, it is simply not possible to talk of a person being able to have any meaningful "will" which can form the basis of the supported exercise of legal capacity.[89]

The Mental Capacity with Support model also does not assume that if decision-making support is offered then autonomous decisions will automatically follow.[90] It is

[81] *Re T (Adult Refusal of Treatment)* [1993] Fam 95, 113 (hereafter, *Re T (Adult Refusal of Treatment)*).
[82] Genevra Richardson, 'Autonomy, Guardianship and Mental Disorder: One Problem, Two Solutions' (2002) 65(5) MLR 702, 704 (hereafter Richardson, 'Autonomy, Guardianship and Mental Disorder').
[83] Szmulker and Kelly 'We Should Replace Conventional Mental Health Law with Capacity-Based Law' (n 21) 450, 453.
[84] Richardson Report (n 41) [2.9]–[2.11].
[85] Szmulker and Kelly, 'We Should Replace Conventional Mental Health Law with Capacity-Based Law' (n 21) 450.
[86] Wilson, 'Right to Life' (n 1) 682; Dawson, 'A Realistic Approach' (n 21) 71; Martin, *Achieving CRPD Compliance* (n 59); David Bilchitz, 'Dignity, Fundamental Rights and Legal Capacity: Moving Beyond the Paradigm Set by the General Comment on Article 12 of the Convention on the Rights of Persons with Disabilities' (2016) 32(3) SAJHR 410 (hereafter Bilchitz, 'Dignity, Fundamental Rights and Legal Capacity').
[87] Martin, *Achieving CRPD Compliance* (n 59) 19.
[88] Bilchitz, 'Dignity, Fundamental Rights and Legal Capacity' (n 86) 417.
[89] Ruck Keene, 'Is Mental Capacity in the Eye of the Beholder?' (n 26) 37.
[90] Donnelly, 'Best Interests in the Mental Capacity Act' (n 35) 324.

concerned with the quality of support, external inhibitors of autonomy such as undue influence, coercion, and manipulation and the interference of other social constructs which inhibit autonomy.[91]

However, the Mental Capacity with Support model does respect the autonomy of persons who are assessed as having mental capacity to make a particular decision without legal restriction. This could be around 40 per cent to 50 per cent of persons admitted into mental health facilities.[92] It is also argued that the 'competence assessment' as it is termed in the United States, protects persons with mental capacity from undue influence by their supporters.[93]

While little is known about the experience of explaining one's wishes and feelings to mental capacity assessors, it is not hard to imagine that it could be undignified if the person does not like or trust the assessor.[94] Case law indicates that capacity assessments may have as much to do with the values of the decision-maker as the person being assessed, including culture and socioeconomic background.[95] While mental capacity assessors in guardianship applications tend to be independent psychologists, in mental health systems the assessment is usually made by the treating psychiatrist. Mental health assessments should also be made by an independent person, with the relevant qualifications, empathy, patience, and experience, to avoid an actual or perceived conflict of interest which may occur when the person who assesses mental capacity also has the responsibility for treatment. An independent person also brings a fresh mind and a different set of qualifications and expertise to the assessment. Further, assessors should be trained to be self-aware and alert to the values they bring to the assessment.[96] At its best, the provision of support gives persons the opportunity to reflect on their wishes and feelings and to develop a personal narrative and sense of self.[97] As Mary Donnelly observes, the process of mental capacity assessment is not just about testing, but is also an opportunity to educate and support.[98]

When a person is assessed to lack mental capacity and autonomy, it is only with respect to a particular decision at a particular time, and does not amount to a global loss of rights.[99] The Mental Capacity with Support model also gives weight to the wishes and feelings of persons who lack mental capacity (although exactly how much weight is still a matter of debate), while permitting other values to be taken into account on occasion. However, it does so without the 'need to go to extreme lengths "to divine the will" where none exists'.[100] Persons who lack mental capacity can then receive treatment which may restore their autonomy and inherent dignity.[101]

However, as argued in Chapter 5 section 5.2.2, dignity has a broader more objective meaning than autonomy and is concerned with recognizing and protecting inherent

[91] ibid 325.
[92] Curley, 'Categorical Mental Capacity' (n 46) 53 and 56.
[93] Scholten and Gather, 'Adverse Consequences of Article 12' (n 43) 5.
[94] Series, 'Relationships, Autonomy and Legal Capacity (n 13) 83.
[95] Ruck Keene, 'Is Mental Capacity in the Eye of the Beholder?' (n 26) 33–34.
[96] ibid 37.
[97] Series, 'Relationships, Autonomy and Legal Capacity' (n 13) 83.
[98] Donnelly, *Healthcare Decision-Making and the Law* (n 40) 111.
[99] Dawson, 'A Realistic Approach' (n 21) 72–73.
[100] Bilchitz, 'Dignity, Fundamental Rights and Legal Capacity' (n 86) 436.
[101] ibid 420.

human worth (even if a person's autonomy may be compromised). As Marie Fallon-Kund and Jerome Bickenbach observe, capacity assessments may be necessary to limit autonomy so as to protect human dignity.[102] Human worth has a number of dimensions including being treated in accordance with one's inherent dignity, behaving in accordance with one's inherent dignity, and being treated equally which is discussed in the next section. In terms of systemic reform, as discussed in Chapter 5 section 5.1, there is a need to reform the mental health system to ensure that persons with mental impairments are treated in accordance with the respect they are entitled to as a result of their inherent human worth. The ability to assess and tailor interventions on an individual basis, rather than to assume mental incapacity regardless of a person's actual ability is in accordance with furthering inherent dignity.[103] Further, as argued in Chapter 5, in some cases, such as extreme self-neglect or harm, interventions may be necessary to preserve a person's dignity. In hard cases, abolition does not provide any answers where a person's 'choice' may place him or her at a serious risk of harm which he or she objectively does not understand.[104]

8.3.3 Equality and Non-Discrimination

The issue of whether the Mental Capacity with Support model is discriminatory and promotes the equality of persons with mental impairments on an equal basis with others is controversial. As discussed in Chapters 6 and 7, much depends on how equality and discrimination in the CRPD are interpreted. If the interpretation of the abolitionists is relied upon, then *any difference* in treatment between persons with and without mental impairment is regarded as an insidious form of discrimination, regardless of its purpose or justification.[105]

However, the Mental Capacity with Support model has a number of strengths. Compared with mental health law, the Mental Capacity with Support model is concerned with a person's actual mental capacity (or incapacity) rather than presuming mental incapacity by law.[106] It recognizes that persons with and without mental impairments are not similarly situated and therefore, in accordance with theories of substantive equality, differential treatment is permissible to the extent of the difference. The separation of the locus of decision-making between the assessor and the person assessed and the ability to apply to a court for a decision with written reasons, makes the Mental Capacity with Support model more transparent than the use of a facilitator

102 Marie Fallon-Kund and Jerome Bickenbach, 'Strengthening the Voice of Persons with Mental Health Problems and Legal Capacity Proceedings' (2016) 5 Laws 29, 29 (hereafter Fallon-Kund and Bickenbach, 'Strengthening the Voice of Persons with Mental health Problems').

103 Mezzina, 'Forty Years of the Law 180' (n 16).

104 Series, 'Relationships, Autonomy and Legal Capacity' (n 13) 87

105 Piers Gooding and Eilionoir Flynn, 'Querying the Call to Introduce Mental Capacity Testing to Mental Health Law: Does the Doctrine of Necessity Provide an Alternative?' (2015) 4 Laws 245, 246 (hereafter Gooding and Flynn 'Querying the Call to Introduce Mental Capacity Testing to Mental Health Law').

106 The idea that the mental capacity model is non-discriminatory as it removes the distinction between persons with mental impairments and general medical patients is well supported in the literature. For example, Donnelly, 'From Autonomy to Dignity' (n 28) 44.

to make an assessment of an individual's will and preferences (see section 8.3.1 above). As Kim Scott argues, substitute decision-making may be inevitable when a person lacks mental capacity, whether or not it is called 'best interests' or the 'best interpretation of will and preferences'.[107]

The Mental Capacity with Support model removes the distinction created by mental health law between persons with mental impairments and persons with other types of disorders. From the perspective of the Mental Capacity with Support model, providing access to medical treatment where a person lacks mental capacity is simply the way in which society responds to persons with mental impairments and other 'vulnerable' persons whose autonomy may be temporarily or permanently compromised for a whole range of reasons due to coercion or undue influence, deception, misinformation, physical disability, illness, tiredness, shock, fatigue, depression, pain, or drugs.[108] Therefore, for the Mental Capacity with Support model, other persons who lack mental capacity for any reason are the appropriate comparators in determining equality. Legal recognition of a lack of independence or autonomous agency where appropriate does not equate to moral inferiority or loss of worth but rather to attention to other vital interests and needs.[109] Given that inherent vulnerability can be conceptualized as a universal human experience and that all persons will be vulnerable at some stage in their life, it can potentially apply equally to everyone in the right circumstances.[110] Some would even go so far as to argue that to this extent the Mental Capacity with Support model applies equally to all persons, not just persons with disabilities.[111]

Nevertheless, the CRPD Committee has rejected the Mental Capacity with Support model and there are a number of arguments made by abolitionists about whether it falls within the meaning of 'non-discrimination' and 'equality' in the CRPD. In particular, these are related to the issues of direct and indirect discrimination and disability neutrality. It also involves challenging what mental capacity assessments themselves are assessing and whether it can be value neutral. I will deal with each of these issues in turn.

8.3.3.1 Direct and Indirect Discrimination and Disability Neutrality

Those who emphasize disability neutrality, interpret the CRPD as not prohibiting coercion per se, but rather prohibiting differential treatment of persons with and without disabilities. That is, the CRPD is interpreted primarily as a non-discrimination treaty

[107] Jillian Craigie and others, 'Legal Capacity, Mental Capacity and Supported Decision-Making: Report from a Panel Event' (2019) 62 Int J Law Psychiatry 160, 164 (hereafter Craigie, 'Panel Event').

[108] *SA (vulnerable adult with capacity: marriage)* [2005] EWHC 2942 (Fam) [37] (hereafter, *SA (vulnerable adult with capacity: marriage)*); Kirsty Keywood, 'The Vulnerable Adult Experiment: Situating Vulnerability in Adult Safeguarding Law' (2017) 53 ibid 88 (hereafter Keywood, 'The Vulnerable Adult Experiment').

[109] Bilchitz, 'Dignity, Fundamental Rights and Legal Capacity' (n 86) 412

[110] Martha Albertson Fineman, 'The Vulnerable Subject and the Responsive State' (2010) 60 Emory Law J 251, 263–64 (hereafter Fineman, 'The Vulnerable Subject').

[111] Martin, *Achieving CRPD Compliance* (n 59) 15; Scholten and Gather, 'Adverse Consequences of Article 12' (n 43) 6.

where involuntary detention and psychiatric treatment would be permitted if the law applied the same way to everyone.[112]

As Jill Stavert observes:

> The pursuit of equal enjoyment of human rights without discrimination does not mean that the human rights of persons with mental disabilities can never be denied or limited. It means that such denial or limitation must be based on the same criteria for all persons and must not be justified on the basis of a person's mental disability. In this connection, the CRPD Committee recognizes that the inability to exercise one's legal capacity is an impediment to the equal enjoyment of all human rights.[113]

Piers Gooding and Eilionoir Flynn argue that a disability neutral ground for intervention would be based on the doctrine of necessity where failure to intervene to protect a person's life or health would constitute criminal or civil negligence.[114] It would apply to persons with and without disabilities.[115] Alternatively, Anna Arstein-Kerslake and Eilionoir Flynn propose that in emergency situations, third parties would be able to intervene by physically stopping a person from completing suicide in order to offer persons with and without mental impairment support to consider their will and preferences (although not involuntary detention or psychiatric treatment). These approaches would still confer the same epistemic privilege to third parties in 'judging' others as having a mental capacity assessment, albeit for a different purpose.[116]

A side effect of the disability neutral approach reflects the observation of Justice Jesse Jackson of the Supreme Court of the United States[117] that states would be less inclined to enact coercive powers against everyone, where they would be more likely to suffer political retribution from the majority, as opposed to arbitrarily singling out a less powerful minority.[118] That said, the rule of law typically allows the law to make exceptions where there are relevant and reasonable grounds of differentiation, including for groups such as children and persons who are assessed to lack mental capacity.

At present the *Mental Capacity Act* 2005 limits capacity assessment to situations where a person has 'an impairment of, or a disturbance in the functioning of, the mind or brain'[119] ('the diagnostic threshold'). The diagnostic threshold was designed to distinguish between those whose perceived failure to cope was a result of a lack of

[112] Martin, *Achieving CRPD Compliance* (n 59) 15.

[113] Jill Stavert, 'Paradigm Shift or Paradigm Paralysis? National Mental Health and Capacity Law and Implementing the CRPD in Scotland' (2018) 7 Laws 26, 2 (hereafter Stavert, 'Paradigm Shift or Paradigm Paralysis?').

[114] Gooding and Flynn 'Querying the Call to Introduce Mental Capacity Testing to Mental Health Law' (n 105) 245, 258.

[115] ibid.

[116] Series, 'Relationships, Autonomy and Legal Capacity' (n 13) 87.

[117] *Railway Express Agency Inc v New York* 336 US 106, 112–13 (1949) cited by Lord Bingham (hereafter, *Railway Express Agency Inc v New York*).

[118] Jill Stavert and Rebecca McGregor, 'Domestic Legislation and International Human Rights Standards: The Case of Mental Health and Incapacity' (2018) 22(1) Int J Hum Rights 70, 5 (hereafter Stavert and McGregor, 'Domestic Legislation and International Human Rights Standards'); *Railway Express Agency Inc v New York* (n 117).

[119] Section 2(1).

inclination or eccentricity rather than a lack of mental capacity.[120] Some argue that the diagnostic threshold is a form of direct discrimination against persons with mental and cognitive impairments, because it is 'discriminatorily applied to people with disabilities'[121] and does not apply to everyone. That is, the diagnostic threshold is not disability neutral.

It is possible to have a Mental Capacity with Support model without the diagnostic threshold, such as in Northern Ireland[122] and with the *Assisted Decision-making Capacity Act* 2015 in Ireland.[123] Wayne Martin and colleagues argue that the diagnostic threshold in the *Mental Capacity Act* 2005 ('MCA') is directly discriminatory, but that the MCA would be CRPD compliant if the diagnostic threshold were removed.[124] There are two concerns with this. The first is that the removal of the diagnostic threshold could result in 'net-widening', that is, it would increase the people who may be found to lack capacity and lead to the potential use of the Mental Capacity with Support model to control those who have unusual, unpopular, or politically threatening views without being able to point to any reason why their autonomy may be compromised.[125] For example, I have previously commented on the controversial decision of the Irish High Court in *Fitzpatrick v K*,[126] where a Jehovah's Witness (and asylum-seeker from the Democratic Republic of Congo) had lost significant amounts of blood during a difficult birth and was found to lack the mental capacity to refuse a potentially life-saving blood transfusion. In that case, the court applied the mental capacity test without considering whether Ms K had a disturbance of the mind and brain and without performing a formal mental capacity assessment. While it is not inconceivable that 'temporary factors' such as the fatigue and strain of the birth, blood loss, and administration of any drugs may have affected Ms K's mental capacity, this argument was never raised. In that case Ms K appeared to the hospital not to take medical advice that she might die without the transfusion or consider the future care of her son whom the hospital thought would be 'orphaned' if she died because she gave priority to her religion.[127] While the distinction between a person's religious faith (which may seem irrational to non-believers) and the irrationality caused by the symptoms of mental impairment (such as delusions, paranoia, and obsessions) is arguable, the mental capacity test is supposed to be able to distinguish between the person who understands all the information and what is at stake for him or her, but rejects it in favour of an alternative belief system like a religion, and the person who is unable to make an informed decision

[120] Beverley Clough, 'New Legal Landscapes: (Re)Constructing the Boundaries of Mental Capacity Law' (2018) 26(2) Med Law Rev 256, 254 (hereafter Clough, 'New Legal Landscapes').

[121] Committee on the Rights of Persons with Disabilities, *General Comment No 1 (2014) Article 12: Equal Recognition before the Law*, 11th Sess, UN Doc CRPD/C/GC/1 (11 April 2014) [15] (hereafter, 'General Comment 1').

[122] MCA NI.

[123] Ruck Keene, 'Is Mental Capacity in the Eye of the Beholder?' (n 26) 32–33.

[124] Martin, *Achieving CRPD Compliance* (n 59) 31.

[125] Gooding and Flynn 'Querying the Call to Introduce Mental Capacity Testing to Mental Health Law' (n 105) 266.

[126] [2008] IEHC 104 (25 April 2008) (H Ct) (Ir); Kay Wilson and Penelope Weller, 'Benevolent Paternalism or a Clash of Values: Motherhood and Refusal of Medical Treatment in Ireland' (2011) 21 (Spring 2011) J of Ment Health Law 108 (hereafter, Wilson and Weller, 'Benevolent Paternalism or a Clash of Values').

[127] ibid 114–15.

because of permanent or temporary factors that disrupt their ability to process relevant information or understand the consequences for them at all. What is problematic from the *Fitzpatrick* case is that when the requirement that a person has a disturbance in the functioning of the mind or brain was missing, it seems to increase the chances that decisions regarding a person's loss of capacity are made based on a clash of values rather than a loss of autonomy. *Fitzpatrick* is an example of where removal of the diagnostic threshold did seem to 'widen the net' and that the 'diagnostic threshold' to protect the competent but eccentric or non-conforming person is justified.

The presumption of capacity also seems to work better if a loss of mental capacity can be linked to the specific way in which a mental impairment or diagnosis is undermining a person's autonomy (eg a person's needle phobia is preventing them from consenting to an operation they want, or a person believes that their psychiatrist is an assassin), and is simpler to apply as it does not require a specific analysis of a person's beliefs.[128] Demonstrating that a person's thinking has not been overtaken by false beliefs or urges caused by mental impairment, also involves a more achievable standard of autonomy than requiring a person to demonstrate a high level of authenticity.[129] Of course, for some people the type or degree of mental impairment may not be sufficient to disrupt a person's autonomy with respect to a particular decision, which should be respected by law.

A diagnostic criterion would also be more harmonious with the ECHR as the exception to the right to liberty in section 5(e) only applies to 'persons of unsound mind'. Nevertheless a finding that a person lacks mental capacity may be sufficient to qualify as a 'person of unsound mind' where that is supported by a mental capacity assessment.[130]

The second difficulty is that simply removing the diagnostic threshold while removing direct discrimination against persons with mental impairments, may still involve indirect discrimination against persons with mental impairments. As Wayne Martin and colleagues observe, there is no dispute that mental capacity testing disproportionately affects those with mental and cognitive impairments.[131] However, they argue that such a disproportionate impact does not necessarily in and of itself constitute indirect discrimination under international law where the reason for differentiation is reasonable and objective and if the aim is to achieve a purpose which is legitimate under the CRPD (See also discussion of the exception to indirect discrimination in section 6.1 above).[132] They argue that the Mental Capacity with Support model does comply in that functional tests conform with the legitimate aims of the CRPD (which as I have argued extend beyond the protection of autonomy) provided the functional test is based on an objective empirically verifiable difference.[133] I will

[128] Donnelly, *Healthcare Decision-Making and the Law* (n 40) 143.

[129] ibid 101.

[130] John Dawson and Annagret Kampf, 'Incapacity Principles in Mental Health Laws in Europe' (2006) 12(3) Psychol, Psychiat and Law 310, 316 (hereafter Dawson and Kampf, 'Incapacity Principles in Mental Health Laws in Europe').

[131] Gooding and Flynn 'Querying the Call to Introduce Mental Capacity Testing to Mental Health Law' (n 105) 256.

[132] Martin, *Achieving CRPD Compliance* (n 59) 8.

[133] ibid 17–18.

discuss the issue of objectivity further in the next section. Further as I have pointed out in Chapter 7, section 7.2, the inability of persons without mental capacity to access care on the same basis as others would also be a form of discrimination.[134]

At this juncture, I should note that I am generally sceptical of claims of disability neutrality or the general claim that neutrality of any kind is ever possible. For instance, abolitionists often argue that the criminal law which applies to everyone is disability neutral, yet the framing of many offences, the background situation of persons with disabilities in society, and the sheer numbers of persons with disabilities who become entangled with the criminal justice system suggests that it is not. Even Tina Minkowitz recognises that disability neutrality is often precluded by the history of a society's thinking about certain issues and for this reason she doubts whether even limited state intervention to restrain a person from completing suicide could ever be disability neutral.[135] I also argue that there are things about certain mental impairments which may predispose persons to fall foul of the criminal law (such as the inability to recognize and respect social boundaries). That is, persons with and without mental capacity are not similarly situated. Accordingly, it is unlikely that changes to the criminal law could be disability neutral, while still applying to and punishing persons with disabilities on an equal basis with others. In my view, no position is neutral, including the abolition of mental health law, and it is far better to be transparent about the values which underpin each position than make fruitless claims about neutrality.

8.3.3.2 Assessing Mental Capacity: A Value Neutral Functional or Substantive Approach?

The Mental Capacity with Support model is often touted as being non-discriminatory because it rests on a 'value-neutral' functional assessment of mental capacity, which ostensibly focuses on process rather than outcome. However, this claim is difficult to sustain both with respect to the theory and implementation of capacity testing.

The CRPD Committee has made two criticisms of mental capacity:

> The concept of mental capacity is highly controversial in and of itself. Mental capacity is not, as is commonly presented, an objective, scientific and naturally occurring phenomenon. Mental capacity is contingent on social and political contexts, as are the disciplines, professions and practices which play a dominant role in assessing mental capacity.[136]

and

> The functional approach 'is flawed for two key reasons: (a) it is discriminatorily applied to people with disabilities; and (b) it presumes to be able to accurately assess the

[134] Kelly 'Human Rights in India' 172.
[135] Tina Minkowitz, 'CRPD and Transformative Equality' (2017) 13(1) In J Law Context 77, 82 (Minkowitz, 'CRPD and Transformative Equality').
[136] General Comment 1 (n 121) [14].

> inner-workings of the human mind and, when the person does not pass the assessment, it then denies him or her a core human right—the right to equal recognition before the law.'[137]

These general criticisms also emerge in several more specific claims. Beverley Clough points out that the development of the mental capacity test in the common law was based entirely on medical evidence and therefore does not give enough weight to non-clinical issues.[138] Mental capacity assessments have been criticized for being notoriously malleable and flexible[139] and for 'lacking uniformity, depth and perceptions about the impact or mental disability and associated risk'.[140] In a similar vein it is difficult for mental capacity assessments to decouple mental incapacity from unwise decisions[141] and to distinguish between a person's impairment and social situation,[142] so that incapacity can essentially mean disagreeing with one's psychiatrist.[143] In addition, incapacity can reflect a failure to give adequate support.[144] It also permits a power imbalance by giving external medical and sometimes legal authorities discretion and epistemic privilege to 'judge' and know a person's 'true' wishes and feelings better than they do themselves.[145]

The question then is whether mental capacity testing, despite its drawbacks, is still capable of being a valid and non-discriminatory basis for intervention? Or at least superior to the alternative proposed by abolitionists?

In beginning this analysis, I propose to take as my starting point, the notion expressed above that no position is value neutral. So that the idea that there exists (or does not exist) such a concept as mental capacity and that it can be assessed, is a position that is based on and expresses certain values. Specifically, that the law should only respect persons' decisions as legally binding where there is evidence that the decision is informed by the relevant information and that the persons understands that information and can apply it to themselves in a rational way.[146] That is, making decisions and accepting their likely consequences should be both deliberate and purposeful. Mental capacity testing also occurs within a social and political context in which the scientific method is valued as an 'objective' process of discovering information about ourselves and the world (which has been challenged by post-modern cultural theorists). However, I do not think that acknowledging the social and political context of the production of science, necessarily undermines science altogether. Rather, the results of scientific investigation need to be carefully interpreted bearing in

[137] General Comment 1 (n 121) [15].
[138] Clough, 'New Legal Landscapes' (n 120) 253.
[139] Richardson, 'Mental Disabilities and the Law' (n 24) 341.
[140] Stavert, 'Paradigm Shift or Paradigm Paralysis?' (n 113) 4.
[141] Gooding and Flynn 'Querying the Call to Introduce Mental Capacity Testing to Mental Health Law' (n 105) 258.
[142] Ruck Keene, 'Is Mental Capacity in the Eye of the Beholder?' (n 26) 31.
[143] Gooding and Flynn 'Querying the Call to Introduce Mental Capacity Testing to Mental Health Law' (n 105) 256.
[144] Ruck Keene, 'Is Mental Capacity in the Eye of the Beholder?' (n 26) 33.
[145] Gooding and Flynn 'Querying the Call to Introduce Mental Capacity Testing to Mental Health Law' (n 105) 256; Series, 'Relationships, Autonomy and Legal Capacity (n 13) 83.
[146] Richardson, 'Mental Disabilities and the Law' (n 24) 340.

mind their inherent limitations and the social and political context in which they are produced. As Wayne Martin and colleagues observe, capacity assessments are effected by social and political forces, but the answer is to try to ensure that the test is done sufficiently rigorously so that it facilitates rather than undermines the objectivity of assessments.[147] The support paradigm also invites sensitivity to the social and environmental context in which persons make decisions and aims to change that environment to where necessary to support persons to exercise their autonomy.

While mental capacity is a legal concept, variations between different persons mental abilities and the mental abilities of the same person over time do exist, and at some point those abilities may not be sufficient for a person to understand the decision he or she is making in the same way that a person with mental capacity does.

As noted by Wayne Martin and colleagues:

> persons suffering from these kinds of conditions are profoundly vulnerable, and one of the threats they face derives from the fact that they have strong desires that are not informed or constrained by decision-making abilities. We arguably have an ethical duty to come to their aid.[148]

I also point out that as observed by Genevra Richardson, it is difficult to design a capacity test where the bar is not so high as to exclude autonomous choices, nor too low to recognize choices which do not represent a person's true wishes.[149] In *PBU & NJE*[150] (discussed above) Justice Bell of the Supreme Court of Victoria, recently held that the mental capacity test in the *Mental Health Act* 2014 (Vic) in relation to involuntary ECT ought not be set too high even where it may involve the refusal of life-saving treatment, so that persons with mental impairments were not expected to have a level of mental capacity above that of the relatively low standard generally required of persons without disabilities.[151]

However, several of the criticisms of the CRPD Committee seem exaggerated. First, while it is true that it is impossible to know *exactly* the inner-workings of the human mind, it is usually possible to make *some* assessment from what persons are able to communicate about their decision-making process, the substance of their wishes and feelings, and their explanation for a decision. In fact, the abolitionist approach does exactly that when it seeks to determine what a person's will and preferences are and even more so when a supporter or facilitator seeks to '*interpret*' a person's will and preferences. The strength of the support paradigm whether it is used on its own, or for the purposes of determining mental capacity and best interests, is that it requires far more time to be spent exploring the inner-workings of the mind of the person with mental impairment and gathering 'evidence' of those workings from the person and those around them, to enable a far deeper, broader, and holistic assessment than assessing mental capacity without support. Both the Mental Capacity with Support

147 Martin, *Achieving CRPD Compliance* (n 59) 22.
148 ibid 41.
149 Richardson, 'Mental Capacity in the Shadow of Suicide' (n 2).
150 [2018] VSC 564.
151 ibid [178].

and the abolitionist approaches, however, require some reconstruction of the inner-workings of the human mind and confer on the assessor a measure of epistemic privilege in 'judging' those inner workings. Both are therefore prone to error. It is also possible that the giving of support and assessing what and how much support to give a person could also be seen as being based on an external judgment of the person, albeit at an earlier stage.[152]

The difference between the two approaches is that the Mental Capacity with Support model will make a mental capacity assessment by comparing the 'evidence' obtained about the inner-workings of the mind of the person assessed against two standards. The first standard is the diachronic interests of the person in terms of their own long-term value commitments and personal narrative, and the second is some broad external 'norms' which are assumed will be part of the decision-making of most persons with mental capacity. There may be some overlap between the two standards, such as expecting persons to act on values integral to their enduring identity (including pre-illness) and to be able to see a future for themselves. Jillian Craigie argues that by using a diachronic perspective, the ability to take into account the consequences to the future self is not just necessary to preserve the interests of the future self, but is necessary to *constitute* the future self, making it an appropriate consideration for the capacity test.[153] Therefore, knowing the trajectory of disorder, it is possible to fairly reliably anticipate that the person's commitments during an episode will undermine their overall interests[154] and jeopardize their most valued life projects.[155] John Dawson argues, using the example of a dairy farmer who was suffering from paranoid delusions but was refusing treatment and was in danger of losing his livelihood and family relationships, that involuntary psychiatric treatment in the community was necessary to allow the dairy farmer to preserve those two aspects of his life he himself had identified as being important to him.[156] On the same basis, George Szmukler argues that a person's 'will' (or long-term value commitments) ought to take precedence over their 'preferences' (which he regards as more short-term and fleeting).[157] Secondly, the external norms are what Fabian Freyenhagen and Tom O'Shea refer to as the 'hidden substance' involved in mental capacity assessments, such as expecting a person to value themselves in their decision-making and act on true beliefs.[158] However, they do not see any problem in acknowledging this substantive element, provided it is countered with increased transparency, democratic discussion of the conditions for capacity

152 Ruck Keene, 'Is Mental Capacity in the Eye of the Beholder?' (n 26) 37.

153 Jillian Craigie, 'Capacity, Value Neutrality and the Ability to Consider the Future' (2013) 9(1) Int J Law Context 4, 11 (hereafter Craigie, 'Capacity, Value Neutrality and the Ability to Consider the Future').

154 ibid 13.

155 Szmulker and Kelly 'We Should Replace Conventional Mental Health Law with Capacity-Based Law' (n 21) 452.

156 Dawson, 'Concepts of Liberty' 35.

157 George Szmukler, 'The UN Convention on the Rights of Persons with Disabilities: 'Rights, Will and Preferences' in Relation to Mental Health Disabilities' (2017) 54 Int J Law Psychiatry 90 (hereafter, Szmulker, 'Rights, Will and Preferences'); George Szmukler, '"Capacity", "Best Interests", "Will and Preferences" and the UN Convention on the Rights of Persons with Disabilities' (2019) 18(1) World Psych 34 (hereafter, Szmukler, ('Capacity,' 'Best Interests', 'Will and Preferences').

158 Fabian Freyenhagen and Tom O'Shea, 'Hidden Substance: Mental Disorder as a Challenge to Normatively Neutral Accounts of Autonomy' (2013) 9(1) Int J Law Context 53, 54, 55, and 62 (Freyenhagen and O'Shea, 'Hidden Substance').

and autonomy and caution where restrictions on liberty are involved (creating a high threshold for intervention).[159] This can be contrasted with the much observed lack of transparency of the will and preferences approach.

Further, when persons are assessed to lack mental capacity, they are not, as asserted by the CRPD Committee, denied the core human right of equality before the law completely—the denial is limited to that particular decision—and as I and others such as John Dawson have argued, it may permit the recognition of other core CRPD rights.[160] Also, where a person's wishes and feelings are given significant weight in determining a person's best interests, the loss may be even more limited.

It will probably always be difficult for a mental capacity assessment to distinguish between lack of mental capacity and an unwise decision, or a person's impairment and their social situation. However, recent case law where judges have found that a person's wishes and feelings were reasonable despite going against social norms indicate that courts are being more careful about distinguishing between mental capacity and prevailing social values.[161] For instance, in *X NHS Trust v Mr B*,[162] where a person with mental impairment refused a life-saving amputation of an infected limb, the Court of Protection recognized that where a person has had a long-term mental impairment it may not be 'helpful to see the person as if he were a person in good health who has been afflicted by illness',[163] but to take a more integrated view of the person and their impairment and to give more weight to their subjective will and preferences.[164] The Court of Protection has also respected the unusual beliefs of a woman who refused life-saving dialysis after a suicide attempt on the basis that her lifestyle revolved around her looks, social life, and material possessions and she didn't want to grow old.[165] A court has also permitted a woman to terminate her pregnancy despite also suffering from paranoia and delusions.[166] Further, in *A NHS Foundation Trust v Ms X*,[167] a case involving a woman with anorexia nervosa and alcoholism with a less than 5 per cent chance of survival and after years of unsuccessful treatment, the Court of Protection recognized that the loss of control and self-determination by involuntarily treatment could itself be severely damaging to the quality of life of a person with mental impairment and even endanger her life.[168] In that case, the court took a 'withdrawal of treatment' approach by considering whether in light of the vehement refusal of treatment by Ms X, the continuation of treatment would be too burdensome and futile to reasonably continue.

159 ibid 66 and 68.

160 Dawson, 'A Realistic Approach' (n 21) 72–73; Wilson, 'Right to Life' (n 1) and my arguments in previous chapters.

161 *Heart of England NHS Foundation Trust v JB* [2014] EWHC 342 (COP) (hereafter *Heart of England NHS Foundation Trust v JB*); *Re SB (A Patient; Capacity to Consent to Termination)* [2013] EWHC 1417 (COP) (hereafter, *Re SB (A Patient; Capacity to Consent to Termination)*).

162 *X NHS Trust v Mr B* [2015] EWCOP 60 (hereafter, *X NHS Trust v Mr B* [2015]).

163 ibid [13].

164 ibid.

165 *Heart of England NHS Foundation Trust v JB* (n 161).

166 *Re SB (A Patient; Capacity to Consent to Termination)* [2013] (n 161).

167 *A NHS Foundation Trust v Ms X (By her Litigation Friend, the Official Solicitor)* [2014] EWCOP 35 (hereafter *A NHS Foundation Trust v Ms X (By her Litigation Friend, the Official Solicitor)*).

168 ibid.

Similarly, in the Victorian case *PBU & NJE*[169] discussed above, Justice Bell interpreted the mental capacity assessment contained in the *Mental Health Act* 2014 (Vic) as a strictly functional assessment of mental capacity which does not depend on the assessors views of the wisdom of the outcome with a strong emphasis on autonomy, dignity, equality, and self-determination so that capacity assessments are 'criteria-focussed, evidence-based, person-centred and non-judgmental'.[170] His Honour held that 'the question is whether the person understands and is able to remember and use or weigh the relevant information, and communicate a decision, in terms of the general nature, purpose and effect of the treatment, not whether the person can make a sensible, rational or well-considered decision'.[171] The issue of whether a person's insight into their diagnosis might interfere with their mental capacity is a matter of fact to be determined rather than presumed in each case.[172] In that case, Justice Bell overturned the decisions of the Mental Health Tribunal and VCAT that PBU and NJE lacked the mental capacity to refuse ECT.

The possibility of persons with mental impairment being able to make a 'reasonable refusal' is part of the Mental Health Acts of some Australian states and territories.[173] Although, as most tribunal findings are not publicly disclosed, it is not possible to know if anyone has successfully argued that they have 'reasonably refused' treatment, although it may be hard to rebut the presumption that rejecting medical advice is always unreasonable.[174] Also, treatment refusal where a person is at risk of harming others may also be regarded as always being unreasonable.[175] However, within a Mental Capacity with Support model, the concept of a 'reasonable refusal' could become a useful supplement to evidence of a person's wishes and feelings and provide evidence of mental capacity. Reasonable refusal is important to be able to determine why a person is refusing treatment as it may not be a lack of capacity but simply knowing what hospitals are like and what goes on there.[176] For instance, a reasonable refusal might include a refusal where a particular treatment has not been beneficial (or only marginally beneficial) in the past, where the side effects were severe and are likely to be permanent, and there are reasonable medical and non-medical alternatives available that the person would accept. These were the also the sorts of examples used by the Expert Committee when describing who would and would not lack mental capacity under their proposal.[177]

As noted by Renu Barton-Hanson a 'more robust application of the current law alone may achieve the desired enhanced participative model'.[178] Similarly, as discussed below, the use of independent advocacy, communication with people who know the

169 [2018] VSC 564.
170 ibid [201].
171 ibid [182].
172 ibid [193].
173 McSherry and Wilson 'The Concept of Capacity' (n 4); *Mental Health and Related Services Act* (NT) s 14B(iii) (hereafter, 'MHRSA NT').
174 ibid.
175 Dawson and Kampf, 'Incapacity Principles in Mental Health Laws in Europe' (n 130) 315.
176 Charlene Sunkel, 'The UN Convention: A Service User Perspective' (2019) 18(1) World Psych 51, 52 (hereafter Sunkel, 'UN Convention: A Service User Perspective').
177 Richardson Report (n 41) [7.9].
178 Barton-Hansen 'Reforming Best Interests' (n 2) 289.

person well, and second opinions guard against incapacity being decided on simply disagreeing with one's doctor.[179]

Brian Murray observes that while the Mental Capacity with Support model may never be able to be an objective and uncontroversial measure of mental capacity, it may nonetheless be the 'least worst' test, especially if clinicians view it holistically.[180]

8.3.4 Participation

As discussed above, the Mental Capacity with Support model is aimed at significantly increasing the participation of persons with mental impairment in personal healthcare decision-making, including through the offering of support to understand people's wishes and feelings as an important factor in determining their best interests. It may also involve ensuring Court hearings involving persons with mental capacity expressing their will and preferences, may result in less restrictive and more individualized measures that promote the autonomy of the person concerned.[181] Under the CRPD, there is a need for independent representation of the will and preferences or wishes and feelings of the person in all hearings and for reasonable adjustments to the court procedures and processes, such as availability of supporters and the use of multidisciplinary panels, informality and regular breaks to maximize the person's participation.[182] However, the decision of the court need not be in agreement with the individual's will and preferences.[183] But, if a person has been included in decision-making and is treated with dignity and respect they are more likely to respect the decision.[184] Participation in proceedings should not depend on mental capacity.[185] The use of court hearings can also provide oversight to ensure that a person has been given sufficient support to make their own decision, provide a check on undue influence or manipulation by supporters, and to ensure that a person's wishes and feelings are not discounted by the unwillingness of doctors and social care professionals to provide certain treatments or services.[186] Court hearings, unlike the use of an informal facilitator, involve the publication of written reasons for scrutiny by other judges on appeal, the profession, and scholarly criticism. It is arguable for instance that the English court's willingness to expand its interpretation of best interests in the anorexia case of *X* discussed above, was influenced by criticism from scholars, like Genevra Richardson, of the earlier anorexia case of *E*.[187]

[179] Szmulker and Kelly 'We Should Replace Conventional Mental Health Law with Capacity-Based Law' (n 21) 450.

[180] Murray, 'Mental Capacity' (n 27).

[181] Fallon-Kund and Bickenbach, 'Strengthening the Voice of Persons with Mental health Problems' (n 102) 29.

[182] ibid 6.

[183] ibid 2–3.

[184] ibid 5.

[185] ibid 6.

[186] Clough, 'New Legal Landscapes' (n 120) 268.

[187] Richardson, 'Mental Capacity in the Shadow of Suicide' (n 2).

8.3.5 Improving the Mental Capacity with Support Model

There are also a number of improvements which could be made to the Mental Capacity with Support model so that it gives more respect to the dignity, equality, and participation of persons with mental impairments. I deal with each of these in turn.

8.3.5.1 Assigning Responsibility for the Provision of Support

The MCA has been criticized for not assigning responsibility for ensuring that the obligation that a person is offered all reasonable support to any particular person and for needing to be expanded and consolidated.[188] The Mental Capacity with support model should remedy these deficits and ensure that someone has responsibility to ensure that a person has been provided with support, record what was provided, and seek further types of support if they are needed.

8.3.5.2 Training and Diversification of Workforce

The need for sensitization and stigma reduction training for clinicians to be able to implement CRPD has been observed by many parties.[189] Other measures include the diversification of the workforce (including peer supporters), training of psychiatrists to make them aware of the norm-laden nature of mental impairment, creative thinking about treatment or care provisions, and where non-consensual treatment is unavoidable robust safeguards.[190]

8.3.5.3 Consideration of the Likely Outcome of Involuntary Detention and Treatment

Mental health law has always been what Terry Carney calls 'ticket for services' type of legislation which aims to connect people with the services they need, without considering how useful those services actually are.[191] One of the strengths of the abolitionist movement is the realization that while involuntary detention and psychiatric treatment can be life-saving and assist recovery, it is not always the case. It can also be experienced as traumatizing and demeaning and the cost of overriding a person's will and preferences to their sense of self should be carefully considered to determine whether it is worth the benefits gained. Evidence of past treatment which has succeeded and failed and the likelihood that involuntary detention and psychiatric treatment will actually lead to success ought to be given significant weight in any 'best interests' assessment. This is further discussed in section 8.3.2 above.

8.3.5.4 Reform of Court Applications

Court applications could be required to set out the details of past and present wishes and feelings of the person, an explanation of why it was not possible to ascertain them and all support that has been provided to the person, as in Scotland.[192]

188 Series, 'Relationships, Autonomy and Legal Capacity' (n 13) 83.
189 Mahomed, 'Involuntary Mental Health Treatment' (n 10) 5.
190 Freyenhagen and O'Shea, 'Hidden Substance' (n 158) 68.
191 Terry Carney, 'Prioritising Supported Decision-Making: Running on Empty or a Basis for Glacial-to-Steady Progress?' (2017) 6 Laws 18, 22 (Carney, 'Prioritising Supported Decision-Making').
192 Stavert, 'Paradigm Shift or Paradigm Paralysis?' (n 113) 9.

8.3.5.5 Judicial Oversight

While current mental capacity legislation largely delegates mental capacity assessments to medical staff, where there is a dispute or doubt about whether a person has capacity or what is in their best interests, the matter is usually referred to court, either for approval 'on the papers' or a full hearing. Institutions refer contentious matters to the court so as not to frustrate the patient's rights under the MCA and confirm that they are acting lawfully, even where there is no legal obligation to do so.[193] While most cases are decided without court intervention, tighter procedures can be developed. For example, mental health law also contains procedures for routine judicial oversight of involuntary detention and psychiatric treatment by the Mental Health Tribunal and in some jurisdictions there is a Consent and Capacity Tribunal. The Expert Committee also proposed judicial oversight by an independent member and a Capacity Tribunal.[194] By contrast, despite Article 12(4) of the CRPD which stipulates the need for legal capacity safeguards, I have not seen any proposals from abolitionists, who are concerned with cutting bureaucratic red-tape, for a system of judicial oversight to deal with difficulties in 'interpreting' a person's will and preferences, other than the use of a facilitator.

8.3.5.6 Judicial Meetings with Persons with Mental Impairment Mandatory

In recent English cases, judges have had an interview with the person concerned before deciding their mental capacity and 'best interests' instead of just relying on the papers. Such meetings have allowed judges to get a sense of the person's wishes and feelings for themselves and allow the person to further participate in the decision-making process. As Justice Mostyn stated after meeting the person whose capacity was in dispute:

> It was an enlightening experience and one which I would recommend to any judge hearing a similar case ... The reason it was enlightening for me was that the person I met was different in many respects to the person described in the papers. CD was engaging and polite. She was articulate. She was amusing. She listened carefully to questions and answered them equally carefully. True, there were comments that suggested powerful delusional forces; and Dr FH explained that she was heavily medicated. But even so, the person I met was a world away from the violent sociopath described in the papers.[195]

A judicial meeting with a person with mental impairment means that decision-makers are able to know the person as a real human being rather than a 'case', it affords the person the dignity of being heard without their voice being filtered by others, and gives the decision-maker the opportunity to do a deeper exploration of their person's wishes and feelings in order to make a more informed and more legitimate decision. Research

[193] Alex Ruck Keene and others, 'Taking Capacity Seriously? Ten Years of Mental Capacity Disputes before England's Court of Protection' (2019) 62 Int J Law Psychiatry 56, 60 (hereafter Ruck Keene, 'Taking Capacity Seriously?').

[194] Richardson Report (n 41) [4.5] and [5.6].

[195] *A Hospital NHS Trust v CD* [2015] EWCOP 74 [31] (hereafter, *A Hospital NHS Trust v CD*).

by Alex Ruck Keene suggests that in England courts only interview the person whose capacity is in question in about a third of cases and this is an area for development.[196]

8.4 Support Except Where There is Harm Model

The Support Except Where There is Harm model prioritizes support and choice in the first instance, but permits limited involuntary detention and psychiatric treatment where there is a risk of harm. Like the other models, the Support Except Where There is Harm model has a number of variations, which range from modifications to existing mental health law to something that looks a lot like the Abolition with Support model, with some ability for involuntary detention and psychiatric treatment in emergency situations where there is a risk of serious harm to oneself or others. It seems to be the approach preferred by law reform bodies and independent reviews in England, Australia, and Canada, but has had less attention in the scholarly literature. As noted above a hybrid Mental Capacity with Support and Support Except Where There is Harm model has been adopted in recent Australian mental health legislation.

The recent Independent Mental Health Act Review in England and Wales[197] is perhaps the latest and most conservative example of the Support Except Where There is Harm model. The independent review recommends a raft of reforms to the Mental Health Act 1983 (UK) aimed at decreasing coercion and increasing support and choice for persons with mental impairments. The most notable reforms include tightening up the civil commitment criteria to limit it to situations of significant harm to self or others and requiring clinicians to identify that specific harm, how detention will reduce this and why alternatives are not available or suitable; a return to voluntary admission as the norm; and various shorter permissible time limits for involuntary detention and psychiatric treatment; and ensuring that treatment is not just appropriate but is likely to be beneficial to the person.[198] It also includes provisions to increase choice and participation by persons with mental impairment by abolishing the nearest relative requirement and allowing people to choose their nominated person; statutory care and treatment plans which require participation from the person with mental impairment; advance choice documents (which when made when a person is certified to have mental capacity will be more or less binding, except where there are compelling reasons to depart from them); advocacy for formal and informal patients; and new rights of appeal.[199] Unlike other approaches this proposal does not use the offering of support as means to try to divert a person away from involuntary detention and treatment in the first place, but it does give rights to choice and participation once a person is detained.

The Australian Law Reform Commission ('ALRC') has proposed a model that gives effect to a person's will and preferences in all cases except where it is necessary to appoint a representative. While it is not entirely clear, it seems that under the ALRC

[196] Ruck Keene, 'Taking Capacity Seriously? (n 193) 60.
[197] 'Wellesley Report' (n 7).
[198] ibid 108–109.
[199] ibid 11.

approach it would be necessary to appoint a representative when it is not possible to determine what a person's current will and preferences are even where a person has been given support. Where a representative is appointed, a decision must be made in the first instance which respects the best interpretation of a person's past will and preferences and where that cannot be determined to 'promote and uphold the person's human rights and act in the way least restrictive of those rights'.[200] However, a person's will and preferences no matter how clear, may be overridden by the representative where it is necessary to prevent harm (bearing in mind that a representative should only be appointed in the first place where a person's current will and preferences cannot be clearly determined).[201] This model prioritizes a person's clear will and preferences in the first instance (presumably allowing persons with clear will and preferences who do not require the appointment of a representative to make decisions independently or with support that may risk harm). However, the caveat that a person's will and preferences can be overridden where a representative is appointed and it is necessary to prevent harm (including death) is ambiguous, especially determining at what point a person requires a representative because he or she cannot make a sufficiently clear decision. It would certainly apply to the 'hard cases' where a person makes no decision, or a decision that is contradictory or not meaningful, that is, where supported decision-making has arguably 'failed'. However, would it apply when a person expresses their wishes to refuse treatment clearly, but his or her decision could be regarded as being 'unclear' because it is based on a different understanding of reality and it appears he or she has not engaged with the consequences of accepting or rejecting treatment at all?

A similar approach has been taken by Michael Bach and Lana Kerzner who have tried to create a Canadian legislative model based on the CRPD.[202] Their model creates three different types of decision-making status: independent decision-making, supported decision-making, and facilitated decision-making (that is, substitute decision-making when there is no one who is capable of interpreting a person's will and preferences in a way that is consistent with their individual life story).[203] Like the ALRC approach, in most situations a person will make an independent or supported decision, but it allows for limited substitute decision-making in situations where there are likely to be 'serious adverse effects', such as a medical emergency when a person is attempting suicide.[204] It is unclear whether a person must also have facilitated decision-making status to permit substituted decision-making in a medical emergency.

More recently, Paul Skowron has argued that 'best interpretation' refers to a process rather than an outcome which applies whenever a supporter seeks to determine what a person's will and preferences are.[205] He argues that 'best interpretation' does not aim to uncover a person's pre-existing 'true' will and preferences, but that in the course of

200 'ALRC Report' (n 97) 77–78.
201 ibid 77–78 (rec 3.3).
202 Michael Bach and Lana Kerzner 'A New Paradigm for Protecting Autonomy and the Right to Legal Capacity' (Law Commission of Ontario, 2010) (hereafter Bach and Kerzner, 'A New Paradigm').
203 ibid 82–98.
204 ibid 133, 147, 156.
205 Skowron, 'Giving Substance to "the Best Interpretation of Will and Preferences" ' (n 6) 126.

receiving information and support a person may discover what their 'true' will and preferences are.[206] However, he acknowledges (departing from the Abolition with Support model) that there may be instances where coercion will be justified where a person's other CRPD rights are in conflict with their will and preferences and coercion is likely to allow that person to participate in the interpretive process.[207] While he does not specify what coercion might involve, presumably it could include involuntary detention and psychiatric treatment, at least enough to avert an emergency involving harm and allow a person to become sufficiently stable to be offered support and to make a decision. He also acknowledges that there are instances where the interpreter ought to acknowledge that they are making a decision constructed from the very limited information they have been able to obtain from the person and the person's CRPD rights, rather than regarding the person with mental impairment as the author of the decision.[208]

8.4.1 Dignity and Autonomy

The Support Except Where There is Harm model permits involuntary detention and psychiatric treatment as a 'necessary measure' whenever a representative needs to be appointed because a person cannot make a clear decision even with support and a person is at risk of harm, which would clearly include suicide and avoidable accidental death. However, it does respect the autonomy of most persons with mental impairment by giving them full responsibility for self-management in aspects of life where their decisions are sufficiently clear and do not require the appointment of a representative. That is, a person with mental impairment would be free to choose any treatment approach from voluntary psychiatric treatment to complementary medicine, peer respite, meditation, massage, diet and exercise, or nothing at all, provided they can make a sufficiently clear decision without the appointment of a representative, and even if their decision is unclear there is no risk of harm. It also prioritizes the provision of support as the first response from the state. Ideally, after accessing support, most people will choose not to complete suicide or engage in life-threatening behaviour, so that there will never be a need for involuntary detention and psychiatric treatment.

John Fanning claims that harm criteria are inherently stigmatizing (and for that reason involve a loss of dignity and equality) and that 'any attempt to "rehabilitate" risk as a structurally significant consideration in mental health law must confront this reality'.[209] The strength of this argument really depends on whether the mere mention of possible harm in legislation, even where it is the exception rather than the rule, is regarded as stigmatizing.

The more important weakness of the Support Except Where There is Harm model is that it is impossible to predict exactly who will complete suicide or die

206 ibid 131.
207 ibid 133.
208 ibid.
209 Fanning, 'Continuities of Risk' (n 8) 431.

from an avoidable accident and when, so that coercion may become an over-inclusive and an *unnecessary* measure to preserve life and prevent non-fatal harm for some people. There is a significant body of literature, which is too large and complex to recount here, concerning the difficulties of precise prediction and the injustice of overriding the individual liberty and autonomy of persons with mental impairment to prevent harm, especially in the context of the possible legal liability and criticism of clinicians for failing to prevent suicide and avoidable accidental death.[210] That said, there are signs of a shift away from the potentially over-broad use of involuntary detention and psychiatric treatment based on a future fear or apprehension of mental deterioration of a person with mental impairment, towards the need for better evidence of actual harm.[211] The definition of actual harm (and whether it only includes physical or other types of harm) can also be tightened. Further, as a practical matter, it is difficult to see how the state could not take seriously situations where persons with mental impairment have engaged in recent suicide attempts, made suicide plans, expressed an intention to complete suicide or self-harm, or have threatened or attempted to or actually harmed others despite the limitations of risk assessment.

As argued above and in Chapter 7, the prevention of harm can be used to restore a person's dignity.

8.4.2 Equality and Non-Discrimination

The Support Except Where There is Harm model treats persons who are capable of making a sufficiently clear decision as having full legal capacity and to this extent, equally with persons without disabilities. The issue is really determining when a decision is sufficiently clear, especially where a person is expressing a definite will and preference which is unclear because the reasoning underpinning it is unclear or contradictory. Obviously, persons who make an unclear decision and are perceived to be likely to engage in harm will be treated without their consent, unlike persons without disabilities. From the abolitionist perspective this would be discriminatory, although once again it is arguable that persons with disabilities who cannot make sufficiently clear decisions with respect to harm or that may undermine their other CRPD rights are not 'the same' as persons without mental impairments. Therefore, differential treatment would not be unequal, especially if it conferred the person with the benefits of not being harmed, the consequences of harming others and of potential recovery.

[210] For example, Genevra Richardson and Gareth Owen George Szmukler, '"Rabone" and Four Unresolved Problems in Mental Health Law' (2013) 37 The Psychiatrist 297 (hereafter, Richardson, 'Rabone');Sascha Callaghan and others, 'Risk of Suicide Is Insufficient Warrant for Coercive Treatment of Mental Illness' (2013) 36 Int J Law Psychiatry 374 (hereafter Callaghan, 'Risk of Suicide is Insufficient Warrant'); Bernadette McSherry, *Managing Fear: The Law and Ethics of Preventive Detention and Risk Assessment*, International Perspectives on Forensic Mental Health (Routledge 2014) 52–55 (hereafter McSherry, *Managing Fear*).

[211] *Pleso v Hungary*, App no 41242/08, 2 January 2013, [65]–[66] (hereafter, *Pleso v Hungary*).

8.4.3 Participation

The Support Except Where There is Harm model, is aimed to maximize individual participation in decision-making through the use of support except where a person cannot make a clear decision and requires the appointment of a representative.

8.5 General Systemic and Social Reforms

Of course, legal reform is only one part of the overall reform 'package' necessary for mental health reform. Regardless of whether mental health law is abolished or not, there is plenty of scope for the state to reform mental health services in consultation with persons with mental impairment to make them more effective services that people actually want to use voluntarily.[212] There is growing awareness that the availability of a range of well-resourced and good quality services is important in reducing the need for coercion in the first place,[213] and that funding shortages (sometimes caused by an increase in population and demand, rather than budget cuts) reduces positive outcomes and the delivery of person-centred care.[214] Some psychiatrists, such as Brendan Kelly and 'post-psychiatrists' (the name certain contemporary critical psychiatrists such as Pat Bracken give themselves),[215] see value in exploring sub-optimal clinical treatments and alternative practices where they are more acceptable to persons with mental impairments. That is, the abolition of mental health law is not the only approach to end the historical abuse and poor treatment of persons with mental impairment which is one of the justifications of abolitionists. The obligation to treat people with dignity is not limited to Article 12.

Abolitionists are concerned that the mental health system is so broken that it is impossible to reform it—that as long as mental health law continues to 'legitimate' involuntary detention and psychiatric treatment, there is no room for other less coercive approaches to become the norm. As Jasna Russo and Diana Rose observe:

> . . . solely working within the human rights framework does not open up the crucial question of how helpful psychiatric interventions are altogether. It may be possible to ensure respect for the dignity of people as well as their right to to make their own decisions and choices, however, if all those choices stay lodged within the biomedical approach to human crisis, then we may continue to neglect the most important avenues for personal growth and living to one's full potential. Work towards these

[212] Peter Bartlett, 'A Mental Disorder of a Kind or Degree Warranting Confinement: Examining Justifications for Psychiatric Detention' (2012) 16(6) Int J Hum Rights 831, 834 (hereafter Bartlett, 'A Mental Disorder of a Kind or Degree Warranting Confinement').

[213] Craigie, 'Panel Event' (n 107) 165–66.

[214] Ruth Vine and Fiona Judd, 'Contextual Issues in the Implementation of Mental Health Legislation' ibid 16, 18 (hereafter Vine and Judd, 'Contextual Issues').

[215] Pat Bracken and Philip Thomas, 'From Szasz to Foucault: On the Role of Critical Psychiatry' (2010) 17(3) Philos Psychiatry Psychol 219 (hereafter, Bracken and Thomas, 'From Szasz to Foucault').

possibilities cannot take place within any framework which focusses exclusively on improving what is already in place . . .[216]

While the scepticism of abolitionists is understandable, I argue that this approach is overly pessimistic. As noted above, there is widespread dissatisfaction with existing the mental health system and broad agreement that coercion is overly used and must be significantly reduced. There is no reason why these social and emotional supports can't be developed along-side mental health law with the view of ensuring that the use of coercion is only a last resort. In fact, most countries have mental health law and many alternatives already exist and *are* already developing and have been some time. For instance, Gooding and colleagues have done a comprehensive literature review of recovery-led and trauma informed practices, 'peer-led' initiatives, family or social network directed initiatives, respite centres, low and no medication options, and home-based support that already exist around the world.[217]

Further, the COVID-19 pandemic has highlighted the importance of the social support on mental health and has made mental health more of a community concern. The growing numbers of persons with mental impairments in the community, the cost of mental impairments to the economy, and the increase of persons with mental impairments receiving disability pensions, have also meant that mental health has been reframed as an economic and productivity issue and for this reason governments have begun to take improving the mental health sector seriously.[218] For example, in Australia the Productivity Commission has estimated that the direct cost of mental ill-health and suicide is $43–70 billion comprised of direct expenditure on health services ($16 billion), lower economic participation and lost productivity ($12–39 billion), and informal care by family and friends ($15 billion).[219] The indirect costs of disability premature death, suicide, and self-inflicted injury are estimated to be $151 billion not including the social and emotional cost.[220] In the past, mental health services have always struggled with funding and a lack of political will and community concern. However, when the cost of *not* investing in mental health care is a very large number then the impetus for governments to invest in it is much greater and can be more easily justified.

A further effect of the CRPD and the call for the abolition of mental health law is a new willingness by governments to reform the mental health system to include greater options. For example, the Victorian Royal Commission into mental health is working on a new mental health model in which mental health law will co-exist with expanding community treatment to avoid involuntary hospital admissions, offering non-hospital based residential care options, making available a range of treatments

[216] Jasna Russo and Diana Rose, '"But What if Nobody's Going to Sit Down and Have a Real Conversation with You?" Service user/Survivor Perspectives on Human Rights' (2013) 12(4) J Public Ment Health 184, 191 (hereafter Russo and Rose, 'But What if Nobody's Going to Sit Down and Have a Real Conversation with You?').

[217] Gooding, *Alternatives to Coercion in Mental Health Settings* (n 15) 11.

[218] For example, Royal Commission into Victoria's Mental Health System, Interim Report, November 2019 (no 87 2018–19) (hereafter, 'Victorian Royal Commission Interim Report'); Productivity Commission, Mental Health Final Report No 95, 30 June 2020 (hereafter, 'Productivity Commission Final Report').

[219] Productivity Commission Final Report (n 218) 3.

[220] ibid.

beyond medication, and bolstering the lived experience workforce including peer supporters.[221] The Productivity Commission has also recommended sweeping changes to create a person-centred mental health system which provides for mental health care to be provided by general practitioners, individual and group talking therapies, telehealth, increased community care and hospital-in-the-home, improving interactions with persons with mental impairments by first responders in emergencies, better gender and age segregated hospitals, and even a role for traditional aboriginal healers.[222]

The power of continued advocacy and education by persons with mental impairments in sharing their lived experience cannot be underestimated. For example, a consumer researcher has admitted that:

> I was not always open to ideas about the reduction of seclusion and restraint. I had always believed that I was never punitive and when I did seek an order for seclusion, I was doing this therapeutically. It was not until I heard the experiences of consumers that my once-held thoughts and beliefs changed.[223]

Similarly, Jacob Jarab points out that (as I note in Chapter 2) the psychiatric profession has always criticized itself (such as through anti-psychiatry) and has always been involved in driving and getting political support for important reforms such as deinstitutionalization and can still do much to assist with independent living under Article 19 of the CRPD.[224] He says:

> More broadly, what can be proposed is dialogue and bridge-building between various types of expertise. In that process, mental health professionals and health care policymakers should accept that human rights standards apply to everyone, including persons with psycho-social disabilities (who are not merely their "patients"), and they should increasingly integrate a human rights-based approach into their work. Human rights training for health professionals in this field would be very beneficial. A critical appraisal of past human rights violations (as abuses of power, and not just wrong medical approaches) would also be most welcome . . .[225]

Abolitionists assume that abolishing mental health law would 'force' the governments to invest in supported decision-making, better services, and social and emotional supports. However, I believe that the opposite is more likely and that there is a real risk that abolishing mental health law without a further development of the health system would instead (following the history of deinstitutionalization) mean that persons with mental impairments will be simply neglected and end up dead, homeless or in the criminal justice system. Moreover, a poorly executed abolition of mental health

221 Victorian Royal Commission Interim Report (n 218).

222 Productivity Commission Final Report (n 218).

223 Sandy Watson and others, 'Care without Coercion—Mental Health Rights, Personal Recovery and Trauma-Informed Care' (2014) 49(4) Aust J Soc Issues 529,543 (hereafter Watson, 'Care without Coercion').

224 Jan Jarab, 'Psychiatry and Human Rights: A Difficult Relationship, But with Growing Potential' (2015) 29 Neuropsychiatrie 106, 107–108 (hereafter Jarab, 'Psychiatry and Human Rights').

225 ibid 111.

law would likely set back the cause for reform even further, as any adverse incidents could cause a public and media outcry for the reinstatement of even tougher mental health laws.

As noted in section 3.3.10 many abolitionists are concerned clinicians will always use involuntary detention and treatment simply because it is 'easier'. However, I believe that this assumption is incorrect. Many psychiatrists understand the delicate balance between the benefits and costs of involuntary detention and psychiatric treatment and agree that it is overused. The real problem is the lack of different options within the mental health system, which relies heavily on medication, and the ability to intervene earlier using less coercive approaches in the community. The creation of a more flexible mental health system with a greater range of treatment options and a stronger voluntary community mental health system would aid in giving clinicians the ability to be more responsive to the will and preferences of persons with mental impairments and pave the way towards more individualized medicine.

Therefore, continued advocacy for the availability of a wider range of talking therapies and non-medical treatment options, improved services and education of the medical profession and governments about the problems with the current mental health system and the experiences of some persons with mental impairments in them is in my view a better focus of activities, than pushing for immediate abolition of mental health law and berating States parties for breaching provisions of the CRPD they never agreed to in the first place.

Broader reforms should focus on redressing the general situation of social disadvantage of persons with mental impairments in most societies including in housing, quality of life, education, and employment. There should also be a focus on quality of relationships which play a huge part in experience of dignity in mental health system and recovery.[226] Communication and interactions between staff and persons with mental impairments are particularly important so that staff come across as humane rather than coldly and distantly professional and people are getting more psychological support than just medication and detention.[227] In fact, sometimes persons with mental impairments report feeling closer to their treating teams than their families and their biggest concern is not being bossed around but rather that nobody cares.[228]

All of these approaches will require significant resources. As Chris Maylea and Asher Hirsh observe:

> The implementation of supported decision-making will not come about as a result of changes to the legislative framework alone, but by an investment in cultural and social change which genuinely supports people to make their own decisions, whatever their mental capacity. This will require a paradigm shift in clinical practice and support service provision built on community engagement and consensus building, resulting in a service system of such high quality and a community so understanding

226 Series, 'Relationships, Autonomy and Legal Capacity (n 13) 89.

227 Russo and Rose, 'But What if Nobody's Going to Sit Down and Have a Real Conversation with You?' (n 216) 189–90.

228 Meredith Stone and others, 'Estranged Relations: Coercion and Care in Narratives of Supported Decision-Making in Mental Healthcare' (2020) 46 Med Humanit 62, 68, 69 (hereafter Stone, 'Estranged Relations').

and supportive that compulsory treatment and involuntary detention is never necessary, upholding the right to choose treatment, not just refuse it.[229]

8.6 Conclusion

It is my contention that the reform of mental health law is preferable to its abolition. In this chapter, I have examined the strengths and weaknesses of the Mental Capacity with Support and Support Except Where There is Harm models as two possible law reform alternatives, in the context of the CRPD principles of dignity, equality, and participation. Of these two reform options, I have argued for the Mental Capacity with Support model as providing the better and more developed option. I have also considered the objections of abolitionists to these two different reform approaches. While the Mental Capacity with Support model is not perfect, it provides a better way of balancing respect for autonomy with a person's other CRPD rights and the CRPD values of inherent dignity, equality, and participation. Even though the Mental Capacity with Support model has been criticized as being malleable, subjective, discriminatory, and demeaning, I have argued that many of its flaws can be overcome by further reforms. The Support Except Where There is Harm model seems to be more a creature of law reform commissions and has not been considered at length in the scholarly literature, but it is a way to increase support for decision-making while ensuring that people at risk of harm to themselves or others still receive treatment. I have also argued for the need for a wider 'package' of legal and systemic reform and why I believe reform is possible while mental health law still remains in place. Any legal reforms would need to be accompanied by adequate resources to be implemented properly.

[229] Chris Maylea and Asher Hirsch, 'The Right to Refuse: The Victorian Mental Health Act 2014 and the Convention on the Rights of Persons with Disabilities' (2017) 42(2) Alt Law J 149, 153, and 155 (hereafter Maylea and Hirsch, 'The Right to Refuse'); McSherry and Wilson 'The Concept of Capacity' (n 4).

9
Conclusion

My book has explored the question of whether mental health law should be abolished or reformed. My answer to that question is that contrary to the arguments of abolitionists, mental health law should not be abolished, but be reformed by decreasing coercion and increasing social support to persons with mental impairments to maximize their dignity (including autonomy), equality, and participation in accordance with the overall object and purpose of the CRPD. I have used two methods. First, I have adopted the CRPD and international human rights law as my conceptual framework to develop a moderate interpretation of the CRPD based on the text, object, and purpose and intention of the parties in negotiating the CRPD (including the ongoing lack of agreement about the abolition of mental health law between disability advocates and States Parties). By using an holistic interpretation of the CRPD I created the 'interpretive compass' of dignity, equality, and participation. Rather than attempt some kind of proportionality analysis to balance conflicting CRPD rights, I instead explored the meaning and scope of dignity, equality, and participation in the CRPD, in the disability, and wider human rights literature. I also used the *interactive* model of social disability which sees disability as an interaction between a person's impairment and their environment, rather than the strong British Social Model of Disability some abolitionists have argued applies to the CRPD. Second, I have used a 'jurisprudential' or 'ethical' analysis that is cogniscent of the social forces shaping mental health law and the debate about its abolition or reform rather than a purely doctrinal method to frame my analysis of the history of mental health law, the call for abolition, and the 'interpretive compass' of dignity, equality, and participation by drawing on both theoretical and empirical research. I summarize my findings as follows.

Contrary to claims of abolitionists that mental health law has more or less stayed the same, my book in Chapter 2 presents a narrative which demonstrates that mental health law has always been in a continual state of reform, the call for abolition perhaps being the latest iteration. In fact, there have already been a number of 'paradigm shifts' within mental health law from legalism and medicalization to rights-based legalism and the first call for abolition—the closure of the asylum and deinstitutionalization. I point out that revolutionary changes like abolition are often self-defeating and the reality rarely lives up to the rhetoric. Instead, I argue, incremental change through reform is preferable.

In Chapter 3, I trace the historical resistance to mental health law, especially as part of the civil rights movement. I set out how mental impairment became subsumed within the disability rights movement and that it is not always a neat fit. Chapter 3 identifies and analyses the key concerns of abolitionists (being, that mental health law is really a system of social control; that mental health law is discriminatory and an unjustified interference with liberty and bodily integrity; that it is inconsistent with

Mental Health Law. Kay Wilson, Oxford University Press. © Kay Wilson 2021. DOI: 10.1093/oso/9780192843258.003.0009

the right to independent living; that it is torture and cruel, inhuman, and degrading treatment and punishment; that it is ineffective and un-therapeutic; and that there are better alternatives). This Chapter summarizes where such concerns come from historically, with a view to setting up how they can be addressed by reforms. My deep analysis of the case for abolition is also important, to counter the impression that I am creating a 'straw man' for my critique and to reassure abolitionists that I understand their position, even if I believe it has some inherent flaws. It also demonstrates that the concerns of abolitionists are selective, focussing on the restoration of autonomy, regardless of the consequences for other CRPD rights. Abolition is seen as a remedy for the historical abuse suffered by persons with mental impairments, although I question whether this is the only or best way in my discussion of the reform of mental health law in Chapter 8.

There is a vast interdisciplinary literature on the meanings of dignity and equality and a lesser one for participation. I have reviewed a reasonably wide sample of that literature in the general human rights and the disability rights context as well as material related to the negotiation of the CRPD and the CRPD literature. Based on that literature I argue that inherent dignity includes but has a wider meaning than respect for autonomy. I argue that autonomy is a state of fact rather than a 'right'. I also note that there is no explicit right to autonomy in the CRPD. 'The freedom to make one's own choices and independence of persons' in Article 3 of the CRPD, can only apply where that is actually possible taking into account the nature of a person's impairment and without undermining other important CRPD rights and values like inherent dignity. While autonomy is an important principle of the CRPD given the history of the will and preferences of persons with disabilities often being completely disregarded and subsumed within the dictates of institutional life, I argue it is not without its limits. When exercising autonomy which involves conduct that is likely to harm others or is self-destructive or violates widely accepted social norms of human dignity (such as, nudity in a public place), autonomy may clash with the protection of inherent dignity. I define dignity has having five distinct components: recognizing a person's inalienable intrinsic human worth, equal treatment, being treated with dignity, and respect for autonomy where autonomy exists and that does not threaten inherent dignity, but also a requirement to behave with dignity. That is, as Deryck Beyleveld and Roger Brownsword argue human dignity can be conceptualized as empowerment where autonomy prevails, *and* as a form of constraint where paternalism and social deference prevail. I argue that the principle of inherent dignity may override autonomy with respect to serious self-destructive and degrading acts especially where there is good reason to believe that a person's autonomy may be compromised and those acts may be irreversible. In accordance with John Kleinig I argue that protecting dignity may not always justify involuntary detention and psychiatric treatment, other approaches should be used first. However, I reject Brendan Kelly's argument that inherent dignity should become the new civil commitment criteria because as a concept it is still too amorphous and contested and is better used as a guiding principle as it is used currently in human rights law.

I also argue that the undignified treatment of persons with mental impairment by the mental health system, which I think sits behind many of the abolitionist's criticisms of mental health law, must be addressed by legal and systemic reform and I give some examples, based on research, of what dignified treatment involves. It is also important to recognize that for many persons with mental impairment their unusual experiences feel real and are meaningful to them and need to be treated respectfully.

I argue that what equality and non-discrimination means in the CRPD is unclear because the CRPD contains an eclectic and incoherent model of equality and non-discrimination. I argue that equality and non-discrimination is broader than treating persons with and without mental impairment exactly 'the same'. I also argue that abolishing mental health law without recognizing the effect of mental impairment on the person may have the effect of exacerbating rather than creating equality in a broader substantive or transformative sense. The focus of abolitionists on achieving formal equality, eliminating direct discrimination and the offering of decision-making support is not sufficient to achieve the comprehensive and ambitious vision of equality and non-discrimination in the CRPD. I set out the difficulties of applying equality and non-discrimination in the CRPD to persons with mental impairment, such as determining equality of what (that is, equality in decision-making may lead to inequality in other areas of life), equality with whom or finding an appropriate comparator (that is, it may not be appropriate to compare persons with and without mental impairment), whether involuntary detention and psychiatric treatment is a detriment or benefit, addressing the sameness and difference of persons with mental impairment and whether supported decision-making is enough to make persons with and without mental impairment 'equal.'

The third component of the interpretive compass is participation which is an important principle in the CRPD and means being consulted about and having one's views taken seriously in the decision-making process. It applies to individual decisions and policy-making. But, I argue that it does not mean that States Parties have to do whatever persons with disabilities say without taking into account other interests. Also, a person's level of participation may vary according to his or her impairments. I also discuss the problem that disabled persons organizations may not be representative of *all* persons with mental impairments—many persons with mental impairments agree with the use of mental health law in certain circumstances and feel they have been sidelined by abolitionists. It may be necessary for persons with mental impairments to have further discussions about issues sidestepped by the CRPD, such as, how and when intervention should occur when people are at risk.

Having discussed the three components of the Interpretive Compass, I am critical of the Abolition with Support Model and I argue in favour of reform using the Mental Capacity with Support Model in recognizing inherent dignity, equality, and participation. While I prefer Mental Capacity with Support, I think that the Support Except Where There is Harm model is promising, but being a creature of various law reform committees I think it is still very under-developed. The Mental Capacity with Support Model respects inherent dignity by creating a process to recognize autonomous decisions and supporting people to reflect on their will and preferences to make autonomous decisions, but it also protects inherent dignity in extreme cases of self-neglect and harm, especially where there is reason to believe that a person may not understand what they are doing. It also supports equality by making the civil commitment criteria equal for all persons who lack mental capacity for whatever reason. However, it also recognizes a legitimate difference between people with and without mental capacity, instead of falsely comparing people who are not similarly situated. The Mental Capacity with Support Model encourages individual participation through the support and assessment process and recent developments include growing participation in court proceedings. I also suggest improvements to the Mental Capacity with Support Model. For example, to ensure that proper support is actually given, to improve mental capacity assessment, to give more weight to individual will, feelings and preferences, to improve treatment options and to improve safeguards such as judicial oversight. Accordingly, I argue that mental health law should be significantly reformed, not abolished.

Bibliography

Articles/Books/Reports

'Advancing the Rights of Users and Survivors of Psychiatry Using the UN Convention on the Rights of Persons with Disabilities—an Interview with Tina Minkowitz' in Helen Spander and others (eds), *Madness, Distress and the Politics of Disablement* (Policy Press 2016)

'The "Crime" of Mental Illness: Extension of "Criminal" Procedural Safeguards to Involuntary Civil Commitments' (1975) 66(3) *The Journal of Criminal Law and Criminology* 25

'Locked in' *The Economist* (3 August 2013)

'Mental Health and Human Rights: Report of the Task Panel on Legal and Ethical Issues' (1978) 20 *Arizona Law Review* 49

'Mental Health, Human Rights and Their Relationship: An Introduction' in Michael Dudley and others (eds), *Mental Health and Human Rights: Vision, Praxis, and Courage* (Oxford University Press 2012) 1

'The Mental Treatment Act 1930' (1930) 2(3637) *The British Medical Journal* 489

'People with Mental Illness Six Times More Likely to Die in an Accident' (2013) September/October *Mental Health Today* 6

A

Ad Hoc Joint Committee on the Mental Capacity Bill 'Report on the Mental Capacity Bill' 25 January 2016 (NIA 353/11-16)

Aho, Kevin, 'Medicalising Mental Health: A Phenomenological Alternative' (2008) 29 *Journal of Medical Humanities* 243

Allderidge, Patricia, 'Hospitals, Madhouses and Asylums: Cycles in the Care of the Insane' (1979) 134 *British Journal of Psychiatry* 321

Amador, Xavier and Henry Kronengold 'Understanding and Assessing Insight' in Xavier Amador and Anthony David (eds), *Insight and Psychosis: Awareness of Illness in Schizophrenia and Related Disorders* (2nd ed, Oxford University Press 2004) 24–25.

Amer, Ahmed Bait, 'Informed Consent in Adult Psychiatry' (2013) 28(4) *Oman Medical Journal* 228

Amering, Michaela and Margit Schmolke, *Recovery in Mental Health: Reshaping Scientific and Clinical Responsibilities* (Peter Stastny trans, Wiley 2009)

Anderson, Joel, 'Vulnerability, Autonomy Gaps and Social Exclusion' in Christine Straehle (ed), *Vulnerability, Autonomy and Applied Ethics* (Routledge 2016)

Appelbaum, Paul, 'Almost a Revolution: An International Perspective on the Law of Involuntary Commitment' (1997) 25(2) *Journal of the American Academy of Psychiatry and the Law* 135

Appelbaum, Paul, 'Protecting the Rights of Persons with Disabilities: An International Convention and Its Problems' (2016) 67(4) *Psychiatric Services* 366

Arnardottir, Oddny Mjoll, 'A Future of Multidimensional Disadvantage Equality?' in Oddny Mjoll Arnardottir and Gerard Quinn (eds), *The UN Convention on the Rights of Persons with Disabilities: European and Scandinavian Perspectives* (Martinus Nijhoff Publishers 2009)

Arstein-Kerslake, Anna, 'An Empowering Dependency: Exploring Support for the Exercise of Legal Capacity' (2016) 18(1) *Scandinavian Journal of Disability Research* 77

Arstein-Kerslake, Anna and Eilonoir Flynn, 'The General Comment on Article 12 of the Convention on the Rights of Persons with Disabilities: A Roadmap for Equality Before the Law' (2016) 20(4) *The International Journal of Human Rights* 471

Arstein-Kerslake, Anna, 'Future Directions in Supported Decision-Making' (2017) 37(1) *Disability Studies Quarterly*

Arstein-Kerslake, Anna and Jennifer Black, 'Right to Legal Capacity in Therapeutic Jurisprudence: Insights from Critical Disability Theory and the Convention on the Rights of Persons with Disabilities' (2020) 68 *International Journal of Law and Psychiatry* 101535

Atkinson, Jacqueline, *Advance Directives in Mental Health: Theory, Practice and Ethics* (Jessica Kingsley Publishers 2007)

Atkinson, Jacqueline and Jacquie Reilly, 'The Recent History of Concepts of 'Dangerousness' in Mental Health Law' (2011) 13(1) *History and Philosophy or Psychology* 45

Australian Institute of Health and Welfare, *Mental Health Services in Australia 2018*, https://www.aihw.gov.au/reports/mental-health-services/mental-health-services-in-australia/report-contents/summary-of-mental-health-services-in-australia (last accessed 25 October 2019)

Australian Institute of Health and Welfare, Admitted Patient Mental Health Related Care https://www.aihw.gov.au/getmedia/71900b8a-fe09-4a6b-9b3c-350698cc82c9/Mental-health-related-admitted-patient-care-2011-12.pdf.aspx. (last accessed 25 October 2019)

Australian Law Reform Commission, *Equality, Capacity and Disability in Commonwealth Laws* (Australian Government 2014)

B

Bach, Michael and Lana Kerzner, 'A New Paradigm for Protecting Autonomy in the Right to Legal Capacity' (Law Commission of Ontario 2010)

Bagenstos, Samuel R, *Law and the Contradictions of the Disability Rights Movement* (Yale University Press 2009)

Baker, John and others, *Equality: From Theory to Action* (Palgrave MacMillan 2004)

Bannister, Emma Waynne and Sridhar Venkatapuram 'Grounding the Right to Live in the Community (CRPD Article 19) in the Capabilities Approach to Social Justice' (2020) 69 *International Journal of Law and Psychiatry* 101551

Barak, Aharon, 'Proportionality and Principled Balancing' (2010) 4(1) *Law & Ethics of Human Rights* 2

Barclay, Linda, 'Justice and Disability: What Kind of Theorizing is Needed?' (2011) 42(3) *Journal of Social Philosophy* 273

Barclay, Linda, 'In Sickness and in Dignity: A Philosophical Account of the Meaning of Dignity in Health Care' (2016) 61 *International Journal of Nursing Studies* 136

Barilan, Y. Michael, 'Respect for Personal Autonomy, Human Dignity, and the Problems of Self-Directedness and Botched Autonomy' (2011) 36 *Journal of Medicine and Philosophy* 496

Bartlett, Peter, 'The Asylum, the Workhouse, and the Voice of the Insane Poor in 19th Century England' (1998) 21(4) *International Journal of Law and Psychiatry* 421

Bartlett, Peter, 'Thinking About the Rest of the World: Mental Health and Rights Outside the 'First World' in Bernadette McSherry and Penelope Weller (eds), *Rethinking Rights-Based Mental Health Laws* (Hart 2010) 397

Bartlett, Peter and Ralph Sandland, *Mental Health Law: Policy and Practice* (Oxford University Press, 3rd ed, 2007)

Bartlett, Peter, 'A Mental Disorder of a Kind or Degree Warranting Confinement: Examining Justifications for Psychiatric Detention' (2012) 16(6) *The International Journal of Human Rights* 831

Bartlett, Peter, 'The United Nations Convention on the Rights of Persons with Disabilities and Mental Health Law' (2012) 75(5) *The Modern Law Review* 752

Barton-Hansen, Renu, 'Reforming Best Interests: The Road Towards Supported Decision-Making' (2018) 40(3) *Journal of Social Welfare and Family Law* 277

Basak, Cali, 'Balancing Human Rights? Methodological Problems with Weights, Scales and Proportions,' (2007) 29 *Human Rights Quarterly* 251

Basser, Lee Ann, 'Human Dignity' in Marcia H Rioux and others (eds), *Critical Perspectives on Human Rights and Disability Law* (Martinus Nijhoff Publishers 2011) 17

Bean, Philip, 'The Mental Health Act 1959: Some Issues Concerning Rule Enforcement' (1975) 2(2) *British Journal of Law and Society* 225

Beckett, Angherd and Tom Campbell, 'The Social Model of Disability as an Oppositional Device' (2015) 30(2) *Disability and Society* 270

Beyleveld, Deryck and Roger Brownsword, *Human Dignity in Bioethics and Biolaw* (Oxford University Press 2001)

Bilchitz, David, 'Dignity. Fundamental Rights and Legal Capacity: Moving Beyond the Paradigm Set by the General Comment on Article 12 of the Convention on the Rights of Persons with Disabilities' (2016) 32(3) SAJHR 410

Bonnie, Richard J, 'Three Strands of Mental Health Law: Developmental Mileposts' in Richard J Bonnie and Lynda E Frost (eds), *The Evolution of Mental Health Law* (American Psychological Association 2001) 31

Boso, Luke, 'Dignity, Equality and Stereotypes' (2017) 92 *Washington Law Review* 1119

Boyle, Aisling, 'The Law and Incapacity Determinations: A Conflict of Governance' (2008) 71(3) *The Modern Law Review* 413

Bracken, Pat and Philip Thomas, 'From Szasz to Foucault: On the Role of Critical Psychiatry' (2010) 17(3) *Philosophy, Psychiatry & Psychology* 219

Brandon, David, 'A Friend to Alleged Lunatics' (2007) (October) *Mental Health Today*

Brandon, Mark, 'Comment: Differences and (in)Equalities' in Austin Sarat (ed), *Law and the Imagining of Difference* (Emerald Publishing Limited 2018) 135

Breakey, William, *The Rise and Fall of the State Mental Hospital*, Series The Rise and Fall of the State Mental Hospital (trans, Oxford University Press 1996)

Broderick, Andrea, *The Long and Winding Road to Equality and Inclusion for Persons with Disabilities: The United Nations Convention on the Rights of Persons with Disabilities* (Intersentia 2015)

Brosnan, Liz, 'Who's Talking About Us Without Us? A Survivor Research Interjection into an Academic Psychiatry Debate on Compulsory Community Treatment Orders in Ireland' (2018) 7 *Laws* 33

Brown, Jennifer, 'The Changing Purpose of Mental Health Law: From Medicalism to Legalism to New Legalism' (2016) 47 *International Journal of Law and Psychiatry* 1

Burch, Matthew, 'Autonomy, Respect, and the Rights of Persons with Disabilities in Crisis' (2017) 34(3) *Journal of Applied Philosophy* 389

Burns, Johnathan, 'Mental Health Inequity: A Human Rights Approach to Inequality, Discrimination and Mental Disability' (2009) 11(2) *Health and Human Rights* 19

Burns, Tom, *Psychiatry: A Very Short Introduction* (Oxford University Press 2006)

Bury, Micheal, 'Social Constructionalism and the Development of Medical Sociology' (2008) 8(2) *Sociology of Health and Illness* 137

Butlin, Sarah Fraser, 'The UN Convention on the Rights of Persons with Disabilities: Does the Equality Act 2010 Measure up to UK International Commitments?' (2011) 40(4) *Industrial Law Journal* 428

Byrne, Bronagh, 'Dis-Equality: Exploring the Juxtaposition of Disability and Equality' (2018) 6(1) *Social Inclusion* 9

C

Callaghan, Sascha and others, 'Risk of Suicide is Insufficient Warrant for Coercive Treatment of Mental Illness' (2013) 36 *International Journal of Law and Psychiatry* 374

Callaghan, Sascha and Christopher Ryan, 'Is There a Future for Involuntary Treatment in Rights-Based Mental Health Law?' (2014) 21(5) *Psychiatry, Psychology and Law* 747

Callaghan, Sascha and Christopher Ryan, 'An Evolving Revolution: Evaluating Australia's Compliance with the Convention on the Rights of Persons with Disabilities in Mental Health Law' (2016) 39(2) *University of New South Wales Law Journal* 596

Campbell, Tom, 'Mental Health Law: Institutionalised Discrimination' (1994) 28 *Australian and New Zealand Journal of Psychiatry* 554

Carey, Benedict, 'The Chains of Mental Illness in West Africa' *The New York Times* 11 October 2015

Carney, Terry, 'Commentary: Regulatory Dividends of Scandal—the Chelmsford Legacy' (2013) 21(3) *Australasian Psychiatry* 220

Carney, Terry, 'Prioritising Supported Decision-Making: Running on Empty or a Basis for Glacial-to-Steady Progress?' (2017) 6 *Laws* 24

Carney, Terry, 'Supported Decision-Making in Australia: Meeting the Challenge of Moving from Capacity to Capacity-Building?' (2017) 35(2) *Law in Context* 44

Cavadino, Michael, *Mental Health Law in Context: Doctor's Orders?* (Dartmouth Publishing Company 1989)

Cavanagh J and others, 'Psychological Autopsy Studies of Suicide: A Systematic Review' (2003) 33 *Psychological Medicine* 395

Celik, Elif, 'The Role of the CRPD in Rethinking the Subject of Human Rights' (2017) 21(7) *The International Journal of Human Rights* 933

Chambers, Mary and others, 'The Experiences of Detained Mental Health Service Users: Issues of Dignity in Care' (2014) 15 *BMC Medical Ethics* 50

Chan, Hui Yun, 'Refusing Treatment Prior to Becoming Incapacitated: Supported Decision-Making as an Approach in Advance Directives' (2018) 24 *European Journal of Health Law* 24

Charland, Louis, 'Benevolent Theory: Moral Treatment at the York Retreat' (2007) 18(1) *History of Psychiatry* 61

Cheng, Ryu, 'Sociological Theories of Disability, Gender and Sexuality: A Review of the Literature' (2009) 19(1) *Journal of Human Behaviour in the Social Environment* 112

Childress, James and others, 'Public Health Ethics: Mapping the Terrain' (2002) 30 *Journal of Law, Medicine and Ethics* 170

Clapperton, Angela and others, 'Relative Risk of Suicide Following Exposure to Recent Stressors, Victoria, Australia' (2019) 43(3) *Australian and New Zealand Journal of Public Health* 254

Clark, Sidney, 'Mental Treatment Act 1930: Temporary Patients' (1933) 2(3793) *The British Medical Journal* 543

Clausen, Christopher, 'John Stuart Mill's "Very Simple Principle"' (2009) Spring *The Wilson Quarterly* 40

Clough, Beverley, 'New Legal Landscapes: (Re)Constructing the Boundaries of Mental Capacity Law' (2018) 26(2) *Medical Law Review* 256

Coghlan, Simon, 'The Moral Depth of Human Dignity' (2018) 41(1) *Philosophical Investigations* 71

Collins, Hugh, 'Discrimination, Equality and Social Inclusion' (2003) 66(1) *The Modern Law Review* 16

Committee, Report of the Expert, *Review of the Mental Health Act 1983 November 1999*, Series Review of the Mental Health Act 1983 November 1999 (trans 1999)

Conly, Sarah, *Against Autonomy: Justifying Coercive Paternalism* (Cambridge University Press 2012)

Conway, Megan A, 'Embodying the Law: Negotiating Disability Identity and Civil Rights' in Austin Sarat (ed), *Law and the Imagining of Difference* (Emerald Publishing Limited 2018) 43

Cook, Judith and Jessica Jonikas, 'Self-Determination among Mental Health Consumers/ Survivors: Using Lessons from the Past to Guide the Future' (2002) 13(2) *Journal of Disability Policy Studies* 87

Cook-Daniels, Loree, 'Supported Decision-Making: Pathway to More Rights or More Wrongs?' (2015) (May/June) *Victimization of the Elderly and Disabled* 5

Corrigan, Patrick and others, 'The Stigma of Mental Illness: Explanatory Models and Methods for Change' (2005) 11 *Applied and Preventive Psychology* 179

Corrigan, Patrick and Ruth Ralph, 'Introduction: Recovery as Consumer Vision and Research Paradigm' in Patrick Corrigan and Ruth Ralph (eds), *Recovery in Mental Illness: Broadening Our Understanding of Wellness* (American Psychological Association 2005) 3

Corrigan, Patrick and others, 'The Effect of New Stories on the Stigma of Mental Illness' (2013) 201(3) *The Journal of Nervous and Mental Disease* 179

Corsi, Jessica Lynn, 'Art.5 Equality and Non-Discrimination' in Ilias Batekas (ed), *The UN Convention on the Rights of Persons with Disabilities: A Commentary* (Oxford University Press 2018)

Cotterrell, Roger, 'Subverting Orthodoxy, Making Law Central: A View of Socio-Legal Studies' (2002) 29(4) *Journal of Law and Society* 632

Council of Australian Governments, *National Disability Strategy 2010-2020* (2011)

Craigie, Jillian, 'Capacity, Value Neutrality and the Ability to Consider the Future' (2013) 9(1) *International Journal of Law in Context* 4

Craigie, Jillian, 'A Fine Balance: Reconsidering Patient Autonomy in Light of the UN Convention on the Rights of Persons with Disabilities' (2015) 29(6) *Bioethics* 398

Craigie, Jillian and others, 'Legal Capacity, Mental Capacity and Supported Decision-Making: Report from a Panel Event' (2019) 62 *International Journal of Law and Psychiatry* 160

Crossley, Nick, 'Not Being Mentally Ill: Social Movements, System Survivors and the Oppositional Habitus' (2004) 11(2) *Anthropology and Medicine* 161

Crossley, Nick, *Contesting Psychiatry: Social Movements in Mental Health* (Routledge 2006)

Curley, Aoife and others, 'Categorical Mental Capacity for Treatment Decisions among Psychiatry Inpatients in Ireland' (2019) 64 *International Journal of Law and Psychiatry* 53

Currie Shawn and others, 'Health Surveillance Data to Examine the Relationship of Depression Prevalence to Social Determinants of Health and Access to Mental Health Services' (2013) 32(1) *Canadian Journal of Community Mental Health* 43

Curtis, George B, 'The Checkered Career of Parens Patriae: The State as Parent or Tyrant?' (1976) 25(4) *DePaul Law Review* 895

D

Dain, Norman, 'Critics and Dissenters: Reflections on "Anti-Psychiatry" in the United States' (1989) 25 *Journal of the History of the Behavioural Sciences* 3

Darwall, Stephen, 'Respect and the Second-Person Standpoint' (2004) 78(2) *Proceedings and Addresses of the American Philosophical Association* 43

Davidson, Gavin and others, 'Supported Decision Making: A Review of the International Literature' (2015) 38 *International Journal of Law and Psychiatry* 61

Davidson, Gavin and others, 'An International Comparison of Legal Frameworks for Supported and Substitute Decision-Making in Mental Health Services' (2016) 44 *International Journal of Law and Psychiatry* 30

Daw, Rowena, 'The Case for a Fusion Law: Challenges and Issues' in Bernadette McSherry and Ian Freckelton (eds), *Coercive Care: Rights, Law and Policy* (Routledge 2013) 93

Dawson, John, 'Randomised Controlled Trials of Mental Health Legislation' (2002) 10 *Medical Law Review* 308

Dawson, John, 'Concepts of Liberty in Mental Health Law' (2009) 12(1) *Otago Law Review* 23

Dawson, John, 'A Realistic Approach to Assessing Mental Health Laws Compliance with the UNCRPD' (2015) 40 *International Journal of Law and Psychiatry* 70

Dawson, John and Annagret Kämpf, 'Incapacity Principles in Mental Health Laws in Europe' (2006) 12(3) *Psychology, Psychiatry and Law* 310

Deas, Murray, 'An Address Delivered at the Opening of the Section of Psychology. Lunacy Legislation and the Lunacy Act 1890' (1891) 2(1596) *The British Medical Journal* 242

Debes, Remy, 'Human Dignity before Kant' in Remy Debes (ed), *Dignity: A History* (Oxford University Press 2017)

Debes, Remy, 'Introduction' in Remy Debes (ed), *Dignity: A History* (Oxford University Press 2017) 1

Deegan, Patricia, 'Recovering Our Sense of Value after Being Labeled Mentally Ill' (1993) 31(4) *Journal of Psychosocial Nursing and Mental Health Services* 7

Degener, Theresia, 'Disability in a Human Rights Context' (2016) 5 *Laws* 35

Degener, Theresia, 'Establishing Equality and Non-discrimination: The United Nations Committee on the Rights of Persons with Disabilities' New Model of Inclusive Equality', Melbourne Social Equity Institute, University of Melbourne, 11 January 2018

Del Villar, Katrine, 'Should Supported Decision-Making Replace Substituted Decision-Making? The Convention on the Rights of Persons with Disabilities and Coercive Treatment under Queensland's Mental Health Act 2000' (2015) 4 *Laws* 173

Delmar, Charlotte, 'The Interplay between Autonomy and Dignity: Summarizing Patients Voices' (2013) 16 *Medical Health Care and Philosophy* 975

Dhanda, Amita, 'Universal Legal Capacity as a Universal Human Right' in Michael Dudley and others (eds), *Mental Health and Human Rights: Vision, Praxis and Courage* (Oxford University Press 2012) 177

Dhanda, Amita, 'From Duality to Indivisibility: Mental Health Care and Human Rights' (2016) 32(3) *South African Journal of Human Rights* 438

Dhir, Aron, 'Human Rights Treaty Drafting through the Lens of Mental Disability: The Proposed International Convention on Protection and Promotion of the Rights and Dignity of Persons with Disabilities' (2005) 41 *Stanford Journal of International Law* 181

Diesfeld, Kate, '"Insight" Unpacking the Concept in Mental Health Law' (2003) 10(1) *Psychiatry, Psychology and Law* 63

Djeffal, Christian, *State and Evolutive Treaty Interpretation* (Cambridge University Press 2015)

Donnelly, Mary, 'From Autonomy to Dignity: Treatment for Mental Disorders and the Focus for Patient Rights' (2008) 26(2) *Law in Context* 37

Donnelly, Mary, *Healthcare Decision-Making and the Law: Autonomy, Capacity and the Limits of Liberalism* (Cambridge Law, Medicine and Ethics 2010)

Donnelly, Mary, 'Best Interests in the Mental Capacity Act: Time to Say Goodbye?' (2016) 24(3) *Medical Law Review* 318

Doyle Guilloud, Suzanne, 'The Right to Liberty of Persons with Psychosocial Disabilities at the United Nations: A Tale of two Interpretations' (2019) 66 *International Journal of Law and Psychiatry* 101497

Dorofeikova, Mariia and others, 'Cognitive Deficit in Patients with Paranoid Schizophrenia: Its Clinical and Laboratory Correlates' (2018) 262 *Psychiatry Research* 542

Dorr, Oliver, 'Article 31' in Oliver Dorr and Kirsten Schmalenbach, *Vienna Convention on the Law of Treaties: A Commentary* (Springer 2012)

Dudley, Michael and Fran Gale, 'Through a Glass, Darkly: Nazi Era Illuminations of Psychiatry, Human Rights and Human Rights Violations' in Michael Dudley and others (eds), *Mental Health and Human Rights: Vision, Praxis and Courage* (Oxford University Press 2012) 211

Duffy, Richard and Brendan Kelly, 'Rights, Laws and Tensions: A Comparative Analysis of the Convention on the Rights of Persons with Disabilities and the Who Resource Book on Mental Health, Human Rights and Legislation' (2017) 54 *International Journal of Law and Psychiatry* 26

Dute, Joseph, 'Should Substituted Decision-Making Be Abolished?' (2015) 22 *European Journal of Health Law* 315

Duwell, Marcus, 'Human Dignity: Concepts, Discussions, Philosophical Perspectives' in Marcus Duwell and others (eds), *The Cambridge Handbook of Human Dignity* (Cambridge University Press 2014)

Dworkin, Ronald, *Justice for Hedgehogs* (Harvard University Press 2011)

Dworkin, Ronald, *Taking Rights Seriously* (Bloomsbury Publishing 2013)

E

Edlinger Monika and others, 'Risk of Violence of Inpatients with Severe Mental Illness—Do Patients with Schizophrenia Pose Harm to Others?' (2014) 213(3) *Psychiatry Research* 450

Edwards, Craig, 'Beyond Mental Competence' (2010) 27(3) *Journal of Applied Philosophy* 273

Ellis, Robert, 'The Asylum, the Poor Law and the Growth of County Asylums in Nineteenth Century Yorkshire' (2008) XLV(2) *Northern History* 279

Ephesus, Soranus of, 'Madness or Insanity (Greek Mania)' in Greg Eghigian (ed), *From Madness to Mental Health: Psychiatric Disorder and Its Treatment in Western Civilisation* (Rutgers University Press 2010) 39

European Agency for Fundamental Rights, 'Equality: Legal Capacity of Persons with Intellectual Disabilities and Persons with Mental Health Problems' (2013) <http://fra.europa.eu/en/publications-and-resources>(accessed 8 October 2019),

F

Failinger, Marie, 'The Paradox in Madness: Vulnerability Confronts the Law' (2012) 1 *Mental Health Law and Policy Journal* 127

Fallon-Kund, Marie and Jerome Bickenbach, 'Strengthening the Voice of Persons with Mental Health Problems and Legal Capacity Proceedings' (2016) 5 *Laws* 29

Fallon-Kund, Marie and Jerome Bickenbach, 'New Legal Capacity Laws and the United Nations Convention on the Rights of Persons with Disabilities: An Overview of Five Countries in Europe' (2017) 24 *European Journal of Health Law* 285

Fanning, John, 'Continuities of Risk in the Era of the Mental Capacity Act' (2016) 24(3) *Medical Law Review* 415

Farrell, Michelle, 'Just How Ill-Treated Were You? An Investigation of Cross-Fertilisation in the Interpretive Approaches to Torture in the European Court of Human Rights and International Criminal Law' (2015) 84(3) *Nordic Journal of International Law* 483

Fazel, Seena and others, 'Schizophrenia and Violence: Systematic Review and Meta-Analysis' (2009) 6(8) *PLoS Medicine* 2

Fennell, Philip, 'Institutionalising the Community: The Codification of Clinical Authority and the Limits of Rights-Based Approaches' in Bernadette McSherry and Penelope Weller (eds), *Rethinking Rights-Based Mental Health Laws* (Hart Publishing 2010) 13

Fennell, Philip and Urfan Khaliq, 'Conflicting or Complementary Obligations? The UN Disability Rights Convention, the European Convention on Human Rights and English Law' (2011) 2011(6) *European Human Rights Law Review* 662

Fina, Valentina Della, 'Article 3 [General Principles]' in V Della Fina and others (eds), *The United Nations Convention on the Rights of Persons with Disabilities* (Springer International Publishing 2017)

Fineman, Martha Albertson, 'The Vulnerable Subject and the Responsive State' (2010) 60 *Emory Law Journal* 251

Fineman, Martha Albertson, 'Equality, Autonomy and the Vulnerable Subject in Law and Politics' in Martha Fineman and Anna Greer (eds), *Vulnerability: Reflections on a New Ethical Foundation for Law and Politics* (Taylor and Francis 2013) 13

Flynn, Eilionoir and Anna Arstein-Kerslake, 'Legislating Personhood: Realising the Right to Support in Exercising Legal Capacity' (2014) 10(1) *International Journal of Law in Context* 81

Flynn, Eilionoir and Anna Arstein-Kerslake, 'State Intervention in the Lives of People with Disabilities: The Case for a Disability-Neutral Framework' (2017) 13(1) *International Journal of Law in Context* 39

Flynn Sandra and others, 'Serious Violence by People with Mental Illness: National Clinical Survey' (2014) 29(8) *Journal of Interpersonal Violence* 1438

Formosa, Paul and Catriona Mackenzie, 'Nussbaum, Kant, and the Capabilities Approach to Dignity' (2014) 17 *Ethical Theory and Moral Practice* 875

Foucault, Michel, *Madness and Civilisation: A History of Insanity in the Age of Reason* (Richard Howard trans, Pantheon Books 1965)

Freckelton, Ian, 'Extra-Legislative Factors in Involuntary Status Decision-Making' in Bernadette McSherry and Penelope Weller (eds), *Rethinking Rights-Based Mental Health Laws* (Hart Publishing 2010)

Fredman, Sandra, *Human Rights Transformed: Positive Rights and Positive Duties* (Oxford University Press 2008)

Fredman, Sandra, 'Emerging from the Shadows: Substantive Equality and Article 14 of the European Convention on Human Rights' (2016) 16 *Human Rights Law Review* 273

Freeman, Melvyn and others 'Reversing Hard Won Victories in the Name of Human Rights: A Critique of the General Comment on Article 12 of the UN Convention on the Rights of Persons with Disabilities' (2015) 2 *Lancet Psychiatry* 844

Freyenhagen, Fabian and Tom O'Shea, 'Hidden Substance: Mental Disorder as a Challenge to Normatively Neutral Accounts of Autonomy' (2013) 9(1) *International Journal of Law in Context* 53

G

Garton, Stephen, 'Seeking Refuge: Why Asylum Facilities Might Still Be Relevant for Mental Health Care Services Today' (2009) 11(1) *Health and History* 25

Gau, SS and AT Cheng, 'Mental Illness and Accidental Death: Case Control Psychological Autopsy Study' (2004) 175 *The British Journal of Psychiatry* 422

Giordano, Simona, 'A Heaven without Giants or Dwarfs: Equality, Gender and Disabilities' (2014) 23 *Cambridge Quarterly of Healthcare Ethics* 22

Glen, Kristen Booth, 'Changing Paradigms: Mental Capacity, Legal Capacity, Guardianship, and Beyond' (2012) 44 *Columbia Human Rights Law Review* 93

Goldschmidt, Jenny, 'New Perspectives on Equality: Towards Transformative Justice through the Disability Convention?' (2017) 35(1) *Nordic Journal of Human Rights* 1

Gooding, Piers, 'Supported Decision-Making: A Rights-Based Disability Concept and Its Implications for Mental Health Law' (2013) 20(3) *Psychiatry, Psychology and Law* 431

Gooding, Piers, 'Change and Continuity in Mental Health Law: The Long Road to the United Nations Convention on the Rights of Persons with Disabilities and Its Implications for Mental Health and the Law Today' (2014) 20(3) *Web Journal of Current Legal Issues* 367

Gooding, Piers, 'Navigating the 'Flashing Amber Lights' of the Right to Legal Capacity in the United Nations Convention on the Rights of Persons with Disabilities: Responding to Major Concerns' (2015) 15 *Human Rights Law Review* 45

Gooding, Piers, *A New Era for Mental Health Law and Policy: Supported Decision-Making and the UN Convention on the Rights of Persons with Disabilities* (Cambridge University Press 2017)

Gooding Piers and others, *Alternatives to Coercion in Mental Health Settings: A Literature Review* (Melbourne Social Equity Institute, University of Melbourne 2018)

Gooding, Piers and Eilinoir Flynn, 'Querying the Call to Introduce Mental Capacity Testing to Mental Health Law: Does the Doctrine of Necessity Provide an Alternative?' (2015) 4 *Laws* 245

Gomory, Toni and others, 'Madness or Mental Illness? Revisiting Historians of Psychiatry' (2013) 23 *Current Psychology* 119

Gosepath, Stefan, 'Equality' in Edward N Zalta (ed), *The Stanford Encyclopedia of Philosophy* (Spring, 2011 ed, 2011)

Gostin, Larry, 'Contemporary Social Historical Perspectives on Mental Health Reform' (1983) 10(1) *Journal of Law and Society* 47

Gostin, Lawrence, *Public Health Law: Power, Duty, Restraint* (University of California Press, 2nd ed, 2008)

Gostin, Lawrence and Lance Gamble, 'The Human Rights of Persons with Mental Disabilities: A Global Perspective on the Application of Human Rights Principles to Mental Health' (2004) *Maryland Law Review* 20

Government Inquiry into Mental Health and Addiction 'He Ara Oranga: Report of the Government Inquiry into Mental Health and Addiction (Crown 2018) https://mentalhealth.inquiry.govt.nz/inquiry-report/he-ara-oranga/

Gurbai, Sandor, 'Beyond the Pragmatic Definition? The Right to Non-discrimination of Persons with Disabilities in the Context of Coercive Interventions' (2020) *Health and Human Rights Journal* https://cdn1.sph.harvard.edu/wpcontent/uploads/sites/2469/2020/06/Gurbai.pdf

Graumann, Sigrid, 'Human Dignity and People with Disabilities' in Jens Braarvig Marcus Duwell, Roger Brownsword, and Dietmar Mieth (eds), *The Cambridge Handbook of Human Dignity* (Cambridge University Press 2014)

Gray, John and others, 'Australian and Canadian Mental Health Acts Compared' (2010) 44(12) *Australian and New Zealand Journal of Psychiatry* 1126

Greer, Steven, '"Balancing" and the European Court of Human Rights: A Contribution to the Habermas-Alexy Debate' (2004) 63(2) *Cambridge Law Journal* 412

Grisso, Thomas and Paul Appelbaum, 'The Macarthur Treatment Competence Study III' (1995) 19(2) *Law and Human Behaviour* 149

Griffin, James, *On Human Rights* (Oxford University Press 2008)

H

Haafkens, J and others, 'Mental Health Care and the Opposition Movement in the Netherlands' (1986) 22(2) *Social Science and Medicine* 185

Harding, Rosie and Ezgi Tascioglu, 'Supported Decision-Making from Theory to Practice: Implementing the Right to Enjoy Legal Capacity' (2018) 8 *Societies* 25

Hellman, Deborah, *When Is Discrimination Wrong?* (Harvard University Press 2008)

Herman, Judith, *Trauma and Recovery: The Aftermath of Violence—from Domestic Abuse to Political Terror* (Basic Books 1992)

Hicks, Donna and Archbishop Emeritus Desmond Tutu, *Dignity: The Essential Role It Plays in Resolving Conflict in Our Lives and Relationships* (Yale University Press 2011)

Hiroeh Urara and others, 'Death by Homicide, Suicide, and Other Unnatural Causes in People with Mental Illness: A Population-Based Study' (2001) 358 *The Lancet* 2110

Hoffman, Steven and others, 'Is the UN Convention of the Rights of Persons with Disabilities Impacting Mental Health Laws in High-Income Countries? A Case Study of Implementation in Canada' (2016) 16(28) *BMC International Health and Human Rights* https://bmcinthealthhumrights.biomedcentral.com/articles/10.1186/s12914-016-0103-1

Holmes, Elisa, 'Anti-Discrimination Rights without Equality' (2005) 68(2) *The Modern Law Review* 175

Howard, Rhonda and Jack Donnelly, 'Human Dignity, Human Rights and Political Systems' (1986) 80(3) *The American Political Science Review* 801

I

Independent Review of the MHA 1983, 'Modernising the Mental Health Act: Increasing Choice, Reducing Compulsion' (UK Government, Final Report, December 2018)

J

Jackson, Emily, 'From "Doctor Knows Best" to Dignity: Placing Adults Whole Lack Capacity at the Centre of Decisions About Their Medical Treatment' (2018) 81(2) *The Modern Law Review* 247

Jamieson, Liz and Pamela Taylor, 'Mental Disorder and Perceived Threat to the Public: People Who Do Not Return to Community Living' (2002) 181 *British Journal of Psychiatry* 399

Jarab Jan, 'Psychiatry and Human Rights: A Difficult Relationship, but with a Growing Potential' (2015) 29 *Neuro-psychiatrie* 106

Jeste, Dilip, 'Supported Decision Making in Serious Mental Illness' (2018) 81(1) *Psychiatry: Interpersonal and Biological Processes* 28

Jones, Kathleen, *Mental Health and Social Policy 1845-1959* (Routledge and Kegan Paul Ltd 1960)

Jones, Nev and Timothy Kelly, 'Inconvenient Complications: On the Heterogeneities of Madness and Their Relationship to Disability' in Helen Spandler (eds), *Madness, Distress and the Politics of Disablement* (Policy Press 2015) 43

K

Kanter, Arlene, *The Development of Disability Rights Under International Law: From Charity to Human Rights* (Routledge 2015)

Kämpf, Annagret, 'Involuntary Treatment Decisions: Using Negotiated Silence to Facilitate Change?' in Bernadette McSherry and Penelope Weller (eds), *Rethinking Rights-Based Mental Health Laws* (Oxford Hart 2010) 129

Katsakou, Christina and others 'Psychiatric Patient's Views on Why Their Involuntary Hospitalisation Was Right or Wrong: A Qualitative Study' (2012) 47 *Social Psychiatry and Psychiatric Epidemiology* 1169

Kayess, Rosemary & Phillip French, 'Out of Darkness into Light? Introducing the Convention on the Rights of Persons with Disabilities' (2008) 8(1) *Human Rights Law Review* 1

Keene, Alex Ruck, 'Is Mental Capacity in the Eye of the Beholder?' (2017) 11(2) *Advances in Mental Health and Intellectual Disabilities* 30

Keene, Alex Ruck, 'Deprivation of Liberty, Restraint, and the CRPD: The View From the German Federal Constitutional Court' Mental Capacity Law and Policy blog-post 4 December 2018 http://www.mentalcapacitylawandpolicy.org.uk/deprivation-of-liberty-restraint-and-the-crpd-the-view-from-the-german-federal-constitutional-court/ (last accessed 21 June 2019).

Keene, Alex Ruck and others, 'Taking Capacity Seriously? Ten Years of Mental Capacity Disputes before England's Court of Protection' (2019) 62 *International Journal of Law and Psychiatry* 56

Kelly, Brendan, 'Dignity, Human Rights and the Limits of Mental Health Legislation' (2014) 31 *Irish Journal of Psychological Medicine* 75

Kelly, Brendan, 'Mental Health, Mental Illness, and Human Rights in India and Elsewhere: What Are We Aiming For?' (2016) 58(2) *Indian Journal of Psychiatry* 168

Keown, Patrick and others, 'Changes in Use of the Mental Health Act 1983 in England 1984/85 to 2015/16' (2018) *The British Journal of Psychiatry* 595

Keys, Mary, 'Article 12 [Equal Recognition Before the Law]' in Valentina Della Fina and others (eds), *The United Nations Convention on the Rights of Persons with Disabilities: A Commentary* (Springer 2017)

Keywood, Kirsty, 'The Vulnerable Adult Experiment: Situating Vulnerability in Adult Safeguarding Law' (2017) 53 *International Journal of Law and Psychiatry* 88

Khaitan, Tarunabh, 'Dignity as an Expressive Norm: Neither Vacuous nor a Panacea' (2012) 32(1) *Oxford Journal of Legal Studies* 1

Khaitan, Tarunabh, *A Theory of Discrimination* (Oxford University Press 2015)

Kidd, Sean and others, 'Mental Health Reform at a Systems Level: Widening the Lens on Recovery Oriented Care' (2014) 59(5) *Canadian Journal of Psychiatry* 243

Kirby, Michael, 'Law Reform, Politics and Mental Health' (1983) 17(1) *Australian and New Zealand Journal of Psychiatry* 39

Kittay, Eva Feder, 'The Ethics of Care, Dependence, and Disability' (2011) 24(1) *Ratio Juris* 49

Kleinig, John, 'Paternalism and Human Dignity' (2017) 11 *Criminal Law and Philosophy* 19

Knight, Fauzia and others, 'Supported Decision-Making: The Expectations Held by People with Experience of Mental Illness' (2018) 28(6) *Qualitative Health Research* 1002

Kogstad, Ragnfrid Eline, 'Protecting Mental Health Clients' Dignity—the Importance of Legal Control' (2009) 32 *International Journal of Law and Psychiatry* 383

Kong, Camillia, 'The Convention for the Rights of Persons with Disabilities and Article 12: Prospective Feminist Lessons against the "Will and Preferences" Paradigm' (2015) 4 *Laws* 709

L

Large, Matthew and others, 'Mental Health Laws That Require Dangerousness for Involuntary Admission May Delay the Initial Treatment of Schizophrenia' (2008) 43(251–256) *Social Psychiatry And Psychiatric Epidemiology* 251

LaVaque-Manty, Mika, 'Universalizing Dignity in the Nineteenth Century' in Remy Debes (ed), *Dignity: A History* (Oxford University Press 2017) 301

Larue Caroline and others 'The Experience of Seclusion and Restraint in Psychiatric Settings: Perspectives of Patients' (2013) 34(5) *Issues in Mental Health Nursing* 317

Leibowitz, Tirza, 'Living in the Community, Access to Justice: Having the Right Makes all the Difference' in Maya Sabatello and Marrianne Schulze (eds), Human Rights and Disability Advocacy (University of Pennsylvania Press 2014)

Lewis, Oliver, 'The Expressive, Educational and Proactive Roles of Human Rights: An Analysis of the United Nations Convention on the Rights of Persons with Disabilities' in Bernadette McSherry and Penelope Weller (eds), *Rethinking Rights-Based Mental Health Laws* (Hart Publishing 2010) 97

Lewis, Oliver and Genevra Richardson, 'The Right to Live Independently and Be Included in the Community' (2020) 69 *International Journal of Law and Psychiatry* 101499

Light, Edwina and others, 'Community Treatment Orders in Australia: Rates and Patterns of Use' (2012) 20(6) *Australasian Psychiatry* 478

Linderfalk, Ulf, 'Is Treaty Interpretation an Art or a Science? International Law and Rational Decision-Making' (2015) 2(1) *The European Journal of International Law* 169

Lindsey, Jaime, 'Developing Vulnerability: A Situational Response to the Abuse of Women with Mental Disabilities' (2016) 24 *Feminist Legal Studies* 295

Linhorst, Donald and others, 'Opportunities and Barriers to Empowering People with Severe Mental Illness through Participation in Treatment Planning' (2002) 47(4) *Social Work* 425

Lord, Janet and others, 'Lessons from the Experience of UN Convention on the Rights of Persons with Disabilities: Addressing the Democratic Deficit in Global Health Governance' (2010) Fall *Journal of Law, Medicine and Ethics* 564

Lord, Janet, 'Shared Understanding or Consensus-Masked Disagreement? The Anti-Torture Framework in the Convention on the Rights of Persons with Disabilities' (2010) 33 *Loyola of Los Angeles International Comparative Law Review* 27

Lord, Janet and Rebecca Brown, 'The Role of Reasonable Accommodation in Securing Substantive Equality for Persons with Disabilities: The UN Convention on the Rights of Persons with Disabilities' in Marcia H Rioux (ed), *Critical Perspectives on Human Rights and Disability Law* (Martinus Nijhoff 2011) 273

Lord, Janet and Michael Ashely Stein, 'Contingent Participation and Coercive Care: Feminist and Communitarian Theories of Disability and Legal Capacity' in Bernadette McSherry and Ian Freckelton (eds), *Coercive Care: Rights, Law and Policy* (Routledge 2013) 31

Love, Laufey and others, 'Achieving Disability Equality: Empowering Disabled People to Take the Lead' (2018) 6(1) *Social Inclusion* 1

Luciano, Mario and others, 'Use of Coercive Measures in Mental Health Practice and Its Impact on Outcome: A Critical Review' (2014) 14(2) *Expert Review of Neurotherapeutics* 131

Lushington, Sydney George, *Archibald's Lunacy: Comprising the Lunacy Acts 1890 and 1891, the Lancashire County (Lunatic Asylums and Other Powers) Act 1891, and All the Statutory Rules, Orders, and Forms of Force Thereunder: Also the Statutes Related to Criminal Lunatics, the Lunacy (Vacating of Seats) Act 1886, and the Idiots Act 1886* (Gale, 4th ed, 1895)

M

Macklin, Ruth, 'Dignity is a Useless Concept' (2003) 327(20–27) *British Medical Journal* 1419

Maclean, Alasdair, *Autonomy, Informed Consent and Medical Law: A Relational Challenge* (Cambridge University Press 2009)

Mackenzie Catriona and Wendy Rogers, 'Autonomy, Vulnerability and Capacity: A Philosophical Appraisal of the Mental Capacity Act' (2013) 9(1) *International Journal of Law in Context* 37

MacKenzie LE and others, 'Hot and Cold Executive Functions in Youth with Psychotic Symptoms' (2017) 47 *Psychological Medicine* 2844

MacQuarrie, Anna and Connie Laurin-Bowrie, 'Our Lives, Our Voices: People with Intellectual Disabilities and Their Families' in Maya Sabatello and Marriane Schulze (eds), *Human Rights and Disability Advocacy* (University of Pennsylvania Press 2013) 25

Maguire, Fiona Brookman and Mike, 'Reducing Homicide: A Review of the Possibilities' (2004) 42 *Crime, Law & Social Change* 325

Mahomed, Faraaz and others 'Involuntary Mental Health Treatment in the Era of the United Nations Convention on the Rights of Persons with Disabilities' (2018) *PLoS Medicine* 1

Manderelli, Gabrielle and others, 'Mental Capacity in Patients Involuntarily or Voluntarily Receiving Psychiatric Treatment for Acute Mental Disorder' (2014) 59(4) *Journal of Forensic Sciences* 1002

Marmot, Michael, 'Social Justice, Epidemiology and Health Inequalities' (2017) 32 *European Journal of Epidemiology* 537

Martin, Wayne and others, *Achieving CRPD Compliance: Is the Mental Capacity Act of England and Wales Compatible with the UN Convention on the Rights of Persons with Disabilities? If Not, What Next?* (University of Essex, Essex Autonomy Project 2014)

Martinez-Pujalte, Antonio 'Legal Capacity and Supported Decision-Making: Lessons from Some Recent Legal Reforms' (2019) 8(4) *Laws* 8010004

Maylea, Chris and Asher Hirsch, 'The Right to Refuse: *The Victorian Mental Health Act 2014* and the Convention on the Rights of Persons with Disabilities' (2017) 42(2) *Alternative Law Journal* 149

Maylea, Christopher, 'A Rejection of Involuntary Treatment in Mental Health Social Work' (2017) 11(4) *Ethics and Social Welfare* 336

McCann, Michael, 'The Unbearable Lightness of Rights: on Sociolegal Inquiry in the Global Era' (2014) 48(2) *Law and Society Review* 245

McCrudden, Christopher, 'Human Dignity and Judicial Interpretation of Human Rights' (2008) 19(4) *The European Journal of International Law* 655

McGrogan, David, 'On the Interpretation of Human Rights Treaties and Subsequent Practice' (2014) 32(4) *Netherlands Quarterly of Human Rights* 47

McGuire, Alan B and others, 'Altered Self-Experience and Goal Setting in Severe Mental Illness' (2015) 18 *American Journal of Psychiatric Rehabilitation* 333

McSherry, Bernadette, 'Protecting the Integrity of the Person: Developing Limitations on Involuntary Treatment' (2008) 26(2) *Journal of Law in Context* 111

McSherry, Bernadette and Penelope Weller (eds), *Rethinking Rights-Based Mental Health Laws* (Hart 2010)

McSherry, Bernadette, 'Legal Capacity under the Convention on the Rights of Persons with Disabilities' (2012) 20 *Journal of Law and Medicine* 22

McSherry, Bernadette, *Managing Fear: The Law and Ethics of Preventive Detention and Risk Assessment*, International Perspectives on Forensic Mental Health (Routledge 2014)

McSherry, Bernadette and Kay Wilson, 'Detention and Treatment Down Under: Human Rights and Mental Health Laws in Australia and New Zealand' (2011) 19(4) *Medical Law Review* 548

McSherry, Bernadette and Kay Wilson, 'The Concept of Capacity in Australian Mental Health Law Reform: Going in the Wrong Direction?' (2015) 40 *International Journal of Law and Psychiatry* 60

McTeague Lisa and others, 'Transdiagnostic Impairment of Cognitive Control in Mental Illness' (2016) 83 *Journal of Psychiatric Research* 37

Megret, Frederic, 'The Disabilities Convention: Human Rights of Persons with Disabilities or Disability Rights?' (2008) 30(2) *Human Rights Quarterly* 494

Megret, Frederic, 'The Disabilities Convention: Towards a Holistic Concept of Rights' (2008) 12(2) *The International Journal of Human Rights* 261

Megret, Frederic, 'Nature of Obligations' in Daniel Moeckli and others (eds), *International Human Rights Law* (Oxford University Press 2014) 97

Megret, Frederic and Dianah Msipa, 'Global Reasonable Accommodation: How the Convention on the Rights of Persons with Disabilities Changes the Way We Think About Equality' (2014) 30 *South African Journal of Human Rights* 253

Meyers, Stephen, 'NGO-Ization and Human Rights Law: The CRPD's Civil Society Mandate' (2016) 5 *Laws* 147

Mezzina, R, 'Forty Years of the Law 180: The Aspirations of a Great Reform, Its Successes and Continuing Need' (2018) 27(4) *Epidemiology and Psychiatric Sciences* 336

Mill, John Stewart, in David Bronwich and George Kateb (eds), *On Liberty* (Yale University Press 2003)

Miller, Peter, 'Critques of Psychiatry' in Peter Miller and Nikolas Rose (eds), *The Power of Psychiatry* (Polity Press 1986) 11

Minkowitz, Tina, 'The United Nations Convention on the Rights of Persons with Disabilities and the Right to Freedom from Nonconsensual Psychiatric Interventions' (2007) 34 *Syracuse Journal of International Law and Commerce* 405

Minkowitz, Tina, 'Abolishing Mental Health Laws to Comply with the Convention on the Rights of Persons with Disabilities' in Bernadette McSherry and Penelope Weller (eds), *Rethinking Rights-Based Mental Health Laws* (Hart Publishing 2010) 149

Minkowitz, Tina 'Submission for Joint CEDAW-CRC General/Recommendation/General Comment on Harmful Practices, Recognizing Forced and Coerced Psychiatric Interventions Against Women, Men and Children as Harmful Cultural Practice' (World Network of Users and Survivors of Psychiatry, 31 August 2011)

Minkowitz, Tina, 'CRPD and Transformative Equality' (2017) 13(1) *International Journal of Law in Context* 77

Mlandenov, Teodor, 'The UN Convention on the Rights of Persons with Disabilities and Its Interpretation' (2013) 7(1) *ALTER European Journal of Disability Research* 29

Mohr, Wanda and Michael Nunno, 'Black Boxing Restraints: The Need for Full Disclosure and Consent' (2011) 20 *Journal of Child and Family Studies* 38

Molas, Andrew, 'Defending the CRPD: Dignity, Flourishing and the Universal Right to Mental Health' (2016) 20(8) *The International Journal of Human Rights* 1264

Moon, Dan, 'The Dangerousness of the Status Quo: A Case for Modernizing Civil Commitment Law' (2014) 20 *Widener Law Review* 209

Moreau, Sophia Reibetanz, 'Equality Rights and the Relevance of Comparator Groups' (2006) 5(1) *Journal of Law and Equality* 81

Morris, Jenny, *Pride Against Prejudice: Transforming Attitudes to Disability* (The Women's Press 1991)

Morse, Stephen, 'A Preference for Liberty: The Case Against Involuntary Commitment of the Mentally Disordered' (1982) 70 *California Law Review* 54

Mosher, Loren, 'Sorteria and Other Alternatives to Acute Psychiatric Hospitalization' (1999) 187 *The Journal of Nervous and Mental Disease* 142

Mullen, Paul, 'Schizophrenia and Violence: From Correlations to Preventive Strategies' (2006) 12 *Advances in Psychiatric Treatment* 239

Mullen, Paul, 'Facing up to Unpalatable Evidence for the Sake of Our Patients' (2009) 6(8) *PLoS Medicine* 1

Mulvany, Julie, 'Disability, Impairment or Illness? The Relevance of the Social Model of Disability to the Study of Mental Disorder' (2000) 22(5) *Sociology of Health and Illness* 582

Munro, Nell, 'Define Acceptable: How Can We Ensure That Treatment for Mental Disorder in Detention Is Consistent with the UN Convention on the Rights of Persons with Disabilities?' (2012) 16(6) *The International Journal of Human Rights* 903

Murali, Vijaya and Femi Oyebode, 'Poverty, Social Inequality and Mental Health' (2004) 10 *Advances in Psychiatric Treatment* 216

Murray, Brian Joseph, 'Mental Capacity: Different Models and Their Controversies' (2017) 23 *British Journal of Psychiatry* 366

N

Nabbali, Essya M, 'A "Mad" Critique of the Social Model of Disability' (2009) 9(4) *The International Journal of Diversity in Organisations, Communities and Nations* 1

National Mental Health Commission, 'A Contributing Life: The 2013 National Report Card on Mental Health and Suicide Prevention' (2013) <http://www.mentalhealthcommission.gov.au/our-report-card/reporting-back-and-looking-forward.aspx>

Nedelsky, Jennifer, *Laws Relations: A Relational Theory of Self, Autonomy, and Law* (Oxford University Press 2011)

Nilsson, Anna and Lucy Series, 'Art. 12 CRPD Equal Recognition before the Law' in Lias Bantekas and others (eds), *The UN Convention on the Rights of Persons with Disabilities: A Commentary* (Oxford University Press 2018)

NHS Digital Mental Health Statistics Annual Figures 2017–2018 (9 October 2018)

Nordenfelt, Lennart, 'The Varieties of Dignity' (2004) 12(2) *Health Care Analysis* 69

Nowak, Manfred, 'Protecting Persons with Disabilities from Torture', Office of the UN High Commissioner for Human Rights', 63rd Sess, UN Doc A/63/150 (July 2008)

Nowak, Manfred, *Report of the Special Rapporteur on Torture and other Cruel, Inhuman or Degrading Treatment or Punishment*, 7th Sess, UN Doc A/HRC/7/3 (15 January 2008)

Nussbaum, Martha, 'The Capabilities of People with Cognitive Disabilities' (2009) 40(3–4) *Metaphilosophy* 331

O

Oaks, David, 'Whose Voices Should Be Heard? The Role of Mental Health Consumers, Psychiatric Survivors, and Families' in Michael Dudley and others (eds), *Mental Health and Human Rights: Vision, Praxis and Courage* (Oxford University Press 2012) 566

O'Donoghue, Brian and others, 'Perceived Coercion in Voluntary Hospital Admission' (2014) 21(1) *Psychiatry Research* 120

O'Hagan, Mary and others, 'Recovery in New Zealand: An Evolving Concept?' (2012) 24(1) *International Review of Psychiatry* 56

OECD, *Making Mental Health Count: The Social and Economic Costs of Neglecting Mental Health Care* (OECD Health Policy Studies, OECD Publishing 2014)

Office of Disability Issues, UK Initial Report on the UN Convention on the Rights of Persons with Disabilities (2011)

Oliver, Mike, 'The Social Model of Disability: Thirty Years On' (2013) 28(7) *Disability and Society* 1024

Owen, Gareth and others, 'Retrospective Views of Psychiatric In-patients Regaining Mental Capacity' (2009) 195 *The British Journal of Psychiatry* 403

P

Palmer, Barton, 'Executive Dysfunction as a Barrier to Authenticity in Decision Making' (2018) 25(1) *Philosophy, Psychiatry & Psychology* 21

Palmisano, Giuseppe, 'Article 19 [Living Independently and Being Included in the Community]' (2017) in V. Della Fina (ed), *The United Nations Convention on the Rights of Persons with Disabilities* 353

Parker, Malcolm, 'Getting the Balance Right: Conceptual Considerations Concerning Legal Capacity and Supported Decision-Making' (2016) 13 *Bioethical Inquiry* 381

Pelka, Fred, *What We Have Done: An Oral History of the Disability Rights Movement* (University of Massachusetts Press 2012)

Perlin, Michael, *International Human Rights and Mental Disability Law: When the Silenced Are Heard* (Oxford University Press 2012)

Perlin, Michael, '"There are No Trials Inside the Gates of Eden" Mental Health Courts, the Convention on the Rights of Persons with Disabilities, Dignity and the Promise of Therapeutic Jurisprudence' in Bernadette McSherry and Ian Freckelton (eds), *Coercive Care: Rights, Law and Policy* (Routledge 2013) 193

Perlin, Michael, '"Striking for the Guardians and Protectors of the Mind": The Convention on the Rights of Persons with Mental Disabilities and the Future of Guardianship Law' (2013) 117(4) *Pennsylvania State Law Review* 1159

Perlin, Michael, '"God Said to Abraham/Kill Me a Son": Why the Insanity Defense and the Incompetency Status are Compatible with and Required by the Convention on the Rights of Persons with Disabilities and Basic Principles of Therapeutic Jurisprudence' (2017) 54 *American Criminal Law Review* 477

Perlin, Michael, '"Temptation's Page Flies Out the Door": Navigating Complex Systems of Disability and the Law from a Therapeutic Jurisprudence Perspective' (2019) 25 *Buffalo Human Rights Law Review* 1

Perry, Donna and others, 'The Right to Life in Peace: An Essential Condition for Realizing the Right to Health' (2015) 17(1) *Health And Human Rights* 148

Perske, Robert, 'The Dignity of Risk and the Mentally Retarded' (1972) 10(1) *Mental Retardation* 1

Pescosolido, Bernice, 'The Public Stigma of Mental Illness: What Do We Think; What Do We Know; What Can We Prove?' (2013) 54(1) *Journal of Health and Social Behaviour* 1

Pickersgill, Martyn, 'How Personality Became Treatable: The Mutual Constitution of Clinical Knowledge and Mental Health Law' (2012) 43(1) *Social Studies of Science* 30

Plumb, Anne, 'UN Convention on the Rights of Persons with Disabilities: Out of the Frying Pan into the Fire?' in Helen Spandler and others (eds), *Madness, Distress and the Politics of Disablement* (Policy Press 2015)

Porter, Roy, *Madness: A Brief History* (Oxford University Press 2002)

Porter, Theodore, 'Funny Numbers' (2012) 4 *Culture Unbound* 585

Pruss, Alexander, 'A Deflationary Theory of Diachronic Identity' (2012) 90(1) *Australasian Journal of Philosophy* 19

Q

Quinn, Gerard and Oddney Mjoll Arnadottir, 'Introduction', in Oddny Mjoll Arnardottir and Gerard Quinn (eds), *The UN Convention on the Rights of Persons with Disabilities: European and Scandinavian Perspectives* (Martinus Njoff Publishers 2009)

Quinn, Gerard and Abigail Rekas-Rosalbo, 'Civil Death: Rethinking the Foundations of Legal Personhood for Persons with Disability' (2016) 56 *Irish Jurist* 286

R

Rasmussen, Tina and Charlotte Delmar, 'Dignity as an Empirical Lifeworld Construction—in the Field of Surgery in Denmark' (2014) 9 *International journal of Qualitative Studies on Health and Well-being* 1

Rees, Neil, 'The Fusion Proposal: A Next Step?' in Bernadette McSherry and Penelope Weller (eds), *Rethinking Rights-Based Mental Health Laws* (Hart 2010) 71

Report of the Expert Committee, *Review of the Mental Health Act 1983* (November 1999)

Ribet, Beth, 'Emergent Disability and the Limits of Equality: A Critical Reading of the UN Convention on the Rights of Persons with Disabilities' (2011) 14 *Yale Human Rights & Development Law Journal* 155

Richards, Kate, *Madness: A Memoir* (Penguin Group 2013)

Richardson, Genevra, 'Reforming Mental Health Law: Principle or Pragmatism' (2001) 54 *Current Legal Problems* 415

Richardson, Genevra, 'Autonomy, Guardianship and Mental Disorder: One Problem, Two Solutions' (2002) 65(5) *The Modern Law Review* 702

Richardson, Genevra, 'Balancing Autonomy and Risk: A Failure of Nerve in England and Wales?' (2007) 30 *International Journal of Law and Psychiatry* 71

Richardson, Genevra, 'Involuntary Treatment, Human Dignity and Human Rights' in Marcia H Rioux and others (eds), *Critical Perspectives on Human Rights and Disability Law* (Martinus Nijhoff Publishers 2011) 137

Richardson, Genevra, 'Mental Disabilities and the Law: From Substitute to Supported Decision-Making' (2012) 65 *Current Legal Problems* 333

Richardson, Genevra, 'Mental Capacity in the Shadow of Suicide: What Can the Law Do?' (2013) 9(1) *International Journal of Law in Context* 87

Riddle, Christopher, 'Defining Disability: Metaphysical Not Political' (2013) 16 *Medicine, Health Care and Philosophy* 377

Rietiker, Daniel, 'The Principle of "Effectiveness" in the Recent Jurisprudence of the European Court of Human Rights: Its Different Dimensions and It's Consistency with Public International Law—No Need for the Concept of Treaty Sui Generis' (2010) 79 *Nordic Journal of International Law* 245

Rioux, Marcia and Christopher Riddle, 'Values in Disability Policy and Law: Equality' in Marcia H. Rioux and others (eds), *Critical Perspectives on Human Rights and Disability Law* (Martinus Nijhoff Publishers 2011) 37

Roberts, Ron and Theodor Itten, 'Laing and Szaz: Anti-Psychiatry, Capitalism and Therapy' (2006) 93(5) *Psychoanalytic Review* 781

Robinson, Darlene, 'Dignity in Older Adults with Schizophrenia Residing in Assisted Living Facilities' (2018) 56(2) *Journal of Psychosocial Nursing* 20

Rodriguez, Philippe-Andre, 'Human Dignity as an Essentially Contested Concept' (2015) 28(4) *Cambridge Review of International Affairs* 743

Rollin, Henry, 'Social and Legal Repercussions of the Mental Health Act, 1959' (1963) 1(5333) *The British Medical Journal* 786

Rose, Diana and others 'Service User and Carer Stakeholder Perspectives on the Public Health Aspects of Diagnosis and Classification of Mental Illness' in Shekhar Saxena and others (eds), *Public Health Aspects of Diagnosis and Classification of Mental and Behavioural Disorders* (American Psychiatric Association and World Health Organisation 2012) 1

Rose, Diana and others 'Service User Perspectives on Coercion and Restraint in Mental Health' (2017) 14(3) *British Journal of Psychiatry International* 59

Rose, Nikolas, 'Law, Rights and Psychiatry' in Peter Miller and Nikolas Rose (eds), *The Power of Psychiatry* (Polity Press 1986) 177

Rose, Nikolas, *Psychiatry: The Discipline of Mental Health,* Series Psychiatry: The Discipline of Mental Health (trans, Polity Press 1986)

Rose, Nikolas, 'Governing Risky Individuals: The Role of Psychiatry in New Regimes of Control' (1998) 5(2) *Psychiatry, Psychology and Law* 177

Rosen, Alan and others 'The Human Rights of People with Severe and Persistent Mental Illness: Can Conflicts between Dominant and Non-Dominant Paradigms be Reconciled?' in Michael Dudley and others (eds), *Mental Health and Human Rights: Vision, Praxis and Courage* (Oxford University Press 2012) 297

Rosen, Michael, *Dignity: Its History and Meaning* (Harvard University Press 2012)

Rosenman, Stephen, 'Mental Health Law: An Idea Whose Time Has Passed' (1994) 28 *Australian and New Zealand Journal of Psychiatry* 560

Rubio, Jose Luis, 'Jumping to Conclusions in Psychosis: A Faulty Appraisal' (2011) 133 *Schizophrenic Research* 199

Russo, Jasna and Diana Rose, '"But what if Nobody's Going to Sit Down and have a Real Conversation with You?" Service User/Survivor Perspectives on Human Rights' (2013) 12(4) *Journal of Public Mental Health* 184

Russo, Jasna and Debra Shulkes, 'What We Talk About When We Talk About Disability: Making Sense of Debates in the European User/Survivor Movement' in Helen Spandler and others (eds), *Madness, Distress and the Politics of Disablement* (Policy Press 2015) 27

Rutherglen, George, 'Disparate Impact, Discrimination and the Essentially Contested Concept of Equality' (2006) 74(4) *Fordham Law Review* 2313

Ryan, Christopher James, 'One Flu over the Cuckoo's Nest: Comparing Legislated Coercive Treatment for Mental Illness with That for Other Illness' (2010) 8 *Bioethical Inquiry* 87

S

Saks, Elyn, 'Psychosis and Identity' (2017) 68(4) *Alabama Law Review* 923

Schiff, David, 'Socio-Legal Theory: Social Structure and Law' (1976) 39(3) *The Modern Law Review* 287

Schlutter, Birgit 'Aspects of Human Rights Interpretation by the UN Treaty Bodies' in Helen Keller and Gier Ulfstein (eds), *UN Human Rights Treaty Bodies: Law and Legitimacy* (Cambridge University Press 2012)

Schopp, Robert, *Competence, Condemnation and Commitment: An Integrated Theory of Mental Health Law* (American Psychological Association 2001)

Schroeder, Doris, 'Dignity: Two Riddles and Four Concepts' (2008) 17 *Cambridge Quarterly of Healthcare Ethics* 230

Schulze, Marianne, *Understanding the UN Convention on the Rights of Persons with Disabilities* (Handicap International 2009)

Scull, Andrew, 'Deinstitutionalization and the Rights of the Deviant' (1981) 37(3) *Journal of Social Issues* 6

Scull, Andrew, *Madness: A Very Short Introduction* (Oxford University Press 2011)

Seatzu, Francesco, 'The Convention on the Rights of Persons with Disabilities and International Human Rights Law' (2018) 7 *International Human Rights Law Review* 82

Seeyle, Katharine and Jess Bigood 'Guilty Verdict for Young Woman Who Urged Friend to Kill Himself' The New York Times, 16 June 2017: http//nyti.ms/2sx11XR

Sen, Amartya, *Inequality Reexamined* (Oxford University Press 1995)

Sensen, Oliver, 'Dignity: Kant's Revolutionary Conception' in Remy Debes (ed), *Dignity: A History* (Oxford University Press 2017) 237

Series, Lucy, 'The Place of Wishes and Feelings in Best Interests Decisions: Wye Valley NHS Trust v Mr B' (2016) 79(6) *The Modern Law Review* 1101

Series, Lucy, 'Relationships, Autonomy and Legal Capacity: Mental Capacity and Support Paradigms' (2015) 40 *International Journal of Law and Psychiatry* 80

Shakespeare, Tom and Nicholas Watson, 'Defending the Social Model' (1997) 12(2) *Disability and Society* 293

Shakespeare, Tom, *Disability Rights and Wrongs* (Routledge 2006)

Shakespeare, Tom, *Disability Rights and Wrongs Revisited* (Routledge 2013)

Shakespeare, Tom and others, 'Rehabilitation as a Disability Equality Issue: A Conceptual Shift for Disability Studies?' (2018) 6(1) *Social Inclusion* 61

Shea, Peter, *Defining Madness*, The Institute of Criminology Monograph Series (Hawkins Press 1999)

Shogren, Karrie and others, 'Supported Decision Making: A Synthesis of the Literature across Intellectual Disability, Mental Health, and Aging' (2017) 52(2) *Education and Training in Autism and Developmental Disabilities* 144

Scholten, Matthe and Jakov Gather, 'Adverse Consequences of Article 13 of the UN Convention on the Rights of Persons with Disabilities for Persons with Mental Disabilities and an Alternative Way Forward' (2017) *Journal of Medical Ethics* 1

Shultziner, Doron, 'Human Dignity—Functions and Meanings' (2003) 3(3) *Global Jurist Topics* 1

Silove, Derrick and others, 'Descent into the Dark Ages: Torture and Its Perceived Legitimacy in Contemporary Times' in Michael Dudley and others (eds), *Mental Health and Human Rights: Vision, Praxis, and Courage* (Oxford University Press 2012) 225

Skorpen, Frode and others, 'Views Concerning Patient Dignity among Relatives to Patients Experiencing Psychosis' (2016) 30 *Scandinavian Journal of Caring Sciences* 117

Skowron, Paul, 'Humility When Responding to the Abuse of Adults with Mental Disabilities' (2017) 53 *International Journal of Law and Psychiatry* 102

Skowron, Paul, 'Giving Substance to "the Best Interpretation of Will and Preferences"' (2019) 62 *International Journal of Law and Psychiatry* 125

Slade, Mike and others, 'Recovery Grows Up' (2012) 21(2) *Journal of Mental Health* 99

Slovenko, Ralph, 'The Transinstitutionalisation of the Mentally Ill' (2003) 29 *Ohio Northern University Law Review* 641

Smith, Damian and others, 'Satisfaction with Services Following Voluntary and Involuntary Admission' (2014) 23(1) *Journal of Mental Health* 38

Spandler, Helen and Jill Anderson, 'Unreasonable Adjustments? Applying Disability Policy to Madness and Distress' in Helen Spandler and others (eds), *Madness, Distress and the Politics of Disablement* (Policy Press 2015) 13

Spigelman, James, 'The Forgotten Freedom: Freedom from Fear?' (2010) 59 *International Comparative Quarterly* 543

Stavert, Jill and Rebecca McGregor, 'Domestic Legislation and International Human Rights Standards: The Case of Mental Health and Incapacity' (2018) 22(1) *The International Journal of Human Rights* 70

Stavert, Jill, 'Paradigm Shift of Paradigm Paralysis? National Mental Health and Capacity Law and Implementing the CRPD in Scotland' (2018) 7 *Laws* 26

Steinert, Tilman, 'The UN Committee's Interpretation of "Will and Preferences" Can Violate Human Rights' (2019) 18(1) *World Psychiatry* 45

Stickley, Theo, 'Should Service User Involvement Be Consigned to History? A Critical Realist Perspective' (2006) *Journal of Psychiatric and Mental Health Nursing* 570

Stone, Meredith and others, 'Estranged Relations: Coercion and Care in Narratives of Supported Decision-Making in Mental Healthcare' (2020) 46 Med Humanit 62, 69

Subcommittee on Prevention of Torture and Other Cruel, Inhuman or Degrading Treatment or Punishment, *Approach of the Subcommittee on Prevention of Torture and Other Cruel, Inhuman or Degrading Treatment or Punishment Regarding the Rights of Persons Institutionalized and Treated Medically without Informed Consent* CAT/OP/27/2 26 January 2016

Sugerman, David, 'Promoting Dialogue Between History and Socio-Legal Studies: The Contribution of Christopher W. Brooks and the "Legal Turn" in Early Modern English History' (2017) 44(S1) *Journal of Law and Society*, S37

Sullivan, Danny and Paul Mullen, ' Mental Health and Human Rights in Secure Settings' in Shekar Saxena (ed), *Public Health Aspects of Diagnosis and Classification of Mental and Behavioural Disorders* (American Psychiatric Association and World Health Organisation 2012) 283

Sulmasy, Daniel, 'Dignity, Disability, Difference and Rights' in DC Ralston and J Ho (eds), *Philosophical Reflections on Disability* (Springer 2010) 183

Sunstein, Cass, *Why Nudge?: The Politics of Libertarian Paternalism* (Yale University Press 2014)

Swinson, Nicola and Jenny Shaw, 'Homicides and Mental Disorders: The National Confidential Inquiry' (2007) 6(11) *Psychiatry* 452

Szasz, Thomas S, 'Ideology and Insanity' (1973) 25(4) *International Social Science Journal* 504

Szmukler, George and Frank Holloway, 'Reform of the Mental Health Act: Health or Safety?' (2000) 177 *British Journal of Psychiatry* 196

Szmukler, George and others, '"Rabone" and Four Unresolved Problems in Mental Health Law' (2013) 37 *The Psychiatrist* 297

Szmukler, George and others, 'Mental Health Law and the UN Convention on the Rights of Persons with Disabilities' (2014) 37 *International Journal of Law and Psychiatry* 245

Szmukler, George and Michael Bach, 'Mental Health Disabilities and Human Rights Protections' (2015) 2 *Global Mental Health* 1

Szmukler, George, '"Compulsion" and "Coercion" in Mental Health Care' (2015) *World Psychiatry* 259

Szmukler, George and Brendan Kelly, 'We Should Replace Conventional Mental Health Law with Capacity-Based Law' (2016) 209 *The British Journal of Psychiatry* 449

Szmukler, George, 'The UN Convention on the Rights of Persons with Disabilities: "Rights, Will and Preferences" in Relation to Mental Health Disabilities' (2017) 54 *International Journal of Law and Psychiatry* 90

Szmukler, George, '"Capacity", "Best Interests", "Will and Preferences" and the UN Convention on the Rights of Persons with Disabilities' (2019) 18(1) *World Psychiatry* 34

T

Theobald, Henry Studdy, *The Law Relating to Lunacy* (Stevens and Sons 1924)

Traustadottir, Rannveig, 'Disability Studies, the Social Model and Legal Developments' in Oddny Mjoll Arnadottir and Gerard Quinn (eds), *The UN Convention on the Rights of Persons with Disabilities: European and Scandinavian Perspectives* (Martinus Nijhoff Publishers 2009)

U

Umama-Agada, Emmanuel and others, 'Variations in Involuntary Admission Rates at Three Psychiatry Centres in Dublin Involuntary Admission Study (DIAS). Can the Differences Be Explained?' (2018) 57 *International Journal of Law and Psychiatry* 17

United Kingdom, *Royal Commission on the Law Relating to Mental Illness and Mental Deficiency 1954-1957 Report* (1957)

UNCHR, 'Report of the Special Rapporteur on Torture and other Cruel, Inhuman or Degrading Treatment or Punishment, Juan E. Mendez' (1 February 2013) UN Doc A/HRC/22/53

Unsworth, Clive, *The Politics of Mental Health Legislation* (Claredon Press, Oxford 1987)

V

Valentina Della Fina, 'Article 3 General Principles' in Della Fina and others (eds), *The United Nations Convention on the Rights of Persons with Disabilities* (Springer International Publishing 2017) 120

Victorian Law Reform Commission, 'Guardianship: Final Report 24' (2012)

Vine, Ruth and Fiona Judd, 'Contextual Issues in the Implementation of Mental Health Legislation' (2019) 62 *International Journal of Law and Psychiatry* 16

Voren, Robert van, 'The Abuse of Psychiatry for Political Purposes' in Derrick Silove Michael Dudley, and Fran Gale (eds), *Mental Health and Human Rights: Vision, Praxis, and Courage* (Oxford University Press 2012) 237

Vorhaus, John, 'Dignity, Capability, and Profound Disability' (2015) 46(3) *Metaphilosophy* 462

W

Wakeham, Scott and Cheryl Sadoski, 'Beyond Equality: Providing Equitable Care for Persons with Disabilities' (2017) 150(4) *CPJ/RPC* 251

Waldron, Jeremy, 'Dignity, Rights, and Responsibilities' (2011) 43(1) *Arizona State Law Journal* 1107

Waldron, Jeremy, 'Dignity and Rank' in Jeremy Waldron and Meir Dan-Cohen (eds), *Dignity, Rank, and Rights* (Oxford University Press 2012) 13

Walvisch, Jamie, 'Defining "Mental Disorder" in Legal Contexts' (2017) 52 *International Journal of Law and Psychiatry* 7

Watson, Joanne and others, 'Supporting End of Life Decision Making: Case Studies of Relational Closeness in Supported Decision Making for People with Severe or Profound Intellectual Disability' (2017) 30 *Journal of Applied Research in Intellectual Disability* 1022

Watson, Sandy and others 'Care without Coercion—Mental Health Rights, Personal Recovery and Trauma-Informed Care' (2014) 49(4) *Australian Journal of Social Issues* 529

Weller, Penelope, 'Legal Capacity and Access to Justice: The Right to Participation in the CRPD' (2016) 5 *Laws* 43

Weller, Penelope, *New Law and Ethics in Mental Health Advance Directives* (Routledge 2013)

Westen, Peter, 'The Empty Idea of Equality' (1982) 95(3) *Harvard Law Review* 537

Wexler, David, *Mental Health Law: Major Issues, Perspectives in Law and Psychology* (Plenum Press 1981)

Windfuhr, Kirsten and Navneet Kapur, 'Suicide and Mental Illness: A Clinical Review of 15 Years of Findings from the UK Confidential Inquiry into Suicide' (2011) 100 *British Medical Bulletin* 101

Wood, Allen and others (eds), *Immanuel Kant, Groundwork for the Metaphysics of Morals* (Yale University Press 2002)

Wicks, Elizabeth, 'The Meaning of "Life": Dignity and Rights to Life in International Human Rights Treaties' (2012) 12(2) *Human Rights Law Review* 199

Williams, Thomas and Jan Olof Bengtsson, 'Personalism' in Edward N Zalta (ed), *The Stanford Encyclopedia of Philosophy* (Spring, 2014 ed, 2014)

Williams, Veronika and others, '"It's the Little Things That Count": Healthcare Professionals' Views on Delivering Dignified Care: A Qualitative Study' (2016) *Journal of Advanced Nursing* 782

Wilson, Kay and Penelope Weller, 'Benevolent Paternalism or a Clash of Values: Motherhood and Refusal of Medical Treatment in Ireland' (2011) 21 (Spring 2011) *Journal of Mental Health Law* 108

Wilson, Kay, 'Law Reform or Systemic Reform? Stakeholder's Perceptions of Resource Constraints in Mental Health in Australia, New Zealand and Canada' (2013) 20(4) *Psychiatry, Psychology and Law* 553–577

Wilson, Kay, 'The Call for the Abolition of Mental Health Law: The Challenges of Suicide, Accidental Death and the Equal Enjoyment of the Right to Life' (2018) 18 *Human Rights Law Review* 651

Wilson, Kay 'The Abolition or Reform of Mental Health Law: How Should the Law Recognise and Respond to the Vulnerability of Persons with Mental Impairment?' (2020) 28(1) *Medical Law Review* 30–64.

Wondemaghen, Meron, 'Testing Equality: Insanity, Treatment Refusal and the CRPD' (2018) 25(4) *Psychiatry, Psychology and Law* 174

Y

Yamin, Alicia Ely, 'Suffering and Powerlessness: The Significance of Promoting Participation in Rights-Based Approaches to Health' (2009) 11(1) *Health And Human Rights* 6

Yamin, Alicia Ely, *Power, Suffering and the Struggle for Dignity: Human Rights Frameworks for Health and Why They Matter* (University of Pennsylvania Press 2016)

Yee, Natalia and others, 'Severe Non-Lethal Violence During Psychotic Illness' (2011) 45(6) *Australian and New Zealand Journal of Psychiatry* 466

Cases

A Hospital NHS Trust v CD [2015] EWCOP 74

A NHS Foundation Trust v Ms X (By her Litigation Friend, the Official Solicitor) [2014] EWCOP 35

D v United Kingdom (1997) 24 EHRR 423

F v West Berkshire HA [1991] UKHL 1 (17 July 1990)

Heart of England NHS Foundation Trust v JB [2014] EWHC 342(COP)

Herczegfalvy v Austria European Court of Human Rights, Chamber, Application No 10533/83, 24 September 1992

Keenan v United Kingdom Application No 27229195, Merits and Satisfaction, 27 Oct 2004

Mammadov v Azerbaijan Application No 4762/05, Merits and Just Satisfaction, 17 March 2010

N v Romania Application No 59132/08 decision of 28 November 2017

PBU & NJE [2018] VSC 564

Perevedentsevy v Russia Application No 39583/05, Merits and Satisfaction, 13 Oct 2004

Pleso v Hungary, Application No 41242/08, Merits and Just Satisfaction, 2 January 2013

Rabone v Penine Care NHS Foundation Trust [2012] UKSC 2

Railway Express Agency Inc v New York 336 US 106

Re SB (A Patient; Capacity to Consent to Termination) [2013] EWHC 1417 (COP)

Reynolds v United Kingdom Application No 2694/08, Merits and Just Satisfaction, 13 March 2012

Rogers v Whitaker (1992) 109 ALR 625

SA (vulnerable adult with capacity: marriage) [2005] EWHC 2942(fam)

Savage v South Essex Partnership NHS Foundation Trust [2008] UKHL 74

Slimani v France Application No 57671/00, Merits and Satisfaction, 27 Oct 2004

Wakenhein v France, Communication No 854/1999, 15 July 2002 CCPR/C/75/854/1999

Wellesley v Beaufort (The Duke of) 2 Russ 20

X NHS Trust v B [2015] EWCOP 60

Legislation

Assisted Decision-Making (Capacity) Act 2015 (Ireland)
Lunacy Act 1890 (Eng & Wales) (repealed)
Lunatic Asylums Act 1845 (Eng & Wales) (repealed)
Mental Capacity Act 2005 (UK)
Mental Capacity Act 2016 (NI)
Mental Health (Compulsory Assessment and Treatment Act) 1992 (NZ)
Mental Health (Review) Amendment Act 2016 (SA)
Mental Health Act 1959 (UK) (repealed)
Mental Health Act 1983 (UK)
Mental Health Act 2007 (UK)
Mental Health Act 2007 (NSW)
Mental Health Act 2009 (SA)
Mental Health Act 2013 (Tas)
Mental Health Act 2014 (Vic)
Mental Health Act 2014 (WA)
Mental Health Act 2015 (ACT)
Mental Health Act 2016 (Qld)
Mental Health Act, RSO 1990, M 7, s 20
Mental Health Amendment (Statutory Review Act) 2014 (NSW)
Mental Treatment Act 1930 (Eng & Wales) (repealed)
National Disability Insurance Scheme Act 2013 (Cth)

Treaties

African Charter on Human and Peoples' Rights, opened for signature 27 June 1981, 1520 UNTS 217 (entered into force 21 October 1986)
American Convention on Human Rights, opened for signature 22 November 1969, 1144 UNTS 143 (entered into force 21 October 1986)
Charter of Fundamental Rights of the European Union (2000) OJ (C364) 1 (7 December 2000)
Convention on the Rights of Persons with Disabilities, open for signature 30 March 2007, UNTS 2515, (entered into force 3 May 2008)
European Convention on Human Rights, opened for signature 1950 (entered into force 1 June 2010)
International Covenant on Civil and Political Rights, opened for signature 16 December 1966, UNTS 999 (entered into force 23 March 1976
Vienna Convention on the Law of Treaties, opened for signature 23 May 1969, 1155 UNTS 331 (entered into force 27 January 1980)

Other

Committee Against Torture, General Comment 2: Implementation of Article 2 by State Parties, 39th Sess, UN Doc CAT/C/GC/2/CRP.1/Rev4 (5-23 November 2007)
Committee on the Rights of Persons with Disabilities, 'Concluding Observations on the Initial Report of Australia, Adopted by the Committee at its Tenth Session' (2–13 September 2013) CRPD/C/AUS/CO/1
Committee on the Rights of Persons with Disabilities 'General Comment No 1 (2014) Article 12: Equal Recognition Before the Law' (10 April 2014) UN Doc CRPD/C/GC/1
Committee on the Rights of Persons with Disabilities, 'Concluding Observations on the United Kingdom' (3 October 2017) CRPD/C/GBR/CO/1)

Committee on the Rights of Persons with Disabilities, 'General Comment No 2 (2014) Article 9: Accessibility,' 11th Sess, UN Doc CRPD/C/GC/2, (11 April 2014)

CRPD Committee, General Comment No. 5 (2017) On Living Independently and being Included in the Community, UN Doc CRPD/C/GC/5, 27 October 2017

CRPD Committee, General Comment No 6: Equality and Non-discrimination (Article 5), 9 March 2018

CRPD Committee, *General Comment on Article 4.3 and 33.3 of the Convention on the Participation with Persons with Disabilities in the Implementation and Monitoring of the Convention*, 16 March 2018

CRPD Committee, Guidelines on Article 14 of the Convention on the Rights of Persons with Disabilities: The Right to Liberty and Security of Persons (14th Session, September 2015)

CRPD declarations and reservations https://treaties.un.org/Pages/ViewDetails.aspx?src=TREATY&mtdsg_no=IV-15&chapter=4&lang=_en&clang=_en

CRPD Negotiation Archives https://www.un.org/development/desa/disabilities/resources/ad-hoc-committee-on-a-comprehensive-and-integral-international-convention-on-the-protection-and-promotion-of-the-rights-and-dignity-of-persons-with-disabilities.html

https://www.health.govt.nz/our-work/mental-health-and-addictions/mental-health/mental-health-and-human-rights-assessment

Testimony from a psychiatric survivor during a question and answer session at an 'afternoon tea' hosted by the National Mental Health Commission, Rydges Hotel Melbourne, 11 October 2013

Thematic Study by the Office of the United Nations High Commissioner for Human Rights on Enhancing Awareness and Understanding of the Convention on the Rights of Persons with Disabilities, UN Doc A/HRC/10/48 (26 January 2009)

UN Human Rights Committee, General Comment 35 Article 9 (Liberty and Security of the Person) 16 December 2014, CCPR/C/GC/35

United Nations, Enable http://www.un.org/disabilities

Universal Declaration of Human Rights

Vienna Declaration and Programme of Action Adopted by the World Conference on Human Rights in Vienna

Index

For the benefit of digital users, indexed terms that span two pages (e.g., 52–53) may, on occasion, appear on only one of those pages.